Recent Praise for the PassKey EA Review Series

Kari Hutchens (Canon City, Colorado)

I passed all three exams with the cheapest study materials out there! Easy to understand and comprehensive. Even from Part 1 of the book (Individuals), I learned so much that I am going to amend two prior year tax returns and get over $1,000 back. Passing all three parts of the EA exam on the first try and getting some extra cash in my pocket gets this book an A+!

Ken Smith (Chicago, Illinois)

I studied like crazy, night and day, and passed all three parts of the EA exam in just eight days. And I passed on the first try!

Michael Mirth (North Las Vegas, Nevada)

I am happy to say I am now an enrolled agent. This was the only source I used to study besides some extra practice tests. The way the book presented the materials made it easy to comprehend. If you are looking for a detailed study guide, this one is for you.

E. Dinetz (Mt. Laurel, New Jersey)

This book is very informative. I have an accounting degree and have done taxes in the past and I learned many new things from this book. I like the fact that after each concept they have a multiple choice quiz/review.

Oliver Douglass

I found this book to be the least expensive and the best guide around. The tests are on the money and the explanations are so easy to comprehend. Thanks for a great book.

Baiye Zebulone

Great books. Straight to the point, and very good examples for SEE preparations. I used all three parts to prepare for the SEE and passed Parts 1 and 3 on the first sitting and Part 2 on the second sitting. I will recommend it to anybody who wants to pass the rigorous EA examination.

Carl Ganster (Wyomissing, Pennsylvania)

I passed all my tests on the first try in five months using the PassKey books. Every topic is covered. It is easy reading, with plenty of examples. I have recommended the books to others who have to take the test. Thanks, PassKey, for writing great test guides. So many of the ones out there are hard to understand.

PassKey EA Review
Part 2: Businesses

IRS Enrolled Agent Exam
Study Guide 2013-2014 Edition

Authors:
Collette Szymborski, CPA
Richard Gramkow, EA
Christy Pinheiro, EA ABA®

PassKey Publications
Elk Grove, CA

Do you want to test yourself?

Then get the PassKey EA Exam Workbook!

PassKey EA Review Workbook:
Six Complete Enrolled Agent Practice Exams

Thoroughly revised and updated for tax year 2012, this workbook features **six complete** enrolled agent practice exams, with detailed answers, to accompany the PassKey EA Review study guides. This workbook includes two full exams for each of the three parts of the EA exam: Individuals, Businesses, and Representation.

You can learn by testing yourself on 600 questions, with all of the answers clearly explained in the back of the book.

Test yourself, time yourself, and learn!

Editor: Cynthia Willett Sherwood, EA, MSJ

PassKey EA Review, Part 2: Businesses, IRS Enrolled Agent Exam Study Guide 2013-2014 Edition

ISBN: 978-1-935664-23-9

First Printing. PassKey EA Review
PassKey EA Review® is a U.S. Registered Trademark

PassKey Publications, PO Box 580465, Elk Grove, CA 95758

www.PassKeyPublications.com

Part 2: Businesses

Tammy the Tax Lady ®

Sorry, but that's not what I meant when I said you had to "pay the piper."

Table of Contents

Introduction

Congratulations on taking the first step toward becoming an enrolled agent, a widely respected professional tax designation. The Internal Revenue Service licenses enrolled agents, known as EAs, after candidates pass a three-part exam testing their knowledge of federal tax law.

This PassKey study guide is designed to help you study for the EA exam, which is formally called the *IRS Special Enrollment Examination* or *"SEE."* The exam covers all aspects of federal tax law, including the taxation of individuals; corporations, partnerships, and exempt entities; ethics; and IRS collection and audit procedures. This guide is designed for the 2013 to 2014 testing season, which begins May 1, 2013 and closes February 28, 2014. Anyone taking the EA exam during this time period will be tested on 2012 tax law.

Exam Basics

The EA exam consists of three parts, which candidates typically take on different dates that do not need to be consecutive. The exam is exclusively administered by the testing company Prometric. You can find valuable information and register online at: ***http://www.prometric.com/IRS***

The yearly pass rates for the SEE vary by exam. In the 2011-2012 testing period, an average of more than 80% of test-takers passed Parts 1 and 3. The pass rate for Part 2 was much lower, averaging about 60%.

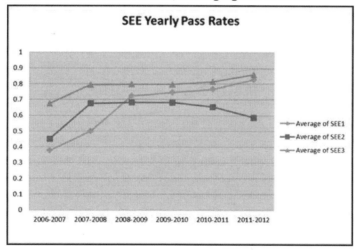

The computerized exam is offered only at Prometric testing centers. The format is multiple choice, with no questions requiring written answers. The length of each part of the exam is 3.5 hours, not including a pre-exam tutorial and post-exam survey.

Computerized EA Exam Format
Part 1 - Individual Taxation-100 Questions
Part 2 - Business Taxation-100 Questions
Part 3 - Representation, Practice, and Procedures-100 Questions

Testing Center Procedures

The testing center is designed to be a secure environment. The following are procedures you'll need to follow on test day:

1. Check in about a half-hour before your appointment time, and bring a current government-issued ID with both a photo and signature. If you don't have valid ID, you'll be turned away and you'll have to pay for a new exam appointment.

2. You'll be given a locker for your wallet, phone, and other personal items. You won't be able to bring any reference materials or other items into the testing room, with the exception of soft earplugs. The center supplies noise-blocking headphones.

3. No food, water, or other beverages are allowed in the testing room.

4. You'll be given scratch paper and a pencil to use, which will be collected after the exam.

5. You'll be able to use an onscreen calculator during the exam, or Prometric will provide you with a handheld calculator. You cannot bring your own.

6. Before going into the testing room, you'll be scanned with a metal detector wand.

7. You'll need to sign in and out every time you leave the testing room. Bathroom breaks are permitted, but the test timer will continue to count down.

8. You're not allowed to talk or communicate with other test-takers in the exam room. Prometric continuously monitors the testing via video, physical walk-throughs, and an observation window.

Violation of any of these procedures may result in the disqualification of your exam. In cases of cheating, the IRS says candidates may be subject to a variety of consequences, including civil and criminal penalties.

Exam-takers who require special accommodations under the Americans with Disabilities Act (ADA) must contact Prometric at 888-226-9406 to obtain an accommodation request form. A language barrier is not considered a disability. [1]

---

[1] *Candidate Information Bulletin* for the Enrolled Agent Special Enrollment Examination.

Exam Content

The IRS introduces multiple versions of new EA exams each May. If you fail a particular part of the exam and need to retake it, don't expect to see the identical questions the next time.

The IRS no longer releases new test questions and answers, although questions from 2003 to 2005 are available on the IRS website for review. (Be aware that tax law changes every year, so make sure you are familiar with recent updates and don't rely too heavily on these sample questions and answers.) Prometric includes broad exam content outlines for each exam part; however, not all of the topics will appear on the exam and there may be other topics that are included.

Your PassKey study guides present an overview of all the major areas of federal taxation that enrolled agents typically encounter in their practices and that are likely to appear on the exam.

Although the PassKey guides are designed to be comprehensive, we suggest you review IRS publications and try to learn as much as you can about tax law in general so that you're well-equipped to take the exam. In addition to this study guide, we highly recommend that all exam candidates read:

- **Publication 17, *Your Federal Income Tax*** (for Part 1 of the exam), and
- **Circular 230, *Regulations Governing the Practice of Attorneys, Certified Public Accountants, Enrolled Agents, Enrolled Actuaries, and Appraisers before the Internal Revenue Service*** (for Part 3 of the exam).

Anyone may download these publications for free from the IRS website.

> **Note:** Some exam candidates take Part 3, *Representation, Practice, and Procedures,* first, rather than taking the tests in order, since the material in Part 3 is considered less complex. The IRS discourages taking the tests out of order by including multiple questions (5% or more at times) of material that relates to taxation of *Individuals* and *Businesses.*

Exam Strategy

Each multiple choice question provides four choices for an answer. There are several different multiple choice formats used:[2]

---

[2] Candidate Information Bulletin for the Enrolled Agent Special Enrollment Examination.

Format One- Direct question

Which of the following entities are required to file Form 709, United States Gift Tax Return?

A. An individual

B. An estate or trust

C. A corporation

D. All of the above

Format Two-Incomplete sentence

Supplemental wages are compensation paid in addition to an employee's regular wages. They **do not** include payments for_____.

A. Accumulated sick leave

B. Nondeductible moving expenses

C. Vacation pay

D. Travel reimbursements paid at the federal government per diem rate

Format Three-All of the following EXCEPT

There are five tests which must be met for you to claim an exemption for a dependent. Which of the following is **not** a requirement?

A. Citizen or Resident Test

B. Member of Household or Relationship Test

C. Disability Test

D. Joint Return Test

There may also be a limited number of questions on the exam that have four choices, with three of them incorrect statements or facts and only one that is a correct statement or fact, which you would select as the right answer.[3] All four of these question-and-answer formats appear in your PassKey study guides. During the EA exam, you need to make sure you read each question thoroughly to understand exactly what is being asked.

Your exam may also include some experimental questions that will not be scored. You won't know which ones they are—the IRS uses them to gather statistical information on the questions before they're added to the exam as scored items.

---

[3] 1-31-13: Telephone interview with Larry Orozco, IRS director of competency and standards.

To familiarize yourself with the computerized testing format, there's a tutorial on the Prometric website. If you're not sure of an answer, you may mark it for review and return to it later. Try to eliminate clearly wrong answers of the four possible choices to narrow your odds of selecting the right answer. But be sure to answer every question, even if you have to guess, because all answers left incomplete will be marked as incorrect. Each question is weighted equally.

In the 3.5 hours of the exam, you'll have 210 minutes to answer questions, or slightly more than two minutes per question. Try to answer the questions you're sure about quickly, so you can devote more time to those that include calculations or that you're not as sure about. Remember that the clock doesn't stop for bathroom breaks, so try to allocate your time wisely.

Scoring

After you finish your exam and submit your answers, you'll learn immediately from a Prometric staff member whether you passed or failed. In either case, you won't receive a printout of the questions you answered correctly or missed.

The IRS determines scaled scores by calculating the number of questions answered correctly from the total number of questions in the examination and converting to a scale that ranges from 40 to 130. The IRS has set the scaled passing score at 105, which corresponds to the minimum level of knowledge deemed acceptable for EAs. Under its testing system, the IRS does not release the percentage of questions that you need to answer correctly in order to pass.

If you pass, you'll receive a score report showing a passing designation, but not your actual score. The IRS considers all candidates who pass as qualified, but does not rank *how* qualified each person may be.

If you fail, you'll receive a scaled score between 40 and 104, so you'll be able to see how close you are to the minimum score of 105. You'll also receive diagnostic information to help you know subject areas you need to focus on when retaking the exam:

- 1: Area of weakness where additional study is necessary. It is important for you to focus on this domain as you prepare to take the test again. You may want to consider taking a course or participating actively in a study group on this topic.
- 2: May need additional study.

- 3: Clearly demonstrated an understanding of subject area.[4]

If necessary, you may take each part of the exam up to four times during the May 1 and February 28 testing window. You'll need to re-register with Prometric and pay fees for each new time you take an exam part.

You can carry over passing scores for individual parts of the exam up to two years from the date you took them.

After Passing

Once you've passed the exam, you must apply for enrollment as an EA, which includes an IRS review of your tax compliance history. Failure to timely file or pay personal income taxes can be grounds for denial of enrollment. You may not practice as an EA until the IRS approves your application and issues you a Treasury Card.

Successfully passing the EA exam can launch you into a fulfilling and lucrative new career. The exam requires intense preparation and diligence, but with the help of Passkey's comprehensive *EA Review*, you'll have the tools you need to learn how to become an enrolled agent.

We wish you much success.

---

[4] *Candidate Information Bulletin* for the Enrolled Agent Special Enrollment Examination.

Ten Steps for the IRS EA Exam

STEP 1-Learn

Learn more about the enrolled agent designation and explore the career opportunities that await you after passing your three-part EA exam. In addition to preparing taxes for individuals and businesses, EAs can represent people before the IRS, just like attorneys and CPAs. Many people who use the PassKey study guides have had no previous experience in preparing taxes, but go on to rewarding new professional careers.

STEP 2-Gather information

Gather more information before you launch into your studies. The IRS publishes basic information about becoming an EA on its website at www.irs.gov/Tax-Professionals/Enrolled-Agents. You'll also find valuable information about the exam itself on the Prometric testing website at www.prometric.com/see. Be sure to download the *Candidate Information Bulletin*, which takes you step-by-step through the registration and testing process.

STEP 3-Obtain a PTIN

A PTIN stands for "Preparer Tax Identification Number." Before you can register for your EA exam, you must obtain a PTIN, which is issued by the IRS.[5] The sign-up system can be found at www.irs.gov/ptin. You'll need to create an account, complete an on-line application, and pay a required fee.

STEP 4-Sign up with Prometric

Once you have your PTIN, you may register for your exam on the Prometric website. After creating an account and paying the required testing fee, you can complete the registration process by clicking on "Scheduling."

STEP 5-Schedule a time, date, and location

You'll be able to choose a test site and time and date that are convenient for you. Prometric has test centers in most major metropolitan areas of the United States, as well as certain other parts of the world. You may schedule as little as two days in advance—space permitting—through the website or by calling 800-306-3926 Monday through Friday. Be aware that the website and the phone line have different inventory of available times and dates, so you may want to check the other source if your preferred date is already full.

---

[5] Foreign-based candidates do not need a PTIN to register to take the exam.

STEP 6-Adopt a study plan

Focus on one exam part at a time, and adopt a study plan that covers all the tax topics on the EA exam. You'll need to develop an individualized study program based on your current level of tax knowledge. For those without prior tax experience, a good rule of thumb is to study at least 60 hours for each of the three exam sections, committing at least 15 hours per week. Start well in advance of the exam date.

STEP 7-Get plenty of rest, exercise, and good nutrition

Get plenty of rest, exercise, and good nutrition prior to the EA exam. You'll want to be at your best on exam day.

STEP 8-Test day has arrived!

On test day, make sure you remember your government-issued ID and arrive early at the test site. Prometric advises to arrive at least 30 minutes before your scheduled examination time. If you miss your appointment and are not allowed to test, you'll forfeit your exam fee and have to pay for a new appointment.

STEP 9-During the exam

This is when your hard work finally pays off. Focus, don't worry if you don't know every question, but make sure you allocate your time appropriately. Give your best answer to every question. All questions left blank will be marked as wrong.

Step 10-Congratulations. You passed!

After celebrating your success, you need to apply for your EA designation. The quickest way is by filling out Form 23, *Application for Enrollment to Practice Before the Internal Revenue Service*, directly on the IRS website. Once your application is approved, you'll be issued a Treasury card, and you'll be official—a brand new enrolled agent!

Essential Business Tax Figures for 2012

Here is a quick summary of key tax figures related to business for the current exam cycle:

2012 Social Security Taxable Wage Base: $110,100. In 2012, the Social Security portion of the FICA tax for employees only is reduced from 6.2% to 4.2%. The employer's portion remains 6.2%. The Social Security tax rate for self-employed persons is similarly reduced, from 12.4% to 10.4%. Therefore, the tax rate for self-employment income earned in calendar year 2012 is 13.3% (10.4% for Social Security and 2.9% for Medicare).

2012 Medicare Taxable Wage Base: No limit.

Section 179 Expense: $500,000 of qualified expenditures/phase-out at $2 million; up to $250,000 in expense for qualified leasehold improvement, restaurant, and retail improvement property.

Bonus Depreciation: Up to 50% for new assets placed in service in 2012.

Mileage Rates:
- Business miles: 55.5¢ per mile
- Medical or moving miles: 23¢ per mile
- Charitable purposes: 14¢ per mile

Exclusion for Employer-Provided Mass Transit:
- $240 per month for parking benefits
- $240 per month in combined highway vehicle transportation and transit passes (increased retroactively for 2012)

Employer Contribution Limits to 401(k) Participant's Plan: $17,000 maximum.

Estate and Gift Tax Exclusion Amount: $5,120,000 (up from $5 million in 2011).

Gift Tax Annual Exclusion: $13,000.

New Rules for Businesses: 2012 Tax Year

S Corporation Built-In Gains Tax (BIG tax): The American Taxpayer Relief Act of 2012 extends the reduced five-year recognition period to sales occurring in 2012 and 2013. The Act also provides that gain on installment sales during these years are subject to the five-year recognition period when it is recognized in future years.

Business Credits: The American Taxpayer Relief Act of 2012 extends and in some cases modifies many credits, including the following:

- Research and Experimentation Credit
- Work Opportunity Tax Credit (expanded target groups that qualify for 2012)
- Employer Credit for Differential Military Pay
- Indian Employment Tax Credit
- New Markets Tax Credit
- Empowerment Zone Employment Credit
- Low Income Housing Credit
- Credit for Alternative Fuel Vehicle Refueling Property
- Credit for Construction of New Energy Efficient Homes
- Credit for Manufacture of Energy Efficient Appliances
- Various credits for producing cellulosic biofuel, alternative fuel mixtures, and wind electricity

Other Extensions Under the Taxpayer Relief Act:

- Enhanced charitable deduction for contributions of food inventory
- Special rules allowing U.S. film and television producers to expense up to $15 million of production costs incurred in the United States ($20 million in economically depressed areas in the U.S.)

Estate and Gift Tax: The estate tax portability election has been made permanent. This is when the surviving spouse's exemption amount is increased by the deceased spouse's unused exemption amount. The single lifetime exemption extending unification of the estate and gift tax has been made permanent.

Other 2012 Business-Related Tax Changes

W-2s: An employee's W-2 must now report both the employer and employee portion of health care insurance costs for 2012.

Farmers' Tax Deadline: Because of delays created by the late tax changes of the fiscal cliff legislation, the IRS will waive penalties for farmers and fishermen who miss the March 1, 2013 tax filing deadline, so long as they file their returns and pay the tax due by April 15.

Cell Phones: The value of employer-provided cell phones has been ruled as excludable as a de minimis fringe benefit, if provided primarily for noncompensatory business reasons.

Nonprofit Relief: Small organizations that lost their tax-exempt status by failing to file e-postcards were eligible for transitional relief in 2012, including possible retroactive reinstatement and a reduced user fee.

Reporting of Nontaxable Exchanges of Property: Both the corporation and certain stockholders involved in a nontaxable exchange of property for stock must attach to their income tax returns a complete statement of all facts pertinent to the exchange. The reporting requirement now applies to stockholders that own 5% or more of a public company or 1% or more of a privately held company.

Unit 1: Business Entities in General

More Reading:
Publication 583, *Starting a Business and Keeping Records*
Publication 1635, *Understanding Your EIN*
Publication 334, *Tax Guide for Small Business*

Overview of EA Exam Part 2: Businesses

For Part 2 of the enrolled agent exam, you will be expected to know a broad range of information related to preparing tax returns for various types of businesses. You will need to understand the different types of business entities and the special tax laws that apply to each: sole proprietorships, partnerships, corporations, tax-exempt organizations; and farmers.

Part 2 of the exam also covers accounting methods and periods; business income; expenses, deductions, and credits; business assets and determining basis; trust and estate income tax; retirement plans; and much more. The material includes taxation issues that affect self-employed businesspersons, which are covered in both the Individual and Business parts of the EA exam, so there is a degree of overlap between the study guides.

We start with an overview of the different types of business entities. There are several types of business entities that are available for taxpayers to use in order to form and run their businesses. Each type has its own drawbacks, risks, and benefits. We briefly review each type below, and we will examine the more complex entities in depth in later units.

Sole Proprietorship

A sole proprietorship is an unincorporated business that is owned and controlled by one person. It may be a single-person business or it may have many employees, but there is only one owner who must accept all the risks and liabilities of the business. As the simplest business type, it is also the easiest to start. An estimated 70% of businesses in the United States are sole proprietorships.[6]

A sole proprietorship cannot be passed on to a new owner as the same business entity because, by definition, a sole proprietorship is owned and operated by a single, specific individual. If a business operated as a sole proprietor-

---

[6] According to the U.S. Census Bureau, in 2008 there were more than 22 million tax returns filed by nonfarm sole proprietors; 3.1 million by partnerships; and 5.8 million for corporations.

ship is sold, it must be registered by the new owner as either a different sole proprietorship or as a different type of business entity.

A taxpayer does not have to conduct full-time business activities to be considered self-employed. Operating a part-time business in addition to having a regular job or business may also be self-employment, and may therefore constitute a sole proprietorship. An activity qualifies as a business if its primary purpose is for profit and if the taxpayer is involved in the activity with continuity and regularity. That means a hobby[7] does not qualify as a business.

Sole proprietors will often receive Form 1099-MISC from their customers showing income they were paid. The amounts reported on Form 1099-MISC, along with any other business income, are reported and taxed on the taxpayer's personal income tax return. Income and expenses from the sole proprietorship are reported on Form 1040, Schedule C, *Profit or Loss from Business*.

			$	Form 1099-MISC	
		3 Other income	4 Federal income tax withheld	Copy B
		$	$	For Recipient
PAYER'S federal identification number	RECIPIENT'S identification number	5 Fishing boat proceeds	6 Medical and health care payments	
		$	$	
RECIPIENT'S name		7 Nonemployee compensation	8 Substitute payments in lieu of dividends or interest	This is important tax information and is being furnished to the Internal Revenue Service. If you are required to file a return, a negligence
		$	$	
Street address (including apt. no.)		9 Payer made direct sales of $5,000 or more of consumer	10 Crop insurance proceeds	

A taxpayer may use the simplified Schedule C-EZ if he or she:

- Had business expenses of $5,000 or less
- Did not claim any depreciation expense
- Used the cash method of accounting
- Did not have inventory at any time during the year
- Did not have a net loss from the business, and had no prior year passive activity losses
- Was the sole proprietor for only one business
- Had no employees during the year
- Did not deduct expenses for business use of his home, and had no depreciation or amortization to report for the year

---

[7] A hobby is an activity typically undertaken for pleasure during leisure time. Income from a hobby is still taxable and reported on Form 1040, Line 21 as "other income." Hobby income is typically not subject to self-employment tax, and the use of losses from a hobby to offset income from other sources is limited.

If a sole proprietor has no employees, he is not required to obtain an Employer identification number (EIN).

Self-employed individuals who have net earnings of $400 or more from self-employment are required to pay self-employment tax by filing Schedule SE, *Self-Employment Tax* along with their Form 1040.

Example: Darlene works as an independent contractor for Right Light Lighting Company. Right Light sends Darlene a Form 1099-MISC that shows she received $25,000 for contract work she did for them. She also receives cash payments of $7,000 from several different individuals for contract work she completed on their homes. Although she did not receive Forms 1099-MISC for the $7,000, Darlene must include the $7,000 cash payments as self-employment income along with the $25,000 on her Schedule C.

Husband and Wife Businesses

Many small businesses are operated jointly by a husband and wife, without incorporating or creating a formal partnership agreement. A husband and wife business may be considered a partnership whether or not a formal partnership agreement is made.

If a husband and wife each materially participates as the only members of a jointly owned and operated business, they may be treated as a *qualified joint venture*. This allows them to avoid the complexity of filing a partnership return, but still gives each spouse credit for Social Security earnings. Items of business income, gain, loss, deduction, and credit are split between the spouses in accordance with their respective interests in the business. The husband and wife then file separate Schedules C and separate Schedules SE. This option is available only to married taxpayers who file joint tax returns.

Partnerships

A partnership is a relationship that exists between two or more persons who join to carry on a trade or business. Each person contributes money, property, labor, or skill, and expects to share in the profits and losses of the business.

A partnership must file an annual information return to report the income, deductions, gains, and losses from its operations, but the partnership itself does not pay income tax. Instead, any profits or losses "pass through" to its partners, who are then responsible for reporting their share of the partnership's income or loss on their individual returns.

A partnership tax return is filed on IRS Form 1065, *U.S. Return of Partnership Income.* Since partners are not employees as such, they should not be issued a Form W-2. The partnership must furnish copies of Schedule K-1 to its partners, showing the income and losses that is allocated to each partner.

A partnership must always have at least one *general partner* whose actions legally bind the business and who is legally responsible for a partnership's debts and liabilities.

A *limited partner* is an investor whose liability is limited to his investment in the business. A limited partner has no obligation to contribute additional capital to the partnership, and therefore does not have an economic risk of loss for partnership liabilities. Income reported by the partnership to limited partners is considered passive income (and is not subject to self-employment tax), while income attributable to general partners is deemed to be active income.

Example: James and Madeline are father and daughter. Together they operate Hunnicutt Business Consulting. Each is active in the business, and each has an equal share in partnership interests and profits. In 2012, Hunnicutt had $80,000 in net profits. The partnership must file a Form 1065 reporting its income and loss for the year. The partnership must also issue two Schedules K-1—one to each partner, James and Madeline. Since they share profits and losses equally, James and Madeline will both have to report $40,000 in self-employment partnership income on their individual tax returns. Partnership income is reported on page 2 of Schedule E, *Supplemental Income and Loss (From rental real estate, royalties, partnerships, S corporations, estates, trusts, REMICs, etc.)*

A partnership can look very different depending on how it is structured—it can be anything from a small business run by a husband and wife to a complex business organization with hundreds of general partners and limited partners as investors. A partnership may have an unlimited number of partners.

Example: Samuel and Jane are siblings who own Devil Dog Publishing, a monthly magazine for tattoo artists. Samuel writes most of the articles, and Jane takes care of the day-to-day operations of the magazine, including paying the bills and securing advertising. Samuel and Jane are in a partnership and must file Form 1065.

An unincorporated organization with two or more members is generally classified as a partnership for federal tax purposes if its members carry on a business and divide its profits. However, a joint undertaking merely to share expenses is not a partnership. For example, co-ownership of rental property is not considered a formal partnership unless the co-owners provide substantial services to the tenants.

> **Example:** Anderson and Sally are good friends who own a rental property together. Each owns a 50% interest. Anderson takes care of the repairs, and Sally collects and divides the rent. They do not have any other business with each other. The co-ownership of the rental property would not be considered a partnership for tax purposes. They would report their income and losses on Schedule E based on their ownership percentage, and then would divide the income and losses on their individual returns.

A partnership return must show the name and address of each partner and the partner's share of taxable income. The return must be signed by a general partner. A limited partner may not sign the return or represent a partnership before the IRS.

If a limited liability company (LLC) is treated as a partnership for federal tax purposes, it must file Form 1065 and one of its general partners or owners must sign the return.

Types of Partnerships Defined

Limited Partnership: A partnership that has at least one limited partner and at least one general partner. Limited partnerships allow investors to invest in businesses while reducing their own personal liability.

Limited Liability Partnership (LLP): An entity that is formed under state law by filing articles of organization as an LLP and is typically used for specific professional services, such as those offered by a law firm. Partners determine the structure of the organization and the distribution of profits and losses. Typically, an LLP allows each partner to actively participate in management affairs but still provides limited liability protection to each partner. A partner in an LLP generally would not be liable for the debt or malpractice of other partners and would only be at risk for the partnership's assets.

C Corporations

Most major companies are treated as C corporations for federal income tax purposes. In forming a corporation, prospective shareholders exchange money, property, or both for the corporation's capital stock.

A C corporation is considered an entity separate from its shareholders and must elect a board of directors who are responsible for running the company. A corporation conducts business, realizes net income or loss, pays taxes, and distributes profits to shareholders.

A C corporation may have an unlimited number of shareholders, both foreign and domestic. The profit of a C corporation is taxed to the corporation when earned, and it may also be taxed to the shareholders when distributed as dividends, resulting in double taxation.

The corporation does not get a tax deduction when it distributes dividends to shareholders, and shareholders cannot deduct any losses of the corporation. A corporation generally takes the same deductions as a sole proprietorship to figure its taxable income, but is also allowed certain special deductions. Corporations must file Form 1120, *U.S. Corporation Income Tax Return.*

S Corporations

S corporations are corporations that elect to pass corporate income, losses, deductions, and credit through to their shareholders for federal tax purposes, in a manner similar to partnerships. Shareholders of S corporations report the flow-through of income and losses on their personal tax returns and are assessed tax at their individual tax rates. This allows the shareholders of S corporations to avoid double taxation on their corporate income. However, the S corporation itself may be responsible for tax on certain built-in gains and passive income. S corporations are subject to the following requirements:

- Be a domestic corporation
- Have only allowable shareholders (partnerships, corporations, and nonresident aliens are not eligible)
- Have no more than 100 shareholders
- Have one class of stock
- Not be an ineligible type of corporation (certain financial institutions, insurance companies, and domestic international sales corporations are not eligible for S corporation status)

An S corporation is required to file a tax return every year, regardless of income or loss, by filing IRS Form 1120S, *U.S. Tax Return for an S Corporation*, and to report each shareholder's applicable share of income or losses to them on Schedules K-1.

Limited Liability Companies (LLC)

A limited liability company (LLC) is a corporation that is formed under state law. Depending upon whether it has a single member (owner) or multiple members, it may choose to be taxed for IRS purposes as a corporation, partnership, or sole proprietorship. Most often, LLCs elect to be taxed as partnerships. Thus, like the owners of S corporations and partnerships, the members of an LLC can avoid double taxation. An LLC can provide the liability protection of a corporation with the tax benefits of a partnership. Unlike a partnership, none of the members of an LLC are personally liable for its debts.

Personal Service Corporations (PSC)

A personal service corporation (PSC) is a corporation that performs services in the fields of health (including veterinary services), law, engineering, architecture, accounting, actuarial science, the performing arts, or consulting. In a PSC, the majority of the stock is owned by employees, retired employees, or their estates. Unlike other corporations, a qualified PSC is always taxed at a flat rate of 35% on taxable income.

A corporation is a personal service corporation if its principal activity during the prior tax year is performing personal services. Personal services include any activity performed in the fields of accounting, actuarial science, architecture, consulting, engineering, health (including veterinary services), law, and the performing arts. A corporation that provides these services will be considered a PSC if substantially all of its compensation is derived from providing personal services.

A person is considered an "employee-owner" of a personal service corporation if both of the following apply:
- He or she is an employee of the corporation or performs personal services for, or on behalf of, the corporation on any day of the testing period.
- He or she owns any stock in the corporation at any time during the testing period.

Unlike other corporations, personal service corporations are always taxed at a flat rate of 35%.

Farmers

The IRS defines the business of farming as someone who cultivates, operates, or manages a farm for profit. Types of farms include livestock, dairy, poultry, fish, and fruit.

Many self-employed farmers, just like Schedule C taxpayers, report income and expenses, and pay regular income tax and self-employment tax on their net profits from farming. However, they report their profit or loss on Schedule F. If the farming business is organized as a corporation or a partnership, the taxpayer files the appropriate tax return for the specific entity type.

Tax-Exempt Organizations (Nonprofit Entities)

The Internal Revenue Code outlines the requirements for tax-exempt organizations, commonly referred to as charitable organizations. They include nonprofit groups that are charitable, educational, and religious in purpose. An organization must be organized and operated exclusively for one of these purposes, and none of its earnings may go to any private shareholder or individual.

Nonprofit organizations may be created as corporations, trusts, or unincorporated associations, but never as partnerships or sole proprietorships. Most organizations must request tax-exempt status by filing Form 23, *Application for Recognition of Exemption.* However, churches, including synagogues, temples, and mosques, do not have to apply for formal exemption, because they are treated as tax-exempt by default.

Exempt organizations file Form 990 to report income and losses. Form 990 is usually an informational return only, but nonprofit organizations may in some instances be subject to tax on activities that are outside the scope of their tax-exempt status.

Employer Identification Number (EIN)

An employer identification number is used for reporting purposes. Unlike Social Security numbers that are assigned to individuals, EINs are assigned to business entities, including the following: sole proprietors, corporations, partnerships, nonprofit associations, trusts and estates.

A business must apply for an EIN if any of the following apply:
- The business pays employees
- The business operates as a corporation, exempt organization, trust, estate, or partnership

- The business files any of these tax returns:
  - Employment
  - Excise
  - Alcohol, Tobacco, and Firearms
- The business withholds taxes paid to a nonresident alien
- The business establishes a pension, profit sharing, or retirement plan

An EIN can also be requested by a sole proprietor who simply wishes to protect his Social Security number for privacy reasons. This way, a sole proprietor can give his EIN rather than his SSN to companies that need to issue him a Form 1099 for independent contractor payments.

If a sole proprietor decides to form a business entity such as a partnership or corporation, he will be required to request an EIN for each separate entity. A new EIN is required for any of the following changes:

- When a sole proprietor or partnership decides to incorporate
- When a sole proprietor takes on a partner and becomes a partnership
- When a partnership becomes a sole proprietorship (for example, when one partner dies)
- When a sole proprietor files for bankruptcy under Chapter 7 or Chapter 11
- When a taxpayer terminates one partnership and begins another partnership
- When a business establishes a pension, profit sharing, or retirement plan

A business does not need to apply for a new EIN in any of the following instances:

- To change the name of a business
- To change the location or add locations (stores, plants, enterprises, or branches of the same entity)
- If a sole proprietor operates multiple businesses (including stores, plants, enterprises, or branches of the same entity)

Further, a sole proprietor who conducts business as a limited liability company (LLC) does not need a separate EIN for the LLC, unless the business is required to file employment or excise tax returns.

Taxpayers can apply for an EIN online or use IRS Form SS-4, *Application for Employer Identification Number.*

Entity Classification Election Rules

Certain business entities may choose how they will be classified for tax purposes by filing Form 8832, *Entity Classification Election*.

An LLC with a single owner is classified as a sole proprietorship for income tax purposes, unless the owner files Form 8832 and chooses to be taxed as a corporation. A single-owner LLC is considered a "disregarded entity" for tax purposes, unless the owner elects to be treated as a corporation.

Similarly, the IRS will treat a domestic LLC with at least two members as a partnership by default unless it files Form 8832 and elects to be treated as a corporation.

An election to change an LLC's classification cannot take effect more than 75 days prior to the date the election is filed, nor can it take effect later than 12 months after the date the election is filed. Once a business entity chooses its classification, it cannot change the election again within five years (60 months).

Example: Kelly and Ned are married and own their own business. They decide to form an LLC for liability protection. Kelly files Form 8832, and she elects to classify their business as a partnership for tax purposes. A few months later, Kelly changes her mind and wants to change classifications and be taxed as a corporation. Kelly must wait at least 60 months in order to change the election.

Business Entities, Liability, Existence, and Taxation Snapshot

Character	Sole Proprietor	C Corporation	S Corporation	Partnership
Formation	No state filing required.	State filing required.	State filing required.	No state filing required.
Existence	Automatically dissolved upon death.	Perpetual life.	Perpetual life.	Varies from state to state.
Liability	Sole proprietor has unlimited liability.	Shareholders are not responsible for the debts of the corporation.	Shareholders are typically not responsible for the debts of the corporation.	General partners are liable for the debts of the partnership.
Operational Requirements	None.	Board of directors, annual meetings, and annual reporting required.	Board of directors, annual meetings, and annual reporting required.	No formal requirements.
Management	Sole proprietor has full control of management and operations.	Managed by the directors, who are elected by the shareholders.	Managed by the directors, who are elected by the shareholders.	Partners may have an oral or written operating agreement.
Taxation	Not a taxable entity. Sole proprietor pays all taxes on his/her individual return.	Taxed at the entity level. Dividends are also taxed at the individual level.	No tax at the entity level. Income/loss is passed through to the shareholders.	Generally, there is no tax at the entity level. Income/loss is passed through to partners.
Pass Through?	Yes.	No.	Yes.	Yes.
Double Taxation	No.	Yes.	No.	No.
Transferability of Interest	No.	Shares of stock are easily transferred.	Yes.	Varies.

Unit 1: Questions

1. A domestic LLC with at least two members that does not file Form 8832 is automatically classified as _____ for federal income tax purposes.

A. An S corporation.
B. A partnership.
C. A qualified joint venture.
D. A personal service corporation.

The answer is B. A domestic LLC with at least two members that does not file Form 8832 is classified as a partnership for federal income tax purposes. ###

2. Which of the following organizations does not require an EIN?

A. An estate.
B. A C corporation.
C. Nonprofit organizations.
D. A sole proprietorship with no employees.

The answer is D. A sole proprietorship without employees does not require an employer identification number. The other choices listed all require an EIN. ###

3. A sole proprietor will be required to obtain a new EIN in which of the following instances?

A. The sole proprietor is required to file excise tax returns.
B. The sole proprietor changes the name of his business.
C. The sole proprietor changes location.
D. The sole proprietor operates multiple locations.

The answer is A. A sole proprietor who is required to file excise tax returns (or employment tax returns) must obtain an EIN. A sole proprietorship is not required to obtain a new EIN when it changes location or its business name. A sole proprietor may operate many different businesses using the same EIN, so long as the businesses are also sole proprietorships. ###

4. In which of the following instances will a partnership not be required to obtain a new EIN?

A. The partners decide to incorporate.
B. The partnership is taken over by one of the partners and is subsequently operated as a sole proprietorship.
C. The general partner ends the old partnership and begins a new one.
D. The partnership adds other business locations.

The answer is D. A partnership is not required to obtain a new EIN simply to add business locations. In all of the other choices listed, the entity would need to obtain a new EIN. ###

5. Which of the following entities is considered separate from its share-holders or owners?

A. A partnership.
B. A C corporation.
C. A sole proprietorship.
D. An LLC.

The answer is B. A C corporation is considered an entity separate from its shareholders. ###

6. A sole proprietor may not be re-quired to file Schedule SE if his net profit for 2012 was _____.

A. Less than $400.
B. $400 or more.
C. Less than $5,000 but more than $400.
D. More than $5,000.

The answer is A. If the net profit was less than $400, a taxpayer should enter the profit on line 12 of Form 1040 and attach Schedule C to the return. Schedule SE is not required unless it was a profit of $400 or more. ###

7. Don and Selma are married, and they run a small pet grooming business together. They would like to treat their business as a qualified joint venture. Which of the following is true?

A. Don and Selma may choose to report their qualified joint venture as a sole proprietorship on two separate Schedules C, so long as they file jointly.
B. Don and Selma may choose to report their qualified joint venture as a sole proprietorship on two separate Schedules C, so long as they file separate tax returns (MFS).
C. Don and Selma must file a partnership tax return for their business activity.
D. Don and Selma may file a single Schedule C, listing Don as the sole proprietor one year and Selma as the sole proprietor the next year.

The answer is A. Don and Selma may choose to report their qualified joint venture as a sole proprietorship on two separate Schedules C, so long as they file jointly. This option is only available to married taxpayers who file jointly. ###

8. Julian is self-employed and has a small business selling used books. The gross income from his business is $20,000 and his business expenses total $9,500. Which schedule must Julian complete to report his business income and expenses?

A. Schedule F.
B. Schedule C.
C. Schedule D.
D. Schedule A.

The answer is B. Julian must complete Schedule C to report his business income and expenses. ###

9. Mandy and her friend, Tammy, work together, making beaded necklaces and selling them at craft shows. They run their business professionally and jointly, always attempting to make a profit, but they do not have any type of formal business agreement. They share with each other the profits or losses of the business. They made $24,900 in 2012 from selling necklaces, and they had $1,900 in expenses. Where and how is the correct way for Mandy and Tammy to report their income?

A. Split the income and report the profits as "other income" on each taxpayer's individual Forms 1040.
B. Each must report her own income and expenses on Schedule C.
C. Mandy and Tammy should calculate income and subtract expenses, and then report the net amount as "other income" on each individual Form 1040.
D. Mandy and Tammy are working as a partnership and should report their income on Form 1065.

The answer is D. Mandy and Tammy are working as a partnership and should report their income on Form 1065, U.S. Return of Partnership Income. Related expenses are deductible, and they are reported as deductions. Each partner would then receive a Schedule K-1 to report their individual items of expenses and income on their Form 1040. ###

10. Catherine is self-employed and would like to use the simplest form available to report her business income and loss. Which of the following expenses would prevent Catherine from using Schedule C-EZ?

A. Auto expenses related to his business activity.
B. Interest paid on business loans.
C. Legal and professional services and fees.
D. Expenses for business use of his home.

The answer is D. Taxpayers cannot use Schedule C-EZ if they deduct expenses for business use of their home. If the taxpayer plans to take a home office deduction, she must use Schedule C. ###

11. All of the statements are true about the following business entities except:
A. S and C corporations may have an unlimited number of shareholders.
B. An LLC typically provides the liability protection of a corporation but the tax benefits of a partnership.
C. "Pass through" entities include LLCs, LLPs, S corporations, and partnerships.
D. A sole proprietorship bears all the liabilities and risks of a business.

The answer is A. Only a C corporation may have an unlimited number of shareholders. An S corporation is limited to no more than 100 shareholders. ###

12. Which of the following is considered a drawback of the C corporation entity?

A. It may have many different shareholders.
B. It may have investors who are nonresident aliens.
C. Profits are subject to double taxation, once at the corporate level and again at the shareholder level when distributed as dividends.
D. It is run by a board of directors.

The answer is C. Corporations are subject to double taxation. The other statements are facts about C corporations but are not considered drawbacks. ###

13. A personal service corporation is always taxed at a_____ rate.

A. 15%.
B. 28%.
C. 35%.
4. 39.6%.

The answer is C. A personal service corporation is created for the purpose of providing personal services to individuals or groups. Personal service corporations not eligible for graduated tax rates, like other C corporations. Personal service corporations pay a 35% flat rate on their taxable income. ###

Unit 2: IRS Business Requirements

More Reading:
Publication 583, *Starting a Business and Keeping Records*
Publication 1779, *Independent Contractor or Employee*
Publication 505, *Tax Withholding and Estimated Tax*

Recordkeeping Requirements for Businesses

Adequate records are important for a taxpayer to monitor business operations, verify his income and expenses, and to support expenses on his tax return. Except in a few cases, the law does not require a business to keep any specific kind of records or use a particular recordkeeping system, so long as the system clearly shows a business's income and expenses.

The taxpayer's recordkeeping system should include a summary of business transactions, which is usually made in the taxpayer's books, such as accounting journals and ledgers. The books must show the business's gross income, as well as the deductions and credits. Additional documents must be kept to support these entries. These include sales slips, paid bills, invoices, receipts, deposit slips, canceled checks, credit card charge slips, cash register tapes, Forms 1099-MISC, invoices, mileage logs, and cell phone records.

Electronic records are acceptable so long as they provide a complete and accurate record of data that is accessible to the IRS in a legible format. They are subject to the same controls and retention guidelines as those imposed on a taxpayer's original hard copy books and records.

Taxpayers must keep records as long as they are needed for the administration of any provision of the Internal Revenue Code. Usually this means that the business must keep records long enough to support income and deductions until the statute of limitations for the tax return has run out. [8]

Generally, a taxpayer must keep records for at least three years from when the tax return was filed or within two years of when the tax was paid, whichever is later. If a business has employees, it must keep all employment tax records for at least four years.

---

[8] The statute of limitations is the period of time in which taxpayers can amend a return to claim a credit or refund or the IRS can assess additional tax.

Taxpayers must keep records relating to property until the period of limitations expires for the year in which the property is disposed of in a taxable disposition. These records are needed to figure any depreciation, amortization, or depletion deduction, and to figure basis for computing gain or loss when the property is sold. A taxpayer may need to keep records relating to the basis of property even longer than the period of limitation since they are important in figuring the basis of the original or replacement property.

Business funds should be kept separate from personal funds. The IRS is more likely to audit a business and deny deductions and business losses if there is no clear separation between business and personal expenses. A separate bank account for business-related transactions is advisable, with business-related bills paid from there rather than from a personal account.

Financial Statements

Financial statements are the formal records of a business's financial activities and are used to examine a business's financial health. There are many types of financial statements, but the two most common ones used for tax reporting purposes are the income statement and the balance sheet.

Income Statement

The income statement is also called the profit and loss statement. It is a financial statement that indicates how revenue is transformed into net income by showing the profit or loss during a certain period, such as a fiscal year or a calendar year. The income statement shows income and expenses, with the profit or loss shown at the bottom of the statement.

Balance Sheet

The balance sheet is a summary of a business's assets, liabilities, and equity on a specific date, such as at the end of its financial year. A balance sheet is often described as a snapshot of a company's financial condition and includes items of assets such as cash, petty cash, accounts receivable, inventory, prepaid insurance, land, buildings, equipment, and goodwill. On the liability side of the balance sheet are items such as accounts receivable, accrued benefits, payroll, and notes payable. Balances on a balance sheet are carried forward from year to year, unlike income statement accounts, which are closed out at year-end and only reflect business operations within a specified period.

Employer Reporting Requirements

Businesses with employees are subject to a number of reporting requirements, including the following:

Forms W-4: When a business hires an employee, it must have the employee complete a Form W-4, *Employee's Withholding Allowance Certificate*

Form W-4 tells the employer the worker's marital status, the number of withholding allowances, and any additional amount to use when deducting federal income tax from the employee's pay.

If an employee fails to complete a Form W-4, the employer must withhold federal income taxes from his wages as if he were single and claiming no withholding allowances.

Forms W-2: A business must complete, file with the Social Security Administration, and furnish to its employees Forms W-2, *Wage and Tax Statement,* showing the wages paid and taxes withheld for the year for each employee. Copies of W-2s must be given to both current and former employees no later than January 31 after the end of the tax year. Employers filing 250 or more Forms W-2 must file electronically unless granted a waiver by the IRS.

In 2012, employers with 250 or more workers have a new reporting requirement for health insurance.[9] *The Affordable Care Act* requires employers to report the cost of health care coverage under an employer-sponsored group health plan. The amount reported includes both the portion paid by the employer and the portion paid by the employee.

Forms 1099: A business must report nonemployee compensation paid during the tax year. It must provide a Form 1099-MISC to any independent contractor paid $600 or more by January 31, and send a copy to the IRS by February 28, or March 31 if the business files 1099s electronically. Specifically, the amounts that businesses are required to report on Forms 1099 include:

- Commissions, fees, and other compensation paid to a single individual when the total amount is $600 or more during the year
- Interest, rents, annuities, and income items paid to a single individual when the total amount is $600 or more

Under current law, most payments to corporations are exempt from Form 1099 reporting requirements. Also under current law, there is no requirement for payments issued in exchange for property, such as purchases of merchandise or equipment.

---

[9] IRS Notice 2012-9.

Forms 1099-MISC should only be used for payments that are made in the course of a trade or business. Personal payments are not reportable.

Example #1: Brett hires a painter to paint his home. The job costs $2,500. Brett is not required to report the payment to the painter, because it is for his personal residence. Because it was a personal payment, Brett cannot deduct the cost on his tax return. However, the painter is still required to report the income on his personal return.

Example #2: The following year, Brett calls the same painter to paint the interior of his business office, which he owns. The job costs $1,000. Since the cost is a business expense, Brett is required to issue a 1099-MISC to the contractor. The $1,000 is fully deductible on his business return as an expense.

Employment Taxes and Self-Employment Tax

Employers must withhold federal income tax from employees' wages. Businesses also withhold part of Social Security and Medicare taxes from employees' wages, and employers pay a matching amount. The IRS issues withholding tables each year so that employers can calculate out how much to withhold from each wage payment.

Employers must report federal income taxes withheld and employees' shares of employment taxes on Form 941, *Employer's Quarterly Federal Tax Return*, or Form 944, *Employer's Annual Federal Tax Return*. Businesses must also make federal tax deposits of employment taxes electronically, generally by using the Electronic Federal Tax Payment System (EFTPS).

In 2012, only the first $110,100 of wages and net earnings are subject to the Social Security portion of tax. There is no cap on the Medicare tax. Self-employed taxpayers figure self-employment tax using Schedule SE (Form 1040). Self-employed taxpayers can deduct half of their SE tax in figuring their adjusted gross income. Wage earners cannot deduct Social Security and Medicare taxes as a tax deduction on their individual returns.

General partners in a partnership are also considered self-employed individuals, and their income is also subject to self-employment tax, just like sole proprietors. Partners in a partnership receive a Schedule K-1 reporting their share of the partnership's income, loss, deductions, and credits.

Social Security and Medicare Taxes	
Social Security tax rate	**2012**
Employer's portion	6.2%
Employee's portion	4.2%
Total for self-employed taxpayer	10.4%
Maximum earnings subject to Social Security taxes	$110,100

Medicare tax rate	**2012**
Employer's portion	1.45%
Employee's portion	1.45%
Total for self-employed individual	2.9%
Maximum earnings subject to Medicare taxes	No limit

Backup Withholding

If a business does not have a payee's Social Security Number or Taxpayer Identification Number, it must withhold federal income taxes at a 28% rate. This is called backup withholding.

Example: Tina is a dentist who hires a cleaning service for her office. The cleaning service refuses to provide a Taxpayer Identification Number, so Tina is required to automatically withhold income tax on her payment to the cleaning service. She must file a Form 1099-MISC for the cleaning service to report the backup withholding amounts.

Trust Fund Recovery Penalty (TFRP)

A trust fund tax is money withheld from an employee's wages (Social Security, Medicare, and income tax) by an employer and held in trust until paid to the Treasury. If a business does not deposit its trust fund taxes in a timely manner, the IRS may assess the trust fund recovery penalty (TFRP). The amount of the penalty is equal to the unpaid balance of the trust fund tax. The TFRP may be assessed against any person who:

- is **responsible** for collecting or paying withheld income and employment taxes, or for paying collected excise taxes, and
- **willfully fails** to collect or pay them.

Once the IRS asserts the penalty, it can take collection action against the personal assets of anyone who is deemed a "responsible person." It is not only the presidents of companies or top finance and accounting personnel who may be held responsible for the TFRP. A "responsible person" may also include the person who signs checks for the company or who otherwise has authority to spend business funds, such as a bookkeeper.

For the IRS to determine that an individual willfully failed to pay the required taxes, the responsible person:

- Must have been, or should have been, aware of the outstanding taxes, and
- Intentionally disregarded the law or was plainly indifferent to its requirements (no evil intent or bad motive is required).

Example: Greta ran her own accounting business and also did the payroll for her local church. The church had four employees, including a choir director. Greta prepared and signed the payroll tax returns and all the checks and then gave them to the pastor to mail. The pastor did not mail the payroll tax reports or remit the payments to the IRS; instead, he took the money to purchase a new organ for the church. Greta knew the pastor was doing this, but did not report it. The IRS assessed the TFRP against the pastor, the church, and Greta. Even though Greta was just the bookkeeper, she knew that the pastor was improperly handling the payroll tax funds, and she did nothing about it, so the IRS can assess the TFRP against Greta.

Using available funds to pay other creditors when the business is unable to pay the employment taxes is an indication of willfulness.

Federal Unemployment (FUTA) Tax

A business reports and pays FUTA tax separately from federal income tax, and Social Security and Medicare taxes. FUTA tax is paid only by the employer—employees do not pay this tax or have it withheld from their pay. The standard FUTA tax rate is 6% on the first $7,000 of wages subject to FUTA. Employers may receive a credit of 5.4% when they file their Form 940, *Employers Annual Federal Unemployment (FUTA) Tax Return*, to result in a net FUTA tax rate of 0.6%.

Employee and Worker Classification

Because employers are responsible for withholding income, employment, and FUTA taxes, an employer must accurately determine whether a person is an independent contractor or an employee. An employer is not required to withhold or pay taxes on payments to independent contractors, which is why many employers will incorrectly classify a worker. An employer must understand the relationship that exists between himself and the person performing the services. A person performing services for business may be:

- An independent contractor
- An employee
- A statutory employee
- A statutory nonemployee

The IRS uses three characteristics to determine the relationship between a business and its workers:

- **Behavioral Control:** covers whether the business has a right to direct or control how the work is done.
- **Financial Control:** covers whether the business has a right to direct or control the financial and business aspects of the worker's job.
- **Type of Relationship:** relates to how the workers and the business owner perceive their relationship.

Examples of true independent contractors include web developers, mobile plumbers, freelance editors, and independent bookkeepers who follow an independent trade in which they offer their services to the public for a fee. However, whether such persons are truly employees or independent contractors depends on the facts in each case.

Example: Roger, an electrician, submits a job estimate to a housing complex for electrical work at $16 per hour for 400 hours. He is to receive $1,280 every two weeks for the next ten weeks. Even if he works more or less than 400 hours to complete the work, Roger will receive $6,400. He also performs additional electrical installations under contracts with other companies that he obtains through advertisements placed in the local paper. Roger is an independent contractor.

Example: Donna is a salesperson employed full-time by Supercargo Dealership, an auto dealer. She works six days a week and is on duty in the showroom on certain assigned days and times. Lists of prospective customers belong to the dealer. She has to develop leads and report results to the sales manager. Because of her experience, she requires only minimal assistance in closing and financing sales and in other phases of her work. She is paid a commission and is eligible for prizes and bonuses offered by the dealership. The business also pays the cost of health insurance and group-term life insurance for Donna. Donna is an employee of the dealership.

Employers who misclassify workers as independent contractors face substantial tax penalties. They are subject to additional penalties for failing to pay employment taxes and failing to file payroll tax forms.

Statutory Employees

Some workers are classified as statutory employees and are issued Forms W-2 by their employers. Statutory employees report their wages, income, and allowable expenses on Schedule C, just like self-employed taxpayers, but they are not required to pay self-employment tax, because their employers must treat them as employees for Social Security tax purposes.

Examples of statutory employees include full-time life insurance salespeople; traveling salespeople; certain commissioned truck drivers; officers of nonprofit organizations; and certain home workers who perform work on materials or goods furnished by the employer. If a person is a statutory employee, the "Statutory Employee" checkbox in box 13 of the taxpayer's Form W-2 should be checked.

Statutory Nonemployees Treated as Independent Contractors

There are two main categories of statutory nonemployees: direct sellers and licensed real estate agents. They are treated as self-employed for all federal tax purposes, including income and employment taxes if:

- Payments for their services are directly related to sales, rather than to the number of hours worked, and
- Services are performed under a written contract providing that they will not be treated as employees for federal tax purposes.

Compensation for a statutory nonemployee is reported on IRS Form 1099-MISC. The taxpayer then reports the income on Schedule C.

Example: Adele works as a full-time real estate agent for Golden Gate Real Estate Company. She visits Golden Gate's offices at least once a day to check her mail and her messages. She manages dozens of listings and splits her real estate commissions with Golden Gate. She does not work for any other real estate company. Adele is a statutory nonemployee. Golden Gate properly issues Adele a Form 1099-MISC for commissions and she files a Schedule C to report her income and expenses.

Directors of a corporation (members of the governing board) are also treated as statutory nonemployees. If an exempt organization compensates board members for performing their duties as directors, the organization should treat them as independent contractors. This is the most common type of statutory nonemployee that may be involved in an exempt organization.

Employing Family Members

The tax requirements for family employees may differ from other employees. The rules vary depending on the family relationship and the business entity type.

1. **Child working for a parent in a sole proprietorship or partnership when each partner is the child's parent:** Payments for the child's services are subject to income tax withholding regardless of age. If the child is under 18, payments are not subject to Social Security and Medicare taxes. If the child is under 21, payments are not subject to FUTA tax. However, all taxes must be withheld if the parent's business is one of three types: a corporation, an estate, or a partnership if only one of the parents is a partner.

2. **Parent working for a child:** Income tax, Social Security, and Medicare taxes are withheld, but not FUTA tax, regardless of the business entity type.

3. **Spouse employed by a spouse:** Income tax, Social Security, and Medicare taxes are withheld, but not FUTA tax. However, FUTA tax is withheld if the spouse works for a corporation or a partnership, even if the individual's spouse is a partner.

Unit 2: Questions

1. U.S. tax law requires businesses to submit a Form 1099-MISC for every contractor paid at least _____ for services during a year.

A. $400.
B. $500.
C. $600.
D. $1,000.

The answer is C. U.S. tax law requires businesses to submit a Form 1099-MISC for every contractor paid at least $600 for services during a year. Each payer must complete a Form 1099-MISC for each individual or business. Corporations are exempt recipients, so if a business makes payments to a corporation, it is not required to issue a 1099-MISC to the corporation. ###

2. Dan is a full-time life insurance salesman and a statutory employee. He receives a Form W-2 for his earnings. How should he report his income?

A. On Form 1040 as regular wage income.
B. On Schedule C, not subject to self-employment.
C. On Schedule C, subject to self-employment tax.
D. On Schedule K.

The answer is B. Statutory employees are unique because they report their wages, income, and allowable expenses on Schedule C, just like self-employed taxpayers. However, statutory employees are not required to pay self-employment tax because their employers must treat them as employees for Social Security tax purposes. ###

3. What is the minimum amount of time an employer should keep employment tax records, such as copies of W-2s?

A. Indefinitely.
B. Three years.
C. Four years.
D. Five years.

The answer is C. The IRS advises employers to keep all employment tax records for at least four years. ###

4. In 2012, an employer with _____ employees or more must report the cost of health care coverage under employer-sponsored group health plans.

A. 50.
B. 100.
C. 200.
D. 250.

The answer is D. Under the Affordable Care Act, employers with 250 or more workers must provide this information on their employees' W-2s in 2012. ###

5. In 2012, what is the threshold for Social Security tax to be withheld from an employee's wages?

A. $106,800.
B. $110,100.
C. $113,700.
D. No cap.

The answer is B. The threshold for Social Security tax is $110,100 in 2012. In tax year 2013, the threshold is $113,700. Medicare taxes are withheld on an employee's wages without regard to income levels. ###

6. All of the following statements are true about the trust fund recovery penalty except:

A. Someone who is simply indifferent to the requirements for paying trust fund taxes will never be assessed the penalty.
B. The IRS can take collection against the personal assets of anyone deemed a "responsible person."
C. A trust fund tax is comprised of income tax and Social Security and Medicare tax that is withheld from an employee's wages and held in "trust" to be paid to the U.S. Treasury.
D. The amount of the TFRP is equal to the unpaid balance of the trust fund tax.

The answer is A. In assessing the trust fund recovery penalty, the IRS may hold someone responsible who intentionally disregarded the law or was "plainly indifferent" to its requirements. No evil intent or bad motive is required. ###

7. The IRS uses all of the following characteristics to assess the relationship between a business and its workers except:

A. Type of relationship.
B. Financial control.
C. Income level.
D. Behavioral control.

The answer is C. Income level is not a factor in determining a worker's status. The main issue involves whether the employer or the worker has the right to direct or control how the work is done, and to control the financial and business aspects of the job. This then helps determine whether a worker is an employee or an independent contractor. ###

8. Caden, age 16, works behind the counter of a juice bar owned by his mother, a sole proprietor. Which of the following taxes, if any, should be withheld from his paycheck?

A. Income tax.
B. Income tax, Social Security and Medicare taxes.
C. Income tax, Social Security and Medicare taxes, and FUTA tax.
D. None of the above.

The answer is A. Family members who work for other family members are subject to different tax requirements. Only income tax is taken out of the paycheck of a child under age 18, so long as he is working for a parent who is a sole proprietor. ####

Unit 3: Accounting Periods and Methods

More Reading:
Publication 334, *Tax Guide for Small Business*
Publication 538, *Accounting Periods and Methods*

Tax Years

The tax year is an annual accounting period for reporting income and expenses. Individuals file their tax returns on a calendar year. Businesses have the option to file their tax returns on either a calendar year or a fiscal year basis.

Calendar tax year: Twelve consecutive months beginning January 1 and ending December 31.

Fiscal tax year: Twelve consecutive months ending on the last day of any month except December. A fiscal year-end does not have to fall on the same date each year. A "52/53-week" tax year is a fiscal tax year that varies from 52 to 53 weeks but does not have to end on the last day of the month. For example, some businesses choose to end their fiscal year on a particular day of the week, such as the last Friday in June.

Example: Paula works for the state of California. The state follows a fiscal year budget that runs from July 1, 2012 through June 30, 2013. This is a 12-month period not ending in December. Most federal and state government organizations operate on a fiscal year basis, as do some corporations.

Short tax year: A tax year of less than 12 months. A short tax year may result in the first or last year of an entity's existence, or when an entity changes its accounting period (for example, from a fiscal year to a calendar year, or vice versa). Even if a business is not in existence for a full year, the requirements for filing the return and paying any tax liability are generally the same as if a full 12-month tax year had ended on the last day of the short tax year.

Example: Eduardo and Jared started a business partnership in 2010. Eduardo died on November 1, 2012; therefore, the partnership is no longer in existence. Jared decides to continue the business as a sole proprietor. He must request a new employer identification number since his business structure has changed. The partnership is dissolved, and a final partnership tax return must be filed for the short tax year from January 1, 2012 to November 1, 2012.

> **Example:** Jillian formed Sorrento Rare Books, Inc. in February 2012. She immediately started having financial troubles and dissolved her corporation in October 2012. Jillian must file a short tax year corporate return for the period that Sorrento Rare Books was in existence.

A business adopts a tax year when it files its first income tax return. Any business may adopt the calendar year as its tax year. A new C corporation may generally elect to use a fiscal year instead. However, the IRS may require use of the calendar year in the following instances:

- The business keeps no books.
- There is no annual accounting period.
- The present tax year does not qualify as a fiscal year.
- The Internal Revenue Code or income tax regulations require use of a calendar year.

IRS Form 1128, *Application to Adopt, Change, or Retain a Tax Year*, is used to request a change in the tax year.

Required Tax Year

Partnerships, S corporations, and PSCs generally must use a required tax year. Unless it can establish a business purpose for a different tax year, a partnership's required tax year must generally conform to its partners' tax years. If a partner owns more than 50% interest in the partnership, this creates a majority interest in the capital and partnership profits. In this instance, the tax year of this partner is the required tax year for the partnership.

> **Example:** Busy Bee Partnership has two partners, both of which are C corporations. Corporation A owns a 30% partnership interest in Busy Bee and operates on a calendar year. Corporation B owns the remaining 70% of the partnership interest and operates on a fiscal year ending February 28. Since Corporation B owns a majority interest in Busy Bee, the partnership will file on the same tax year as Corporation B.

If there is no majority interest tax year, the partnership must use the tax year of all of the principal partners (those who have an interest of 5% or more in the capital and partnership profits). If there is no majority interest tax year and the principal partners do not have the same tax year, the partnership must use the tax year that would result in the *least aggregate* deferral of income to its partners.

Example: Andrew and Bella each have a 50% interest in the Chef Supplies Partnership. Andrew uses the calendar year and Bella uses a fiscal year ending November 30. Chef Supplies must adopt a fiscal year ending November 30 because this results in the least aggregate deferral of income to the partners, as shown in the following table.

With Year End 12/31:	Year End	Interest	Months of Deferral	Interest × Deferral
Andrew	12/31	50%	0	0
Bella	11/30	50%	11	5.5
Total Deferral				**5.5**
With Year End 11/30:	Year End	Interest	Months of Deferral	Interest × Deferral
Andrew	12/31	50%	1	0.5
Bella	11/30	50%	0	0
Total Deferral				**0.5**

Unless it can establish a business purpose for using a fiscal year, an S corporation or PSC must generally use a calendar year. A partnership, an S corporation, or a PSC can file IRS Form 1128, *Application to Adopt, Change, or Retain a Tax Year* to support its business purpose for using a fiscal year. For example, a seasonal business (such as a ski resort) may elect a fiscal year based on a genuine business purpose. It is not considered a legitimate business purpose to elect a particular fiscal tax year so that partners or shareholders may defer income recognition.

Section 444 Election

A partnership, an S corporation, or a PSC can request to use a tax year *other than* its required tax year by filing Form 8716, *Election to Have a Tax Year Other Than a Required Tax Year*. This is known as a section 444 election and it *does not apply* to any business that establishes a genuine business purpose for a different accounting period.

A partnership or an S corporation that makes this election must make certain required payments based upon the value of the tax deferral the owners receive by using a tax year different from the required tax year. A PSC that makes the election must make certain distributions to its owner-employees by December 31 of each applicable year.

A business can request a section 444 election if it meets all of the following requirements:

- It is not a member of a tiered structure.
- It has not previously had a section 444 election in effect.
- It elects a year that meets the deferral period requirement.

The deferral period depends on whether the entity is using the election to retain its tax year or to adopt or change its tax year. If it intends to retain its tax year, it may only do so if the deferral period is three months or less. The deferral period is the number of months between the beginning of the retained year and the end of the first required tax year.

If the entity is requesting adoption or a change to a tax year other than the required tax year, the deferral period is the number of months from the end of the new tax year to the end of the required tax year. Generally, the IRS will allow a section 444 election only if the deferral period is less than the shorter of:

- Three months, or
- The deferral period of the tax year being changed

> **Example:** Davidson Partnership, a newly formed partnership owned by two calendar-year partners, begins operations on December 1, 2012. Davidson wants to make a section 444 election to adopt a September 30 tax year. Davidson's deferral period for the tax year beginning December 1, 2012 is three months, the number of months between September 30 and December 31.

The section 444 election remains in effect until it is terminated. If the election is terminated, another section 444 election cannot be made for any tax year. The election also ends automatically when any of the following occurs:

- The entity changes to its required tax year.
- The entity liquidates.
- The entity becomes a member of a tiered structure.
- The IRS determines that the entity willfully failed to comply with the required payments or distributions.
- The entity is an S corporation and the S election is terminated. However, if the S corporation immediately becomes a PSC, it can continue the prior section 444 election.
- A PSC ceases to be a PSC. Again, however, if a PSC becomes an S corporation, it can continue the prior election.

If a business files its first tax return using the calendar tax year and later changes its business structure (such as moving from a sole proprietorship to a partnership), the business must continue to use the calendar year unless it receives IRS approval or is otherwise forced to change in order to comply with the IRC. A taxpayer's death marks the end of his final tax year as an individual and the following day is the beginning of the first tax year for his estate. The executor or personal representative of the estate is responsible for filing the individual's final income tax return (Form 1040), income tax returns for the estate (Form 1041), and possibly an estate tax return (Form 706).

Example: Desmond is an unmarried physician. On July 1, 2012, he dies, and his son, Raleigh, is named the executor of his father's estate. Raleigh is responsible for filing Desmond's final individual tax return (Form 1040). The final Form 1040 covers the income earned between January 1 and July 1. In addition, he must file income tax returns for the estate for the period that begins on July 2 and ends when the estate's assets have been distributed. Raleigh must request an EIN for his father's estate, which is considered a separate legal entity for tax purposes. Desmond's assets are valued at approximately $15 million on the date of his death. Therefore, in addition to income tax returns, Raleigh is also required to file an estate tax return (Form 706).

The executor chooses the estate's tax period when he files its first income tax return. Generally, the estate's first tax year is any period of 12 months or less that ends on the last day of a month. If the executor selects the last day of any month other than December, the estate has adopted a fiscal tax year. The due date for Form 1041 is the fifteenth day of the fourth month following the end of the entity's tax year.[10]

Filing Due Dates for Entities

April 15th of each year is the normal due date for filing most individual and partnership returns. Any time a return due date falls on a Saturday, Sunday, or legal holiday, the due date is delayed until the next business day.

Corporate tax returns are due on March 15th, if the corporation is on a calendar year. If the corporation is on a fiscal year, the tax return is due on the fifteen day of the third month following the end of the tax year. Nonprofit organizations must file their information returns by May 15 if they are on a calendar-year reporting period. If the exempt entity is on a fiscal year, the

---

[10] More detail on estates can be found in Unit 20, *Trusts and Estate Income Tax.*

return is due on the fifteenth day of the fifth month following the end of the tax year.

> **Example:** A calendar year C corporation dissolved on July 22, 2012 and ceased all operations. Its final return is due by October 15, 2012 (the fifteenth day of the third month following the close of their short tax year). The return will cover the short period from January 1, 2012 through July 22, 2012.

Accounting Periods and Income Tax Return Due Dates

Entity Type	Accounting Period	Due Date of Return
Sole Proprietor-ship	Adopts the same tax year as the owner, typically a calendar year.	**April 15** (same as individuals) . May request a 6 month extension.
Partnership	Adopts the same tax year as the partners who own more than 50% of the business, usually the calendar year.	**April 15,** or the 15th of the 4th month following the end of the tax year. May request a 5 month extension.
C Corporation	Fiscal year or calendar year.	**March 15,** or the 15th of the 3rd month following the end of the tax year. May request a 6 month extension.
S Corporation	Calendar year unless a valid section 444 election is made.	**March 15,** or the 15th of the 3rd month following the end of the tax year. May request a 6 month extension.
Exempt Entities	Fiscal year or calendar year.	**May 15,** or the 15th of the 5th month following the end of the tax year. May request a 3 month extension, and then a second 3 month extension.
Estates and Fiduciary returns (Form 1041 and Form 706)	Generally a fiscal year (the tax year begins on the day after the decedent's date of death and the executor then selects a tax year when the first return is filed.)	Form 1041 is due the 15th of the 4th month following the end of the tax year. Form 706 is due nine months after the date of death. A six month extension is available.

Extensions

Entities and individuals may request an extension of time to file their federal income tax returns. An extension does not grant the entity additional time to pay any tax due. It only provides additional time to file the return. Any estimated tax due must be paid by the filing deadline, or the entity will be subject to interest and penalties on the amount of unpaid tax.

Accounting Methods

An accounting method is a set of rules used to determine when and how income and expenses are reported. No single accounting method is required of all taxpayers. However, the taxpayer must use a system that reflects income and expenses, and it must be used consistently from year to year.

A business owner may use different accounting methods if he has two *separate and distinct* businesses. According to the IRS, two businesses will not be considered *separate and distinct,* however, unless a separate set of books and records is maintained for each business.

Example: Blake is a self-employed enrolled agent. He prepares tax returns from January through April every year. He is also a motivational speaker and does speaking engagements on martial arts because he is an accomplished martial artist. He decides to report his tax preparation business using the accrual method and his martial arts business using the cash method. He keeps separate books and records for each business. Blake may use different accounting methods because he has two separate and distinct businesses with separate sets of records.

Acceptable Accounting Methods

Businesses report taxable income under the following accounting methods:

- Cash method

- Accrual method

- Special methods of accounting for certain items of income and expenses

- Hybrid method using elements of the methods above

Different rules apply to each accounting method. The most common accounting method is the *cash method*, which is used by most individuals and small businesses. The *accrual method* is used by most large corporations and is a more accurate method of recognizing income and expenses, because it reflects when taxable income is actually earned.

Cash Method

The cash method of accounting is the simplest method to use, but the IRS restricts its use to certain types of businesses. The following types of businesses are required to use the accrual method:

- A corporation (other than an S corporation) with average annual gross receipts exceeding $5 million
- A partnership with a corporate partner (other than an S corporation) with average annual gross receipts exceeding $5 million
- Any business that carries or produces inventory, unless the business has average annual gross receipts of $1 million or less
- Any tax shelter, regardless of its size
- Any corporation with long-term contracts

> **Example:** Cameron and William Davis form the Davis and Davis Architectural Corporation, which is a C corporation. In 2012, the income for the corporation is $4.2 million. The Davis and Davis Corporation may still use the cash method because it has gross receipts under $5 million and does not have any inventory.

> **Example:** Corinne and her husband, Doug, run Bicycles-R-Us as a husband-and-wife partnership. Bicycles-R-Us designs and sells custom bicycles and carries a substantial inventory. In 2012, Bicycles-R-Us had gross receipts of $2.3 million. Bicycles-R-Us cannot use the cash method because it produces inventory and its average annual gross receipts exceed $1 million.

Exceptions: The following entities may use the cash method of accounting:
- A qualified family farming corporation with gross receipts of $25 million or less
- A qualified personal service corporation
- Artists, authors, and photographers who sell works that they have created by their own efforts

Gross Receipts Test

An entity (other than a tax shelter) that meets the gross receipts test can use the cash method. An entity generally meets the test if its average annual gross receipts are $5 million or less, determined by adding the gross receipts for that tax year and the two preceding tax years and dividing the total by three.

Gross receipts for a short tax year are annualized. An entity that fails to meet the gross receipts test for any tax year is prohibited from using the cash method and must change to the accrual method, effective for the tax year in which the entity fails to meet the test.

If a business produces or sells merchandise, it usually has inventory. Businesses that have inventory must use the accrual method unless their average annual gross receipts are $1 million or less.

Example: Green Bay Corporation produces inventory and its gross receipts are $200,000 for 2010, $800,000 for 2011, and $1,100,000 for 2012. The company's average annual gross receipts are therefore $700,000 ([$200,000 + $800,000 + $1,100,000] ÷ 3 = $700,000). Green Bay Corporation is allowed to continue to use the cash method.

Example: Crape Company makes golf car parts. The company carries inventory throughout the year. Crape's gross receipts have never exceeded $900,000. Therefore, Crape may continue to use the cash method.

The 12-Month Rule

Under the cash method, taxpayers generally deduct expenses when they are actually paid based upon the presumption that the expenses relate to the current tax year and are not deductible if paid in advance. This means that businesses generally may not attempt to lower their taxable income by paying expenses applicable to future years. The taxpayer would instead capitalize the costs paid in advance and deduct them in the years to which they apply. However, there is an exception called the 12-month rule. Under the 12-month rule, the cash-basis taxpayer is *not* required to capitalize amounts paid that do not extend beyond the earlier of the following:

- 12 months after the benefit begins, or
- The end of the tax year after the tax year in which payment is made.

Example: Sherry is a calendar-year sole proprietor and pays $3,000 in 2012 for an insurance policy that is effective for three years (36 months), beginning on July 1, 2012. This payment does not qualify for the 12-month rule. Therefore, only $500 (6/36 x $3,000) is deductible in 2012, $1,000 (12/36 x $3,000) is deductible in 2013, $1,000 (12/36 x $3,000) is deductible in 2014, and the remaining $500 is deductible in 2015, when the policy expires.

Example: Garrison Partnership is a calendar-year business. It pays $15,000 on July 1, 2012 for a business liability policy that is effective for one year beginning on July 1, 2012. The 12-month rule applies, and the full $15,000 is deductible in 2012.

Example: Mikayla is a sole proprietor who rents retail space for her eyebrow threading business. She pays two years of rent in advance in order to receive a substantial discount from her landlord. She cannot use the 12-month rule because the benefit from her advance payment exceeds the 12-month time period. She must amortize the expense for rent over the time period to which the payment applies.

Constructive Receipt

Under the cash method, taxpayers report income when it is actually or "constructively" received during the tax year. Income is constructively received when the amount is credited to the taxpayer's account or made available without restriction so that the taxpayer or his agent has access to the funds. The taxpayer does not need to have physical possession of the payment.

Example: Patel Brothers Partnership operates on the cash method. Interest income is credited to Patel's bank account in December 2012, but the partners do not withdraw it until January 2013. The partnership must include the interest income in its gross income for 2012, not 2013. The partnership had ownership and control of the income in 2012, so it is taxable in the year received.

Income is not considered to be constructively received if actual control of the income is restricted.

Example: Better Jail Bonds LLP is a cash-basis partnership that bills a customer on December 10, 2012. The customer sends the company a check postdated to January 2, 2013. The check cannot be deposited until 2013 because it was postdated. Better Jail Bonds would include this income in gross income for 2013, since constructive receipt did not occur until then.

Accrual Method

Under the accrual method of accounting, an entity reports income in the year earned and deducts or capitalizes expenses as they are incurred. The purpose of the accrual method is to match income and expenses in the correct year. Under the accrual method, a business generally records income when a sale occurs or income is earned, regardless of when the business gets paid. Income is reported on the *earliest* of the following dates:

- When payment is received
- When the taxpayer earns the income

- When the income is due to the taxpayer
- When title has passed

A business that uses the accrual method must apply it to reporting expenses as well as income. Expenses are reported as soon as they are incurred. It does not matter when the business actually pays for the expenses.

The accrual method gives a more accurate assessment of a business's financial situation than the cash method. Income earned in one period is more accurately matched against the expenses that correspond to that period, so a business gets a better picture of net profits for each period.

Example: Ali's Computer Inc. is a calendar-year, accrual-basis corporation. The business sold a computer on December 28, 2012 for $2,500. Ali billed the customer in the first week of January 2013, but did not receive payment until February 2013. Ali must include the $2,500 in his 2012 income, the year the company actually *earned* the income.

Advance payments are generally included in income in the year they are received. However, an accrual basis taxpayer may postpone reporting the income for services to be performed in the next tax year. Advance payments for the sale of goods may be subject to an alternative method. The advance payment would be included in income in the earlier of:

- The tax year in which the business includes advance payments in gross receipts for its normal accounting method; or
- The tax year in which the business includes the income in financial reports, such as those provided to shareholders.

Hybrid Accounting Method

Businesses may also use a hybrid accounting method that is a combination of the cash, accrual, and other special methods if the hybrid method clearly reflects income and is used consistently. The following restrictions to the hybrid method apply:

- If an inventory is necessary to account for income, the business must use an accrual method for purchases and sales. The cash method can be used for other income and expense items.
- If an entity uses the cash method for reporting income, it must use the cash method for reporting expenses.
- If an entity uses the accrual method for reporting expenses, it must use the accrual method for reporting income.

Changing Accounting Methods

A business may choose any permitted accounting method when it files its first tax return. Subsequent changes, either in the overall accounting method or the treatment of a material item, generally require that the taxpayer obtain IRS approval. Prior approval is needed for:

- Changes from cash to accrual or vice versa, unless the change is required by tax law
- Changes in the method used to value inventory (such as switching from LIFO to FIFO)
- Changes in the accounting method to figure depreciation

The taxpayer must file Form 3115, *Application for Change in Accounting Method*, to request a change in either an overall accounting method or the accounting treatment of any item. However, IRS consent is not required for the following:

- Switching to straight-line depreciation from accelerated methods (once a taxpayer switches to straight-line for an asset, he cannot switch back)
- Making an adjustment in the useful life of a depreciable or amortizable asset (but a taxpayer cannot change the recovery period for MACRS or ACRS property)
- Correcting a math error or an error in figuring tax liability
- A change in accounting method when the change is required by tax law, such as when a business's average gross receipts exceed $5 million

Example: Gary is a general partner in Ultimate Consumer Goods, and discovers a major error in the useful life of a depreciable asset—the asset should have been depreciated over 15 years, rather than five. Ultimate Consumer Goods does not have to ask the IRS for permission in order to correct the depreciation error.

Inventory Tracking and Valuation

A business that produces or sells products must track its inventory in order to correctly calculate income. Businesses often make a full physical inventory count at the end of each tax year, as well as at other reasonable intervals. The recorded inventory balances are then adjusted to agree with the actual counts. Physical inventory counts may identify irregularities such as theft, as well as damaged goods and obsolete products.

Example: Wrightwood Grocery Store takes a physical inventory once a month. During the physical inventory, store employees are required to record any damaged goods such as dented cans and ripped packaging. When the physical inventory is completed, the manager does a reconciliation based to her records. She may also discover that a portion of the inventory is missing, apparently due to theft. She adjusts the books to record the theft losses and damaged merchandise.

A business's inventory should include all of the following, if applicable:
- Merchandise or stock in trade
- Raw materials
- Work in process
- Finished products
- Supplies that physically become a part of the item intended for sale (labels, packaging, etc.)

Merchandise that is included in inventory includes:
- Purchased merchandise if the title has passed to the taxpayer, even if the merchandise is still in transit or the business does not have physical possession of it for another reason.
- Goods under contract for sale that have not yet been segregated and applied to the contract.
- Goods out on consignment.
- Goods held for sale in display rooms or booths located away from the taxpayer's place of business

For mail order businesses, merchandise is generally included in the closing inventory until the buyer pays for it. The following merchandise is not included in inventory:
- Goods the business has sold, but only if legal title (ownership) has passed to the buyer.
- Goods consigned to the taxpayer.
- Goods ordered for future delivery if the business does not yet have title.

Land, buildings, and equipment used in a business are never included in inventory.

Shipping Terms and Transfer of Ownership

Certain shipping terms dictate when a taxpayer must recognize income or take an item out of inventory. The terms indicate the point at which ownership of goods transfers from shipper to buyer. The three most common terms are:

1. **FOB destination:** Title (ownership) of the goods passes to the buyer at the point of destination (when the goods arrive at the buyer's location).

2. **FOB shipping point:** Title (ownership) of the goods passes to the buyer at the point of shipment (when the goods leave the seller's premises). FOB shipping point is also called "FOB origin."

3. **C.O.D.** ("cash on delivery" or "collect on delivery"): Collection of the payment upon delivery. COD title does not pass until payment is remitted for the goods.

Example: Weitzman Furniture Company is a calendar-year, accrual-basis corporation that manufactures custom household furniture. For purposes of its financial reports, the company accrues income when it ships furniture. For tax purposes, it does not accrue income until the furniture has been delivered and accepted by the buyer. In 2012, the company receives an advance payment of $8,000 for an order of furniture to be custom manufactured for a total price of $20,000. Weitzman ships the furniture FOB destination to the customer on December 26, 2012, but it is not delivered and accepted by the customer until January 3, 2013. For tax purposes, Weitzman must include the $8,000 advance payment in gross income for 2012, and must include the remaining $12,000 of the contract price in gross income for 2013, after the furniture was accepted and the title passed to the buyer.

Acceptable Inventory Methods

There are several common inventory accounting methods, which identify the cost of items in inventory. They include the specific identification method, the weighted average cost method, FIFO, and LIFO.

Specific Identification Method

This method is used when it is possible to identify and match the actual cost to specific items in inventory. It is most useful with an inventory that includes a limited number of highly specific and high-dollar items, such as custom goods or rare items like artwork or gemstones. The business simply accounts for each individual item as it is sold.

Example: The Classic Custom dealership sells rare collectible and classic cars. Each car is inventoried and tracked individually by the license plate number. The cost of each car is tracked on a separate spreadsheet. When a car is sold, the vehicle is taken out of inventory. This is an example of specific identification inventory valuation.

Average Cost Method

This method is commonly used when a company has large quantities of items that are largely interchangeable rather than individually unique. It allows the company to calculate an average cost per unit without tracking the individual units as they are purchased, manufactured, or sold. The formula for figuring average cost is:

Average Unit Cost = (Total Cost of Units Purchased or Manufactured)/ (Total Quantity of Units)
Aggregate Inventory Cost = (Average Unit Cost) x (Units in Current Inventory)

Example: The Average Cost Method

Anna owns a pet store. She purchases five dog leashes at $10 apiece. The following week, the price of the leashes goes up, and she purchases five more leashes at $20 apiece. Anna then sells five leashes the following week. The weighted average cost of Anna's inventory is calculated as follows:

Total cost of leashes:
(Five leashes at $10 each) = $50
(Five leashes at $20 each) = $100
Total number of units = 10 leashes
Weighted average = $150 / 10 = $15

$15 is the average cost per leash for the 10 leashes Anna has purchased. If she applies this average cost to the five leashes unsold at the end of the week, the calculated cost of the leashes on hand would be $75 ($15 times 5 leashes).

First-In, First-Out (FIFO)

The first-in, first-out (FIFO) method is used by most major corporations to assign cost to their inventory.

With FIFO, the assumption is that inventory is sold in the order that it is acquired or produced, with the oldest goods sold first and the newest goods sold last (such as rotating stock in a grocery store). The actual quantities in inventory at the end of the tax year are assigned costs based upon the cost of items of the same type that the business most recently purchased or produced. The formula for figuring inventory based on the FIFO method is as follows:

> **Unit Cost per item = (Cost/Quantity) for the most recent lot of the item that was purchased or produced**
>
> **Aggregate Inventory Cost = (Unit Cost per item x Quantity) for each item**

In an economy with rising prices (inflation),[11] the use of FIFO will typically assign a higher value to ending inventory than other methods, and thus result in reporting higher taxable income.

Example: FIFO Method

Rabbata Electronics, a cash-basis, calendar-year taxpayer, sells car audio equipment. Beginning inventory on January 1 included 300 car stereos with cost of $20. On January 10 the business purchased 600 stereos at $20.10; on January 16 it purchased 400 stereos for $20.20; and on January 25 it purchased 500 stereos for $20.30. In January the business sold 1,200 car stereos. Under FIFO it is assumed that the oldest merchandise is sold first. Rabbata Electronics had a beginning inventory of 300 stereos—those units are assumed to leave inventory first, followed by the units purchased on January 10 and January 16. Thus, the cost assigned to the units on hand at the end of January is determined as follows:

Beginning inventory	**300**
January 10 purchases	600
January 16 purchases	400
January 25 purchases	500
Total units available	1,800
Units sold	(1,200)
Units in inventory at end of January	**600**

Composition based upon FIFO assumption:

January 25 purchases	500 @ 20.30 =	10,150
Unsold portion of January 16 purchases	100 @ 20.20 =	2,020
Total inventory at end of January	600	$12,170

---

[11] This concept of "rising prices" has been on numerous prior exams. Know the difference between LIFO and FIFO with regard to inventory valuation and how it affects income reporting.

Last-In, First-Out (LIFO)

The last-in, first-out (LIFO) method assumes that the newest inventory purchased or produced is sold first, and the oldest inventory is sold last. Since the prices of goods, labor, and materials generally rise over time, this method will typically result in assigning a lower aggregate cost to inventory on hand, higher amounts as the cost of sales, and thus lower taxable. As a result, use of the LIFO method is subject to close scrutiny by the IRS and highly complex rules governing its calculation.

The formula for figuring inventory using the LIFO method is as follows:

> **Unit Cost per item = (Cost/Quantity) for the oldest lot of the item that was purchased or produced**
>
> **Aggregate Inventory Cost = (Unit Cost per item x Quantity) for each item**

Example: LIFO Method

Using the same background information for Rabbata Electronics outlined before, but using a LIFO assumption rather than FIFO, the 300 units on hand at January 1 are assumed to have a LIFO cost per unit of only $10 because Rabbata has been in business for twenty years and the unit costs of its purchases have approximately doubled in that period due to inflation. Therefore, the cost assigned to the units on hand at the end of January is determined as follows:

Beginning inventory	**300**
January 10 purchases	600
January 16 purchases	400
January 25 purchases	500
Total units available	1,800
Units sold	(1,200)
Units in inventory at end of January	**600**

Composition based upon LIFO assumption:

Beginning inventory	300 @ 10.00 =	3,000
Unsold portion of January 10 purchases	300 @ 20.10 =	6,030
Total inventory at end of January	600	$9,030

In comparison to the FIFO example above, the aggregate cost assigned to ending inventory using LIFO would be lower. Since the income generated by Rabbata in January from selling 1,200 would be the same using either accounting method for inventory, its taxable income would be higher using FIFO instead of LIFO.

Unless a business has used the LIFO method from its inception, it must obtain permission from the IRS to change to the LIFO from another method of inventory valuation. Permission is requested by filing Form 970, *Application To Use LIFO Inventory Method*.

Differences between FIFO and LIFO

Economic Climate	FIFO	LIFO
Periods of Rising Prices (Inflation)	(+) Higher value of inventory	(-) Lower value of inventory
	(-) Lower cost of goods sold	(+) Higher cost of goods sold
Periods of Falling Prices (Deflation)	(-) Lower value of inventory	(-) Higher value of inventory
	(+) Higher cost of goods sold	(+) Lower cost of goods sold

Valuing Inventory

The value of a business's inventory is a major factor in figuring taxable income. In addition to the inventory accounting methods described above, the following methods are commonly used to assign value to inventory: cost, lower of cost or market, and retail.

Cost Method: All direct and indirect costs are included.

- For merchandise on hand at the beginning of the tax year, cost means the ending inventory price of the goods.
- For merchandise purchased during the year, cost means the invoice price minus appropriate discounts, plus transportation or other charges incurred in acquiring the goods. It may also include other costs that must be capitalized under the uniform capitalization rules (covered later in this unit).
- For merchandise produced during the year, cost means all direct and indirect costs, including those that have to be capitalized under the uniform capitalization rules.

A trade discount is sometimes given for volume or quantity purchases. The cost of inventory must be reduced by trade discounts.

Lower of Cost or Market Method: The market value of each item on hand is compared with its cost and the lower amount is used as its inventory value. This is a good way to record the actual value of inventory when the inventory loses value quickly, such as happens with fashion clothing. This method applies to the following:

- Goods purchased and on hand

- The basic elements of cost (direct materials, direct labor, and certain indirect costs) of goods being manufactured and finished goods on hand

The lower of cost or market method cannot be used in conjunction with the LIFO method.

Example: Lower of Cost or Market

Graham makes leather motorcycle accessories at his factory. Under the lower of cost or market method, the following items would be valued at $600 in closing inventory.

Inventory Item	Cost	Market	Lower
Leather jacket	$300	$500	$300
Motorcycle helmets	$200	$100	$100
Leather motorcycle chaps	$450	$200	$200
Total	**$950**	**$800**	**$600**

Graham must value each item in the inventory separately. He cannot value the entire inventory at cost ($950) and at market ($800) and then use the lower of the two figures.

Retail Method: Under the retail method, the total retail selling price of goods on hand at the end of the tax year in each department or of each class of goods is reduced to approximate cost by using an average markup expressed as a percentage of the total retail selling price. For example, if a store marks up its merchandise by 35%, that percentage would be used as a basis for estimating the cost of its current inventory.

Cost of Goods Sold (COGS)

Part of the inventory equation consists of figuring cost of goods sold (COGS), which is deducted from a business's gross receipts to determine its gross profit. If an expense is included in COGS, it cannot be deducted again as a business expense. The following are types of expenses that go into figuring COGS:

- The cost of products or raw materials, including freight
- Storage
- Direct labor costs (including contributions to pensions or annuity plans) for workers who produce the products
- Factory overhead

Postage or shipping costs to deliver a finished product to a buyer are not included in inventory costs.

Example: In calculating COGS, American Custom Shoes includes the cost of leather and thread in the shoes it manufactures, as well as wages for the workers that produce the shoes. The shipping cost of sending its finished shoes to customers is not included in COGS, and is deductible as a current expense.

The equation for cost of goods sold is as follows:

Beginning Inventory + Inventory Purchases – Ending Inventory = Cost of Goods Sold

COGS is recorded as an expense as the company sells its goods.

Example: Doggie Delights Inc. is a cash-basis corporation that manufactures custom dog sweaters. In January, Doggie Delights has $20,000 in overall sales. In the same month, the corporation also has a number of expenses, including wages for the sweater designers ($5,000) and the cost of raw materials, including yarn, appliqué, rhinestones, and other raw materials ($3,000). The wages and the cost of the raw materials are directly related to the production of the inventory (the sweaters) and must be included in the cost of goods sold calculation. Other expenses not directly related to the manufacture of the sweaters, which might include items like a receptionist's salary ($1,500), telephone charges ($130), and advertising ($1,200) are also expensed, but are not part of COGS. The income statement for January would look like this:

Gross income from sales:	$20,000
COGS: ($5,000 + $3,000)	($8,000)
Gross profit	$12,000
Other expenses: ($1,500 + $130 + $1,200)	($2,830)
Net income for January	**$9,170**

Other Inventory Requirements

Goods that cannot be sold at normal prices or are unusable because of damage, imperfections, shop wear, changes of style, odd or broken lots, or other similar causes should be valued at their actual selling price minus the direct cost of disposition, no matter which method is used to value the rest of the entity's inventory.

When a business incurs a casualty or theft loss of inventory, it increases the cost of goods sold by properly reporting opening and closing inventories.

The business can also choose to take the loss separately as a casualty or theft loss. If the entity chooses to report a casualty loss, it must adjust opening inventory to eliminate the loss items and avoid counting the loss twice.

If a taxpayer removes items from inventory for personal use, he is required to subtract the cost of personal use items from total purchases.

Uniform Capitalization Rules (UNICAP)

The uniform capitalization rules (commonly referred to as UNICAP) provide detailed guidance regarding the direct costs and certain indirect costs related to the production of goods or the purchase of merchandise for resale that businesses must capitalize as the cost of inventory.

These costs cannot be expensed and deducted when incurred. They must be capitalized and deducted later, when the inventory is used or sold.

Example: Creative Costumes manufactures Halloween and stage costumes. During August, Creative Costumes purchases raw materials to produce costumes for the upcoming holiday. All the materials and shipping costs associated with the inventory must be capitalized rather than expensed. As the Halloween costumes are sold, Creative Costumes expenses the costs associated with the inventory as cost of goods sold. At the end of each month, Creative Costumes does a physical inventory count and adjusts COGS for any damaged or stolen inventory.

Example: MTG Studios produces movies for Hollywood. Film production is subject to the uniform capitalization rules, so MTG must capitalize all of its costs, including set design, costumes, special effects, film editing, and salaries for actors and production workers. When a film is finally completed and distributed, MTG Studios is allowed to deduct the production costs as COGS.

Most types of businesses are subject to the uniform capitalization rules, including the following:

- Retailers or wholesalers (if they produce or purchase merchandise for resale),
- Manufacturers who produce property for sale; and
- Taxpayers who construct assets for their own trade or business.

However, the uniform capitalization rules do not apply to the following:

- Resellers of personal property with average annual gross receipts of $10 million or less for the three prior tax years.
- Nonbusiness property (such as a hobby that produces occasional income).
- Research and experimental expenditures.
- Intangible drilling and development costs of oil and gas or geothermal wells.
- Property produced under a long-term contract.
- Timber raised, harvested, or grown, and the underlying land.
- Qualified creative expenses incurred as self-employed writers, photographers, or artists that are otherwise deductible on their tax returns.
- Loan originations.
- Property provided to customers in connection with providing services. It must be *de minimis* and not be included in inventory in the hands of the service provider.
- The costs of certain producers who use a simplified production method and whose total indirect costs are $200,000 or less.

Unit 3: Questions

1. Which of the following date ranges would be considered a fiscal tax year?

A. January 1, 2012 to December 31, 2012.
B. February 15, 2012 to February 15, 2013.
C. July 1, 2012 to June 30, 2013.
D. May 1, 2012 to May 31, 2013.

The answer is C. A fiscal tax year is any tax year that is 12 consecutive months and ends on the last day of any month except December. Answer A is incorrect because this is a calendar year, not a fiscal year. Answer B is incorrect because a fiscal year must end on the last day of the month. Answer D is incorrect because it is more than 12 consecutive months. ###

2. Which of the following dates would not be considered the end of an acceptable tax year?

A. January 31.
B. April 15.
C. December 31.
D. The last Friday in February.

The answer is B. April 15 is the IRS due date for individual tax returns, not the end of a tax year. Answer A is incorrect because January 31 is the last day of the month, which qualifies as a fiscal tax year-end. Answer C is incorrect because December 31 is a calendar year-end. Answer D is incorrect because a tax year that ends on the same day of the week every year is a 52/53-week tax year, which is a legitimate type of fiscal year. ###

3. What is the definition of the calendar year?

A. A calendar year is always from January 1 to December 31.
B. A calendar year is always a 12-month period ending on the last day of any month.
C. A calendar year can end on any day of the month, so long as the period spans 12 months.
D. A calendar year starts on April 15 and ends on April 15 the following year.

The answer is A. A calendar year is always the 12-month period from January 1 to December 31. ###

4. A business must adopt its first tax year by what date?

A. The due date (including extensions) for filing a return.
B. The due date (not including extensions) for filing a return.
C. The date the EIN is established.
D. The first time the business pays estimated payments.

The answer is B. A business must adopt its first tax year by the due date (not including extensions) for filing a return for that year. A business adopts a tax year when it files its first income tax return. ###

5. Vargas Cellular Corporation was organized on April 1, 2012. It elected the calendar year as its tax year. When is the first tax return due for Vargas Cellular for this short tax year?

A. April 15, 2013.
B. April 15, 2012.
C. March 15, 2013.
D. May 15, 2013.

The answer is C. Since the corporation chose a calendar year, its first tax return is due March 15, 2013. This short period return will cover April 1, 2012 through December 31, 2012. Corporate tax returns are due on the fifteenth day of the third month after the end of the corporation's taxable year. ###

6. Which of the following entities may use the cash method of accounting?

A. A family farming corporation with average gross receipts of $22 million.
B. A C corporation with average gross receipts of $50 million.
C. A tax shelter with $50,000 in average gross receipts.
D. A corporation with long-term contracts and average gross receipts of $900,000.

The answer is A. A family farming corporation may use the cash method of accounting if its average annual gross receipts are $25 million or less. A tax shelter must always use the accrual method, regardless of its gross receipts. A corporation with long-term contracts must always use the accrual method. A C corporation with gross receipts exceeding $5 million is required to use the accrual method. ###

7. Which of the following changes in accounting method does not require prior approval from the IRS?

A. A change from FIFO to LIFO inventory valuation.
B. A change from the cash method to the accrual method.
C. A change in the overall method of figuring depreciation.
D. A correction of a math error in depreciating an asset.

The answer is D. The correction of a math error does not require prior approval from the IRS. Consent from the IRS is not required for the following changes:
•Correction of a math error for computing tax liability or other mathematical error.
•A correction in depreciable life or correction of a depreciation error.
•An adjustment to an asset's useful life. ###

8. Helen Banner is the owner of Banner's Custom Lamps, Inc., a calendar-year, accrual-basis S corporation. She sells five lamps to Sonny's Interior Design on December 21, 2012, billing Sonny's for $2,500. Sonny's Interior Design pays the invoice on January 15, 2013. Banner's Custom Lamps would include this income in which tax year?

A. 2012.
B. 2013.
C. 2014.
D. None of the above.

The answer is A. The income would be included in Banner's 2012 tax return, because Banner is using the accrual method of accounting for income and expenses. Under the accrual method, income is reported in the year earned and expenses are deducted in the year incurred. Since Banner sold the lamps in 2012, the income would be reported in 2012, regardless of when payment is actually received. ###

9. A company can choose to compute taxable income under which of the following methods?

A. Hybrid method.
B. Accrual method.
C. Cash method.
D. All of the above.

The answer is D. Unless specifically prohibited by the IRC or income tax regulations, a company can choose to compute its taxable income under any of the listed methods. Any accounting method may be acceptable if it clearly reflects income and is applied consistently from year to year. ###

10. Ben owns a jewelry store. All of the following transactions are examples of constructive receipt of income in 2012 except?

A. Ben receives a check payment on December 31, 2012, but does not deposit the check in the bank until January 2, 2013.
B. Ben receives a direct deposit of funds to his bank account on December 15, 2012, but does not withdraw any of the funds until March 2013.
C. Ben receives a signed IOU from a delinquent account in November 2012. He receives payment on this account on January 10, 2013.
D. An escrow agent receives a payment on Ben's behalf that is restricted for his use. It is an advance payment for a custom ring, but he cannot access any of the funds until the ring is delivered and inspected. On December 25, 2012, the ring is delivered and the restriction is lifted. Ben picks up the cash on January 9, 2013.

The answer is C. According to the doctrine of constructive receipt, income is included in gross income when a person has an unqualified right to the funds. Constructive receipt must be more than just a billing, an offer, or a mere promise to pay. The amount promised to Ben as an IOU, therefore, does not have to be included in income for 2012. ###

11. Which of the following entities may not use the cash method of accounting?

A. A partnership that produces inventory for sale to customers and has $1.2 million in average annual gross receipts.
B. A C corporation without inventory that has $4.5 million in average annual gross receipts.
C. A qualified family farming corporation with $24 million in average annual gross receipts.
D. A sole proprietor with inventory and $500,000 in average annual gross receipts.

The answer is A. Generally, an entity cannot use the cash method if it has average annual gross receipts exceeding $5 million. However, if a company has inventory, the threshold for gross receipts is $1 million. A qualified family farming corporation may use the cash method if its average gross receipts do not exceed $25 million. ###

12. Ray operates a retail store using the accrual method of accounting and reports income on Schedule C, Net Profit or Loss from Business. He also runs a lawn care service that operates only in the summer months. Which of the following statements is true?

A. The lawn care business is required to use the accrual method of accounting because Ray has already elected this method for his other business, and all businesses operated by one individual must use the same method of accounting.
B. The lawn care business may use either the cash or accrual method of accounting, so long as both businesses have separate and distinct records.
C. Ray may keep one set of records for the two businesses and use different methods of accounting for each one.
D. Ray must combine the income for both businesses and keep one set of record books for both.

The answer is B. A taxpayer may use different methods of accounting for two distinct and separate businesses. Separate accounting books must be kept for each business. ###

13. The following are all acceptable methods of accounting for inventory except:

A. Specific identification.
B. Coupon method.
C. FIFO.
D. LIFO.

The answer is B. FIFO, LIFO, and specific identification are all acceptable inventory methods. The "coupon method" is not. ###

14. Jenny owns a small side business selling makeup door-to-door. She reports her income and loss on Schedule C. Occasionally, she takes items out of inventory for her own personal use. In 2012, she took $250 worth of makeup for her own use. What is the proper tax treatment of this action?

A. Jenny must reduce the amount of her total inventory purchases by $250.
B. Jenny may take an expense of $250 on Schedule C for the personal use items.
C. Jenny must increase the cost of her purchases by the value of her personal use items.
D. Jenny may deduct the $250 on Schedule A as an employee business expense.

The answer is A. Taxpayers are required to subtract the cost of personal use items from total purchases, if they remove items for personal use from business inventory. ###

15. Under the lower of cost or market method of valuing inventory, what is the value of the inventory as a whole, based on the table below?

Item	Cost	FMV
Shirts	$200	$500
Shoes	$300	$200
Shorts	$225	$150
Total	**$725**	**$850**

A. $725.
B. $850.
C. $750.
D. $550.

The answer is D. To value inventory using the "lower of cost or market" method, compare the cost and the fair market value of each of the items in inventory, and choose the lower of the two to obtain the inventory's value. The answer is calculated as follows:
(Shirts $200 + Shoes $200 + shorts $150) = $550 inventory valuation. ###

16. Which of the following activities would make a taxpayer subject to the uniform capitalization rules?

A. A taxpayer produces items as a hobby and occasionally sells them at a profit.
B. A taxpayer produces property for sale to wholesale retailers.
C. A taxpayer acquires raw land and holds it for investment.
D. A taxpayer refurbishes multiple automobiles for his own use.

The answer is B. A taxpayer is subject to the uniform capitalization rules if he produces real property or personal property for use in a trade or business. Producing items for personal use or as a hobby does not qualify. ###

17. Which of the following types of property are not exempt from the uniform capitalization rules?

A. Qualified expenses of a writer, photographer, or performing artist.
B. Timber and the underlying land.
C. Services provided to customers.
D. A corporation that produces audio recordings.

The answer is D. A corporation that produces audio recordings or films would be subject to UNICAP. Generally, the uniform capitalization rules apply to a taxpayer that produces property for use or resale in a business. A company that provides only services would not carry an inventory, so it is not subject to UNICAP. Independent (self-employed) authors, writers, and artists are exempt from the rules. ###

18. All of the following activities are exempt from the uniform capitalization rules except:

A. Resellers of personal property with average annual gross receipts of $25 million.
B. Intangible drilling and development costs of oil and gas or geothermal wells.
C. Research and experimental expenditures.
D. Property produced under a long-term contract.

The answer is A. Resellers of property with annual gross receipts of $10 million or less are exempt from UNICAP. A reseller with average annual gross receipts of $25 million would be subject to UNICAP. ###

19. Chris is the owner-shareholder of Chris's Clothing Company, an S corporation. He manufactures clothing items for resale to the general public and also sells them to wholesale distributors. Chris is trying to figure out his inventory calculations in order to file his 2012 tax return. Which of the following items should be included in his yearend inventory?

A. 2,000 t-shirts out on consignment for another retailer to sell.
B. The machinery used to manufacture the clothing.
C. An order of fabric that was in transit, FOB destination (the title had not yet passed to Chris).
D. 1,000 shirts that were shipped COD to a retailer that had not arrived at the buyer's warehouse.

The answer is A. Chris should include the consigned goods in his own inventory, since goods on consignment are not actually sold to the retailer, and title remains with Chris. Merchandise sent COD is included in inventory until it reaches the buyer, because title does not pass to the buyer until the item is delivered and paid for. Machinery and other fixed assets are not· included in inventory. They are depreciated separately. ###

20. All of the following practices are acceptable methods of accounting for inventory except:

A. The taxpayer accounts for inventory and includes only direct costs associated with manufacturing the goods.
B. The taxpayer has a theft loss of inventory when a disgruntled employee steals substantial amounts of merchandise. The taxpayer chooses to increase his cost of goods sold to account for the stolen items, and properly reports his beginning and closing inventory.
C. The taxpayer values his inventory using the lower-of-cost or market method, using the lowest value for each item in his inventory valuations.
D. The taxpayer has two businesses, and chooses to use LIFO for the first business and FIFO for the second one. He keeps a separate set of books for each business.

The answer is A. Taxpayers must include direct and indirect costs in inventory. Taxpayers may claim a casualty or theft loss of inventory through the increase in the cost of goods sold by properly reporting opening and closing inventories. Taxpayers may choose to use different accounting methods for different businesses, so long as the businesses are kept separate and distinct accounting records are maintained for each. ###

21. Tuxedo House, a clothing retailer, had the following expenses in 2012. Based on the information below, what is Tuxedo House's cost of goods sold for the year?

Tuxedos purchased for resale: $20,000
Freight in $3,000
Freight out to customers $6,000
Beginning inventory $15,600
Ending inventory $12,000

A. $23,000.
B. $26,600.
C. $28,600.
D. $42,500.

The answer is B. The COGS is $26,600 ($15,600 beginning inventory + $20,000 purchases + $3,000 freight in, minus $12,000 ending inventory). Freight in and merchandise purchased for resale are part of the COGS, but freight out is not. ###

22. Thomas is a cash-basis sole proprietor who reports income and loss on Schedule C. He purchases a bulk order of watches for his mail order business. The watches cost $5,000, and the related shipping cost is $350. What is the correct treatment of the shipping cost he paid for delivery of the watches?

A. Thomas may elect to deduct the shipping cost on his tax return as a regular expense.
B. Shipping cost paid on the watches must be added to the basis of the inventory.
C. Thomas cannot deduct the shipping cost and cannot capitalize it.
D. Thomas may elect to deduct the shipping cost as an itemized deduction on Schedule A.

The answer is B. The shipping cost increases the asset's basis. If the property is merchandise bought for resale (such as inventory), the shipping cost is part of the cost of the merchandise and must be capitalized and later recovered as cost of goods sold when the watches are resold. ###

23. All of the following costs must be included in inventory except:

A. Shipping raw materials to the business's factory.
B. Shipping finished product orders to customers.
C. Raw materials.
D. Direct labor costs.

The answer is B. Shipping finished products to customers is not an expense that should be included in inventory. This cost is a current expense and would be deductible as postage, rather than capitalized as a cost of inventory. ###

Unit 4: Business Income

More Reading:
Publication 525, *Taxable and Nontaxable Income*
Publication 538, *Accounting Periods and Methods*
Publication 334, *Tax Guide for Small Business*

Gross income to a business includes all types of income, unless specifically exempt, in the form of money, property, or services. Sources of income for a business include all of the following:

- Income received for services
- Income received for manufacturing or selling merchandise
- Gains from the sale of business property or investment property
- Income from the discharge of indebtedness (debt forgiveness income)
- Income from an interest in an estate or trust
- Portfolio income from investments
- Fair market value of property or services received through bartering
- Rental activities and royalties

Just like individual taxpayers, businesses sometimes earn income that is exempt from tax. More often, businesses engage in transactions that *defer* income to a later date. An example is a section 1031 exchange, which allows for deferral of income on the exchange of business or investment property.

Sole proprietors report business income on Schedule C (Form 1040), or Schedule F (Form 1040) for farmers and fishermen. A partnership reports its income on Form 1065.

Corporations file Form 1120, while S corporations use Form 1120S. In this unit, we will review the details of various types of business income.

Bartering Income

Bartering occurs when a taxpayer exchanges goods or services without exchanging actual money. An example of bartering is a plumber doing repair work for a dentist in exchange for dental services. The fair market value of goods and services received in exchange must be included in income in the year received.

> **Example:** Ethan is a self-employed social media marketer. He and Bryce, a house painter, are members of a barter club where members get in touch with one another directly and bargain. In return for Ethan's marketing services, Bryce paints Ethan's home. Ethan must report the exchange as income on Schedule C. Bryce must include in income the fair market value of the services Ethan provided.

Income from Canceled Debt

If a business-related debt is canceled or forgiven, other than as a gift or bequest, the business generally includes the canceled amount in income. However, a cash-basis business is not required to realize income from a canceled debt to the extent that the payment of the debt would have led to a business deduction.

> **Example:** Barbells Partnership is a cash-basis business. The company orders computer repair services on credit but later has trouble paying its debts. The computer repair company forgives the repair bill. The partnership is not required to recognize the canceled debt as income because payment of the repair bill would have been deductible as a business expense anyway.

In the above example, the canceled debt of an accrual-basis business would be considered income, because the deduction for the expense already would have been recorded.

If a taxpayer owes a debt to a seller for property he bought and the seller then reduces the amount owed, the taxpayer generally does not have income from the reduction. Unless the taxpayer is bankrupt or insolvent, the amount of the reduction is treated as a purchase price adjustment, and the basis in the property is reduced.

Real Estate Income

Businesses may have income from rental activity, which is any amount of money received or accrued as payment for the use of property. Types of rental income may also include rent payments and deposits from renters.

Generally, the IRS deems rental income as passive income, which is not subject to employment taxes. However, rental income is not passive income and is subject to employment taxes when the taxpayer is a professional real estate dealer. A taxpayer qualifies as a real estate dealer if he is primarily engaged in the business of selling real estate to customers. Rent received from real estate held for sale to customers is subject to self-employment tax, while income received from real estate held for investment is not subject to SE tax. Rental income is reported on the following forms:

- **Schedule C,** *Profit or Loss from Business* (used for professional real estate dealers)

- **Schedule E**, *Supplemental Income and Loss* (from rental real estate, royalties, partnerships, S corporations, estates, trusts, REMICs, etc.)

Self-employed real estate dealers or owners of a hotel, boarding house, or apartment building who provide services for guests must report their rental income and expenses on Schedule C, subject to self-employment tax. The services must be ones that are *not* normally provided with the rental of rooms for occupancy only, such as maid service, rather than services that *are* normally provided for the occupants' convenience, such as providing heat and light, cleaning stairways and lobbies, and collecting trash.

If a taxpayer is not a professional real estate dealer, he must report the rental income and expenses on Schedule E, Form 1040.

Example: Joe owns two residential rental properties. He manages them and collects rents. He also has a full-time job as a restaurant manager. He is not a real estate dealer. Joe must report his rental income and losses on Schedule E. His rental income is considered passive income and is not subject to self-employment tax.

Example: Evelyn is a licensed real estate agent. She sells properties and also maintains several rental properties. She works as a real estate agent full-time, and manages all the rental properties herself. Evelyn elects to treat her rental income on Schedule C, not Schedule E. Her losses are not limited, and the income is subject to self-employment tax.

Lease cancellation payments received from a tenant are reported as income in the year received. Advance rental payments received under a lease must be recognized in the year received, regardless of what accounting method or period is used. This means that a taxpayer who owns rental properties and receives rent in advance cannot delay recognizing the income, even if the taxpayer is on the accrual basis.

85

Personal Property Rents

A taxpayer in the business of renting personal property, such as equipment, vehicles, or formal wear, includes the rental income on Schedule C. Prepaid rent can also be received for renting personal property, and must be recognized in the year received.

Advance Payment for Services

Generally for accrual-based taxpayers, an advance payment for services to be performed in a later tax year is taxable in the year the payment is received. But if there is an agreement that the service will be completed by the end of the next tax year, the recognition of that income can be postponed and included in income the next year. The taxpayer cannot, however, postpone the recognition of income beyond the next year.

Service agreement: If a taxpayer receives an advance payment for a service agreement on property he sells, leases, builds, installs, or constructs, he can postpone reporting income. This applies only if the taxpayer offers the property without a service agreement in the normal course of business. Postponement is not allowed if:

- The taxpayer will perform any part of the service after the end of the tax year immediately following the year he receives the advance payment.
- The taxpayer will perform any part of the service at any unspecified future date that may be after the end of the tax year immediately following the year he receives the advance payment.

Example: Ross is an accrual-based, calendar-year taxpayer who owns a television repair business. In 2012, he receives payments for one-year contracts that specify he will repair or replace certain TV components that break. Ross includes the payments in gross income as he earns them.

Example: The Best Service Tennis Club is a calendar-year, accrual-based taxpayer that holds tennis clinics for new players. On November 1, the club receives payment for a one-year contract for 24 one-hour clinics beginning on that date. The club gives six clinics in 2012. Under this method of including advance payments, the club must include one-fourth (6/24) of the payment in income for 2012 and three-fourths (18/24) of the payment in 2013. This is true even if the club does not give all of the clinics by the end of 2013.

Guarantee or warranty: Generally, a taxpayer cannot postpone reporting income received under a guarantee or warranty contract.

Advance Payment for Sales

Special rules apply to including income from advance payments on agreements for the future sale of goods to customers, such as gift certificates or cards that can be redeemed later for goods. Under the accrual method, the advance payment is generally included in income in the year in which it is received.

However, there is an alternative method in which the advance payment can be included in gross receipts under the method of accounting the taxpayer uses for tax purposes or the method of accounting used for financial reports, whichever is earlier.

Example: Tangerine Specialty Foods uses the accrual method of accounting for tax and financial reporting purposes and accounts for the sale of goods when it ships the goods. A customer purchases a $100 gift card from Tangerine's website on Dec. 28, 2012 using a credit card. Tangerine ships the gift card to the customer on January 3, 2013. Under the alternative method of reporting income for advance payment of sales, Tangerine may recognize the $100 in gross receipts in either 2012 (the tax year in which it received the payment) or 2013 (the tax year in which it shipped the gift card.)

Business Interest and Dividend Income

Businesses can earn interest just like individuals do. This is especially true if the business lends money to other businesses and individuals. In any business, interest received on notes receivable that have been accepted in the normal course of business is reported as business income.

A common example of this is when a C corporation owns stock in another corporation. The C corporation earns dividends and interest on its investments, just like an individual does.

For most sole proprietors, dividend income is nonbusiness income and reported on Form 1040. However, dividends are treated as business income to professional stockbrokers and securities dealers.

Business-Related Court Awards and Damages

The IRC excludes from taxation most types of court awards and settlements that grant compensation for physical injuries or illness.

Most other types of court awards and settlements are taxable income, which are included in business income, such as:

- Damages for:
    - Patent or copyright infringement,
    - Breach of contract, or
    - Interference with business operations.
- Compensation for lost profits
- Interest earned on any type of court award
- Punitive damages related to business income or business activity[12]

If a business owner or employee is injured by equipment and later receives a court settlement, the income is not taxable to the employee, but it is still deductible as a business expense by the company that issues the settlement.

Amounts Not Considered Business Income

Just as with individual taxpayers, there are types of business-related income and property transfers that are not taxable or reportable. Some of these transactions may be partially taxable, and some are transactions where the recognition of income is delayed until a later date. Examples include:

- Issuance of stock from the sale of Treasury stock
- Most business loans (these are debt, not income)
- State and local sales taxes that are collected and then remitted to state or local governments
- Like-kind exchanges of property
- Gain from an involuntary conversion, if the gain is reinvested properly
- Consignments (inventory that is owned by another business)
- A volunteer workforce for an exempt entity
- Workers' compensation for injuries or sickness
- A pension, annuity, or similar allowance for personal injuries or sickness resulting from active service in the armed forces
- Refundable security deposits (if returned to the renter after relinquishing the property)

---

[12] Punitive damages may be awarded in addition to compensatory damages for actual monetary losses. Punitive damages are subject to income tax, but not subject to self-employment tax (FICA).

Unit 4: Questions

1. Which of the following would not be considered income for tax purposes?

A. Interest earned on a court award.
B. Damages received in a suit or settlement for personal physical injuries.
C. Barter income from consulting services.
D. Legal damages awarded for copyright infringement.

The answer is B. Certain items of income are excluded from gross income by provisions in the Internal Revenue Code. Gross income does **not** include certain types of compensation for physical injuries. ###

2. Evelyn is a self-employed bookkeeper who performs services for a client, a small corporation. In exchange for her services, the corporation gives Evelyn 500 shares of stock with a fair market value of $4,000. How would the transaction be reported?

A. Evelyn must report the stock as a capital gain.
B. This is not a taxable event. Evelyn would not have to recognize the income until she sold the stock.
C. Evelyn must recognize the stock as interest income.
D. Evelyn must include the fair market value of the shares in her ordinary income.

The answer is D. Since the fair market value of the stock is $4,000, she must include that amount in her income. Bartering is an exchange of property or services. Evelyn must include the FMV of property or services received in her gross income. ###

3. When are advance rental payments taxable?

A. In the year they are received.
B. In the period in which they are accrued.
C. They are not taxable.
D. They are taxable when the checks are cashed.

The answer is A. Advance rental payments received under a lease must be recognized in the year received. This is true no matter what accounting method or period is used. This means that a taxpayer who owns rental properties and receives rent in advance cannot delay recognizing the income, even if the taxpayer is on the accrual basis. ###

4. The Vitrano Tool Corporation rents large tools and machinery for use in construction projects. The company always charges a refundable security deposit and a nonrefundable cleaning deposit when someone rents a machine. Vitrano Tool Corporation received the following amounts in 2012:

Rental income	$50,000
Security deposits	$4,050
Cleaning deposits	$1,500

What amount should be included in the corporation's gross income?

A. $50,000.
B. $51,500.
C. $54,050.
D. $55,550.

The answer is B. The refundable security deposits are not taxable income, because those amounts are returned to the customer. The amounts included in gross income would be the rental income and the nonrefundable cleaning deposits ($50,000 + $1,500 = $51,500). ###

5. When is a business not required to realize income from a canceled debt?

A. Canceled debt is always taxable to a business.
B. A business does not have to realize canceled debt income to the extent that the payment of the debt would have led to a business deduction.
C. Canceled debt is never taxable income to a business.
D. Canceled debt is realized income to a sole proprietorship, but not to a C corporation or an S corporation.

The answer is B. Canceled debt is not realized income to a business to the extent that the payment of the debt would have led to a business deduction. All of the other answers are incorrect. ###

6. Camille, a calendar-year, accrual-based taxpayer, owns a studio that teaches ballroom dancing. On October 1, 2012, she receives payment for a one-year contract for 96 one-hour lessons beginning on that date. She gives eight lessons in 2012 and the rest in 2013. How and when must she recognize this payment as income?

A. All income must be recognized in 2012.
B. All income may be deferred until 2013 since that is when most of the lessons are given.
C. 8/96 of the income must be recognized in 2012 and the rest, 88/96, in 2013.
D. All of the income can be split equally between 2012 and 2012.

The answer is C. Under the rules of advance payment for services, Camille must recognize income from the eight lessons she gives in 2012 and recognize the rest in 2013, regardless of whether she actually has given all of the lessons by the end of 2013. ###

7. Assume the same facts as in the previous question, except the payment is for a two-year contract for 96 lessons. Camille gives eight lessons in 2012; 48 lessons in 2013; and 40 lessons in 2014. How and when must she recognize this payment as income?

A. All income must be recognized in 2012.
B. 8/96 of the income must be recognized in 2012; 48/96 in 2013; and 40/96 in 2014.
C. 8/96 of the income must be recognized in 2012 and 88/96 in 2013.
D. All of the income can be deferred and split equally between 2013 and 2014.

The answer is A. Camille must include the entire payment in income in 2012 since some of the services may be performed after the following year. ###

8. Harley is a real estate professional who owns two duplexes and an office building, all of which he rents to tenants. He works on his rental activity full-time. How should Harley report his rental income?

A. On Schedule E.
B. On Schedule C.
C. On Schedule D.
D. Harley's rental income is not taxable because he is a real estate professional.

The answer is B. Normally, the IRS considers rental income as passive income, not subject to employment taxes, and it is reported on Schedule E, Supplemental Income and Loss. However, as a real estate professional, Harley's income is not passive and is subject to employment taxes. He must report his rental income on Schedule C, Profit or Loss for Business. ###

Unit 5: Business Expenses

More Reading:
Publication 535, *Business Expenses*
Publication 538, *Accounting Periods and Methods*
Publication 15-B, *Employer's Tax Guide to Fringe Benefits*
Publication 587, *Business Use of Your Home*
Publication 463, *Travel, Entertainment, Gift, and Car Expenses*

Business expenses are the costs of carrying on a trade or business, and are usually deductible if the business operates to make a profit. Some expenses must be treated differently than others, and some must be capitalized and depreciated.

Expenses under the Accrual Method

Under the accrual method of accounting, [13] a taxpayer generally deducts or capitalizes business expenses when both of the following apply:

- The **all-events test** has been met, which is defined as all events have occurred that fix the fact of liability, and the liability can be determined with reasonable accuracy.
- **Economic performance** has occurred.

Economic performance occurs as the property or services are provided or the property is used.

Example: Tessa is an accrual-based, calendar-year taxpayer. She orders office supplies in December 2012 and receives them later in the month. She does not pay the bill for the supplies until January 2013. She can deduct the expense in 2012 because all events have occurred to fix the liability, the amount of the liability can be determined, and economic performance occurred in 2012.

Exception for recurring items: Expenses for certain recurring items may be treated as incurred during the tax year even though economic performance has not occurred. In the above example, office supplies may qualify as a recurring item. If so, the taxpayer can deduct them in 2012, even if the supplies are not delivered until 2013 when economic performance occurs.

---

[13] Under the cash method of accounting, a taxpayer generally deducts expenses in the tax year in which he actually pays them. There is an exception for certain payments under the 12-month rule, covered in Unit 3, *Accounting Methods.*

The exception for recurring items applies if all of the following requirements are met:

- The "all-events" test is met.
- Economic performance occurs by the earlier of the following dates:
  - 8½ months after the close of the year.
  - The date the taxpayer files a timely return, including extensions, for the year.
- The item is recurring in nature and the taxpayer consistently treats similar items as incurred in the tax year in which the all-events test is met.

Either:

- The item is not material, or
- Accruing the item in the year in which the all-events test is met results in a better match against income than accruing the item in the year of economic performance.

To determine whether an item is recurring and consistently reported, the taxpayer must consider how frequently he has this same expense and how he reports it for tax purposes. A new expense or an expense that is not incurred every year can be treated as recurring if the taxpayer reasonably expects to incur it regularly in the future.

The exception does not apply to workers' compensation or tort liabilities.

Allowable Expenses

To be deductible, a business expense must be both "ordinary" and "necessary." An ordinary expense is one that is common and accepted in the taxpayer's industry. A necessary expense is one that is helpful and appropriate for the particular trade or business. However, an expense does not have to be "indispensable" to be considered necessary.

Before a business can deduct an item as an expense, it must first distinguish whether the expense is one used to figure cost of goods sold,[14] or whether it is a capital expense, or whether it is a personal expense. None of these are deductible as expenses. The following rules apply:

- If an expense is included in the cost of goods sold, it cannot be deducted again as a business expense. Some expenses must be capitalized rather than deducted.
- Personal, family, and living expenses generally cannot be deducted as business expenses.

---

[14] A fuller explanation of cost of goods sold (COGS) can be found in Unit 3, *Accounting Methods*.

In the remaining portion of this unit, we will review the types of business expenses that are allowable as deductions.

Employee Wages

An employer can deduct the pay it gives its employees if the pay is reasonable and for services performed by the employee. "Supplemental wages" refers to compensation paid in addition to an employee's regular wages. Supplemental wages include the following:

- Bonuses
- Commissions
- Overtime pay
- Accumulated sick leave
- Severance pay
- Taxable awards
- Prizes
- Back pay
- Retroactive pay increases
- Payments for nondeductible moving expenses

Supplemental wages are taxable to the employee just like regular wages and deductible as a wage expense by the employer. Businesses are responsible for federal income tax withholding, Social Security and Medicare taxes, and Federal Unemployment Tax Act (FUTA) taxes.

These taxes are withheld from an employee's paycheck, and the business owner remits them to the IRS. Most businesses are then required to deposit these taxes electronically using the Electronic Federal Tax Payment System (EFTPS), although some very small businesses may still opt to pay employment taxes with their payroll tax returns.

In order for a business to deduct employee compensation, the expense must meet all of the following tests:

- The payments must be ordinary and necessary expenses directly related to the trade or business.
- The amounts must be reasonable. Reasonable pay is the amount that like businesses would normally pay for the same or similar services.
- There must be proof that services were actually performed (unless the compensation qualifies as supplemental wages, such as maternity leave, sick pay, or vacation pay).
- The expenses must have been paid or incurred during the tax year.

If the IRS determines pay is excessive, it can disallow the excess as a deduction.

Transfers of property to an employee can also be considered compensation, and the fair market value of the property on the date of transfer is deductible by the business and taxable to the employee as wages. A gain or loss is recognized on the transfer of the difference between the FMV and the basis of the property.

In addition to deducting employees' pay, a business may deduct expenses paid to independent contractors.

Employers are also able to deduct fringe benefits they provide to employees, which we cover in detail in Unit 6.

Business Gifts: the $25 Limit

Companies are allowed to spend up to $25 per year *per employee*, tax-free, for a business gift. This does not include cash gifts. Any amount in excess of $25 is disallowed as a business deduction. The $25 limit for business gifts does not include incidental costs — for example, packaging, insurance, and mailing costs, or the cost of engraving jewelry. Related costs are considered incidental only if they do not add substantial value to a gift.

Any additional costs for postage and wrapping paper, etc. may be deducted separately by the business.

> **Example:** Roggan Corporation gives each of its 75 employees a $25 fruit basket during the holidays. The company may deduct the cost of the gifts ($1,875 = $25 X 75). The gift is not taxable to the employee, and the fair market value of the gift is not included in the employee's wages.

A business may also deduct business-related gifts to clients and customers. The amount is still limited to $25 given to any person during the year. If a taxpayer and a spouse *both* give gifts, they are treated as one taxpayer for the purpose of the deduction, even if they both have separate businesses. A gift to the *spouse* of a business customer or client is generally considered an indirect gift to the customer or client.

> **Example:** Hawaii Fruit Corporation gives a large fruit and nut basket to its best customer, Dominic's Produce Company. The fruit basket costs $57, and the shipping and mailing of the basket costs $17. Hawaii Fruit Corporation can deduct $25 for the basket and $17 for the cost of mailing, for a total gift deduction of $42.

> **Example:** Miguel sells tools to Hammer's Hardware Store. He gives three fancy candy boxes to each of the store's owners to thank them for their patronage. Miguel pays $80 for each package, or $240 total. He can deduct a total of $75 ($25 limit × 3) for the packages. The remainder of the gift expense is disallowed.

Exceptions to the Gift Limit

Exceptions to the gift limit: The following items are considered promotional and not gifts for purposes of the $25 limit:

- An item that costs $4 or less with the business name clearly imprinted on it (examples include imprinted pens, desk sets, and plastic bags)
- Signs, display racks, or other promotional materials to be used on the business premises of the recipient

> **Example:** Betty's Beekeeper Company gives 150 imprinted pens to her customers and their employees. The pens cost $4 each and they are imprinted with Betty's business name, website, and phone number. She also gives ten of her best customers a beautiful wood rack to display her honeybee products in their stores. The display racks cost $100 each. None of these items is subject to the $25 gift limitation, since they are all promotional items and follow the IRS guidelines.

Business Travel, Meals, and Entertainment

To be deductible for tax purposes, business expenses for travel, meals, and entertainment must be incurred while carrying on a genuine business activity. Generally, the business must be able to prove that entertainment expenses, including meals, are directly related to the conduct of business.

Deductible Meal Expense: the 50% Limit

Travel and transportation costs are 100% deductible, but only 50% of the cost of meals and entertainment is deductible as a business expense. The 50% limit applies to business meals or entertainment incurred while:

- Traveling away from home (whether eating alone or with others) on business
- Entertaining customers at a restaurant or other location
- Attending a business convention or reception, business meeting, or business luncheon

Related expenses that are also subject to the 50% limit include:

- Taxes and tips on a business meal or entertainment activity
- Cost of a room in which the business holds a dinner or cocktail party

The 50% limit applies to meal and entertainment expenses incurred for the production of income, including rental or royalty income. It also applies to the cost of meals incurred while obtaining deductible educational expenses, such as meals during a continuing education seminar. The cost of transportation to a business meal or a business-related entertainment activity is not subject to the 50% limit.

Example: Karen is a business owner who takes a client to lunch. The total restaurant bill is $88. She also pays cab fare of $10 to get to the restaurant. Karen's deductible expense for this event is $54, figured as follows:

Deductible meal expense	$88 X 50% =$44
Deductible travel expense	$10
Total deductible expense	**$54**

Exceptions to the 50% Limit

There are some exceptions to the 50% limit. The following meals are 100% deductible by the employer:

- Meals that are included in employees' wages as taxable compensation
- Meals that qualify as a *de minimis* fringe benefit, such as occasional coffee and doughnuts
- Meals that are made available to the general public as part of a promotional activity, such as a real estate broker who provides dinner to potential investors at a sale presentation
- Meals furnished to employees when the employer operates a restaurant or catering service
- Meals furnished to employees as part of a teambuilding activity, such as a company picnic
- Meals that are required by federal law to be furnished to crew members of certain commercial vessels
- Meals furnished on an oil or gas platform or drilling rig located offshore or in Alaska

DOT Meals: Special 80% Allowance

There is also an exception for businesses subject to the U.S. Department of Transportation (DOT) "hours of service" limits. In 2012, the following qualified individuals can deduct 80% of meal expenses while traveling away from their tax home:

- Interstate truck operators and bus drivers who are under DOT regulations

- Air transportation workers (such as pilots, crew, dispatchers, mechanics, and control tower operators) who are under Federal Aviation Administration regulations
- Railroad employees (such as engineers, conductors, train crews, dispatchers, and control operations personnel) who are under Federal Railroad Administration regulations
- Merchant marines who are under Coast Guard regulations

Businesses are also allowed to deduct employees' meals at the 80% rate when DOT hours of service regulations apply.

The Per Diem Rate for Business Travel

To ease recordkeeping requirements, a business may use the federal per diem rate as an alternative to keeping track of employees' actual expenses during business travel away from home.

Per diem is a daily allowance paid to a business's employees for lodging, meals, and incidental expenses incurred when traveling. The allowance is in lieu of paying their actual travel expenses. There is a per diem rate for combined lodging and meal costs, and a per diem rate for meal costs alone. An employer may use either per diem method for reimbursing employee travel expenses. A self-employed person can only use per diem for the meal costs. Per diem payments that are not in excess of the federal rate are not included in an employee's wages and are not taxable to the employee, if an employee submits an expense report to the employer. An expense report must show the time, place, and business purpose of the employee's travel.

The per diem rates differ based on domestic and foreign travel, and also vary by location. For example, the per diem rate in large cities like Los Angeles and New York is higher than for small cities. The IRS publishes the per diem rates every year in Publication 1542, *Per Diem Rates.* Taxpayers who choose to use the per diem rate still need to prove the time, place, and business purpose of the travel and meals.

In lieu of using the per diem rates for specific destinations, an employer may rely on simplified "high-low" rates established annually for travel within the continental United States. This method treats some cities as high-cost localities for all or part of the year, with a single per diem rate of $242 in 2012 and others as lower-cost cities with a per diem rate of $163 in 2012.[15]

---

[15] The rate schedule is updated every October 1 for the start of the federal government's fiscal year. However, rates remained unchanged from January-September 2012 to October-December 2012 so the same high-low rates apply for the entire tax year.

Taxpayers that do not choose to use the per diem rate must keep adequate records of their travel expenses, including receipts, bills, or canceled checks. An exception is made for meals that cost under $75.

Regardless of whether the per diem rate is used or actual expenses are tracked, all travel expenses must be "ordinary and necessary" expenses incurred for business.

Entertainment Expenses: Business-Related

A business is allowed to deduct 50% of business-related entertainment expenses that are incurred for entertaining a client, customer, or employee. Once again, however, the expense must be both ordinary and necessary. It is not necessary to prove that the entertainment actually resulted in business income or other business benefit for the expense to be deductible.

General Rules: Deductible Entertainment Expenses	
General rule	Expenses to entertain a client, customer, or employee are deductible.
Definitions	Entertainment includes any activity generally considered to provide entertainment, amusement, or recreation, and includes meals provided to a customer or client.
Tests	**Directly-related test**
	• Entertainment takes place in a clear business setting, or
	• The main purpose of entertainment is the active conduct of business, and
	• The taxpayer engages in business during the entertainment, and
	• The taxpayer has more than a general expectation of getting income or some other specific business benefit.
	Associated test
	• Entertainment is associated with the taxpayer's business, and
	• Entertainment occurs directly *before* or *after* a substantial business discussion.
Other rules	A business generally can deduct only 50% of entertainment expenses.
	A taxpayer cannot deduct expenses that are lavish or extravagant.

Entertainment expenses that are generally not deductible are those that occur solely at a nightclub, theater, sporting event, cocktail party, or at a hunting lodge, on a fishing trip, or on a yacht.

The IRS looks at whether there is a "clear business setting" associated with the entertainment and whether there are "substantial distractions" at the location that prevent business from being conducted. If a taxpayer takes a client to a special event, he may not deduct more than the face value of the ticket, regardless of the amount paid. Then the taxpayer must apply the 50% limitation for entertainment expenses.

Example: Following a day of business meetings, Erik wants to take his best two best clients to a basketball game, but the tickets are sold out. So Erik pays a scalper $390 for three tickets. The actual face value of each ticket is $52. Erik may only use the face value of the ticket as a basis for his deduction, and then he must further apply the 50% limit. Therefore, his deductible entertainment expense is $78, figured as follows:

Cost of three event tickets (face value only $52 X 3):	$156
Then, apply the 50% limit ($156 X 50%):	$78

There is an exception for tickets to sports events that benefit a charitable organization. A taxpayer can take into account the full cost paid for a ticket, even if it is more than the face value, if the entire net proceeds go to a qualified charity; its main purpose is to benefit the charity; and the event uses volunteers to do substantially all the event's work.

Recordkeeping for Travel, Entertainment & Gift Expenses				
Expense	**Amount**	**Time**	**Description**	**Business Purpose**
Travel	Record of each expense for travel, lodging, and meals.	Dates for each trip and number of days spent on business.	Destination (name of city, town, etc.)	Business purpose for the expense.
Entertainment	Cost of each separate expense.	Date of entertain-ment.	Location of place of enter-tainment.	Business purpose for the expense.
Gifts	Cost of the gift.	Date of the gift.	Description of the gift.	Relationship: Information about the recipients that shows the busi-ness relationship.
Transportation	Cost of each separate expense.	Date of the expense. For car expenses, the date of the use of the car.	The business destination.	Business purpose for the expense.

Deductible Travel and Transportation Expenses

Taxpayers who travel away from home on business may deduct related expenses, including the cost of reaching their destination, the cost of lodging and meals, and other ordinary and necessary expenses.

Ordinarily, expenses related to use of a car, van, pickup, or panel truck for business can be deducted as transportation expenses. In order to claim a deduction for business use of a car or truck, a taxpayer must have incurred business-related costs related to one or more of the following:

- Traveling from one work location to another within the taxpayer's tax home area. (Generally, the tax home is the entire city or general area where the taxpayer's main place of business is located, regardless of where he actually lives.)[16]
- Visiting customers.
- Attending a business meeting away from the regular workplace.
- Getting from home to a temporary workplace. (A "temporary workplace" can be either within or outside the taxpayer's tax home area.)

Taxpayers are considered "traveling away from home" if their duties require them to be away from home substantially longer than an ordinary day's work and they need to sleep or rest to meet the demands of their work.

Travel business expenses incurred while away from home overnight are deductible expenses.[17] However, if a taxpayer uses his personal car while traveling away from home overnight on business, the rules for claiming car or truck expenses are the same as stated above.

If the travel includes some element of personal travel, the taxpayer must keep records showing how much is related to business and then figure the amount of personal travel because that portion is not deductible as a business expense.

> **Example:** Paul flies to New Orleans on business and takes his wife with him so she can vacation there. Paul pays $190 for each airline ticket and $200 for a double hotel room. The cost of a single hotel room is $150. Paul can deduct the cost of his plane ticket and the cost of $150 for the hotel room. His wife's expenses are not deductible as a business expense.

Businesses must determine the nonbusiness portion of the expense by multiplying it by a fraction. The numerator of the fraction is the number of nonbusiness days during the travel and the denominator is the total number of days spent traveling.

Standard Mileage Rate

Most businesses may choose to use either the standard mileage rate or actual car expenses in order to figure the deduction for automobile expenses. A

---

[16] Costs related to travel between a taxpayer's home and regular place of work are commuting expenses and not deductible as business expenses.

business owner is free to choose whichever method gives him a larger deduction.

In 2012, the standard mileage rate for business is 55.5 cents per mile. A taxpayer who chooses this standard rate may not deduct actual expenses of operating a vehicle, such as gas, oil, and insurance. Business-related parking fees and tolls may be deducted in *addition* to the standard mileage rate.

If a business chooses to use the standard mileage rate the first year an automobile is put into service, it will have to use the straight line method of depreciation if it later changes to using actual expenses.[18]

> ***Note:** The standard mileage rate can now be used by cars for hire, such as a taxi. This law changed in 2011.

A business is prohibited from using the standard mileage rate if it:

- Operates five or more cars at the same time
- Claims a depreciation deduction using any method other than straight line
- Claims a section 179 deduction on a car
- Claims the special depreciation allowance on the car
- Claims actual car expenses for a car that was leased

The standard mileage rate cannot be used by C corporations. Only self-employed individuals, including partners in a partnership, can use the standard mileage rate. However, a C corporation can choose to reimburse an employee shareholder for mileage under an accountable plan.

Actual Vehicle Expenses

Actual vehicle expenses include the costs of the following items:
- Depreciation
- Lease payments
- Registration
- Garage rent
- Repairs and maintenance
- Gas, oil, and tires
- Insurance, parking fees, and tolls

If business use of the vehicle is less than 100%, expenses must be allocated between business and personal use. Only the business use percentage of the automobile expense is deductible.

---

[18] Revenue procedure 2004-64.

> **Example:** Brandon uses a delivery van in his landscaping business. He has no other car, so the van is used for personal travel on the weekends. Brandon chooses to deduct actual costs, rather than the standard mileage rate. Based on his records, Brandon's total automobile expenses in 2012 are $6,252, which includes the cost of diesel fuel, oil changes, tire replacement, and repairs. Brandon uses the vehicle 75% for business, so his allowable auto expense deduction using the actual expense method is $4,689 ($6,252 x 75%).

A business may also deduct the amounts reimbursed to employees for car and truck expenses.

Recordkeeping Requirements for Auto Expenses

To claim the standard mileage rate, a taxpayer needs to keep records that identify the vehicle and prove ownership or a lease, plus a daily log showing miles traveled, destination, and business purpose.

For actual expenses, a mileage log is also necessary, because it helps establish business use percentage.

For depreciation purposes, a taxpayer needs to show the original cost of the vehicle and any improvements as well as the date it was placed in service.

Business Rent Expense

Businesses may deduct expenses for renting property. Rented property includes real estate, machinery, and other items that an entity uses to conduct business. The cost of acquiring a lease is not considered rent and must be amortized.

Generally, rent paid in a trade or business is deductible in the year paid or accrued. If a taxpayer pays rent in advance, he can deduct only the amount that applies to his use of the rented property during the tax year. The rest of the payment can be deducted only over the period to which it applies.

Expenses applicable to a property that is used for multiple activities or purposes must be allocated among each activity.

> **Example:** The Barista Coffee Corporation owns a large building. It uses half of the building for its own manufacturing activity and rents the other half to tenants who run various unrelated businesses. One half of the corporation's building expenses (such as utilities, mortgage expense, and property tax) would be allocated to the rental activity, and the other portion of the building expenses would be allocated to Barista's regular business and manufacturing activity.

Partial Business Use of Property

If a taxpayer has both business and personal use of rented property, he may only deduct the amount actually used for business. To compute the business percentage, the taxpayer must compare the size of the property used for business to the entire size of the property. The resulting percentage is used to figure the business portion of the rent expense. Two commonly used methods for figuring the percentage are:

- Divide the area (length multiplied by width) used for business by the total area of the property.
- If rooms are approximately the same size, divide the number of rooms used for business by the total number of rooms.

Example: Ainsley rents a business office to use as a studio for painting and also to run her tutoring business. Her total rental payments for the year are $11,000. The office is 1,000 square feet; she uses 800 square feet for the tutoring business and the remaining 200 square feet for her painting area. Therefore, she uses the office 80% for her business and 20% for personal purposes. The deductible portion of the rent expense is $8,800 (80% × $11,000).

Home Office Deduction

Taxpayers may be able to deduct certain expenses for the part of their home used for business, if the space is used regularly and exclusively as:

- The principal place of business, and/or
- Exclusively as the place to meet with patients, clients, or customers in the normal course of business; or
- In direct connection with the business, if the taxpayer uses a separate structure that is not attached to the home.

Because of the exclusive use rule, taxpayers are not allowed to deduct business expenses for any part of their home that is used for both personal and business purposes.

Self-employed people must fill out a special form to claim the home office deduction. Schedule C businesses must complete Form 8829, *Expenses for Business Use of Your Home,* and then transfer the total to their Schedule C when they file their income tax return (Form 1040).

Taxes as an Expense

Businesses deduct taxes in the year they pay them, regardless of what method of accounting the business uses. Under the accrual method, a business can deduct a tax before it pays it, if it meets the exception for recurring items discussed earlier in this unit.

Real Estate Taxes

In order for real estate taxes to be deductible, the taxing authority must calculate the property taxes on the assessed value of the real estate. If the property is sold, the deductible portion of the real estate taxes must be allocated between the buyer and the seller according to the number of days in the property tax year that each owned the property. The seller is treated as paying the taxes up to but not including the date of sale. The buyer is treated as paying the taxes beginning with the date of sale.

Not Deductible: Taxes for Local Improvements

Businesses cannot deduct taxes charged for local benefits and improvements that tend to increase the value of property. These include assessments for streets, sidewalks, water mains, sewer lines, and public parking facilities. A business must increase the basis of its property by the amount of the assessment.

A business may deduct taxes for local benefits if the taxes are for maintenance, repairs, or interest charges related to those benefits.

> **Example:** Lawrence owns a business office on Main Street. In 2012, the city charges an assessment of $4,000 to each business on Main Street to improve the sidewalks. Lawrence cannot deduct this assessment as a current business expense. Instead, he must increase the basis of his property by the amount of the assessment.

> **Example:** Waterfront City converts a downtown area into an enclosed pedestrian mall built to improve local businesses. The city assesses the full cost of construction, financed with 10-year bonds, against the affected properties. The city pays the principal and interest with the annual payments made by the property owners. The assessments for construction costs are not deductible as taxes or as business expenses, but are depreciable capital expenses. The part of the payment used to pay the interest charges on the bonds is deductible as taxes.

Taxes: Special Rules

Federal income taxes are never deductible. However, corporations and partnerships can deduct state and local income taxes imposed on them as business expenses.

A self-employed individual who reports income on Schedule C may deduct state and local income taxes only as an itemized deduction on Schedule A (Form 1040).

> **Example:** Reiner Company is a calendar-year C corporation incorporated in Iowa. Iowa imposes a 10% state tax on Reiner's corporate earnings. In 2012, Reiner pays $12,000 in state income tax to Iowa. This state tax would be deductible as a business expense on the corporation's federal tax return **(Form 1120).**

Interest charged on unpaid income tax assessed on individual income tax returns is not a business deduction, even when the tax due is related to income from a trade or business. This interest should be treated as a business deduction only in figuring a net operating loss deduction. Penalties on underpaid deficiencies and underpaid estimated tax are not deductible as interest.

Employment Taxes

A business's deduction for wages paid is not reduced by the Social Security, Medicare, and income taxes it is required to withhold from employees. Businesses can deduct the employment taxes they must pay from their own funds as taxes.

> **Example:** A partnership pays its secretary $18,000 a year. However, after withholding various taxes, the employee receives $14,500. The business pays an additional $1,500 in employment taxes. The full $18,000 should be deducted as wages. The business can also deduct the $1,500 (employer's portion of the FICA) paid as taxes.

Employers may also deduct any required state unemployment taxes or state disability fund taxes.

Self-Employment Tax

Self-employed individuals can deduct one-half of their self-employment tax as a business expense in figuring adjusted gross income. This deduction only affects income tax. It does not affect net earnings from self-employment or self-employment tax.

Other Deductible Taxes

1. **Franchise taxes:** Corporate franchise taxes are deductible as a business expense.
2. **Personal property tax:** Taxes imposed by a state or local government on personal property used in a taxpayer's trade or business are deductible.
3. **Occupational taxes:** A business may deduct any tax imposed by a state or local government on personal property used in its trade or business.
4. **Excise taxes:** Excise taxes that are ordinary and necessary expenses of carrying on a trade or business are deductible. Excise taxes are taxes paid

when purchases are made on a specific good, such as gasoline, or activity, such as highway usage by trucks. Under the Affordable Care Act, indoor tanning salons are subject to a 10% excise tax, which is a deductible business expense.

Insurance Expenses

The following types of business-related insurance premiums are deductible as business expenses:

- Insurance that covers fire, storm, theft, accident, or similar losses
- Credit insurance that covers losses from business bad debts
- Group hospitalization and medical insurance for employees, including long-term care insurance[19]
- Liability insurance
- Malpractice insurance
- Workers' compensation insurance[20]
- Contributions to a state unemployment insurance fund
- Business interruption insurance that pays if a business is shut down due to a fire or other cause
- Car insurance that covers vehicles used in a business (not deductible if a business uses the standard mileage rate to figure car expenses)
- Group-term life insurance for employees

If a cash-basis business pays an insurance premium for years in advance, it can only deduct the portion that applies to the current tax year, regardless of whether it prepaid the entire amount. The 12-month rule applies for cash-basis taxpayers.[21]

> **Example:** Rick's Racing Bikes is a cash-basis business on a calendar year. On May 1, 2012, Rick's pays $2,000 for business insurance covering one year. The insurance policy begins May 1, 2012 and ends May 30, 2013. The 12-month rule applies. Rick's Racing Bikes may deduct the full $2,000 in 2012. The benefit does not extend beyond 12 months after the right to receive the benefit begins.

---

[19] If a partnership pays accident and health insurance premiums for its partners, it generally can deduct them as guaranteed payments to partners. If an S corporation pays accident and health insurance premiums for its more than-2% shareholder-employees, it generally can deduct them but must also include them in the shareholder's wages subject to federal income tax withholding.

[20] The same rules apply as detailed in the above footnote.

[21] Under the 12-month rule, a cash-based business is not required to capitalize amounts paid that do not extend beyond the earlier of the following: (1) 12 months after the benefit begins, or (2) The end of the tax year after the tax year in which payment is made.

Example: Luxe Chocolate Corporation is a cash-basis business on a calendar year. On October 1, 2012, Luxe Chocolates pays $3,600 in advance for business insurance policy covering three years. The policy coverage begins October 1, 2012 and ends September 30, 2015. Since the advance payment covers more than 12 months (36 months), a portion of the $3,600 must be deducted ratably over the three-year period. To figure the monthly premium amount, the policy cost is divided by the coverage period: ($3,600 ÷ 36 = $100). The months of coverage in each tax year is then multiplied by the monthly premium:

      2012: deduction $300 ($3,600 ÷ 36 x 3).
      2013: deduction $1,200: ($3,600 ÷ 36 x 12).
      2014: deduction $1,200 ($3,600 ÷ 36 x 12).
      2015: deduction $900 ($3,600 ÷ 36 x 9).

Self-Employed Health Insurance Deduction

A self-employed individual may be able to deduct premiums paid for medical and dental insurance and qualified long-term care insurance for himself, his spouse, and his dependents. To qualify, a taxpayer must have a net profit reported on his Schedule C (Form 1040). He cannot take the deduction for any month he was eligible to participate in any employer-subsidized health plan (including one that his spouse was eligible for), even if he or his spouse did not actually participate in the plan.

As a result of the Affordable Care Act,[22] employees may now elect to include children under 27 years of age under their health coverage. The child does not have to be a dependent in order to qualify for this expanded benefit.

Interest Expense

Entities can deduct interest paid or accrued during the tax year on debts related to the business. If the interest relates to a business expense or purchase, it is deductible. It does not matter what type of property secures the loan. A business deducts interest as follows:

- **Cash method:** A business may deduct only the actual interest paid during the tax year, and cannot deduct a promissory note because it is a promise to pay and not an actual payment.
- **Accrual method:** A business may deduct only interest that has accrued during the tax year.

A taxpayer cannot receive a tax deduction by paying interest early. Interest paid in advance can only be deducted in the tax year in which it is due. If a business uses the accrual method, it cannot deduct interest owed to a related

---

[22] The *Affordable Care Act* was enacted on March 23, 2010.

person who uses the cash method until payment is made and the interest is includable in the gross income of that person.

Business Bad Debts

Most business bad debts are a result of credit sales to customers for goods or services that have been sold but not yet paid for. These are recorded in a business's books as either accounts receivable or notes receivable. If, after a reasonable amount of time a business has tried to collect the amount due but is unable to do so, the uncollectible part becomes a business bad debt.

A debt becomes worthless when there is no longer any chance the amount owed will be paid. A business does not have to wait for the debt to be due or to obtain a court judgment to show the debt is uncollectible.

A business bad debt is a loss from the worthlessness of a debt that was either:

- Created or acquired in the trade or business, or
- Closely related to a taxpayer's trade or business when it became partly or totally worthless.

To be considered closely related to a taxpayer's trade or business, the primary motive for incurring the debt must be business related.

A taxpayer may claim a business bad debt deduction only if the amount owed was previously included in his gross income.

If a business loans money to a client, supplier, employee, or distributor for a business reason and the loan later becomes worthless, the business may deduct the loan as a bad debt. The loan must have a genuine business purpose in order for this treatment to qualify.

> **Example:** Carol is an accrual-based taxpayer who owns an eyeglass manufacturing company. One of her salesmen, Bryson, loses all his samples and asks Carol for a loan to replace them. Carol loans Bryson $3,000 to replace his eyeglass samples and sample bags. Bryson later quits his job without repaying the debt. Carol has a business-related bad debt that she may deduct as a business expense.

If a taxpayer receives property in partial settlement of a debt, the debt should be reduced by the property's FMV, which becomes the property's basis. The remaining debt can be deducted as a bad debt when and if it becomes worthless.

Sometimes an entity will recover an old debt that was previously written off as worthless. If a business recovers a bad debt that was deducted in a prior year, the recovered portion must be included as income in the current year tax return. There is no need to amend prior year tax returns.

Business Start-up and Organizational Costs

Most of the costs associated with starting a business must be treated as capital expenditures. However, businesses are allowed to deduct a limited amount of start-up and organizational costs.

In 2012, businesses may deduct $5,000 in start-up expenses. If expenses exceed $50,000, there is a dollar-for-dollar reduction until the deduction is eliminated.

Any remaining start-up expenses must be amortized ratably over 180 months (15 years) on Form 4562, *Depreciation and Amortization*. Start-up costs can be deducted in the tax year they are incurred, and the amortization period starts with the month the taxpayer begins operating the business.

Example: Bronco Corporation has start-up expenses of $51,000 in 2012. Bronco is $1,000 over the $50,000 threshold so it must reduce its deduction for start-up expenses by the amount that it is over the threshold. Bronco can deduct $4,000 of its start-up expenses: $5,000 allowable deduction, minus the excess $1,000. The remaining amount of start-up expenses, $47,000 ($51,000 - $4,000 allowable expense) must be amortized over 180 months.

Example: Clean Water Inc. opened for business on November 1, 2012. Prior to opening, the company incurred $21,200 in start-up expenses for advertising and manager training. Since Clean Water had less than $50,000 of start-up costs, the company is allowed to deduct the full $5,000, *plus* an additional $360 in amortization on its 2012 tax return [($21,200 - $5,000)/180 x 2 (two months, November and December)].

If a taxpayer completely disposes of a business before the end of the amortization period, he can deduct all the deferred start-up costs. However, the business can deduct these deferred start-up costs only to the extent they qualify as a loss.

Qualifying Start-up Costs

Business start-up costs are the expenses incurred before a business actually begins operations, and include any amounts paid in anticipation of the activity becoming an active trade or business.

Start-up costs are amounts paid or incurred for:

- Creating an active trade or business; or
- Investigating the creation or acquisition of an active trade or business.

Start-up costs may include:

- An analysis or survey of potential markets
- Advertisements for the opening of the business

- Salaries and wages for employees who are being trained and their instructors
- Travel and other necessary costs for securing prospective distributors, suppliers, or customers
- Salaries and fees for executives and consultants, or for similar professional services

For costs in excess of $5,000, the amortization period starts with the month the business begins operating its active trade or business.

> **Example:** Moonlight Corporation received its corporate charter on September 12, 2012. The company paid $15,500 in Internet and television advertising; $2,000 in training for employees; and $4,000 in consultant fees, all incurred before opening for business. Moonlight opens for business on January 8, 2013. The company can elect to expense $5,000 as a start-up cost in the 2012 tax year. It can then amortize the remaining $16,500 beginning in January 2013.

Start-up costs do not include deductible interest, taxes, or research and experimental costs.

Qualifying Organizational Costs

The costs of organizing a corporation or partnership are also deductible up to $5,000 in 2012, reduced by the excess of cost over $50,000. Just as with start-up costs, any remaining organizational costs must be amortized ratably over 180 months.

To qualify as an organizational cost it must be an expense:
- For the creation of the business
- Chargeable to a capital account
- For partnerships, the cost must be incurred by the due date of the tax return (excluding extensions) for the year business begins
- For corporations, the cost must be incurred before the end of the first tax year in which the corporation is in business

Examples of qualifying organizational costs include:
- The cost of temporary directors
- The cost of organizational meetings
- Filing fees for partnerships
- State incorporation fees for corporations
- Legal and accounting fees for setting up the business

Nonqualifying Organizational Costs

The following items are not qualifying organizational costs, and cannot be amortized:

- Costs for issuing and selling stock or securities, such as commissions, professional fees, and printing costs
- Costs associated with the acquisition of assets to the corporation or partnership
- The cost of admitting or removing partners, other than at the time the partnership is first organized
- The cost of making a contract concerning the operation of the partnership trade or business including a contract between a partner and the partnership
- The cost of issuing and marketing partnership interests such as brokerage, registration, and legal fees and printing costs

Start-up and organizational expenses are claimed as an "other deduction" on business returns (such as Form 1065 for partnerships or Form 1120 for corporations). Self-employed taxpayers claim start-up expenses as an "other expense" on Schedule C or Schedule F.

If a business is completely dissolved, disposed of, or sold at a later date, the business may deduct any remaining deferred organizational or start-up costs on the final tax return.

> **Example:** Rainbow Party Products formed five years ago. In 2012, the corporation experienced financial difficulties and eventually closed. At the time of dissolution, the corporation had $14,000 in remaining unamortized start-up and organizational costs. These costs are deductible immediately on the corporation's final tax return.

If a business never materializes after claiming start-up or organizational costs, the costs are treated differently depending on the entity type. In the case of a corporation, all investigatory costs are deductible as a business loss. In the case of an individual, the costs incurred before making a decision to acquire a business are considered personal costs and are generally not deductible.

Charitable Contributions by Businesses

Among business entities, only C corporations are permitted to deduct charitable deductions. The deduction is limited to 10% of taxable income, which is explained in detail in Unit 14, *Corporate Transactions*. Self-employed taxpayers may not deduct charitable contributions as business expenses, only as expenses on Schedule A if they itemize deductions.

Miscellaneous Business Expenses

There are many other types of expenses that are deductible for a business. Deductibility often depends on the facts and circumstances of the case. Some expenses that would be inappropriate in one line of business may be completely acceptable in another. The following are some common expenses businesses are allowed to deduct:

- Advertising
- Credit card convenience fees
- Certain franchise or trademark fees
- Education and training for employees
- Internet-related expenses, such as domain registration fees
- Interview expense allowances for job candidates
- Outplacement services provided to employees
- Legal and accounting fees directly related to operating a business
- Tax preparation fees for business returns
- License and regulatory fees paid annually to state or local governments
- Penalties paid for late performance or nonperformance of a contract
- Repairs to business property, including the cost of labor and supplies
- Subscriptions and memberships to trade magazines and professional organizations
- Supplies and materials consumed and used during year
- Utilities, including heat, lights, power, telephone service, and water and sewage

Costs That Can be Deducted or Capitalized

There are certain costs that businesses may choose to deduct or capitalize. There are specific rules about the special circumstances in which each may be deducted and how to amortize additional amounts. The following are costs that are generally capital expenses but that a business may elect to deduct:

- Research and experimental costs
- Carrying charges that a taxpayer pays to carry or develop real or personal property
- Certain intangible drilling costs
- Certain domestic exploration and development costs for mines or other natural deposits (other than oil or gas wells)
- Circulation costs for publishers of newspapers and magazines
- Certain environmental cleanup costs
- Qualified expenses in federally-declared disaster areas, such as control or abatement of hazardous substances; removal of debris or demolition of structures; or repair of business-related property damaged in a disaster area
- Reforestation costs up to $10,000

- Film and television production costs (only through 2012)

Nondeductible Expenses

The IRS does not allow the following types of expenses as business deductions:

- Political contributions, including indirect contributions such as advertising in a convention program of a political party
- Lobbying expenses
- Dues for country clubs, golf and athletic clubs, and hotel and airline clubs, even if the club is used for business activity
- Penalties and fines paid to any governmental agency for breaking the law, such as parking tickets or fines for violating local zoning codes
- Legal and professional fees for work of a personal nature, such as drafting a will or damages arising from a personal injury; legal fees paid to acquire business assets (these are added to the basis of a property)

Unit 5: Questions

1. Alexa is a self-employed accountant who reports income and loss on Schedule C. She goes to a continuing education seminar out-of-state. She pays $400 for the seminar and $35 for a train ticket to the event. She also incurs $26 in restaurant meal expenses and $10 in taxi fare on the way to the restaurant. What is her deductible expense for this event?

A. $400.
B. $435.
C. $458.
D. $465.

The answer is C. The answer is $458 ($400 + $35 + $10 + [26 x 50%]). Her meal expenses are subject to the 50% rule, but the taxi fare is fully deductible. The cost of the train ticket and the seminar are also fully deductible. ###

2. In 2012, Helton Partnership, a cash-basis partnership, borrowed $50,000 to purchase machinery. $2,500 in interest on the loan was due in December 2012. Rather than pay the interest, the partnership refinanced the loan and the interest into a new loan amount totaling $53,800: the original loan amount plus interest and an additional $1,300 in loan origination fees. The first payment on the new loan was due January 29, 2013. How much interest is deductible?

A. $0.
B. $2,500.
C. $2,800.
D. $3,800.

The answer is A. The partnership is on the cash basis; therefore, it can only deduct interest actually paid during the year. Since the partnership did not actually pay any interest, it does not have a deductible expense. The fact that the loan was refinanced has no bearing on the deductibility of the interest in the current tax year. ###

3. Norman is the sole proprietor of McGowan Trucking Company. He is subject to the Department of Transportation rules for hours of service. In 2012, what percentage of his meals is he able to deduct while working as an interstate truck driver?

A. 50%.
B. 75%.
C. 80%.
D. 100%.

The answer is C. A taxpayer who is subject to the Department of Transportation's hours of service may deduct a larger percentage of his meal expenses when traveling away from his tax home. For the DOT hours of service limits, multiply meal expenses incurred while away from home on business by 80% in 2012. ###

4. Kimberly is a sole proprietor and files a Schedule C. How should she report the $2,000 in charitable contributions she made on behalf of her business in 2012?

A. The contributions may be deducted on Schedule A as an itemized deduction.
B. The contributions may be deducted on Schedule C as a business deduction.
C. The contributions may not be deducted.
D. Up to 10% of the taxpayer's charitable contributions may be deducted on Schedule C. The remaining amount must be carried over to the next taxable year.

The answer is A. Self-employed taxpayers may deduct these contributions on their Schedule A. The contributions cannot be deducted as a business expense on Schedule C. Only C corporations may deduct charitable contributions as a business expense. ###

5. Which of the following tests is not required in order for entertainment expenses to be deductible?

A. Business was engaged in during the entertainment event.
B. The main purpose of the entertainment was the conduct of business.
C. There was more than just the general expectation of business benefit.
D. The entertainment resulted in profit for the business.

The answer is D. The taxpayer is not required to prove that the entertainment event actually produced a profit. The taxpayer must meet all the following tests in order to deduct an entertainment expense:

•Business was engaged in during the entertainment event.
•The main purpose of the entertainment was the conduct of business.
•There was more than just the general expectation of business benefit. ###

6. Marion owns a shoe repair shop. In 2012, she had the following income and expenses:

Repairs to shop floor $1,000
City tax on her business assets $2,000
Assessment for sidewalks $5,800
Utilities for her store $1,800

What is the tax treatment of the above expenditures?

A. Deduct repairs, property tax, and utilities as expenses. The assessment must be added to the basis of the property and depreciated.
B. All the above expenses are currently deductible.
C. The property tax must be deducted on Schedule A, and the rest of the expenses may be deducted as business expenses on Schedule C.
D. Only the utilities and repairs may be deducted.

The answer is A. The repairs, property tax, and utilities are all deductible as current expenses. The property tax is deductible as a business expense on Schedule C (rather than on Schedule A) because it is assessed on business property. Assessments for streets, sidewalks, sewer lines, and other public services generally add value to the property and must be added to the basis of the property rather than deducted as current expenses. ###

7. Delia, a self-employed real estate agent, traveled to a business convention by train. The train ticket cost $100. At the convention, she purchased a new computer that cost $2,100 for use in her business. She also purchased a computer game for $50. Delia spent $80 on meals and $90 on her hotel room during the convention. How much is deductible as a current business expense?

A. $190.
B. $230.
C. $2,280.
D. $2,430.

The answer is B. Delia may deduct the cost of her hotel room, one-half of her meals expense, and her train ticket to attend the convention.

$100 + $90 + (80 X 50%) = $230

The cost of the computer game is a personal expense and not deductible. The cost of the computer is not a current expense, but instead must be capitalized and depreciated over its useful life. ###

8. Mountain Suppliers made a business loan to Sugarhill Corporation, a supplier, in the amount of $10,000. After paying $2,000, Sugarhill Corporation defaults, and the debt becomes worthless. How much may Mountain Suppliers deduct as a business bad debt?

A. $0.
B. $2,000.
C. $8,000.
D. $10,000.

The answer is C. Loans to a client, customer, employee, or distributor for a business reason can be deducted as a business bad debt. The amount of the loan, minus what was repaid, is the deduction on Mountain Supplier's tax return: $10,000- $2,000 = $8,000. ####

9. On January 1, 2012, Galveston Seafood Partnership, a calendar-year, cash-basis business, purchases a fire insurance policy for its business. The policy is for three years and is required to be paid in full the first year. Galveston Seafood pays $1,800 for the policy. How much of this policy is deductible in 2012?

A. $0.
B. $600.
C. $800.
D. $1,800.

The answer is B. If a cash-basis business pays an insurance premium in advance, it can only deduct the portion that applies to the current tax year, regardless of whether it prepaid the entire amount. Therefore, Galveston Seafood may only deduct the part of the policy that applies to the current year, figured as follows: $1,800 ÷ 36 (months) =$50 per month; $50 X 12 = $600, the current year insurance expense. The exception to this is the "12 month rule," in which the amounts paid do not create a benefit that does not exceed the earlier of:

•12 months after the first date on which the business receives the benefit; or
•The end of the tax year following the tax year in which payment is made. ###

10. Bob owns Jackpot Pawn Shop. He makes a business loan to a client in the amount of $5,000. Bob also loans his brother $1,000 so he can buy a car. His brother, Keith, used to work sporadically at the shop as an employee. Both of the loans are now uncollectible. How much can Bob deduct as a business bad-debt expense?

A. $1,000.
B. $4,000.
C. $5,000.
D. $6,000.

The answer is C. Only the loan to the client would be deductible as a business bad-debt expense. A loan to a client, customer, employee, or distributor for a business reason can be deducted as a business bad debt. Since Keith is a related person and not a regular employee and the loan was for personal reasons, Bob may not deduct the loan to his brother as a business bad debt. ###

11. Lily owns a dress shop. In 2009, she correctly deducted a $10,000 business bad debt after a fabric supplier defaulted on a loan. Then, in 2012, the fabric supplier wishes to do business with Lily again and repays $9,000 of the loan that was once in default. How must Lily report this payment?

A. Lily must amend her 2009 tax return to reflect the incorrect $10,000 bad debt deduction.
B. Lily must reflect this recovery of $9,000 as income in 2012.
C. Lily must reflect income of $9,000 in 2009 by going back and filing an amendment for that year.
D. Lily must amend her 2009 tax return, but she may still reflect $1,000 in bad debt deduction.

The answer is B. Lily is not required to amend her prior year return to report the recovery of the bad debt. Sometimes a business will recover an old debt that was previously written off as worthless. Since Lily recovers a bad debt that was deducted properly in a prior year, she must include only the recovered portion as income in her current year tax return. ###

12. Mike borrowed $100,000 to purchase a machine for his business. The machine cost $90,000. The rest of the money went into Mike's business account, and he purchased a jet ski with the money later in the year. However, the loan was secured entirely by his business assets. Which of the following statements is true?

A. Mike cannot purchase personal items with a business loan; therefore, none of the interest is deductible.
B. All of the interest is deductible, because it is secured by his business assets.
C. Only the amount of interest allocated to the business machine is deductible.
D. None of the answers is correct.

The answer is C. Generally, interest on a business loan is fully deductible. However, debt incurred for personal reasons is not deductible as a business expense. The amount of interest allocated to the business machine is deductible, but not the amount for the jet ski, which is a personal expense. ###

13. Brady owns Super Sweets Company. He gives business gifts to one of his best customers, as follows:

•Glass display for Super Sweets: $500
•Fruit basket: $50
•20 imprinted pens: $35
•Postage for the fruit basket: $20

How much can Brady deduct on his tax return as a business gift expense?

A. $25.
B. $525.
C. $580.
D. $605.

The answer is C. There is a $25 limit per person per tax year for business gifts; however, there are exceptions to this rule. Incidental costs, such as packaging, insuring, and mailing, are not included in determining the cost of a gift for purposes of the $25 limit. The following items are also not considered gifts for purposes of the $25 limit:

•An item that costs $4 or less with the business name imprinted on it
•Signs, display racks, or other promotional material to be used on the business premises of the recipient

Therefore, the business may deduct $580, figured as follows:

1. Glass display $500
2. Fruit basket $25 (only $25 is deductible as a gift expense)
3. 20 imprinted pens $35
4. Postage for basket $20
($500 + $25 + $35 + $20) = $580.

###

14. Maddie rents a small storage unit for her business on February 1, 2012. She is given a discount if she pays the full amount of the lease upfront, which is $1,620 for a three-year lease. What is the amount of Maddie's 2012 deductible expense for leasing the storage unit?

A. $495.
B. $540.
C. $560.
D. $1,620.

The answer is A. If a taxpayer pays for rent or a lease in advance, only the amount that applies to the current year is deductible. The balance must be deducted over the period over which it applies. The answer is figured as follows:

Deductible lease expense for 2012:

$1,620 / 36 (months) = $45 per month
$45 X 11 months (February-December 2012) = $495. ###

15. A corporation may deduct all the following taxes except:

A. Federal income taxes.
B. State income taxes.
C. Local income taxes.
D. Corporate franchise taxes.

The answer is A. Federal income taxes are never deductible as a business expense, no matter what the entity. Penalties assessed on delinquent taxes are also never deductible. ###

16. Garrett operates his printing business out of rented office space. He uses a truck to deliver completed jobs to customers. Which of the following statements is not correct?

A. Garrett can deduct the cost of round-trip transportation between customers and his print shop.
B. Garrett can deduct traveling costs between his home and his main workplace.
C. Garrett can deduct the cost of mileage to deliver completed jobs to the post office to mail.
D. Garrett can deduct the costs to travel to his customers who are disabled and cannot come to his shop.

The answer is B. A taxpayer cannot deduct the costs of driving a car between his home and his main workplace. These costs are personal commuting expenses. The costs of driving to meet with clients or do other business-related errands are deductible. ###

17. Carrie is the sole proprietor of a flower shop. She drove her van 20,000 miles during the year: 16,000 miles to deliver flowers to customers and 4,000 miles for personal use. Carrie wants to use actual costs instead of the standard mileage rate. What is Carrie's percentage of business use for the van?

A. 10%.
B. 20%.
C. 80%.
D. 90%.

The answer is C. Carrie can claim only 80% (16,000 ÷ 20,000) of the cost of operating her van as a business expense. She cannot count the personal miles and therefore must prorate the mileage to reflect her percentage of business use. ###

18. The Castellano Partnership paid the following penalties in 2012. Which are deductible?

A. A penalty paid to the county for violating construction regulations.
B. A penalty imposed by the IRS for late filing of a Form 1065 partnership return.
C. A penalty paid to the city for violating its sign ordinance.
D. A penalty for late performance of a contract.

The answer is D. Penalties paid for the late performance or non-performance of a contract are deductible. Penalties or fines paid to any government entity because of a violation of law are not deductible. ###

19. Which of the following costs qualify as business start-up costs?

A. State and local taxes.
B. Research and experimental costs.
C. A survey of potential markets.
D. Both B and C.

The answer is C. A business may deduct up to $5,000 in start-up costs in 2012. Start-up costs are costs incurred in creating an active trade or business or investigating the creation or acquisition of an active trade or business. Start-up costs include amounts paid for:
•An analysis or survey of potential markets, products, and labor supply
•Advertisements for the opening of the business
•Salaries and wages for training employees
•Salaries and fees for executives and consultants.
The other costs listed are not qualifying start-up costs. ###

20. Actual car expenses include the costs of the following items except:

A. Depreciation.
B. Lease payments.
C. Mileage.
D. Registration.

The answer is C. A taxpayer may choose to take the standard mileage rate or actual expenses. A taxpayer may not take both. If a taxpayer does not choose to use the standard mileage rate, he may deduct actual car or truck expenses. ###

21. Monique opens a bakery on October 16, 2012. Before the business opens, she had $53,000 in start-up expenses. How much may she deduct in start-up costs for 2012?

A. $0.
B. $3,000.
C. $5,000.
D. $2,850.

The answer is D. Because Monique's expenses exceed $50,000, she must reduce the initial year deduction by $1 for every $1 over $50,000. Thus, the $5,000 start-up costs deduction is reduced to $2,000. She figures the amortization on $51,000 ($53,000 - $2,000.) Her monthly amortization amount is $283 ($51,000 ÷ 180), so her first year amortization deduction is $850 ($283 X 3) for the three months her business is open. Her total start-up expense deduction for 2012 is $2,850. ###

22. Under the accrual method, a taxpayer generally deducts or capitalizes business expenses when the all-events test has been met and _____ has occurred.

A. The 12-month rule.
B. The recurring items exception.
C. Economic performance.
D. All of the above.

The answer is C. Economic performance occurs as the property or services are provided or the property is used. ###

23. All of the following statements are correct regarding the deductibility of business expenses except:

A. If an expense is included in the cost of goods sold, it must be deducted as a business expense.
B. Only some expenses may be deducted; others must be capitalized.
C. An expense does not have to be indispensable in order to be considered necessary.
D. Personal, family, and living expenses cannot be deducted as business expenses.

The answer is A. If an expense has already been included in the cost of goods sold, it cannot be deducted again as a business expense. All of the other statements are correct. ###

24. In December 2012, Nicholas travels to an industry meeting in San Francisco. His company uses the high-low method of per diem rates, and San Francisco is designated a high cost city with a rate of $242 a day. Which of the following statements is correct?

A. Nicholas does not need to submit an expense report if his company is using the per diem method for reimbursements.
B. Nicholas will be taxed on the $242 per diem reimbursement his company gives him.
C. The $242 rate only covers lodging and not meals.
D. Per diem rates are designed for the convenience of businesses, since employers do not have to keep track of and pay the actual travel expenses for their employees.

The answer is D. Per diem rates make reimbursing business travel easier for businesses. They are in lieu of employers paying the actual travel expenses of employees. Each of the other statements is incorrect. ###

25. For entertainment expenses to be deductible, the directly-related and _____ tests must be met.

A. Substantial.
B. Associated.
C. Profitability.
D. All of the above.

The answer is B. In addition to the directly-related test, deductible entertainment expenses must meet the associated test, meaning the entertainment is associated with the taxpayer's business and the entertainment occurs directly before or after a substantial business discussion. ###

26. In all of the following situations, a business is prohibited from using the standard mileage rate except:

A. If it is a C corporation.
B. If it deducts expenses for gas, oil, and insurance.
C. If it operates a fleet of four cars.
D. If it claims a section 179 deduction on a car.

The answer is C. A business is allowed to use the standard mileage if it operates a fleet of four cars. If it operates five or more cars at the same time, it is prohibited from using the standard mileage rate, which in 2012 is 55.5 cents per mile. ##

27. Leonora is a sole proprietor who is figuring her business deductions for 2012. What is the total amount she may deduct on her Schedule C?

•Bad debt from a bankrupt client: $350
•Business website charges: $240
•Electricity, gas, and water for her home office (400/1,600 square feet is business use): $1,200
•Continuing education seminars: $850
•Subscription to professional journals: $200
•Credit card convenience fees for her business: $150
•Health club dues: $600
•Bookkeeping for her business: $300
•Salvation Army donation: $150
•Health insurance for herself: $4,800
•Business interruption insurance: $300
•Trip to state capital to lobby for less regulation: $800

A. $2,690.
B. $7,490.
C. $8,290.
D. $8,390.

The answer is B. All the expenses are legitimate business deductions except for the health club dues, the charitable donation, and the lobbying trip to the state capital. Leonora must allocate the business portion of her utilities' expense, which is $300 (one-quarter business usage of $1,200.) Thus, the answer is figured as follows: $250 + $240 + $300 + $850 + $200 + $150 + $300 + $4,800 + $300 = $7,490. ###

28. On January 7, 2012, Edgar leased retail space for his gift shop business for five years for $7,200 per year. Edgar paid the full $36,000 during the first year of the lease. What is Edgar's rental deduction for 2012?

A. $6,800.
B. $7,200.
C. $28,800.
D. $36,000.

The answer is B. Edgar may only deduct the amount owed in 2012, $7,200. Generally, rent paid in a trade or business is deductible in the year paid or accrued. If a taxpayer pays rent in advance, he can deduct only the amount that applies to his use of the rented property during the tax year. Edgar can deduct the rest of his payment only over the period to which it applies. ###

29. During 2012, Kerry had the following expenditures related to commercial real estate that she owns:

County property tax	$1,975
State property tax	$980
Assessment for sewer construction	$1,500

What amount Kerry may deduct on her commercial real estate property?

A. $2,955.
B. $4,455.
C. $3,765.
D. $5,265.

The answer is A. Only the property taxes are deductible as a current expense. The assessment for sewer construction is not deductible, but instead must be added to the property's basis. ###

30. Which of the following costs would qualify as business organizational costs?

A. Costs for issuing and selling stock in the new company.
B. State and local taxes.
C. Legal fees to draw up contracts for new partners.
D. State incorporation fees.

The answer is D. The costs of organizing a corporation or partnership are deductible up to $5,000 in 2012, reduced by the excess of cost over $50,000. Any remaining organizational costs must be amortized ratably over 180 months. Expenses must be for the creation of the business, and include the cost of temporary directors, organizational meetings, filing fees for partnerships, and state incorporation fees for corporations. Legal and accounting fees for setting up the business are allowable expenses, but costs of making partnership contracts are not. Printing expenses and other costs related to issuing stock or securities in the new company, also do not qualify as organizational costs. ###

Unit 6: Employer-Provided Fringe Benefits

More Reading:
Publication 15, *Employer's Tax Guide*
Publication 15-A, *Employer's Supplemental Tax Guide*
Publication 15-B, *Employer's Tax Guide to Fringe Benefits*

Fringe Benefits for Employees

A fringe benefit is a form of pay to employees for the performance of services. Some fringe benefits are taxable to the employee, and some are not. The IRS position is that any fringe benefit provided to employees is taxable and must be included in the recipient's pay *unless* the law specifically excludes it.

For Part 2 of the EA exam, you must understand how these benefits are treated from the employer's perspective. In this unit, we review the main types of fringe benefits employers offer their employees.

Taxable Fringe Benefits

An employer must include in a recipient's pay the amount by which the value of a fringe benefit is more than the sum of the following amounts:

- Any amount the law excludes from pay
- Any amount the recipient paid for the benefit

If the recipient of a taxable fringe benefit is an employee, the benefit is subject to employment taxes and must be reported on Form W-2. If the recipient of a taxable fringe benefit is not an employee, the benefit is not subject to employment taxes, but it may have to be reported on Form 1099-MISC for independent contractors or Schedule K-1 for partners.

Cafeteria Plans

A cafeteria plan, including a flexible spending arrangement, provides employees an opportunity to receive certain benefits on a pretax basis. The plan may make benefits available to employees, their spouses, and dependents. It may also include coverage of former employees. Participants in a cafeteria plan must be permitted to choose among at least one taxable benefit, such as cash, and one qualified benefit that is nontaxable. Generally, a cafeteria plan may not offer a benefit that defers pay. However, a cafeteria plan can include a qualified 401(k) plan as a benefit. Employee benefits may include:

- Accident, dental, vision, and medical benefits.
- Adoption assistance.
- Dependent care assistance
- Group term life insurance coverage

- Health savings accounts

Plans That Favor Highly Compensated Employees (HCEs)

If a cafeteria plan favors highly compensated employees, the value of their benefits become taxable. There cannot be special rules that favor eligibility for HCEs to participate, contribute, or benefit from a cafeteria plan. This is to discourage companies from offering spectacular tax-free benefits to their highly compensated executives, while ignoring the needs of lower-paid employees.

An HCE is any of the following:

- an officer
- a shareholder who owns more than 5% of the voting power or value of all classes of the employer's stock
- an employee who is highly compensated based on the facts and circumstances; or
- a spouse or dependent of a person described above.

Employer-provided benefits also cannot favor "key employees," defined as:

- An officer with annual pay of more than $165,000 in 2012, or
- An employee who is either a 5% owner of the business or a 1% owner of the business whose annual pay was more than $150,000 in 2012.

The law for highly compensated employees includes a "look-back provision," so employees who were previously considered HCEs are generally still considered HCEs for 2012 plan year testing.

If a plan favors HCE or key employees, the employer is required to include the value of the benefits they could have selected in their wages. A plan is considered to have "favored" HCEs if more than 25% of all the benefits are given to HCEs.

A benefits plan that covers union employees under a collective bargaining agreement is not included in this rule.

Simple Cafeteria Plans

Starting in 2011, eligible employers meeting certain requirements could establish a new type of "simple" cafeteria plan. A simple cafeteria plan is treated as automatically satisfying the nondiscrimination requirements that apply to cafeteria plans. The following rules apply:

- Employers must employ an average of 100 or fewer employees during either of the two preceding years.

- All employees who had at least 1,000 hours of service for the preceding plan year must be eligible to participate and able to select any benefit available under the plan. [23]
- Employers must make a contribution to provide qualified benefits on behalf of each qualified employee in an amount equal to:
    - A uniform percentage of not less than 2% of the employee's compensation for the plan year, or
    - An amount which is at least 6% of the employee's compensation for the plan year or twice the amount of the salary reduction contributions of each employee, whichever is less.

Fringe Benefit Exclusion Rules

Certain fringe benefits exclude all or part of the value of certain benefits from the recipient's pay. In this next section, we provide an overview of the exclusion rules for these fringe benefits. Each of these benefits has its own definitions of who is considered a highly compensated employee and other exceptions as to who is covered or what income is taxable.

Accident and Health Benefits

An employer may exclude contributions it makes to an accident or health plan for an employee, including the following:

- Contributions to the cost of accident or health insurance, including long-term care insurance.
- Contributions to a separate trust or fund that directly or through insurance provides accident or health benefits
- Contributions to Archer MSAs or health savings accounts

Accident and health plans may provide benefits for employees, their spouses, their dependents, and their children.

Achievement Awards

Employers may generally exclude from an employee's wages the value of awards given for length of service or safety achievement.

An employer's deduction for employee achievement awards given to a single employee is limited to the following:

- $400 for awards that are not qualified plan awards
- $1,600 for all awards, whether or not they are qualified plan awards

---

[23] Employers may elect to exclude employees who are under age 21, have less than a year of service during the plan year, are covered under a collective bargaining agreement, and are nonresident aliens working outside the United States whose income did not come from a U.S. source.

A qualified plan award is one that does not discriminate in favor of highly compensated employees. The exclusion for employee awards does not apply to awards of cash, gift cards, or other intangible property such as vacations or tickets to sporting events.

Adoption Assistance

An adoption assistance program is a separate written plan that provides payments or reimbursements for qualifying employee expenses. The payments or reimbursements are not taxable to the employee.[24]

Athletic Facilities

The value of an employee's use of athletic facilities may be excluded from wages only if the facility is on premises that the employer owns or leases. Substantially all the use of the gym or athletic facilities must be for a company's employees, their spouses, and their dependent children.

De Minimis (Minimal) Benefits

An employer may exclude the value of a de minimis benefit provided to an employee from the employee's wages. This is a property or service an employer provides that has so little value that accounting for it would be impractical. Examples of de minimis benefits include the following:

- Occasional personal use of a company copying machine
- Holiday gifts with a low fair market value
- Occasional parties for employees and their gifts

Cash and gift cards are never excludable as de minimis benefits, no matter how little the amount, except for occasional meal money or transportation fare.

Dependent Care Assistance

An employer can exclude the value of benefits provided to an employee for care of qualified dependents. The services must be provided to allow an employee to work.[25]

For 2012, an employee can generally exclude from gross income up to $5,000 of benefits ($2,500 if MFS) received under a dependent care assistance program each year. However, the exclusion cannot be more than the smaller of the earned income of either the employee or his or her spouse.

---

[24] An adoption program cannot favor HCEs, defined in this case as a 5% owner at any time during the year or preceding year, or who received more than $115,000 in pay for the preceding year, unless he was not also in the top 20% of employees when ranked by pay in the preceding year.

[25] The same HCE rules apply to dependent care assistance benefits.

Educational Assistance

An employer can offer employees educational assistance for the cost of tuition, fees, books, supplies, and equipment. The payments may be for either undergraduate or graduate-level courses, and do not have to be work-related.

In 2012, $5,250 may be excluded per year per employee. If an employer pays more than $5,250, the excess is taxed as wages to the employee.

Not covered is the cost of courses involving sports, games, or hobbies, unless they are related to the business or are required as part of a degree program. The cost of lodging, meals, transportation is also not included in education expenses.

Tuition reduction: An educational organization can exclude the value of a qualified undergraduate tuition reduction to an employee, his or her spouse, or dependent child. Graduate education only qualifies if it is for the education of a graduate student who performs teaching or research activities for the educational organization.

Employee Discounts

Employers can exclude the value of employee discounts from wages up to the following limits:

- For a discount on services, 20% of the price charged nonemployee customers for the service.
- For a discount on merchandise, the company's gross profit percentage multiplied by the price nonemployee customers pay for the property.[26]

Employer-Provided Cell Phones

The value of the business use of an employer-provided cell phone is excludable from an employee's income to the extent that, if the employee paid for its use, the payment would be deductible. The IRS has ruled that there must be substantial "noncompensatory" reasons for use of a phone which relate to the employer's business. Legitimate reasons include the employer's need to contact the employee at all times for work-related emergencies and the employee's need to be available to speak with clients away from the office.

However, a cell phone provided simply to promote an employee's morale or to attract a prospective employee is considered a form of compensation. In those cases, the value of a cell phone would no longer be a de minimis benefit and must be added to an employee's wages.

---

[26] An HCE is defined in this case as a 5% owner at any time during the year or preceding year, or who received more than $115,000 in pay for the preceding year, unless he was not also in the top 20% of employees when ranked by pay in the preceding year.

If an employer provides an employee with a cell phone primarily for noncompensatory business purposes, personal use of the phone also is excludable from an employee's income as a *de minimis* fringe benefit.[27]

Group-Term Life Insurance Coverage

An employer can exclude the cost of up to $50,000 of group-term life insurance from the wages of an insured employee. Any coverage above that amount must be included in the employee's wages, reduced by the amount the employee paid toward the insurance.

With some exceptions, life insurance is not group-term life insurance unless a business provides it to at least 10 full-time employees at some time during the year. [28]

Health Savings Accounts (HSAs)

An HSA is an account owned by a company's employee or former employee. Any contributions an employer makes become the employee's property and cannot be withdrawn by the employer. Contributions to the account are used to pay current or future medical expenses of the account owner, his or her spouse, and any qualified dependent. The medical expenses must not be reimbursable by insurance or other sources.

1. **Eligibility:** A qualified individual must be covered by a high deductible health plan with a deductible in 2012 of at least $1,200 for self-only coverage or $2,400 for family coverage. Annual out-of-pocket expenses to the beneficiary are limited to $6,050 for self-only coverage and $12,100 for family coverage. There are no income restrictions on an individual's eligibility to contribute to an HSA, nor is there a requirement the account owner have earned income to contribute.

2. **Employer contributions:** In 2012, an employer can contribute up to $3,100 for self-only coverage or $6,250 for family coverage to a qualified individual's HSA. The contribution amounts are increased by $1,000 for qualified individuals who are age 55 or older at any time during the year. No contributions can be made to an individual's HSA after he becomes enrolled in Medicare Part A or Part B.

3. **Nondiscrimination rules:** An employer's contribution amount to an employee's HSA must be comparable for all employees who have comparable cov-

---

[27] IRS Notice 2011-72.

[28] For this exclusion, a plan cannot favor key employees, defined as an officer having annual pay of more than $165,000; an individual who for 2012 was either a 5% owner of the business or a 1% owner of the business whose annual pay was more than $150,000. A plan does not favor key employees as to participation if it benefits at least 70% of the company's employees and at least 85% of the participating employees are not key employees.

erage during the same period, or there will be an excise tax equal to 35% of the amount the employer contributed to all employees' HSAs. However, the Tax Relief and Health Care Act of 2006 allows employers to make larger HSA contributions for a non-highly compensated employee than for a highly compensated employee.[29]

Meals and Lodging Provided to Employees

An employer may exclude the value of meals and lodging it provides to employees if they are:

- On the employer's business premises, and
- For the employer's convenience.

For lodging, there is another rule: it must be required as a condition of employment.

Lodging can be provided for the taxpayer, the spouse, and the taxpayer's dependents, and still not be taxable.

Example: Henry is a project supervisor for Franklin Construction. He is provided free hotel lodging at remote job sites, where he is required to stay for many months while timber is cleared and the grounds are prepared for construction projects. The value of the lodging is excluded from income, because it is for his employer's convenience. The cost of the hotel is deductible by Franklin Construction as a business expense.

The exclusion from taxation does not apply if the employee can choose to receive additional pay instead of lodging.

Meals for the Convenience of the Employer

Meals provided to employees for the convenience of the employer are 100% deductible by the employer but are not taxable to the employees. Meals must be taken on the business premises, such as in the following instances:

- Workers such as police officers, firefighters, and other emergency personnel need to be on call for emergencies during the meal period
- The nature of the business requires short meal periods
- Eating facilities are not available in the area of work
- Meals are furnished to all employees on a regular basis, so long as meals are furnished to substantially all the employees for the convenience of the employer

---

[29] An HCE is defined in this case as a 5% owner at any time during the year or preceding year, or who received more than $115,000 in pay for the preceding year, unless he was not also in the top 20% of employees when ranked by pay in the preceding year.

- Meals are furnished immediately after working hours because the employee's duties prevented him or her from obtaining a meal during working hours

> **Example:** Paramedic Transport regularly provides meals to employees during working hours so that paramedics are available for emergency calls during the meal. The meals are therefore excludable from the employee's wages and still deductible by the employer.

> **Example:** An employer has pizza delivered to the office at a group meeting because the business requires the meeting be kept short, and there are no alternative restaurants in the immediate area.

If over half of a business's employees are furnished meals on the business premises for the *employer's* convenience, the business may treat all the meals furnished to the employees on the business premises as furnished for the "employer's convenience."

In the case of food service employees, meals furnished to restaurant employees before, during, or after work hours are considered furnished for the employer's convenience.

Moving Expense Reimbursements

An employer can generally exclude qualifying moving expense reimbursements from an employee's wages. The exclusion applies only to reimbursement of moving expenses that the employee could deduct if he or she had paid or incurred them without reimbursement. Deductible moving expenses include only the reasonable expenses of:

- Moving household goods and personal effects from the employee's former home to the new home, and
- Traveling, including lodging, from the former home to the new home.

Expenses for meals are not included, and the move must meet both the distance test and the time test. The distance test is met if the new job location is at least 50 miles farther from the employee's old home than the old job location was. The time test is met if the employee works at least 39 weeks during the first 12 months after arriving in the general area of the new job location.

No-Additional-Cost Services

An employer can exclude a service provided to an employee if it does not cause the business any substantial additional cost. The service must be offered to customers in the ordinary course of the line of business of the employer. Typically, no-additional-cost services are excess capacity services, such as airline, bus, or train tickets; hotel rooms; or telephone services provided free or at a reduced price to employees working in those lines of business.[30]

Retirement Planning Services

Employers with qualified retirement plans may exclude from an employee's wages the value of any retirement planning advice or information the business provides to employees or spouses. The exclusion does not apply to services for tax preparation, accounting, legal, or brokerage services.

Transportation (Commuting) Services

Employers may provide transportation benefits to their employees up to certain amounts without having to include the benefit in the employee's income. Qualified transportation benefits include transit passes, paid parking, a ride in a commuter highway vehicle between the employee's home and workplace, and qualified bicycle commuting reimbursement.

In 2012, employees may exclude:

- $240 per month in combined commuter highway vehicle transportation and transit passes,[31] and
- $240 per month in parking benefits.

This nontaxable benefit is a combined maximum of $480 per month in 2012. Employees may receive transit passes and benefits for parking during the same month; they are not mutually exclusive.

An employer may also reimburse an employee for a bicycle that is used for commuting purposes. A qualified bicycle commuting reimbursement is a reimbursement of up to $20 per month for reasonable expenses incurred by the employee in conjunction with his commute to work by bike.

However, if an employer allows an employee to use a company vehicle for commuting, the value of the vehicle's use is taxable to the employee. Personal use of an employer's vehicle is also considered taxable wages to the employee.

---

[30] An HCE is defined in this case as a 5% owner at any time during the year or preceding year, or who received more than $115,000 in pay for the preceding year, unless he was not also in the top 20% of employees when ranked by pay in the preceding year.

[31] Congress's fiscal cliff legislation of January 2, 2013 retroactively reinstated parity between the benefits for parking and transit benefits for 2012. The parity had expired at the end of 2011, so that for all of 2012 employers had expected the amount excluded for commuter highway vehicles or transit passes to be $125 a month, not $240. The IRS has issued guidance on FICA tax refunds and W-2 adjustments for businesses that gave transit benefits of more than $125 a month in 2012. Employers that treated the excess as wages can make adjustments, but they will have to reimburse their employees for the over-collected FICA tax before doing so.

Working Condition Benefits

This exclusion from wages applies to property and services an employer provides so that the employee can perform his or her job. A common example is an employee's use of a company car for business.

An employer who provides a car for an employee can exclude the amount that would be allowable as a deductible business expense if the employee paid for its use. Employers may instead choose to include the entire annual lease value of the car in the employee's wages. The employee can then claim any deductible business expense for the car as an itemized deduction on his personal income tax return.

A qualified nonpersonal-use vehicle is one that an employee is unlikely to use more than minimally for personal purposes because of its design. These include the following vehicles:

- Police, fire, and public safety vehicles
- An ambulance or hearse
- Any vehicle designed to carry cargo with a loaded gross vehicle weight over 14,000 pounds
- Delivery trucks with seating for the driver only
- A 20-person or more passenger bus
- School buses
- Tractors and other farm vehicles
- Vehicles such as cement mixers, garbage trucks, forklifts, and moving vans

Pickup trucks and vans of 14,000 pounds or less are qualified nonpersonal vehicles if they have been specially modified for business purposes, such as painted with advertising or marked with permanent decals, and have been fitted with certain special equipment specific to the business.

Accountable Plans

A business can reimburse employees for business-related expenses. Depending upon the type of plan the employer has, the reimbursement for business travel may or may not be taxable to the employee. There are two types of reimbursement plans:

- **Accountable Plans** - An accountable plan is not taxable to the employee and has strict substantiation requirements. Amounts paid under an accountable plan are not wages and are not subject to income tax withholding and payment of Social Security, Medicare, and Federal Unemployment (FUTA) taxes.

- **Nonaccountable Plans** - A nonaccountable plan is taxable to the employees as wages and is subject to all employment taxes and withholding. Generally, there are no substantiation requirements for a nonaccountable plan.

Example: Dana is a saleswoman for Sunshine Cosmetics. She takes two potential clients out to dinner and pays for the meal. She also keeps track of her business mileage on a spreadsheet. The following week, she submits her receipts and the spreadsheet to Sunshine Cosmetics for reimbursement. Dana's employer reimburses her for the out-of-pocket expenses she incurred. This arrangement is considered an accountable plan. The reimbursement is not taxable to Dana and is deductible by the employer as a regular business expense.

For expenses to qualify under an accountable plan, the employee must follow guidelines in order to have the expenses reimbursed. An accountable plan requires employees to meet all of the following requirements:
- Have incurred the expenses while performing services as employees
- Adequately account for the expenses within a reasonable period of time
- Adequately account for their travel, meals, and entertainment expenses
- Provide documentary evidence of their travel, mileage, and other employee business expenses
- Return any excess reimbursement or allowance within a reasonable period of time if paid in advance

Under an accountable plan, a business owner may *advance* money to employees in anticipation of an expense; however, certain conditions must be met. The cash advance must be reasonably calculated to equal the anticipated expense, and the business owner must make the advance within a reasonable period of time.

Unit 6: Questions

1. Evermore Inc. reimburses employees for their business travel. Which of the following is taxable to the employee?

A. Travel reimbursements made under an accountable plan.
B. Travel reimbursements made under a nonaccountable plan.
C. Parking passes at a cost of $240 per month.
D. A qualified bicycle commuting reimbursement.

The answer is B. Travel reimbursements made under a nonaccountable plan are taxable to the employee as wages. ###

2. All of the following are excludable from wages except:

A. An outstanding employee achievement award valued at $300.
B. Occasional snacks provided by the employer in the employee break room.
C. Employer-provided vehicles that employees may also use for personal purposes.
D. Meals furnished during work hours for the benefit of the employer.

The answer is C. The value of a vehicle for personal use by an employee is a taxable benefit. If an employer provides a car for an employee's use, the amount that can be excluded as a working condition benefit is the amount that would be allowable as a deductible business expense if the employee paid for its use. There are exceptions for emergency personnel such as police officers who are required to use their emergency vehicles. Employee achievement awards are exempt up to $1,600. Meals are exempt if either furnished for the employer's convenience or if de minimis. Snacks would usually be considered a de minimis benefit. ###

3. The Pancake House has a qualified benefit plan for its employees. The following benefits were offered to the employees. Which of these is fully taxable to the employee?

A. Qualified group term life insurance of $50,000.
B. Qualified dependent care of up to $5,000.
C. A membership to the local athletic club.
D. Free transit passes.

The answer is C. Memberships to athletic facilities are a taxable benefit. A workout area on the employer's premises is the exception. The other benefits are not taxable as part of a fringe benefit plan to employees. ###

4. Heart-Wise Ambulance Services provides meals and lodging for ten employees at the workplace as a condition of employment because the paramedics are not allowed to leave the premises when they are on a shift. The employees eat and sleep for free. Which of the following is true?

A. All the costs of meals and lodging can be excluded from the employees' wages and deducted as an expense by the employer.
B. The meals and lodging are not taxable to the employee, but the employer can only deduct 50% of the meal expense.
C. The meals and lodging are taxable to the employee and deductible by the employer. The employee may then deduct the cost as an employee-business expense.
D. None of the above.

The answer is A. Employers may exclude the value of meals and on-site lodging from an employee's wages. Lodging provided for the convenience of the employer is also excludable from an employee's wages. Since the employees are required to remain on the employer's premises, the value of the meals and lodging is a nontaxable benefit to the employees. Meals provided to employees for the convenience of the employer are 100% deductible by the employer, but are not taxable to the employees. To be considered "for the convenience of the employer," they must be taken on the business premises, and there are also other restrictions. ###

5. Which of the following benefits must be included in an employee's income?

A. Child care reimbursed under a qualified flexible spending plan.
B. Employee discounts on products.
C. A holiday gift of $50 in gas cards.
D. A holiday gift of a $25 canned ham.

The answer is C. Gifts in cash or cash equivalents such as gift cards must always be included in income. Fringe benefits that may be excluded from income include employee discounts, qualified transportation passes, parking, and de minimis holiday gifts. ###

6. Right Angles Engineering offers its employees an education reimbursement. Renee is a full-time employee working for Right Angles. In 2012, she takes graduate accounting courses and has $5,900 in tuition expenses and $300 in expenses for required books. Right Angles reimburses Renee for all the expenses. How should this reimbursement be treated?

A. All of the amounts are excluded from the employee's income, and the amounts are deductible by the employer as a qualified fringe benefit.
B. The first $5,250 of the educational expenses is excluded from the employee's wages as a qualified fringe benefit, and the remaining amount is taxable as wage income to Renee.
C. Only $5,900 (the tuition costs) of the educational expenses are excluded from the employee's wages as a qualified fringe benefit, and the remaining amount is taxable as wage income to Renee. The cost of the books is not a qualified educational expense.
D. All of the reimbursement is taxable as wages, because graduate courses do not qualify for reimbursement under a fringe benefit plan.

The answer is B. Although all of the expenses are qualified educational expenses, only the first $5,250 of the educational expenses is excluded from the employee's wages as a qualified fringe benefit, and the remaining amount is taxable as wage income to Renee. $5,250 is the maximum excluded benefit in 2012. If an employer pays more than $5,250 for educational benefits for an employee during the year, the excess is taxed as wages. ###

7. Antonio is employed by the GR Accounting Firm. When he travels for his audit work, he submits his meal and travel receipts for reimbursement by the firm, which has an accountable plan for its employees. Which of the following statements is true?

A. Under an accountable plan, the reimbursed amounts are taxable to Antonio and will be clearly listed on his Form W-2.
B. Under an accountable plan, Antonio may deduct his travel and meal expenses on his tax return, even though they have already been reimbursed by his employer.
C. Under an accountable plan, Antonio's employer may only deduct 50% of Antonio's meal expenses, even though Antonio was reimbursed in full for the expense.
D. Under an accountable plan, reimbursed expenses are usually taxable to the employee as wages, and the employer should deduct the expenses as wage expense.

The answer is C. The expenses for entertainment and meals must be reduced by 50%, regardless of whether the employer reimburses the employee for the full amount of the meals. Under an accountable plan, employee reimbursements are not included in the employee's income. The employer can deduct the expenses as current expenses on his tax return. ###

8. A simple cafeteria plan is _____:

A. A type of plan that makes all fringe benefits a company wants to offer nontaxable to employers and employees.
B. A plan that only offers benefits which defer pay.
C. A flexible spending arrangement.
D. A type of plan that allows employers with 100 or fewer employees to meet the nondiscriminatory requirements and offer certain benefits under a cafeteria plan.

The answer is D. A simple cafeteria plan is a newer form of cafeteria plan established under health care reform. It is designed for employers with 100 or fewer employees and gives employers a way to bypass some of the complicated nondiscriminatory requirements of regular cafeteria plans while offering similar benefits. ###

9. Which of the following is not a fringe benefit that may be excluded from an employee's pay?

A. Dependent care assistance of up to $5,000 a year.
B. A cell phone given to an employee for excellent job performance.
C. Moving expense reimbursements.
D. Retirement planning services.

The answer is B. The value of an employer-provided cell phone is only excludable from an employee's wages if it is given for a noncompensatory business purpose. A cell phone used to boost morale or, in this case, as a type of financial bonus would be taxable to the employee. ###

10. For cafeteria plans, a "key" employee in 2012 is defined as all of the following except:

A. An officer with annual pay of more than $165,000.
B. A 1% owner of the business with annual pay of more than $150,000.
C. A 10% owner of the business.
D. Both A and B.

The answer is C. Under the rules for cafeteria plans, a key employee is a 5% owner of the business, not a 10% owner. Both A and B are correct in describing key employees. ###

11. Certain types of fringe benefits cannot favor highly compensated employees. In 2012, how is an HCE defined for the following types of fringe benefits: adoption, dependent care, and educational assistance; employee discounts; lodging and meals on premises; and no-additional-cost services?

A. An employee with annual pay of more than $150,000 the preceding year.
B. An officer with annual pay of more than $165,000 the preceding year.
C. A 5% owner of the company, or one with annual pay of more than $150,000 the preceding year.
D. A 5% owner of the company, or one with annual pay of more than $115,000 the preceding year.

The answer is D. For the fringe benefits listed, an HCE is a 5% owner of the company or one with annual pay of more than $115,000 the preceding year. The second test can be disregarded if the employee was not also among the top 20% of employees when ranked by pay for the preceding year. Benefit plans cannot favor highly compensated employees to the detriment of other employees. ###

12. Which of the following statements is not correct about health savings accounts?

A. Contributions cannot be made to an individual's HSA after he becomes enrolled in Medicare.
B. Only taxpayers with gross income below $200,000 may contribute to an HSA.
C. Qualified individuals must be covered by high deductible insurance plans.
D. Contributions to an HSA are used to pay current or future medical owners of the account owner, his or her spouse, and qualified dependents.

The answer is B. There are no income restrictions on who may contribute to an HSA. ###

Unit 7: Business Credits & Deductions

> **More Reading:**
> Instructions for Form 3800, *General Business Credit*
> Publication 334, *Tax Guide for Small Business*
> Publication 536, *Net Operating Losses for Individuals, Estates, and Trusts*
> Instructions for Form 8903, *Domestic Productions Activities Deduction*
> Instructions for Form 4626, *Alternative Minimum Tax-Corporations*

Net Operating Losses (NOLs)

A net operating loss (NOL) is when a business has tax deductions that exceed its current income, resulting in negative taxable income. This happens when a business has more expenses than revenues during a given tax year. A loss from operating a business is the most common reason for an NOL.

By applying a net operating loss to preceding tax years, a business can receive a refund of previously paid taxes. The NOL can also be used to reduce future tax payments. A business may choose whether or not to "carry back" or "carry forward" an NOL.

The default election, called the carryback period, is to carry back a net operating loss two years. Then the business can carry forward any remaining NOL for up to 20 years. A business may also elect not to carry back an NOL and only carry it forward.

A valid election must be made in order to forgo the carryback period and only carry forward an NOL. If a taxpayer fails to file a return on time and does not make the proper election, he is forced to carryback the NOL.

> **Note:** Any net operating loss that is not absorbed in the carryback (generally two years) and carryforward (20 years) periods is lost. It cannot be deducted in any other tax year.

In order for a sole proprietor to have an NOL, the loss must be caused by the following expenses:

- Deductions from a trade or business that result in an overall loss
- Deductions from work as an employee
- Casualty or theft losses (personal or business-related)
- Losses from rental property
- Moving expenses
- Losses from a farming business

An individual taxpayer may have a net operating loss if his adjusted gross income minus the standard deduction (or itemized deductions) is a negative number; this is most commonly caused by losses from a Schedule C business.

Longer Carryback Periods

There are certain instances in which a business qualifies for a longer NOL carryback period. The following are exceptions to the two-year carryback rule:

- If the NOL is due to a farming loss, qualified farmers are eligible for a five-year carryback period.
- "Qualified small businesses"[32] may carry back a loss three years if the loss is due to a federally declared disaster.
- Net operating losses due to a casualty or theft may be carried back three years.
- Product liability losses have a ten-year carryback period. An example would be when a business sells an item that is later subject to a recall and lawsuits.

Reporting Net Operating Losses

In order to claim a refund from an NOL, an individual taxpayer may choose to amend a prior year tax return, or may use IRS Form 1045, *Application for Tentative Refund*, to apply for a quick tax refund resulting from the carryback of an NOL.

If the taxpayer is self-employed, the net operating loss does not change the amount of self-employment tax to any of the years to which it is carried forward or back. Also, if a business or individual owes interest and penalties in a prior year, the NOL carryback will not abate them.

Example: Gregory operates a farming business and files his return on Schedule F. In 2012, he has a net operating loss of $35,000. He had income of $25,000 in the prior year, so he elects to carry back his NOL in order to receive a refund of the income tax he paid. Gregory also owed self-employment taxes in 2011, but the NOL will not abate them. The NOL only offsets income tax.

The following items are not allowed when a business figures an NOL:

- Any deduction for personal exemptions
- Capital losses in excess of capital gains
- The exclusion of gain from the sale of qualified small business stock
- Nonbusiness deductions in excess of nonbusiness income (hobby losses)
- A net operating loss from *another* year (a carryback or a carryforward)

---

[32] A "qualified small business" for purposes of this rule is a sole proprietorship or a partnership that has average annual gross receipts of $5 million or less during the three-year period ending with the tax year of the NOL.

- The domestic production activities deduction (DPAD) cannot create or increase an NOL carryback or carryforward
- A self-employed taxpayer's contribution to a Keogh plan (a type of retirement plan for sole proprietors)

Income from other sources may eliminate or reduce a net operating loss for the year. For example, if a taxpayer has income from wages, as well as a net operating loss from a small business, then the wage income will offset the amount of the NOL.

Example: Jim runs an auto detailing business as a sole proprietor. In 2012, he had an $8,000 NOL from his Schedule C business. Jim files jointly with his wife, Elaine. She has $23,000 in taxable income from wages. On their jointly filed return, Jim's net operating loss is absorbed by Elaine's $23,000 in wages, making their joint AGI $15,000 ($23,000 - $8,000 NOL).

Business Credits

There are a variety of tax credits for business. Credits are generally more valuable than deductions because they are subtracted directly from a business's tax liability. However, most tax credits are available in limited situations, applying only to certain industries or to very specific activities.

General Business Credit

Many business credits fall under the umbrella of the general business credit (GBC). The GBC is not a single credit but is instead a combination of 32 business credits. [33] Each business credit is claimed on a separate form, and then the credits are added in aggregate on Form 3800, *General Business Credit.*

The GBC is a nonrefundable credit that is subtracted directly from tax, reducing an entity's tax liability dollar for dollar. Generally, credits cannot be claimed to the extent that they would reduce a business's tax bill below its tentative minimum tax. The General Business Credit may not offset any of a business's employment tax liabilities.

Carryback and Carryforward

A business's GBC for the year consists of its carryforward of business credits from prior years plus the total of its current year business credits. If dollar limitations on the GBC prevent a business from claiming all of it in the year that it was earned, it can generally be carried back to the prior year and forward to the following 20 years.

---

[33] The number of general business credits for the 2012 tax year. Specific credits and their requirements vary from year to year.

List of Business Credits

The following are some of the more widely-used general business credits. The starred credits (marked like this: ***) are those most likely to be tested on the EA exam, according to the exam specifications on the Prometric website.

***Investment Credit (Form 3468)

The Investment Credit is the sum of the following five credits: Rehabilitation and Energy Credits, and the Advanced Coal, Advanced Energy, and Gasification projects.

- **Rehabilitation Credit:** This credit is given to businesses that rehabilitate pre-1936 buildings (10%) or certified historic structures (20%) of qualified expenditures. For 2012, the credit is temporarily increased to 13% for pre-1936 buildings and 26% for historic structures that are located in certain disaster zones.
- **Energy Credit:** This credit is given to businesses that use solar energy to generate electricity or that use geothermal deposits to power their equipment. The credit is between 10% and 30% for qualified fuel cell and other solar energy property,
- **Advanced Coal, Gasification, and Advanced Energy Project Credits:** These credits are designed to reduce greenhouse emissions by retrofitting existing technology to make it cleaner or spurring investment in alternative energy. In the case of the Advanced Energy Credit, qualifying projects must re-equip, expand, or establish a manufacturing facility for the production of solar, wind, or geothermal energy, or electric cars.

The Investment Credit allows businesses to take a deduction for a percentage of certain investment costs from their tax liability *in addition* to the normal allowances for depreciation. In general, a business cannot claim the Investment Credit for property that is:

- Used mainly outside the United States
- Used by a governmental unit or foreign person or entity
- Used by a tax-exempt organization
- Used for lodging or in the furnishing of lodging ; or
- Any property that has already been expensed under section 179 (accelerated depreciation)

***Disabled Access Credit (Form 8826)

This is a nonrefundable tax credit for an eligible small business that incurs expenses to provide access to persons who have disabilities. The expenses must be incurred in order to allow the business to comply with the Americans with Disabilities Act. The amount of the Disabled Access Credit is 50% of qualified expenses, with a maximum credit per year of $5,000. To be eligible, a business must have earned $1 million or less or had no more than 30 full-time employees during the year.

***Work Opportunity Tax Credit (Form 5884)

The WOTC provides a credit to for-profit employers of as much as $9,600 per veteran who was hired and began work before the end of 2012. The credit for qualified tax-exempt organizations is a maximum of $6,240. The amount of this credit varies depending on factors such as the length of the veteran's unemployment before being hired.

Prior to 2012, businesses could take a Work Opportunity Credit equal to 40% of the first $6,000 of wages paid to new hires of one of eight targeted groups. These groups include welfare and food stamp recipients, ex-felons, summer youth employees, and SSI recipients. For 2012, the credit was amended to allow only the hiring of certain qualified veterans.

However, the *American Taxpayer Relief Act of 2012* extended all of these credits retroactively to cover workers hired in 2012. Since employers claiming the WOTC are required to have a state agency certify workers as credit eligible within a month of hiring, it is not clear how the retroactive reinstatement of the credit will be implemented.

Alternative Motor Vehicle Credit (Form 8910)

This credit consists of the following credits for certain alternative motor vehicles placed in service during the year:

- Qualified fuel cell motor vehicle credit
- Advanced lean burn technology motor vehicle credit
- Qualified hybrid motor vehicle credit
- Qualified alternative fuel motor vehicle credit
- Qualified plug-in electric drive motor vehicle conversion credit.

This credit is unusual because it is allowed for both personal and business-use vehicles. If the credit is claimed for a personal vehicle, the credit is a nonrefundable personal credit and will reduce the taxpayer's regular tax as well as the alternative minimum tax.

If the credit is claimed for a business-use vehicle, the credit becomes part of the General Business Credit, so it is available for carryback and carryforward treatment.

Other Credits

Qualified Plug-in Electric Drive Motor Vehicle Credit (Form 8936): This is a $2,500 to $7,500 credit for each new qualifying plug-in electric vehicle purchased or leased during the year.

Credit for Alternative Fuel Vehicle Refueling Property: This credit allows a 30% credit for the cost of installing clean-fuel vehicle refueling property to be used in a business, up to $30,000 a year.[34]

Energy Efficient Appliance Credit (Form 8909): This credit is available for manufacturers of eligible dishwashers, clothes washers, refrigerators. The amount of the credit is based on how little energy a particular appliance uses[35].

Energy Efficient Home Credit (Form 8908): This credit ranges from $1,000 to $2,000, and is available for eligible contractors of certain energy-efficient homes sold for use as residences. [36]

Credit for Employer Social Security and Medicare Taxes Paid on Certain Employee Tips (Form 8846): This credit is generally equal to the employer's portion of Social Security and Medicare taxes paid on tips received by employees of restaurants and other food service establishments where tipping is customary. An employer must meet both of the following requirements to qualify for the credit:

- The business has employees who received tips from customers for serving food or beverages.
- The business paid employer Social Security and Medicare taxes on these tips.

The credit does not apply to other tipped employees, such as hairdressers or bellhops.

Credit for Employer Differential Wage Payments (Form 8932): This credit provides certain small businesses with an incentive to continue to pay wages to an employee performing services on active duty in the uniformed services of the United States for a period of more than 30 days.[37]

Credit for Employer-Provided Childcare Facilities and Services (Form 8882): This credit applies to the qualified expenses a business incurs for employee childcare, childcare resources, and childcare referral services. The credit

---

[34] Expired at the end of 2011, but retroactively extended through 2013 by the American Taxpayer Relief Act of 2012.
[35] Also retroactively extended through 2013.
[36] Also retroactively extended through 2013.
[37] Also retroactively extended through 2013.

is up to 25% of the cost of the childcare facility plus 10% of resource and referral costs. A business is limited to a credit of $150,000 per tax year.

Credit for Small Employer Health Insurance Premiums (Form 8941): This credit applies to the cost of health insurance premiums that an eligible small business provides certain employees. For tax-exempt small businesses, the credit is generally limited to 25% of premiums paid. For all other small employers, the credit is generally 35% of premiums paid. For purposes of this credit, an eligible business must have had fewer than 25 full-time equivalent employees for the tax year, with average annual wages of less than $50,000.

Credit for Small Employer Pension Plan Start-up Costs (Form 8881): This credit applies to pension plan start-up costs of a new qualified defined benefit or defined contribution plan (including a 401(k) plan), SIMPLE plan, or simplified employee pension plans. In order to qualify, the business must not have employed more than 100 employees in the preceding year. The credit is 50% of eligible costs up to a maximum credit of $500 per year for the first three years of the retirement plan.

Credit for Increasing Research Activities: A credit for expenses related to qualified research intended for use in developing new or improved technology that would be used in a taxpayer's business.[38]

Other, more obscure, general business credits include ones for everything from maintaining railroad tracks and training mine rescue teams to makers of orphan drugs and distilled spirits. EA exam-takers do not need to know specifics of these narrowly-based credits.

In addition to credits designed to spur specific economic investment, Congress frequently passes other specific incentives for businesses to engage in certain types of business activity. In 2012, section 181 allows film and television producers to expense the first $15 million of production costs incurred in the United States ($20 million if in economically depressed areas), rather than capitalizing the costs under normal uniform capitalization rules.[39]

Domestic Production Activities Deduction (DPAD)

The domestic production activities deduction, authorized by IRC section 199, is designed to stimulate domestic manufacturing and farming. In 2012, the DPAD is equal to 9% of the *lesser* of:

---

[38] Expired at the end of 2011, but retroactively extended through 2013 by the American Taxpayer Relief Act of 2012.

[39] Also retroactively extended through 2013.

- The business's qualified production activities income, or
- Taxable income determined without regard to the DPAD.

The deduction is limited to 50% of wages paid on Form W-2 by the company for the year. Therefore, if a company does not have any employees, it is not eligible for this deduction. This provision is to encourage domestic employment and to discourage outsourcing.

> ***Note:** Payments made to independent contractors and reported on Form 1099 are not wages and do not qualify for purposes of the DPAD.

> **Example:** Brent Wise Corporation manufactures building components in the United States that it wholesales to building contractors. All of Brent Wise's manufacturing activity is in the U.S., and therefore qualifies for the DPAD. In 2012, Brent Wise had gross sales of $650,000 from its manufacturing activity and paid $225,000 in wages to its employees. Brent Wise's DPAD deduction would therefore be the lesser of:
>
> •9% of the $650,000 in sales, or
>
> •50% of the $225,000 wages.
>
> Thus, Brent Wise's DPAD would be $58,500 (.09 x $650,000).

Eligible Activities for the DPAD

The following activities are qualified production activities eligible for claiming the DPAD:

- Manufacturing goods in the United States
- Selling, leasing, or licensing items that have been manufactured in the United States
- Selling, leasing, or licensing motion pictures that have been produced in the United States (except for pornography)
- Construction of real property in the United States
- Engineering and architectural services relating to a U.S.-based construction project
- Software development in the United States
- The production of water, natural gas, and electricity in the United States (simply transmitting or distributing these goods does not qualify)
- The growth and processing of agricultural products and timber

In order to figure the deduction, a business must correctly calculate its domestic production gross receipts (DPGR).

Example: Raiser Ranch Inc. is a slaughtering plant that has various locations in the United States as well as two locations in Brazil. Although the type of production activity is qualified for the DPAD, Raiser Ranch must track how much of its production occurs in the United States, because only the U.S. production qualifies for the DPAD. Raiser Ranch must allocate its gross receipts between the factory production in the United States and Brazil to calculate DPGR.

Reporting the DPAD Deduction

The DPAD is reported on IRS Form 8903, *Domestic Production Activities Deduction*. The deduction is available to individuals, trusts and estates, C corporations, partnerships, and other pass-through entities such as S corporations and LLCs.

Individual taxpayers (Schedule C and Schedule F) claim the deduction as an adjustment to income on Form 1040. Individual partners or shareholders include their share of the DPAD from pass-through entities, such as partnerships, LLCs taxed as partnerships, and S corporations. C corporations claim the deduction directly on Form 1120.

In 2012, the deduction may not exceed 9% of a C corporation's taxable income or 9% of AGI for sole proprietors, partners in a partnership, and owner-shareholders of S corporations. Estates and trusts are also eligible for the DPAD, but only if the income is not passed through to beneficiaries.

Not Qualified DPAD Activities

The following types of business are specifically excluded from claiming the DPAD:

- Construction services that are cosmetic in nature, such as drywall and painting.

- Leasing or licensing items to a related party.

- Selling food or beverages prepared at restaurants or dining establishments.

- The *transmission* or distribution of electricity, natural gas, or water (although the *production* of electricity, natural gas, or potable water in the United States is a qualified activity).

- Any advertising, product placement, customer service businesses, and other telecommunications services.

- Most service type businesses.

Alternative Minimum Tax

Federal tax law gives special treatment to certain types of income and allows deductions and credits for certain types of expenses. Business taxpayers who benefit from this special treatment may have to pay at least a minimum amount of tax through an additional alternative minimum tax (ATM).

First enacted by Congress in 1969, the AMT is an effort to ensure that individuals and corporations pay at least a minimum amount of tax.[40]

The AMT is the excess of the tentative minimum tax over the regular tax. Thus, the AMT is owed only if the tentative minimum tax is greater than the regular tax. The tentative minimum tax is calculated separately from the regular tax. In general, the tentative minimum tax is computed by:

1. Starting with AGI less itemized deductions, or with AGI for taxpayers who are not claiming itemized deductions, for regular tax purposes,
2. Eliminating or reducing certain exclusions, deductions, and credits that are allowed in computing the regular tax, to derive alternative minimum taxable income (AMTI),
3. Subtracting the AMT exemption amount,
4. Multiplying the amount computed in (3) by the AMT rate, and
5. Subtracting the AMT Foreign Tax Credit.

When calculating the AMT using this formula, businesses must include a number of "tax preference items." After AMT adjustments, these tax preference items are added back into taxable income to determine the AMTI (see step two). For business taxpayers, tax preference items include depletion, excess intangible drilling costs, tax-exempt interest on private activity municipal bonds; accelerated depreciation on property placed in service before 1987; and exclusion of gain on qualified small business stock.[41]

For sole proprietors and partners of a partnership, the AMT is calculated on Form 6251, *Alternative Minimum Tax-Individuals.* For corporations, the AMT is

---

[40] The American Taxpayer Relief Act retroactively increased the AMT exemption amounts for 2012. Lawmakers also created a permanent fix to the AMT, which has been modified 19 times since 1969. Going forward, the AMT will be indexed to inflation, meaning the income threshold for being subject to the AMT will rise automatically each year.

[41] For the EA exam, test-takers should not have to calculate the AMT, but should be able to recognize specific tax preference items for business.

calculated on Form 4626, *Alternative Minimum Tax-Corporations.* A corporation is treated as a small corporation exempt from the AMT if its gross receipts for the last three years are less than $7.5 million, or $5 million for the company's first three-year testing period.

Unit 7: Questions

1. The General Business Credit is defined as:

A. A single business credit for small businesses.
B. A set of various credits available to businesses.
C. The credit for dependent care.
D. A collection of charitable deductions for businesses.

The answer is B. The General Business Credit consists of various credits available to businesses. The GBC is also the total of the carryforward of business credits from prior years plus the total current year business credits. ###

2. Farwell Corporation is a qualified small business for purposes of the General Business Credit. The corporation could not use all of its credits in 2012. What is the carryover period for the GBC?

A. The GBC may be carried back two years and carried forward 5 years.
B. The GBC may be carried back five years and carried forward 10 years.
C. The unused GBC cannot be carried over to another tax year.
D. The GBC may be carried back one year and carried forward for 20 years.

The answer is D. Normally, businesses can carry back unused business credits one year and carry them forward 20 years. ###

3. Stacy owns the Peach Pit Cannery. In 2012, she renovated her cannery to come into compliance with the Americans with Disabilities Act. The Peach Pit Cannery had gross receipts of $750,000 and spent $15,000 on disabled access upgrades. What is Stacy's current year Disabled Access Credit?

A. $2,500.
B. $5,000.
C. $7,500.
D. $15,000.

The answer is B. The amount of the Disabled Access Credit is 50% of the qualified expenses, but the maximum credit per year is $5,000. ###

4. The standards of the Disabled Access Credit conform to the _____ ?

A. Architectural Standards Act.
B. U.S. Department of Labor.
C. Americans with Disabilities Act.
D. National Organization on Disability.

The answer is C. The Disabled Access Credit is a nonrefundable tax credit for an eligible small business that pays expenses to provide access to disabled persons. The taxpayer must pay or incur the expenses to enable the business to comply with the Americans with Disabilities Act. ###

5. In 2012, the Work Opportunity Tax Credit provides a credit for businesses that do which of the following?

A. Provide job training for out-of-work individuals.
B. Give severance to laid-off workers.
C. Invest in federal empowerment zones.
D. Hire unemployed veterans and other individuals in targeted groups.

The answer is D. The WTOC offers credits to businesses who hire out-of-work veterans, as well as other individuals in eight different targeted groups. ###

6. Which of the following is not part of the Investment Credit in 2012?

A. Gasification Project Credit.
B. Hydroelectric Power Credit.
C. Rehabilitation Credit.
D. Energy Credit.

The answer is B. The Investment Credit is the sum of five credits that are designed to spur investment in activity that reduces greenhouse emissions and rehabilitates historic property. In 2012, the Investment Credit consists of the Rehabilitation and Energy Credits, and the Advanced Coal, Advanced Energy, and Gasification Projects. There is no credit for hydroelectric power. ###

7. Bettina owns her own photography business, and she has an NOL in the current year. She elects to carry back her losses to a previous period. How long may she carry back and carry forward her NOL?

A. Back 5 years, forward 20 years.
B. Back 2 years, forward 20 years.
C. Back 3 years, forward 25 years.
D. Back 2 years, forward 5 years.

The answer is B. In general, a net operating loss may be carried back two previous years, and the remaining loss may be carried forward to each of the subsequent 20 years. ###

8. Which event would create a genuine NOL?

A. Selling a personal used car for a loss.
B. Selling a primary residence for a loss.
C. Casualty loss from a fire on a business location.
D. Large losses from the sale of corporate stock.

The answer is C. Only the casualty loss is potentially deductible for purposes of the net operating loss. Losses from the sale of stock are capital losses and cannot be used to create an NOL. Losses from the sale of personal-use property or a primary residence are not deductible. ###

9. Gabriel is a small business owner who reports income and loss on Schedule C. He had an NOL in 2012 due to a business casualty loss. His losses occurred in a presidentially declared disaster area. What is the earliest year that Gabriel can carryback his losses?

A. 2008.
B. 2009.
C. 2010.
D. 2011.

The answer is B. In the case of a loss due to a federally declared disaster area, qualified small businesses may carry back a loss three years instead of the normal two-year carryback period. ###

10. Which of the following items is allowed when figuring a net operating loss?

A. Capital losses in excess of capital gains.
B. A net operating loss from another year (a carryback or a carryforward).
C. The domestic production activities deduction.
D. The loss from the theft of business property.

The answer is D. Only the losses due to the theft of business property would be allowed in figuring a net operating loss. ###

11. Which of the following does not qualify for the domestic production activities deduction (section 199)?

A. Manufacturing goods in the United States.
B. Construction of buildings in the United States.
C. Selling food or beverages prepared at restaurants.
D. Software development in the United States.

The answer is C. Selling food or beverages prepared at restaurants is specifically disallowed for purposes of the DPAD. Most U.S.-based manufacturing qualifies for the DPAD. ###

12. All of the following statements are correct regarding the DPAD except:

A. The DPAD cannot be more than 25% of the wages a business pays its employees.
B. Businesses with both domestic and foreign business activity must use only their domestic income in calculating the DPAD.
C. In 2012, the DPAD can be as much as 9% of a company's qualified taxable income.
D. The DPAD is authorized by section 199 of the Internal Revenue Code.

The answer is A. The DPAD cannot be more than 50%, not 25%, of the wages a business pays its employees. All of the other statements are correct about this business deduction designed to stimulate manufacturing and other production activities in the United States. ###

13. Which of the following is not a tax preference item for the AMT?

A. Excess intangible drilling costs.
B. Interest on private-activity municipal bonds.
C. Accelerated depreciation.
D. Health care premiums for employees.

The answer is D. Many factors may trigger the AMT for a business. These are called tax preference items, but health care premiums for employees are not among them. ###

Unit 8: Basis of Business Assets

More Reading:
Publication 551, *Basis of Assets*
Publication 547, *Casualties, Disasters, and Thefts*

A business asset is any type of property used in the conduct of a trade or business: land, buildings, machinery, furniture, trucks, patents, and franchise rights are all examples. Some assets are tangible, and others are intangible. Taxpayers must capitalize the cost of business assets, rather than deduct them in the year the cost is incurred.

Basis is the amount of a taxpayer's investment in property for tax purposes. In order to compute gain or loss on the sale of an asset, a business must be able to determine its basis in the property sold. The basis of property is also used to determine depreciation, amortization, depletion, and casualty losses. If a business cannot determine the basis of an asset, the IRS will deem it to be zero.

Cost Basis of Business Assets

The basis of property is usually its cost—the amount a business pays for an asset. The basis of an asset also includes amounts paid for the following items:

- Sales tax on the purchase
- Freight to obtain the property
- Installation and testing
- Excise taxes
- Legal and accounting fees to obtain property
- Revenue stamps
- Recording fees
- Real estate taxes (if assumed by the buyer)
- Settlement costs for the purchase of real estate
- The assumption of any liabilities on the property

Example: Naomi pays $4,000 for a commercial dryer for her laundromat. Naomi also pays $500 for shipping and sales tax. The installation cost for the dryer is $250. These costs are added to the purchase price, resulting in a basis of $4,750.

Certain events that occur during the period of ownership may increase or decrease the basis, resulting in an *adjusted basis.* The basis of property is *increased* by the cost of improvements that add to the value of the property. The basis of property is *decreased* by depreciation, insurance reimbursements for casualty and theft losses, and certain other items such as rebates.

Basis of Real Property

Real property, often called real estate, is land and anything built on or attached to it. When a taxpayer buys real property, certain fees and other expenses become part of the cost basis in the property.

Real estate taxes: If a taxpayer pays real estate taxes on property he buys that the seller owed, those taxes are added to the basis and cannot be deducted.

Settlement costs: Settlement fees and closing costs for buying a property are added to its basis. These include abstract fees; charges for installing utility services; legal fees, including title search and preparation of the sales contract and deed; recording fees; surveys; transfers; owner's title insurance; and any amounts the seller owes that the taxpayer agrees to pay, such as charges for improvements or repairs and sales commissions.

Assumption of mortgage: If a taxpayer buys property with an existing mortgage, the basis includes the amount he pays for the property plus the amount of the mortgage that he assumes.

> **Example:** The Oceanside Partnership purchases a commercial building for $200,000 in cash and assumes a related mortgage of $800,000. The partnership also pays $5,500 in legal fees to a real estate attorney to handle the purchase. Oceanside's basis in the building is $1,005,500 ($200,000 + $800,000 + $5,500).

Constructing assets: If a taxpayer builds property or has assets built for him, the expenses of construction are added to the basis. These expenses include land; labor and materials; architect's fees; building permit charges; payments to contractors; payment for rental equipment; inspections; employee wages paid for the construction work; and the cost of building supplies and materials used in the construction. The value of the taxpayer's own labor or any other labor he did not pay for are not included in the basis.

Demolition Costs: Demolition costs *increase* an asset's basis rather than decrease it because they are necessary expenses in order to prepare a property for use. Costs incurred to demolish a building are added to the basis of the land on which the demolished building was located. The costs associated with clearing land for construction also must be added to the basis of the land. For example, if a business pays to demolish an existing building and clear the lot of debris so new construction can begin, all of the costs associated with the preparation of the land are added to the land's basis.

> **Example:** Tony buys a lot with a badly damaged building on it for $25,000. He demolishes the building and prepares the land for a new structure. The demolition costs $13,000. Tony's new basis in the land is $38,000 ($25,000 + $13,000).

Rehabilitation Costs: Rehabilitation costs increase basis. However, any rehabilitation credits allowed for the expenses must first be subtracted.

Not Included in the Basis of Real Property

The following settlement fees and closing costs cannot be included in the basis of a property:

- Casualty insurance premiums
- Rent or utility costs related to occupancy of the property before closing
- Any charges for acquiring a loan, such as mortgage insurance premiums, loan assumption fees, cost of a credit report, fees for appraisal reports, fees for refinancing a mortgage, and points.

Points are prepaid interest on a loan and are deducted as interest over the life of the loan, rather than added to an asset's basis.

Improvements to Business Property

There are many costs that will increase an asset's basis, such as making additions or improvements to business property. The costs of making improvements to an asset are capitalized if the improvements:

- Add to the value of the asset,
- Appreciably lengthen the time a business can use it, or
- Adapt it to a different use.

Any cost that is added to the basis of an asset cannot be deducted currently. Examples of improvements include installation of new electric wiring, a new roof, adding central air conditioning, or renovation of a kitchen.

In contrast, a repair keeps a property in operating condition but does not add to its value or substantially prolong its life. Examples include repainting a property or replacing broken windows.

Example: Douglas repairs a leaky toilet in a rental duplex. The repair may be deducted as a current expense. The following year, Douglas replaces the entire plumbing system in the duplex with new pipes and bathroom fixtures. This is an improvement that increases the value of the property. Douglas must capitalize the cost of the new plumbing, and thus increase the property's basis, and depreciate the cost of this improvement over its useful life.

Since improvements increase a property's basis, a taxpayer must keep accurate records to distinguish between the costs of repairs and improvements.

Repair vs. Improvements (Capitalization Rule Changes)

In December 2011,[42] the IRS released temporary regulations that will require major changes in determining whether certain costs are repairs or

---

[42] Federal Register, Dec. 27, 2011.

improvements, and thus whether they need to be expensed or capitalized. Under the changes, an improvement is redefined as a cost involving:

- The **betterment** of a **unit** of property,
- The **restoration** of a **unit** of property, or
- The **adaptation** of a **unit** of property to a new or different use.

The new IRS improvement standards apply to the building structure and to each of the building's major component systems separately. The guidelines divide a building into nine different structural components called "building systems," such as those for plumbing, heating and air conditioning, and electrical.

The effects of a repair on a specific building system, rather than the building as a whole, must be evaluated under the new, narrower definition of an improvement. The result will be to make costs more difficult to classify as repairs, meaning the taxpayer will be less likely to deduct them as expenses and more likely to capitalize them.

For example, under current guidelines significant repairs to an elevator may "better" the elevator but would not be significant to the building as a whole, so the repair could be expensed. Under the new guidelines, the costs would be significant to the *elevator system* and would have to be capitalized.

Example: A landlord purchases an apartment building in 2010 for $750,000. In 2012 he spends $8,000 to fix wiring in the electrical system. Under the old IRS rules, the $8,000 likely would be considered a repair because it is relatively small compared to the overall cost of the building. Under the new rules, the electrical system is a separate structural component. This means that the $8,000 must be compared with the cost of the electrical system alone, not the cost of the whole building. This makes the expense more significant and more likely to constitute an improvement.

The final regulations are still being revised, and the IRS announced in December 2012 that it was delaying full implementation until 2014.[43] For the 2012 tax year, taxpayers have the choice to use the current rules or adopt the new ones.

Other Increases to Basis of Business Property

Among the items that increase the basis of property are the following:

- The cost of extending service lines to the property
- Impact fees
- Legal fees, such as the cost of defending and perfecting title

---

[43] IRS Notice 2012-73.

- Zoning costs

Government assessments for items such as paving roads and sidewalks increase the value of an asset, and therefore must be added to an asset's basis. A business cannot deduct assessments as taxes, but may deduct charges for maintenance, repairs, or interest charges related to the improvements.

Decreases to Basis

A business must decrease the basis of property by items that represent a return of capital for the period during which the business holds the property. For example, rebates and casualty losses are among the items that decrease an asset's basis.

Example: Kristin buys a copier that costs $1,200 to use in her business. She sends in a rebate receipt and receives a $50 rebate from the manufacturer. The correct way to account for this rebate is to reduce the basis of the asset to $1,150 ($1,200 - $50).

Items that reduce the basis of property also include the following:

- Deductions for amortization, depreciation, section 179, and depletion (covered in Unit 9, *Depreciation of Business Assets*)
- Nontaxable corporate distributions
- Exclusion of subsidies for energy conservation measures
- Residential energy credits, vehicle credits, the Investment Credit, and the Credit for Employer-Provided Child Care
- Certain canceled debt excluded from income
- Easements

Casualty Losses

Deductible casualty losses and insurance reimbursements reduce the basis of property. A casualty is defined as the damage, destruction, or loss of property resulting from an identifiable event that is sudden, unexpected, or unusual.

Deductible casualty losses related to business and income-producing property (such as rental property)are reported on IRS Form 4684, *Casualties and Thefts*, and are deductible without regard to whether they exceed the $100 and 10% of AGI thresholds that apply for personal use property.

> **Example:** Ramon has a fire at his home that destroys his couch and coffee table, which are personal-use property. The loss for his personal furniture is $5,000. This loss must be reduced by $100, and Ramon can deduct the portion that exceeds 10% of his AGI. The same fire also damages a business asset, an expensive laptop that he had brought home that day in order to catch up on his work. The computer is destroyed and results in a business casualty loss of $3,000 that is fully deductible.

A casualty loss is not deductible if the damage or destruction is caused by progressive deterioration due to normal wear and tear from weather conditions or insect damage. If an entity has business property that is stolen or destroyed, the loss is figured as follows:

> **The taxpayer's adjusted basis in the property**
> **MINUS**
> **Any salvage value**
> **MINUS**
> **Any insurance or other reimbursement received**

Theft Losses

Many businesses are victims of theft, which is defined as the taking of money or property by the following means: blackmail, burglary, embezzlement, extortion, kidnapping for ransom, larceny, and robbery. The taking of property must be illegal under the state law where it happened, and it must have been done with criminal intent.

> **Example:** Jeff owns a sports shop that sells memorabilia. Several years ago, Jeff purchased some signed football jerseys for display for $150, which is his adjusted basis in the property. Jeff's jerseys were stolen in 2012. The FMV of the jerseys was $1,000 just before they were stolen, and insurance did not cover them. Jeff's deductible theft loss is $150, which is his basis in the jerseys.

Casualty losses are generally deductible only in the tax year during which the casualty occurred, even if a business does not repair or replace the damaged property until a later year. Theft losses that are not reimbursable can be deducted only in the year the business discovers the property was stolen.

Insurance Reimbursements: If a business has property that is covered by insurance, it must file an insurance claim for reimbursement, or it will not be able to deduct the loss as a casualty or theft. The portion of the loss not covered by insurance, such as a deductible, is not subject to this rule.

Example: Howard and Gayle are partners and have a gourmet food truck that is used 100% for business purposes. Howard has an accident that causes $2,350 in damage to the truck. He and Gayle decide to pay the repair bill out-of-pocket so their business insurance costs will not increase. The insurance policy has a $500 deductible. Because the insurance would not cover the first $500 of a vehicle collision, only the $500 would be deductible as a casualty loss. This is true even when the business does not file an insurance claim, because the policy would not have reimbursed the deductible.

A business that has a casualty or theft loss must decrease its basis in the property by any insurance or reimbursement it receives and by any deductible loss. The result is the adjusted basis in the property.

A business must increase its basis in the property by the amount spent on repairs that restore the property to its pre-casualty condition. If a business's casualty or theft loss deduction causes deductions to be more than its income for the year, it has a net operating loss. The NOL could be carried back to an earlier year for tax the business already paid, resulting in a refund, or the NOL could be carried forward to lower tax in a later year.

Basis of Securities

The basis of stocks, bonds, and other securities is the purchase price plus any costs of purchase, such as commissions and recording or transfer fees. Stock is generally purchased in various quantities. A taxpayer must keep track of the basis per share of all stock bought and sold.

Example: In 2012, Yuen Corporation purchases 2,000 shares of Catalyst Corporation stock. The cost of the stock is $24,000, and Yuen pays a broker's fee of $550 on the purchase and transfer. Therefore, the basis of the stock is $24,550 ($24,000 + $550).

Events that occur after the purchase of the stock can require adjustments to the per share basis of stock. The original basis per share can be changed by events such as stock dividends, stock splits, and DRIP (dividend reinvestment plan) activity.

- Stock dividends involve the issuance of additional shares to current shareholders. The taxpayer's ownership total basis is unchanged but is spread over more shares, which decreases the basis per share.
- A stock split is similar to a stock dividend. For example, a two-for-one stock split increases the number of outstanding shares two-fold and decreases the value and the basis per share by half.

The total basis remains the same in a stock split. For example, if a taxpayer has 100 shares at $50 per share, his basis is $5,000. Assuming a 2 for 1 stock split, the taxpayer now has 200 shares at $25, which still equals $5,000.

> **Example:** In 2012, Zollinger Partnership purchases 100 shares of Better Electronics for $11,000. There is an additional $200 in broker's commissions, so the original basis per share is $112 ([$11,000 + $200] ÷ 100). Later in 2012, Zollinger receives 40 additional shares of Better Electronics' stock as a nontaxable stock dividend. The $11,200 basis must now be spread over 140 shares (100 original shares plus the 40-share stock dividend). The adjusted stock basis is $80 per share ([$11,200 ÷ 140).

Basis Other Than Cost

There are many times when a taxpayer cannot use cost as basis. In these cases, the fair market value or the adjusted basis of the property can be used.

Property received for services: If a taxpayer receives property for his services, he must include its FMV in income. The amount included in income becomes the basis. If the services were performed for a price agreed on beforehand, it will be accepted as the FMV of the property if there is no evidence to the contrary.

When property is transferred in lieu of wages, the employer is entitled to deduct its fair market value at the time of the transfer. A gain or loss is realized if there is a difference between the fair market value and the adjusted basis of the property.

Bargain purchases: A bargain purchase is a purchase of an item for less than its FMV. If, as compensation for services, a taxpayer buys goods or other property at less than the FMV, the difference between the purchase price and the property's FMV must be included in his income. His basis in the property is its FMV (the purchase price plus the amount included in income.)

Unit 8: Questions

1. Jade purchases a condemned warehouse for her business, but it is in such bad condition that she decides to demolish it and build a new one. The demolition costs $15,600. How must Jade report these costs on her tax return?

A. The cost for the demolition is added to the basis of the land where the original demolished structure was located.
B. The demolition may be expensed on her tax return on Schedule E.
C. The demolition cost is an itemized deduction on her Schedule A.
D. The demolition cost must be amortized over 180 months.

The answer is A. Demolition costs or other losses related to the demolition of any building are added to the basis of the land. ###

2. What item would not be included in an asset's basis?

A. Sales tax.
B. Installation charges.
C. Recording fees.
D. Interest paid on a loan to purchase the asset.

The answer is D. Interest charges are not added to an asset's basis. Interest is a currently deductible expense. ###

3. Ian buys a building. He makes a $15,000 down payment in cash. He also assumes a mortgage of $180,000 on it and pays $1,000 in title fees and $2,000 in points. What is Ian's basis in the building?

A. $15,000.
B. $195,000.
C. $196,000.
D. $198,000.

The answer is C. Ian's basis is $196,000. The title fees, mortgage amount, and the down payment are added together to figure the original cost basis of the building. The points are not included in the basis. ###

4. Irina owns a bookstore. In 2012, she has a business loss of $14,000 due to water damage from a storm. The loss is completely covered by insurance. However, Irina will not be reimbursed by her insurance company until 2013. How should she treat this loss?

A. She should claim the entire loss as a casualty loss in 2012 and then claim the income from the insurance company reimbursement in 2013.
B. She must reduce the amount of her inventory loss in 2012. For 2013, she must include the insurance reimbursement as income.
C. She does not need to make any adjustments to her tax return, since she knows she will receive a reimbursement within a short period of time.
D. She must reduce her cost of goods sold in 2012 to reflect the loss and then claim the reimbursement as income in 2013.

The answer is C. Irina expects to be fully reimbursed for her loss, so no adjustments are necessary. If Irina was reimbursed by her insurance company and her reimbursement either exceeded her losses or was less than her losses, then an adjustment would be necessary. ###

5. All of the following items decrease the basis of property except:

A. Casualty or theft loss deductions and insurance reimbursements.
B. The cost of defending a title.
C. Depreciation.
D. Amortization.

The answer is B. The cost of defending title to a property increases its basis. ###

6. Under new IRS rules, what are the categories for determining what constitutes an improvement to property?

A. Betterment, restoration, or adaptation.
B. Prolonging life and creating value.
C. Renovation, amelioration, or restoration.
D. Enhancement and repair.

The answer is A. Under the new rules, an improvement is redefined as a cost involving a betterment of the unit of property, a restoration of the unit of property, or an adaptation of the unit of property to a new or different use. ###

7. How does a stock split affect basis?

A. There is no effect.
B. It increases the basis of stock.
C. It decreases the basis of stock.
D. It decreases the basis of a share of stock but does not affect the total basis of the stock.

The answer is D. A stock split increases the number of outstanding shares, which decreases the per-share value, but it does not change the basis of the stock as a whole. ###

8. Priscilla's Pastries, a sole proprietorship, bought a building for $250,000 in cash in March 2012. Priscilla paid the title company $13,000 in settlement fees to purchase the property. She also assumed an existing mortgage of $35,000 on the property. Legal fees of $9,500 were incurred in a title dispute with the former owner in April 2012. The title was finally transferred to Priscilla in May 2012. Property taxes in the amount of $2,600 were incurred on the property after ownership was transferred. What is Priscilla's basis in the building in December 2012?

A: $250,000.
B: $285,000.
C: $307,500.
D: $310,100.

The answer is C. The basis is $307,500 ($250,000 + $13,000 + $35,000 + $9,500). The settlement fees, mortgage assumed by the buyer, and the legal fees for defending a title are all included in the basis of the property. Priscilla cannot deduct the cost of the legal fees on her tax return as an expense. Instead, the amount must be added to the basis and depreciated. The property taxes are not included in the basis of the building because they were incurred when Priscilla was already the legal owner. Instead, the property taxes may be deducted as a current expense. ###

9. Which is not a correct statement regarding repairs vs. improvements under IRS rules?

A. A repair generally may be deducted as a current business expense.
B. A repair keeps a property in operating condition but does not add to its value or substantially prolong its life.
C. An improvement adds value to an asset, or appreciably lengthens the time a business can use it.
D. A taxpayer may choose whether to expense or capitalize improvements.

The answer is D. Improvements to a property cannot be deducted as expenses; they must be capitalized. ###

10. Arrowhead Model Builders is constructing a custom home. Calculate the basis of the property from the following information:

•$125,000 land purchase price
•$40,000 construction loan
•$3,000 points on construction loan
•$12,000 real estate taxes
•$20,000 tear-down of existing home
•$10,000 clearing brush
•$50,000 construction workers' wages
•$25,000 value of owner's labor
•$300,000 construction materials

A. $227,000.
B. $557,000.
C. $560,000.
D. $582,000.

The answer is B. All items are added to the property's basis except for the points on the loan (this is an expense that is deducted over the life of the loan) and the value of the owner's labor. ###

11. Franco purchases 50 shares of Canine Country stock for $3,500. He pays a broker's fee of $100. He later receives 40 additional shares of Canine Country stock. The following year, the company does a two-for-one stock split. Calculate the total basis of Franco's Canine Country stock and his per share basis:

A. Stock basis: $3,500; per share basis: $38.88.
B. Stock basis: $3,500; per share basis: $19.44.
C. Stock basis: $3,600; per share basis: $20.
D. Stock basis: $3,600; per share basis: $40.

The answer is C. The basis is the stock's purchase price plus the broker's fee ($3,500 + $100 = $3,600). After the stock split, Franco has 180 shares of stock (50 shares + 40 shares X 2 = 180). The stock split reduces his per share basis by half to $20 ($3,600 ÷ 180 shares of stock = $20). ###

Unit 9: Depreciation of Business Assets

More Reading:
Publication 946, *How to Depreciate Property*

Capital Expenditures

Under the Internal Revenue Code, certain costs and purchases must be capitalized, including the following:

- The expenses of going into business (start-up costs),
- The cost of business assets, and
- The cost of business improvements.

Capital expenditures are generally not currently deductible, but many of these costs may instead be recognized as depreciation or amortization expense over lives assigned to individual assets.

> **Example:** Better Produce, Inc. is a canning company that processes fruits and vegetables. In 2012, it has an older canning machine that ceases to function. Better Produce has the option to purchase a new machine for $500,000, or completely rebuild its old machine, which will extend its useful life for another five years. Better Produce chooses to rebuild the machine at a cost of $125,000. The $125,000 cost must be capitalized and depreciated over its useful life, which in this case is five years.

Depreciation Overview

A depreciable asset usually has value well beyond the year in which it is purchased. Depreciation is an income tax deduction that allows a business to recover the cost or other basis of property. It is an annual allowance for the wear and tear, deterioration, or obsolescence of an asset. The amount allowed as an annual depreciation deduction is intended to roughly approximate the reduction in the value of a capital asset as it ages. Tax depreciation is based on the original, historical cost of the asset and is not indexed for inflation.

The cost of land and many land improvements cannot be depreciated. Most other types of tangible property, such as buildings, machinery, vehicles, furniture, and equipment, are depreciable. Likewise, certain intangible property, such as patents, copyrights, and computer software, is amortizable.

In order to be depreciated or amortized, an asset must meet all the following requirements:

- The taxpayer generally must own the property. However, taxpayers may also depreciate capital improvements for property they lease (for example, a fence that is built on property that the business leases from another party).

- A taxpayer must use the property in business or in an income-producing activity. If a taxpayer uses the property for *both* business and personal use, he can only deduct an amount of depreciation based on the business-use percentage.
- The property must have a useful life of more than one year.

The property ceases to be depreciable when the business has fully recovered the property's cost or when the taxpayer sells or retires it from service, whichever happens first. In order to properly depreciate an asset, a taxpayer must identify the following:

- The depreciable basis of the property
- Whether the taxpayer elects to expense any portion of the asset
- The depreciation method for the property
- The class life of the asset (which is representative of the asset's useful life)
- Whether the property is listed property
- Whether the taxpayer qualifies for any bonus first year depreciation

The following assets are not depreciable:

- Property with a useful life of one year or less.
- Property placed in service and disposed of in the same year.
- Equipment that is used to build capital improvements.
- Section 197 intangibles such as copyrights and patents, which must be amortized, not depreciated.

Example: Natalie is a self-employed bookkeeper who is required to purchase new income tax return preparation software every year. She cannot depreciate the software but may instead deduct its cost as a business expense since the item only has a useful life of one year.

Taxpayers must use Form 4562, *Depreciation and Amortization* to:

- Claim deductions for depreciation and amortization,
- Make an election under section 179 to currently expense certain depreciable property, and
- Provide information on the business/investment use of automobiles and other listed property.

Example: Ron's Business Rentals made a down payment on a rental property and assumed the previous owner's mortgage. Ron owns the property and now may depreciate it.

> **Example:** Harris's Doughnut Shop bought a new van that will be used only for business. Harris will be making payments on the van for the next five years. Harris owns the van and can depreciate it.

Modified Accelerated Cost Recovery System (MACRS)

The modified accelerated cost recovery system (MACRS) is the depreciation method generally used for most *tangible* property, such as machinery, buildings, and automobiles. Under MACRS, all assets are divided into nine separate classes that dictate the number of years over which their cost will be recovered. Each MACRS class has a schedule that specifies the percentage of the asset's cost that is depreciated each year. For example, trucks are depreciated over five years, and fruit trees are depreciated over ten years.

MACRS Class Life Table

Property Class	Asset Type
3-year property	Certain tractor units; race horses over two years old; qualified rent-to-own property.
5-year property	Computers; office machinery; automobiles, taxis, buses, and trucks; breeding cattle and dairy cattle; appliances, carpets, and furniture used in residential retail activity; certain geothermal, solar, and wind property.
7-year property	Office furniture and fixtures; agricultural machinery and equipment; any other property that does not have a designated class life.
10-year property	Vessels and water transportation equipment; trees or vines bearing fruit or nuts; single purpose agricultural or horticultural structures.
15-year property	Improvements to land such as fences, roads, and bridges; municipal wastewater treatment plants; qualified restaurant and retail improvement property; qualified leasehold improvement property.
20-year property	Certain municipal sewers; farm buildings (other than single purpose agricultural or horticultural structures).
25-year property	Certain municipal sewers; water utility property.
27.5-year property	Residential rental property, if more than 80% of its gross rental income is from dwelling units.
39-year property	Section 1250 nonresidential real property, such as office buildings, stores, and warehouses.

The depreciation calculations spread out deduction of the asset's cost over a recovery period roughly consistent with the asset's estimated useful economic life. Certain assets, such as computers, office furniture, and cars, are assigned the same recovery period in all industries.

Real property is depreciated using the straight-line method, with an equal amount of expense each year. The recovery periods for buildings vary depending upon the property's use. For example, nonresidential buildings, such as office buildings, shopping malls, and factories, are depreciated over a 39-year recovery period. Residential buildings, such as apartment complexes and residential rentals, are depreciated over a 27.5-year period.

Placed-in-Service Date

Depreciation begins when a taxpayer places property in service for the production of income. This is called the placed-in-service date.

Example: Donald buys a machine for his business that is delivered on December 20, 2012. However, the machine is not installed and operational until January 12, 2013. It is considered placed in service in 2013, and the first depreciation expense deduction can be claimed in 2013.

If the machine had been ready and available for use when it was delivered, it would have been considered placed in service in 2012 even if it were not actually used until 2013.

Example: On June 23, 2012, Sue bought a house to use as residential rental property. She made several repairs and had it ready for rent on September 5, 2012. At that time, she began to advertise the home for rent in the local newspaper. Sue can begin to depreciate the rental property in September because it is considered placed in service when it is ready and available for rent.

Salvage Value (Scrap Value)

An asset cannot be depreciated below its salvage (or scrap) value. Salvage value is the asset's estimated FMV at the end of its useful life. Salvage value is affected both by *how* a business uses the property and *how long* it uses it. If it is the business's policy to dispose of property that is still in good operating condition, the salvage value can be relatively large. If the business's policy is to use property until it is no longer usable, its salvage value can be zero.

Example: Cooper Trucking operates a trucking fleet that delivers produce. Cooper Trucking purchases a new delivery truck in 2012 for $125,000. The MACRS class life of the truck is five years. At the end of five years, Cooper Trucking estimates it will sell the used delivery truck at auction for $30,000, so it uses this amount as salvage value. The basis of the truck is $125,000, but the *basis for depreciation* is $95,000 ($125,000- $30,000), since the business expects to recover $30,000 at the end of the asset's useful life.

Common Depreciation Methods

A business generally may use any accepted depreciation method. However, once it chooses a depreciation method for an asset, the business must generally use the same method for the life of the asset.

Straight-Line Depreciation

This is the simplest method. To use the straight-line method, a business must first determine the asset's basis, salvage value, and class life. If the asset has a salvage value, it is subtracted from the basis. The balance is the total depreciation expense deduction the business can take over the useful life of the property. For an asset that originally cost $200, has an estimated salvage value of zero, and a five-year recovery period, the straight-line depreciation allowance would be $40 ($200 ÷ 5) each year for five years.

Straight-line Depreciation = (Cost - Salvage Value) ÷ Useful Life

A business may switch to the straight-line method at any time during the useful life of the property without IRS consent. However, after a business changes to straight-line, it cannot change back to any other method for a period of ten years without written permission from the IRS.

Example: On April 1, 2012, the Redstone Granite Corporation purchases a computer system for $40,000. The system has a five-year class life under MACRS. There is no salvage value. Depreciation is figured as follows:
Depreciation for 2012 = ($40,000 ÷ 5 years) x (9 months ÷ 12) = **$6,000.**
Depreciation for 2013 = ($40,000 ÷ 5 years) x (12 ÷ 12) = **$8,000.**

The Double-Declining Balance Method

This method uses a flat percentage depreciation rate over the class life of the asset. For example, if five years is the asset's cost recovery period, the double-declining balance method has a depreciation rate of [2 ÷ 5], or twice the straight-line depreciation rate. Instead of spreading the cost of the asset evenly over its life, this method expenses the asset by applying a constant rate to the declining balance of the asset, which results in declining depreciation expense each successive period.

The logic for the double-declining balance method is that there should be a greater deduction in the earlier years when the asset is more productive.

Example: For an asset that originally cost $200 and has a five-year recovery period, double-declining balance depreciation is $80 = ([2 ÷ 5]x $200) in the first year; $48 = ([2 ÷ 5]x[$200 - $80]) in the second year; $28.80 = ([2 ÷ 5]x[$200 - $80 - $48]) in the third year; and so on.

Although assets are usually depreciated according to the MACRS tables, there are other depreciation methods that are not based on a term of years. This is common in manufacturing businesses, where the useful life of machinery can vary based on production.

A business can elect to exclude certain property from MACRS by making an election on Form 4562.

Unit-of-Production Method

This method allocates depreciation based on the asset's units of activity, rather than on a set number of years. For example, airplanes may be depreciated based on air miles, delivery trucks based on miles driven, and machinery based on the number of units produced.

Depreciation is computed by dividing the total cost of the asset (minus salvage value) by its projected units-of-production capacity. Then, to determine depreciation expense each period, the business multiplies the depreciation per unit of production (or activity) by the number of units during the period.

Example: The Kumar Company owns a machine that produces computer components. It was purchased for $500,000 and the machine is expected to produce 240,000 units over its useful life. The salvage value of the machine is estimated at $20,000. Using the units of production method, the machine's depreciable basis is $480,000 ($500,000 - $20,000 salvage value). The depreciable basis is divided by the number of units that the machine is expected to produce ($480,000 ÷ 240,000). This equals depreciation of $2 per unit produced. If the machine produces 30,000 components in 2012, depreciation for the year will be $60,000 ($2 x 30,000 units). If the machine produces 25,000 parts in 2013, its depreciation will be $50,000 ($2 x 25,000 units). The depreciation will be calculated similarly each year until the asset's accumulated depreciation reaches $480,000. At that point, even if the machine is still in use, it will be considered fully depreciated, and the depreciation will stop.

Section 179 Deduction

The section 179 deduction is a special allowance that allows certain small businesses to elect to take a full deduction for the cost of new or used property in the first year they place it in service, rather than depreciating it over its useful life. However, a business may choose to use standard depreciation methods for its assets instead of electing to use the section 179 deduction.

To qualify for the section 179 deduction, the property must meet all the following requirements:

- It must be tangible property, with the exception of off-the-shelf computer software
- It must be acquired for business use (and used more than 50% for business in the year placed in service)
- It must have been acquired by purchase (not as a gift)
- It must not have been purchased from a related party, including a spouse, ancestors, or lineal descendants

Eligible property generally includes the following:

- Machinery and equipment.
- Property contained in or attached to a building (other than structural components), such as refrigerators, grocery store counters, office equipment, printing presses, testing equipment, and signs.
- Gasoline storage tanks and pumps at retail service stations.
- Livestock, including horses, cattle, hogs, sheep, goats, and mink and other furbearing animals.
- Computer software ("off-the-shelf" computer software is one of the few *intangible* assets that is eligible for section 179)
- Business vehicles with a gross vehicle weight in excess of 6,000 pounds

Section 179 Limits and Phase-Outs

The section 179 deduction may not exceed taxable income for the year. For example, if a business's taxable income is $150,000, the section 179 deduction cannot exceed $150,000. However, an amount disallowed due to this limitation may be carried over for an unlimited number of years.

The deduction can be elected for individual qualifying assets, up to a maximum of $500,000 for 2012. The deduction amount may be increased by up to $35,000 for businesses in qualifying enterprise zones and up to $100,000 for businesses in federally declared disaster areas. However, to the extent the cost of qualifying section 179 property placed in service by the taxpayer exceeds $2 million, the maximum is reduced on a dollar-for-dollar basis, and eliminated if the total cost of qualifying property is at least $2.5 million.[44]

Qualified Real Property (QRP)

Businesses generally may not deduct the costs of real property under section 179. However, a special provision presently allows businesses to use up to

---

[44] The section 179 deduction limits were increased in 2010 and 2011, but were scheduled to decrease in 2012. However, the American Taxpayer Relief Act of 2012 retroactively reinstated the $500,000 deduction and $2 million dollar phase-out for tax year 2012 and extended these levels through 2013.

$250,000 of the $500,000 limit described above for costs of qualified real property (QRP).[45]

This provision applies only to the following:

- Qualified leasehold improvement property
- Qualified restaurant property (such as renovation of a restaurant building)
- Qualified retail improvement property (such as an interior upgrade of a retail clothing store)

Example: Armando owns an Italian restaurant. In 2012, he renovates the interior by upgrading the booths and remodeling the kitchen at a cost of $260,000. He also purchases a computer for use in his business at a cost of $5,000. Therefore, Armando has the following qualifying expenses for the section 179 deduction:

Computer:	$5,000
Qualified real property :	$260,000
Total asset purchases in 2012:	**$265,000**

Since the limit for expensing QRP under section 179 is $250,000, Armando may only expense $250,000 of the renovation costs. However, he may still take the section 179 deduction for the full cost of the computer, since the limit for other qualifying property is $500,000 in 2012. Armando's allowable section 179 deduction is therefore limited to $255,000 ($5,000 computer + $250,000 of QRP). The excess amount of $10,000 may be depreciated over the useful life applicable for this type of real property.

Example: In 2012, Ashby Corporation purchases refurbished manufacturing equipment costing $2.1 million. The cost of the equipment is $100,000 more than $2 million limit, so Ashby Corporation must reduce its section 179 dollar limit to $400,000 ($500,000 – $100,000). The remaining cost basis of $1.7 million ($2.1 million - $400,000 deducted under section 179) may be recovered using regular depreciation methods. ***Note:** the equipment in this scenario is not eligible for bonus depreciation because it is used.

Trade-in Property: If a business buys qualifying property with cash and a trade-in, its depreciable basis for purposes of the section 179 deduction includes *only* the cash the business paid.

---

[45] Congress also retroactively reinstated the QRP provision for 2012 and extended it through 2013.

> **Example:** Soccer Time, a retail sports shop, traded two wood displays with a total adjusted basis of $680 for a new glass display that cost $1,320. Soccer Time received an $800 trade-in allowance for the old displays and paid an additional $520 in cash for the new glass display. The shop also traded a used van with an adjusted basis of $4,500 for a new van costing $9,000. Soccer Time received a $4,800 trade-in allowance on the used van and paid $4,200 in cash for the new van. Only the portion of the new property's basis paid by cash qualifies for the section 179 deduction. Therefore, Soccer Time's qualifying costs for the section 179 deduction are $4,720 ($520 + $4,200).

Bonus Depreciation

If the cost of business property cannot immediately be deducted as a section 179 expense, a business may elect to take bonus depreciation for certain types of new property (***Note:** Unlike section 179, bonus depreciation does **not** apply to used property). This provision allows a business to write off 50% of certain property costs in the first year, with the remaining cost depreciated over the asset's useful life. Applicable section 179 deductions are generally used first, followed by bonus depreciation, unless the business has an insufficient level of taxable income.

The bonus depreciation allowance generally applies to tangible personal property with a recovery period of 20 years or less, as well as to certain buildings and leasehold improvements, office equipment, and purchased computer software. The property must be new and in original use condition (unlike the requirement for section 179 deduction, which is allowed for both new and used property.)

Bonus depreciation is useful to businesses that spend large amounts on equipment during the year because it is not subject to the same $2 million phase-out as the section 179 deduction.

Listed Property

Special rules apply to listed property, which includes cars and other vehicles used for transportation; property used for entertainment, recreation, or amusement such as photographic or video-recording equipment; and certain computers. If an item is used for both business and personal purposes, deductions for depreciation and section 179 are based on the percentage of business use. Further, if business use is not more than 50%, section 179 deductions and bonus depreciation allowances are not allowed, and depreciation must be calculated using the straight-line method.

> **Example:** In 2012, Eleanor buys and places into service a new computer that costs $4,000. She uses the computer 80% for her business and 20% for personal purposes. The business part of the cost of the property is $3,200 (80% × $4,000), which she may deduct under section 179.

Property that is 100% business-use, such as a desktop computer and printer used exclusively at a business location (including a qualified home office), is not considered listed property. Further, the IRS no longer categorizes cellular telephones as listed property.

Heavy Sports Utility Vehicle Exception:[46] A taxpayer cannot elect to expense under section 179 more than $25,000 of the cost of any heavy sport utility vehicle (SUV) and certain other vehicles placed in service during the tax year. This rule applies to vehicles weighing between 6,000 and 14,000 pounds. Ambulances, hearses, taxis, transport vans, clearly marked emergency vehicles, and other qualified non-personal use vehicles are excluded from the $25,000 limit.

Section 280F "Luxury Automobile" Depreciation Limits: For certain other passenger vehicles weighing less than 6,000 pounds and used more than 50% for business purposes, the total depreciation deduction is also limited, as outlined under section 280F. Although the term "luxury" automobile is used in section 280F's caption, it does not appear in the general rule, and the depreciation limits affect most new cars. The IRS releases guidance regarding tax treatment for specific makes and models of vehicles each year, adjusted for inflation. In 2012, bonus depreciation is capped at $11,160 for cars and $11,360 for trucks and vans during the first year they are placed into service.[47]

Depletion

Depletion is similar in concept to depreciation, and is the method of cost recovery for mining and agricultural activities. Depletion refers to the exhaustion of a natural resource as a result of production, such as using up of natural resources by mining, quarrying, or felling (of timber).

Mineral property, timber, and natural gas are all examples of natural resources that are subject to the deduction for depletion. There are two ways of figuring depletion:

- Cost depletion
- Percentage depletion

---

[46] This use of the section 179 deduction became known as the "Hummer Tax Loophole" because it allowed businesses to buy large SUVs and write them off. The IRS has since modified the tax code with the limits described above. EA exam-takers should be familiar with the limits on vehicle depreciation.
[47] Revenue Procedure 2012-14.

Cost Depletion

This method allocates the cost of a natural resource over the total anticipated volume to yield cost depletion per unit (expressed in tons, barrels, etc.) A depletion deduction is then allowed each year based on the units exploited.

After a business determines the property's basis, estimates the total recoverable units, and knows the number of units sold during the tax year, it can calculate the cost depletion deduction as follows:

Divide the property's basis for depletion by estimated total recoverable units
= **Rate per unit**
Multiply the rate per unit by actual units sold = **Cost depletion deduction**

Example: In 2012, Brian buys a timber farm, and he estimates the timber can produce 300,000 units when cut. At the time of purchase, the adjusted basis of the timber is $24,000. Brian then cuts and sells 27,000 units. Brian's depletion rate for each unit is $.08 ($24,000 ÷ 300,000). His deduction for depletion in 2012 is $2,160 (27,000 × $.08).

Percentage Depletion

This is an alternative method of computing depletion. Under this method, a flat percentage of gross income from the property is taken as the depletion deduction. Percentage depletion may not be used for timber and its use for oil and gas properties is subject to strict limits.

To figure percentage depletion, businesses multiply a certain percentage, specified for each mineral, by gross income from the property during the year. The percentage depletion deduction generally cannot be more than 50% (100% for oil and gas property) of taxable income from the property, before the depletion deduction and the domestic production activities deduction (DPAD).

Some businesses employ cost depletion at the outset of operations when a large number of units of the deposit are extracted and sold, and then convert to percentage depletion later when percentage depletion yields a more sizable deduction.

Amortization

Intangible assets include goodwill, patents, copyrights, trademarks, trade names, and franchises. Amortization is used to deduct the cost of an intangible asset over the projected life of the asset, in a manner similar to the straight-line method of depreciation.

The basis of an intangible asset is usually the cost to buy or create it and must be determined before the asset can be amortized. Businesses determine yearly amortization by dividing the cost of the intangible asset by the useful life of the intangible asset.

> **Example:** Sean spent $125,000 to purchase a copyright. The copyright has a remaining life of 15 years; the amount amortized each year is $8,333.
>
>
> **Initial Cost ÷ Useful Life = Amortization per Year**
>
> ($125,000 ÷ 15 = $8,333 per year)
>
>

> **Example:** Charlotte purchases a trademark from another company. The trademark costs $28,880. The trademark has 16 years remaining before expiration. She must amortize the asset over 16 years (192 months). Therefore, the monthly amortization expense is $150 ($28,880 ÷ 192).

> **Example:** On April 1, 2012, Frank buys a patent for $5,100. The patent will expire in 17 years. He amortizes the patent using the straight-line method over its useful life of 17 years. He divides the $5,100 basis by 17 years to get his $300 yearly deduction. He only owned the patent for nine months during 2012, so he multiplies $300 by 9/12 to get his deduction of $225 for the first year. In 2013, Frank can deduct $300 for the full year.

Patents: The basis of a patent is generally the cost of its development, such as research and experimental expenditures, drawings, working models, and legal and governmental fees. If the business is allowed to deduct research and experimental expenditures as current business expenses, it cannot include these same costs in the basis of the patent. The value of an inventor's time is not considered part of the basis, unless compensation cost is incurred (as in the case where the inventor is an employee of a business).

Copyrights: The basis of a copyright will usually be the costs of obtaining the copyright, including copyright fees, attorney fees, and clerical assistance.

The useful life of a patent or copyright is the lesser of the life granted by the government or the remaining life when the business acquires it (if it is purchased or acquired from the original owner).

> **Example:** Jackson purchases a patent for an electrical power strip. He plans to manufacture the power strip and sell it to customers. The patent has nine years left before expiration, so Jackson may depreciate the cost over nine years.

However, if the patent or copyright becomes valueless before the end of its useful life, the remaining cost can be deducted as an expense in the year that happens.

> **Example:** Harriet purchases a patent for a popular toy design that has a useful life of 10 years. However, two years after the purchase, the toy design is deemed hazardous to children, and all the toys are recalled. The patent is now considered worthless, and the remaining cost can be expensed.

Patents and copyrights are not eligible for section 179 deductions or any other accelerated depreciation method.

A business may amortize the capitalized costs of section 197 intangibles over a 15-year period (180 months). Section 197 intangibles are assets that are created in connection with the acquisition of a business, and include goodwill, formulas and trademarks, franchise licenses, and intangibles such as favorable relationships with customers or suppliers that are carried over from the business being purchased. These intangible assets are not eligible for accelerated or bonus depreciation.

Unit 9: Questions

1. The maximum section 179 expense a business can elect to deduct for qualified real property placed in service in 2012 is:

A: $179,000.
B: $250,000.
C: $500,000.
D: $2 million.

The answer is B. In 2012, there is a special provision that allows taxpayers to deduct up to $250,000 of qualified real property (QRP) under section 179. This special allowance for QRP is included within the maximum $500,000 section 179 limit. For example, a taxpayer can have $250,000 of QRP and $250,000 of other business property to make up the $500,000 section 179 depreciation allowance. ###

2. The Friendship Spirit Partnership bought the Andrews Brothers Partnership. The goodwill and covenant not to compete associated with the purchase was valued at $100,000. Per section 197, what is the number of years over which goodwill can be amortized?

A. 5 years.
B. 10 years.
C. 15 years.
D. 25 years.

The answer is C. Goodwill is a section 197 intangible. A business must amortize over 15 years (180 months) the capitalized costs of section 197 intangibles. ###

3. Which of the following would not qualify for a depletion deduction?

A. Oil well.
B. Timber.
C. Diamond mine.
D. Gasoline refinery factory.

The answer is D. A gasoline refinery would not qualify since it is not the depletion of a natural resource but is instead a factory that refines the product. Depletion is the exhaustion of natural resources, such as mines, wells, and timber, as a result of production. ###

4. Tom owns a construction business. He would like to switch his assets to straight-line depreciation for easier accounting and tracking of the assets. All of the following statements are correct except:

A. A business may switch to the straight-line method at any time during the useful life of the property without IRS consent.
B. A business must always request permission from the IRS to switch to the straight-line method.
C. When the change to straight-line is made, depreciation is figured based on the taxpayer's adjusted basis in the property at that time.
D. Tom can choose to switch all of his assets to straight-line no matter what type of depreciation method he has been using previously.

The answer is B. A business does not need to request IRS permission to switch to the straight-line method of depreciation. No special consent is required. ###

5. Levi owns a convenience store. He purchases two computers from his grandfather and places both in service in 2012 as part of a bona fide business transaction. The computers cost $750 each. Which of the following is true?

A. Levi can take a section 179 deduction for the computers.
B. Levi can take regular MACRS depreciation on the computers.
C. Levi is not allowed to depreciate the computers since they were purchased from a related party. But he may take bonus depreciation on the computers.
D. Levi may take either section 179 or bonus depreciation on the computers.

The answer is B. The computers do not qualify as section 179 property because Levi and his grandfather are related persons, meaning Levi cannot claim a section 179 deduction. However, Levi may still depreciate the computers using the MACRS depreciation schedule. ###

6. Which of the following types of business property qualifies for the section 179 accelerated depreciation deduction?

A. A delivery truck.
B. A business building.
C. A residential rental property.
D. A patent.

The answer is A. To qualify for the section 179 deduction, the property must be tangible personal property. Buildings, houses, and other real property generally do not qualify for section 179 treatment. Intangible assets, such as patents and copyrights, must be amortized over their useful life. ###

7. Camarillo Mexican Cantinas bought a restaurant for $500,000 on January 15, 2012. Included in the purchase price were business assets as follows:

•Certificate of deposit: $100,000
•Accounts receivable of $50,000
•Truck with FMV of $80,000 and adjusted basis of $68,000
•Industrial oven with FMV of $20,000 and adjusted basis of $18,000

For depreciation purposes, what portion of the $500,000 lump-sum payment is allocated to the combination oven?

A. $18,000.
B. $53,320.
C. $20,000.
D. $50,000.

The answer is C. Absent any information indicating the seller was a related party, their adjusted basis would not be relevant to how Camarillo Mexican Cantinas allocates the total purchase price among the individual assets acquired. Instead, since the total paid ($500,000) to acquire the business exceeds the total FMV of the assets acquired ($250,000), they would allocate value based in proportion to (but not more than) the FMV of each individual asset, and the remainder would be allocated to goodwill. ###

8. Mary purchases a new computer that costs $1,100. She uses the property 75% for her business and 25% for personal purposes. What is Mary's section 179 depreciation deduction?

A. $0.
B. $275.
C. $825.
D. $1,100.

The answer is C. The business part of the cost of the property is $825 (75% × $1,100). ###

9. Lou is a sole proprietor who buys a cellular phone for $720 in 2012. Based on his phone records, Lou uses the cell phone 45% for business use and 55% for personal use. What is Lou's section 179 deduction for 2012?

A. $0.
B. $324.
C. $396.
D. $720.

The answer is A. When a taxpayer uses property for both business and non-business purposes, he can elect the section 179 deduction only if he uses the property more than 50% for business in the year the asset is placed into service. Lou may still choose to use another depreciation method for the business portion of the phone. ###

10. Kerman Corporation is a calendar-year, cash-basis corporation that specializes in constructing office buildings. Kerman bought a truck on December 1, 2012 that had to be modified to lift materials to second-story levels. The truck is 100% business-use. After the lifting equipment was installed, Kerman accepted delivery of the modified truck on January 10, 2013. The truck was placed in service on January 23, 2012, the date it was ready and available to perform the function for which it was bought. When can Kerman start depreciating the truck?

A. 2012.
B. 2013.
C. 2014.
D. Never.

The answer is B. Kerman may not depreciate the truck until it is placed in service for business use, which was in 2013. ###

11. Which of the following property is a business not able to depreciate?

A. Property placed in service and disposed of in the same year.
B. Intangible assets.
C. Machinery.
D. Buildings.

The answer is A. Property placed in service and disposed of in the same year is not depreciated. Business property ceases to be depreciable when the taxpayer has fully recovered the property's cost or when the taxpayer disposes of it. If a business buys and then disposes of an asset in the same year, it would not be depreciated. ###

12. Which of the following vehicles is considered listed property for tax purposes?

A. An ambulance.
B. A passenger automobile weighing 6,000 pounds or less.
C. A taxi.
D. A marked police car.

The answer is B. The IRS considers regular passenger automobiles weighing 6,000 pounds or less as listed property. ###

13. In 2012, Vanner Partnership placed in service section 179 property with a total cost of $2,025,000. The partnership's taxable income in 2012 was $600,000. What is Vanner's allowable section 179 deduction for 2012?

A. $0.
B. $475,000.
C. $500,000.
D. $600,000.

The answer is B. The partnership must reduce its section 179 dollar limit by $25,000, the amount of its qualifying purchases that exceeds the $2 million limit ($2,025,000 – $2,000,000). Its maximum section 179 deduction is $475,000 ($500,000 – $25,000). The partnership's taxable income from the active conduct of all its trades or businesses for the year was $600,000, so it can deduct the full $475,000. ###

14. Alex is having financial difficulties, so he sells his office building to Cheryl, a real estate investor, who plans to use it as a business rental property. Alex was liable for $5,000 in delinquent real estate taxes on the property, which Cheryl agrees to pay. How should Cheryl treat this transaction?

A. Cheryl cannot deduct these taxes as a current expense; she must add the amount to the basis of the property.
B. Cheryl can deduct these taxes as a current expense on her Schedule A.
C. Cheryl can deduct these taxes as a current expense on her Schedule E.
D. Cheryl can deduct these taxes as a current expense on her Schedule C.

The answer is A. Cheryl may not deduct the taxes as a current expense, since they are delinquent real estate taxes and the person who is legally liable for the debt is Alex. However, the taxes may be added to the property's basis and depreciated as part of the purchase price, since Cheryl intends to use the property as a rental. ###

15. TJ buys and places in service professional video-recording equipment in 2012. He pays $15,000 cash and receives a $3,000 trade-in allowance for used video equipment. He used both the old and new video-recording equipment 90% for business and 10% for personal purposes. His allowable section 179 deduction is:

A. $16,200.
B. $13,500.
C. $12,600.
D. $15,000.

The answer is B. The section 179 deduction applies only to the amount actually paid in cash and not to the value of his trade-in allowance, and further applies only to the portion used for business purposes. Thus, the deduction is limited to 90% of $15,000, or $13,500. ###

17. Lucy and Jessica are equal partners in a restaurant. In 2012, they purchase a new $30,000 pizza oven for the restaurant and want to take the section 179 deduction for the full cost of the oven. The partnership's ordinary income before the section 179 deduction is $25,000. There were no other qualifying section 179 purchases during the year. What is the amount of section 179 deduction that Lucy can deduct on her individual tax return?

A. $0.
B. $6,000.
C. $12,500.
D. $15,000.

The answer is C. The section 179 deduction for the $30,000 oven is limited by the partnership income. The section 179 deduction cannot exceed overall income for the year, so it is limited to $25,000. Then the deduction is split between the two partners ($25,000 X 50%) = $12,500. Section 179 is a separately stated item on a partnership tax return. ###

18. Using MACRS, what is the recovery period for depreciating a commercial office building?

A. 20 years.
B. 25 years.
C. 27.5 years.
D. 39 years.

The answer is D. Commercial real property is depreciated over a 39-year recovery period. ###

Unit 10: Disposition of Business Assets

More Reading:
Publication 544, *Sales and Other Dispositions of Assets*

Business assets may be sold, traded, exchanged, abandoned, or destroyed. A business may recognize a gain or loss if it:

- Sells property for cash
- Exchanges property for other property
- Receives payment from a tenant for the cancellation of a lease
- Receives payment for granting the exclusive use of a copyright
- Receives property to satisfy a debt
- Abandons property
- Receives insurance reimbursement for damaged property

A taxpayer may fully depreciate an asset until its adjusted basis is zero, but continue to use the asset thereafter until it is no longer useful. If an asset is sold, the amount received is compared to the asset's adjusted basis to determine whether a gain or loss should be recognized.

To properly report the disposition of an asset, a taxpayer must first determine whether it is a *capital asset*, a *noncapital asset,* or a *section 1231 asset.*

Capital assets

Capital assets include personal-use assets; collectibles; and investment property such as stocks, bonds, and other securities (unless held by a professional securities dealer). A personal residence and personal-use car are both examples of capital assets. A gain from the disposition of personal-use property is a capital gain, but a loss is generally not deductible, except for certain casualty losses.

> **Example:** Jim collects toy mechanical banks as a hobby, and he owns 15 of them, which have appreciated in value. He is not a professional dealer. Jim's mechanical banks are considered capital assets.

Noncapital assets

Noncapital assets include inventory, accounts receivable, and other assets used in a trade or business, as residential rental property, or to produce royalties. The definition of a "capital asset" varies based on the type of asset, and for how long the asset is held.

> **Example:** In February 2012, Ines purchases a black-and-white copy machine for use in her business. The machine cost $6,000, but by July she realizes she needs a color copier instead. It is too late to return it to the store, so Ines sells the used black-and-white copier for $3,000. The copier is a business asset held for less than a year, so it is treated as a noncapital asset. She recognizes an ordinary loss that may be deducted on her business's income tax return.

Section 1231 Assets

Section 1231 assets include business (noncapital) assets that have been held for more than one year, as well as certain business and investment property disposed of in involuntary conversions.

The tax code gives special treatment to transactions involving disposition of section 1231 assets. If the taxpayer has a net loss from all section 1231 transactions, the loss is treated as ordinary loss. If the section 1231 transactions result in a net gain, the gain is generally treated as capital gain (except for depreciation recapture, which is taxed as ordinary income, as discussed below).

> **Example:** Philip owns an antique vase that he purchased at auction two years ago. He also owns a residential rental property that he purchased three years ago, as well as two vehicles. One is a pizza delivery van he bought five years ago that he uses exclusively in his restaurant business. The other vehicle is his personal-use SUV that he uses for commuting and everyday errands. Phillip's assets are categorized as follows:
>
> **1. Antique vase:** A capital asset, because it is a collectible
>
> **2. Residential rental property:** Section 1231 rental property (held over one year and business-use)
>
> **3. Pizza delivery van:** Section 1231 business property (held over one year and business-use)
>
> **4. SUV:** A capital asset, because it is a personal-use vehicle

Section 1231 Transactions

Section 1231 assets include depreciable business property such as buildings, machinery, timber, unharvested crops, livestock, and leaseholds. Section 1231 assets can also include nondepreciable real property (such as land that is purchased for business use) and property that is held for the production of income but that is involuntarily converted due to theft, casualty, or condemnation. Other examples of section 1231 assets include the following:

- Machinery used in business
- A patent, copyright, or other intangible asset used in a business

- Hotels, office buildings, warehouses, residential apartment complexes, and other residential rental property
- Any asset held for more than one year that is used for the production of income and has been involuntarily converted

In order to qualify as section 1231 property, the property must have been held for more than one year. Gain or loss on the following transactions is subject to section 1231 treatment:

1. **Sale or exchange of cattle and horses:** They must be held for draft, breeding, dairy, or sporting purposes and held for 24 months or longer.
2. **Sale or exchange of other livestock:** Other livestock includes hogs, mules, sheep, goats, donkeys, and other fur-bearing animals. They must be held for draft, breeding, dairy, or sporting purposes and held for 12 months or longer.
3. **Sale or exchange of depreciable (or amortizable) property:** Business property that is held for more than one year. Examples include machinery and trucks, as well as amortizable section 197 intangibles such as patents or copyrights.
4. **Sale or exchange of business real estate:** The property must be used in a business activity and held for more than one year. Examples include barns and office buildings.
5. **Sale or exchange of unharvested crops:** The crops and land must be sold, exchanged, or involuntarily converted at the same time and to the same person, and the land must have been held longer than one year. Growing crops sold with a leasehold on the land, even if sold to the same person in a single transaction, are not included.

Example: Harwell Inc. manufactures shipping containers. Harwell has owned the land and the building that houses its manufacturing operations for many years. The land and the building are therefore section 1231 assets, because they are used in a business and have been held for more than one year. Harwell also has unsold shipping containers in inventory. Inventory is generally not a section 1231 and its sale in the ordinary course of business results in ordinary income or loss.

Example: Six years ago, Superior Design Inc. purchased a computer for $10,000. The company sells it this year for $700. Superior Design had depreciated the computer down to its salvage value, which was estimated at $1,000. The company has a loss of $300 on the sale of the computer ($1,000 salvage value minus $700 sale price). The computer is a section 1231 asset and the loss is an ordinary loss.

Section 1231 and Involuntary Conversions

The sale, exchange, or involuntary conversion of inventory is not a section 1231 transaction. This applies to business property or a capital asset held in connection with a trade or business or a transaction entered into for profit, such as investment property, but not to property held for personal use, such as a personal residence. The business property in these transactions must have been held for more than a year.

The sale of a copyright, literary, musical, or artistic composition is not a section 1231 transaction if a taxpayer's personal efforts created the property, or if it was received as a gift from a previous owner whose personal efforts created it. The sale of such property results in ordinary income and generally is reported on Form 4797, *Sales of Business Property.*

> **Example:** Debbie is a self-employed writer who reports her income on Schedule C. She writes a popular crockpot cookbook and publishes it. A few years later, Debbie sells the copyright of the manuscript to a publisher. The sale is ordinary income and must be reported on Form 4797. This is not a section 1231 transaction, because the copyright was self-created.

Depreciation Recapture

Depreciation recapture is required when a business sells previously depreciated or amortized property at a gain. In this instance, the business may have to recapture the portion of the gain attributable to depreciation and treat this amount (even if otherwise nontaxable) as ordinary income. The balance of the gain in excess of the recaptured depreciation is treated as capital gain.

> **Example:** Jeff runs Hammerton Dairy Farm, which is a calendar-year sole proprietorship. In February 2010, Jeff buys a tractor (5-year property) that costs $10,000. MACRS depreciation deductions for the tractor are $1,500 in 2010 and $2,550 in 2011 (based upon MACRS table A-14 for 150% declining balance depreciation using a half-year convention). Jeff sells the tractor in May 2012 for $7,000. The MACRS deduction in 2012 is $893 (½ of $1,785). The gain on the sale of the tractor that must be treated as ordinary income is figured as follows:
>
> | | |
> |---|---:|
> | Amount received in the sale | $7,000 |
> | Original purchase price | $10,000 |
> | MACRS depreciation deductions ($1,500 + $2,550 + $893) | ($4,943) |
> | Adjusted basis | $5,057 |
> | Gain realized ($7,000 - $5,057) | $1,943 |
>
> The realized gain is less than the amount of depreciation subject to recapture, so the entire amount is treated as ordinary income.

In determining depreciable recapture for property sold at a gain, there is a critical distinction between two types of property: section 1245 and section 1250. For section 1245 property, any gain attributable to previously deducted depreciation allowance is taxed as ordinary income. For section 1250 property, the depreciation recapture is limited to the portion of previously deducted depreciation allowances in excess of deductions that would have been taken if computed using the straight-line method.

> **Example:** The Drake Partnership owns a $20,000 business machine that has been depreciated $12,000 over the years, so the partnership's adjusted basis in it is $8,000. In 2012, the partnership sells the machine for $25,000. The total gain on the sale is $17,000 ($25,000 - $8,000). The partnership must recognize ordinary income of $12,000 (to recapture depreciation deductions taken on the machine) and the remaining $5,000 ($17,000 - $12,000) is treated as a capital gain.

> **Example:** Years ago, Mabel purchased a painting for her corporate office for $125,000. Mabel has taken depreciation deductions of $39,000 and her adjusted basis in the painting in 2012 is $86,000. The painting has appreciated in value, and, Mabel sells it in December 2012 for $180,000 and realizes a gain of $94,000 ($39,000 of ordinary income from depreciation recapture and $55,000 in long-term capital gain).

Section 1245 Property

Section 1245 property is defined by either:

1. Personal (tangible or intangible) property[48], or
2. Other tangible property (not including buildings) that is depreciable and that is:
    a. Used as an integral part of certain specified activities (manufacturing, production, extraction, or furnishing transportation, communications, electrical energy, gas, water, or sewage disposal services), or
    b. A facility used for the bulk storage of fungible[49] commodities (examples of highly fungible commodities are crude oil, wheat, etc.)

---

[48] Personal property is **not the same** as "personal-use" property. In its most general definition, personal property includes any asset other than real estate. The distinguishing factor between personal property and real estate is that personal property is movable and real property is fixed permanently to one location, such as land or buildings.

[49] A fungible good or asset is one that is essentially interchangeable with other goods or assets of the same type, such as a specific grade of a particular commodity. Another example is a dollar bill—it does not matter where or when the dollar bill was produced, because there is no difference between one dollar and another dollar.

For example, a grain silo would be considered section 1245 property rather than section 1250 property, even if it was attached permanently to the land. Storage structures for oil and gas and other minerals would be considered section 1245 property.

Example: Several years ago, Crystal purchased a used binding machine at auction for her business. The cost of the machine was $1,000. Crystal has claimed $400 in depreciation on the machine. In 2012, Crystal sells the machine for $1,100. Her gain is as follows:

Sale price of the machine:	$1,100
Minus adjusted basis ($1,000 - $400):	$600
Crystal's gain on the sale of the machine:	$500

A portion of the gain is ordinary income ($400 of depreciation recapture for section 1245 property), and the remainder of $100 is long-term capital gain.

Section 1250 property

Section 1250 property generally consists of buildings (including their structural components), other inherently permanent structures, and land improvements of general use and purpose. Examples of section 1250 property include residential rental property, factory buildings, and office buildings. Since buildings are generally depreciated using the straight-line method, taxpayers usually get more favorable treatment of depreciation recapture for section 1250 property.

Example: Maeve has owned an apartment building for almost twenty years. She originally purchased the building for $2.5 million. After taking straight-line depreciation deductions, her adjusted basis in 2012 is $800,000 and she sells the property for $4.5 million. Her gain is as follows:

Sale price	$4,500,000
Minus adjusted basis	$800,000
Gain on sale	$3,700,000

Because the building is section 1250 property and Maeve has only taken straight-line depreciation, there is no depreciation recapture, and the entire amount of the gain is treated as long-term capital gain.

Installment Sales

An installment sale involves a disposition of property in which the seller receives at least a portion of the sales proceeds during a year subsequent to the year of the sale. The resulting gain is typically reported using the installment method. If a business elects out of using the installment method, it must report the entire gain in the year of the sale, even though it may not receive the remaining proceeds until later years. Each payment received on an installment sale transaction may include the following components:

- Return of the seller's adjusted basis in the property
- Gain on the sale
- Interest income (attributable to financing the sales over a period of time)

The taxpayer must calculate a gross profit percentage, representing the ratio of the gain on the sale (numerator) to the total proceeds to be paid less any interest portion (denominator). The denominator will also equal the total of the gain and the return of the seller's adjusted basis in the property. Each year, including the year of sale, the total payments received less the portion attributable to interest is multiplied by the gross profit percentage to determine the portion of the gain that must be recognized. The gain is reported on Form 6252, *Installment Sale Income.* In certain circumstances, the business may be treated as having received a payment, even though it has not received cash. For example, the receipt of property or the assumption of a mortgage on property sold may be treated as a payment.

Example: A business sells a machine for a price of $6,000, with a gross profit of $1,500, and it will receive payments totaling $6,000 plus interest over four years. The gross profit percentage is 25% ($1,500 ÷ $6,000). After subtracting the applicable interest portion from each payment, the business will apply the gross profit percentage to each installment, including the down payment, and report the resulting amount as installment sale income for each tax year in which it receives payments. The remainder of each payment is the tax-free return of the machine's adjusted basis.

Example: In 2012, the Greenbelt Partnership sells land to a buyer under an installment sale. The land has a basis of $40,000, and the sale price is $100,000. Therefore, the gross profit is $60,000. Greenbelt receives a $20,000 down payment and the buyer's note for $80,000. The note provides for four annual payments of $20,000 each, plus 8% interest, beginning in 2013. Greenbelt's gross profit percentage is 60%. Greenbelt reports capital gain of $12,000 for each payment of $20,000 received in 2012 and 2013. In 2014, Greenbelt and the buyer agree to reduce the purchase price to $85,000, and payments during 2014, 2015, and 2016 are reduced to $15,000 for each year. The new gross profit percentage is 46.67%. Greenbelt will report capital gain of $7,000 (46.67% of $15,000) for each of the $15,000 installments paid in 2014, 2015, and 2016.

If the arrangement is modified at a later date or the full amount of the sale price is not paid, the resulting gross profit on the sale may also change.

An installment sale may trigger depreciation recapture. If a business reports the sale of property under the installment method, any applicable depreciation recapture under section 1245 is taxable as ordinary income in the year of sale, even if no payments are received in that year. If the gain is more than the depreciation recapture amount, the remainder of the gain would be recognized using the installment method rules.

An installment sale does not apply to:

- The sale of inventory, even if the business receives a payment after the year of sale
- A sale that results in a loss
- The sale of publicly traded property (such as stocks or bonds)
- The sale of depreciable property between related parties

Like-Kind Exchanges (Section 1031)

A like-kind exchange occurs when a business or individual exchanges business or investment property for similar property. IRC section 1031 provides that income from the exchange is not taxable currently, but is deferred until the acquired property is later sold or otherwise disposed.

The simplest form of 1031 exchange is a simultaneous swap of one property for another. However, it may also be arranged as a deferred exchange, in which the disposition of one property and the later acquisition of a replacement property are mutually dependent parts of an integrated transaction. In contrast, simply selling a property and using the proceeds to purchase another similar property is a taxable transaction.

A common type of 1031 exchange is an exchange of real property (real estate). Generally, real property can be exchanged even if the properties are substantially different. For example, an exchange of farmland for a commercial building will still qualify for nonrecognition treatment. However, entities may exchange other types of business property, such as machinery and vehicles, and intangible assets, such as patents and copyrights. To qualify as a like-kind exchange, the property traded and the property received must be similar, with both either business property or investment property.

All of the following can be exchanged as like-kind property:

- Condos, raw land, apartment buildings, duplexes, commercial buildings, residential rentals, and retail buildings
- A single business property exchanged for two or more properties and vice versa

- Water rights, mineral rights, oil and gas interests, copyrights, trademarks, and other intangible assets (but not partnership interests or securities)
- Livestock (but not livestock of different sexes)

Certain property does not qualify for section 1031 exchange treatment, including the following:

- Inventory, or any property purchased for resale

- Stocks, bonds, notes, or other securities

- Livestock of different sexes

- Real property within the United States and real property outside the United States

- Exchanges of shares of corporate stock in different companies

- Exchanges of partnership interests or LLC membership interests

- A personal residence, or personal-use property, such as a personal car

- Land under development for resale

- Corporation common stock

Strict rules and timetables apply to a section 1031 exchange if it does not entail a simultaneous exchange of properties. The exchanger has a maximum of 45 days after the sale to identify a list of potential replacement properties and 180 days after the sale to acquire one of those properties.

Example: A corporation purchases a medical office building for $300,000. After four years, the fair market value of the property is $350,000. If the corporation were to sell the property, it would recognize a gain of $50,000, of which a portion attributable to recapture of any accelerated depreciation would be treated as ordinary income. If the corporation instead arranges a like-kind exchange through which it would either receive a similar property in exchange, or invest the proceeds from the sale of the building in a similar property, the taxable gain would be deferred.

Section 1031 requires that a qualified intermediary be used to facilitate tax-deferred exchanges. This is an independent party who acquires the relinquished property and transfers it to the buyer. The intermediary holds the sales proceeds to prevent the taxpayer from having actual or constructive receipt of the funds. The intermediary then acquires the replacement property and transfers it to the taxpayer to complete the exchange within the allowable time limits. If a qualified intermediary is not used, the exchange will not be allowed.

Example: Otis owns a piece of raw land in Texas he wants to exchange, and he arranges a 1031 exchange transaction. When the land sale closes, his escrow company holds the proceeds. Within 45 days Otis identifies an apartment building he wants to buy in Arkansas and successfully negotiates a contract to buy the building. Within the required 180 days, the escrow company releases the funds he needs to close the purchase, and the exchange transaction is complete. The escrow company is considered a qualified intermediary, and Otis has successfully postponed recognition of any gain related to disposition of the original property.

Boot in an Exchange

Boot is a term used to describe cash or other property that is included in an exchange or other transaction that might otherwise qualify for nonrecognition of gain. The party that receives boot will typically be required to recognize taxable gain to the extent of the amount received.

A typical transaction involves one party exchanging property to another party for like-kind property and either additional cash or property that does not qualify as like-kind. The taxpayer who receives the boot may have to recognize a taxable gain to the extent of the fair market value of the boot received. However, this gain cannot exceed the amount of gain that would have been recognized if the property had been sold in a taxable transaction. Boot received can be offset by qualified costs paid during the transaction.

Example: Stephen and Tricia decide they will exchange rental properties. Stephen's rental property is more valuable, so Tricia agrees to exchange her rental property and an additional $10,000 in cash. Therefore, Stephen will be required to recognize $10,000 of gain on the transaction.

Example: Andrew wishes to exchange his rental property in a 1031 exchange. His relinquished rental property has an FMV of $60,000 and an adjusted basis of $30,000. Andrew's replacement property has an FMV of $50,000, and he also receives $10,000 in cash (boot) as part of the exchange. Andrew, therefore, has a realized gain of $30,000 on the actual exchange, and he has a taxable gain of $10,000— equal to the cash (boot) received in the exchange. The rest of his gain is deferred until he sells or disposes of the new property at a later date.

Sometimes, boot is recognized when two people exchange properties that are subject to liabilities. Liabilities on property are netted against each other. The taxpayer is treated as having received boot only if he is relieved of a greater liability than the liability he assumes. This is called debt reduction boot, and it occurs when a taxpayer's debt on the replacement property is less than the debt on the relinquished property. This occurs most often when a taxpayer is acquiring a less expensive or valuable property.

A business or individual may have to recognize gain on a partially taxable like-kind exchange, but would never recognize a loss. However, a loss on a like-kind exchange would affect the taxpayer's basis in the property received, and the tax treatment when it is ultimately sold or disposed.

Basis of Property Received in a Like-Kind Exchange

The basis of the property received is generally the adjusted basis of the property transferred.

Example: Judy has a rental house with an adjusted basis of $70,000. In 2012, she trades the rental house for an empty lot with a FMV of $150,000. Judy's basis in the empty lot is $70,000, equal to the adjusted basis of her previous property.

If a taxpayer trades property and also pays money, the basis of the property received is the basis of the property given up, increased by any additional money paid.

Example: Peyton buys a new diesel truck for use in her delivery business. She pays $43,000 cash, and she trades in her old truck for a trade-in allowance of $13,600. The old truck cost $50,000 two years ago. Peyton has taken depreciation deductions of $39,500 on the old vehicle. Even though she deducted depreciation of $39,500, the $3,100 gain on the exchange ($13,600 trade-in allowance minus her $10,500 adjusted basis) is not reported because the gain is postponed under the rules for like-kind exchanges. Her basis in the new truck is $53,500, the total of the cash paid ($43,000) and her adjusted basis of $10,500 in the old truck.

Example: Jorge trades a plot of land (adjusted basis $30,000) for a different plot of land in another town (FMV $70,500). He also pays an additional $4,000 in cash. Jorge's basis in the new land is $34,000 (his $30,000 basis in the old land plus the $4,000 additional money he paid).

The basis of any additional property received is its fair market value on the date of the trade. The taxpayer is taxed on any gain realized, but only up to the amount of the boot received (any cash and the fair market value of nonqualified property).

Like-Kind Exchanges Between Related Parties

Like-kind exchanges are allowed between related parties, which for purposes of a section 1031 exchanges are defined as:

- Family members (siblings, spouses, ancestors, and lineal descendants.)
- An individual and an entity (corporation or partnership) in which the individual owns either directly or indirectly more than 50% in value of the entity. This includes ownership by a spouse or close family member.
- Two entities in which the same individual owns directly or indirectly more than 50% of each.
- An estate in which the taxpayer is either the executor or beneficiary of the estate.
- A trust in which the taxpayer is the fiduciary and the related party is a beneficiary either of that same trust or a related trust or a fiduciary of a related trust.

Exchanges between related parties get close scrutiny by the Internal Revenue Service, because they are often used by taxpayers to evade taxes on gains.

Although section 1031 does not prohibit related-party exchanges, it requires a longer holding period to deter taxpayers from exchanging assets with family members or related businesses in order to dispose of them immediately and shift the gain.

For exchanges between related parties, the nonrecognition treatment will not apply if either property in the exchange is disposed of within two years. Exceptions to this rule include:

- If one of the parties originally involved in the exchange dies, the two-year rule does not apply.
- If the property is subsequently converted in an involuntary exchange (such as a fire or a flood), the two-year rule does not apply.
- If the exchange is genuinely not for tax avoidance purposes, the subsequent disposition generally will be allowed.

Example: Tim and John are brothers. Tim owns a residential rental property and John owns a tract of land. In 2012, they exchange the properties. Since they are related parties, they each must hold the properties for at least two years or the exchange will be disallowed and treated as a sale. In early 2013, John dies. In this case, the 1031 exchange is still valid, because the holding period rule does not apply if one of the parties in a related exchange dies before the two-year period expires.

Involuntary Conversions/Section 1033

An involuntary conversion occurs when a taxpayer's property is destroyed, stolen, condemned, or disposed of under the threat of condemnation, and he receives other property or money in payment, such as insurance or a condemnation award. In order to qualify as an involuntary conversion, the destruction or condemnation must be beyond the taxpayer's control.

Gain or loss from an involuntary conversion of property is usually recognized for tax purposes unless the property is a main home. A taxpayer cannot deduct a loss from an involuntary conversion of property held for personal use unless the loss resulted from a casualty or theft. However, a taxpayer may be able to avoid reporting gain on an involuntary conversion if he receives or invests in property similar to the converted property. This is called a section 1033 conversion. The gain on the involuntary conversion is then deferred until a taxable sale or exchange occurs at a later date.

> **Example:** Denise owns a residential rental property with an adjusted basis of $50,000. It is destroyed by a hurricane in 2012. Her property is insured, so Denise receives insurance reimbursement for $100,000, the fair market value of the property. Denise buys a replacement rental property six months later for $100,000. Her gain on the involuntary conversion is $50,000 ($100,000 insurance settlement minus her $50,000 basis). However, Denise does not have to recognize any taxable gain in 2012 because she reinvested all the insurance proceeds in another, similar property.

The replacement period for an involuntary conversion generally ends two years after the end of the first tax year in which any part of the gain on the condemnation is realized.

> **Example:** Anders owns a trophy business. On May 30, 2012, a tornado destroys a garage with Anders's trophies and other business supplies. His insurance company reimburses him for the entire loss. Anders has until December 31, 2014 to replace the garage and supplies using the insurance proceeds. He is not required to report the insurance proceeds on his 2012 tax return. So long as he reinvests all the insurance proceeds in replacement property, he will not have taxable gain until he disposes of the replacement property.

A three-year replacement period is allowed for real property that is held for investment, such as office buildings or residential rentals. The replacement period is four years for livestock that is involuntarily converted because of weather-related conditions. If the property is subject to an involuntary conversion in certain federally declared disaster areas, the replacement period can be up to five years.

208

Property Type	Replacement Period
Most property except those noted below.	Two years.
Real property held for investment or business use. This includes residential rentals, office buildings, etc.	Three years.
Livestock, due to weather-related conditions.	Four years.

The replacement property must be purchased before the end of the tax year in which the replacement *deadline* applies. If the involuntary conversion property is not replaced within the allowed time period, an amended tax return would have to be filed for the year the involuntary conversion occurred, reporting a taxable transaction.

If a taxpayer reinvests in replacement property similar to the converted property, the replacement property's basis is the same as the converted property's basis on the date of the conversion.

Usually, the taxpayer's basis in the new property will be its cost, reduced by any gain realized on the old property that was not recognized. However, the basis may be increased by any gain the taxpayer recognizes on the involuntary conversion and decreased by the following:

- Any loss the taxpayer recognizes on the involuntary conversion
- Any reimbursement he receives and does not reinvest in similar property

Example: Cody is a general contractor who uses a truck for his business. The truck is destroyed in an accident. It had been partially depreciated, and its adjusted basis was $40,000. The insurance company sends a check for $55,000 to replace the truck. Two months later, Cody uses all the insurance money to purchase a replacement truck, and he pays an additional $2,000 out-of-pocket in order to purchase the new vehicle. The basis in the new truck is $42,000 ($40,000 basis of the old truck + $2,000 additional out-of-pocket cost). Another way of reaching the same answer is as follows: Cody paid a total of $57,000 for the new truck, including the insurance proceeds of $55,000 plus an additional $2,000. This cost is reduced by the amount of gain that he has not recognized on the involuntary conversion, $15,000 (replacement proceeds of $55,000 less adjusted basis of $40,000), to derive the basis of the new truck: $42,000. This does not have to be reported as a taxable transaction because it is a qualified involuntary conversion of business property.

Example: Paula owns a rental condo in Virginia with a basis of $125,000. The building was destroyed by flooding, and Paula receives an insurance settlement of $200,000. A year later, she decides to purchase another condo in Maryland for $175,000. Paula's realized gain on the involuntary conversion is $75,000 ($200,000 - $125,000 basis). Paula must recognize $25,000 of gain, because she received an insurance payment of $200,000, but only spent $175,000 on the replacement property. Her basis in the new property will be $150,000, which is calculated as the cost of the new property in Maryland minus the deferred gain ($175,000 - $25,000 = $150,000), or alternatively, as the basis of the old property plus the recognized gain ($125,000 + $25,000 = $150,000). If Paula had used all the insurance proceeds and invested it in the new property, she would not have to report any taxable gain.

Condemnations

An involuntary conversion may result from a condemnation, when the government or another organization with legal authority seizes private property from its original owner for public use. The owner generally receives a condemnation award (money or property) in exchange for the property that is taken. A condemnation is like a forced sale, the owner being the seller and the government being the buyer.

Example: The state government informs Troy that it is condemning his motel in order to widen a highway. Troy goes to court to try to keep his property. The court decides in favor of the government, which takes his property and pays him $400,000 in exchange. Troy's basis in the motel was $80,000. He decides not to purchase replacement property. Therefore, he has a taxable gain, and $320,000 must be recognized as income ($400,000 - $80,000 = $320,000). If Troy were to purchase replacement property with the condemnation award, he would have a nontaxable section 1033 exchange.

Amounts taken out of the condemnation award to pay debts on the property are considered paid to the taxpayer and included in the amount of the award.

Example: The city awarded Katie $200,000 after condemning her land to build a conference center. However, she was paid only $148,000 because the city paid $50,000 to her mortgage company and $2,000 for accrued real estate taxes. Katie is considered to have received the entire $200,000 as a condemnation award.

Unit 10: Questions

1. Which of the following dispositions of depreciable property can trigger depreciation recapture?

A. Installment sale.
B. Gift.
C. Transfer at death.
D. Section 1031 exchange where no money or unlike property is received.

The answer is A. An installment sale can trigger recapture. If a business reports the sale of previously depreciated property using the installment method, any applicable depreciation recapture under section 1245 or 1250 is taxable as ordinary income in the year of sale. ###

2. Arbordale Acres is a farming corporation. In 2012, Arbordale sells a used tractor for $25,000. The original cost of the tractor was $20,000, and it is fully depreciated. What is the tax treatment for Arbordale's sale of the tractor?

A. There is no gain or loss on the sale of the tractor.
B. Arbordale has a gain of $25,000. The first $20,000 is considered section 1245 recapture and is taxed as ordinary income. The remaining $5,000 is considered section 1231 capital gain.
C. Arbordale has a gain of $25,000. The first $15,000 is considered section 1245 recapture and is taxed as ordinary income. The remaining $10,000 is considered section 1231 capital gain.
D. The entire gain is a section 1245 gain and will be taxed as depreciation recapture as ordinary income.

The answer is B. The first $20,000 is considered section 1245 recapture and is taxed as ordinary income. The remaining $5,000 is considered section 1231 capital gain. ###

3. Which of the following is not section 1245 property?

A. Computer.
B. Office building.
C. Display shelving.
D. Grain silo.

The answer is B. Section 1245 property does not include real estate such as buildings and structural components; therefore, the office building would not be included. Storage structures such as oil and gas storage tanks, grain storage bins, and silos are not treated as buildings but as section 1245 property. ###

4. Which of the following assets is not section 1231 property?

A. An office building.
B. Unharvested crops.
C. A business asset held for less than one year.
D. A patent.

The answer is C. In order to qualify as section 1231 property, the property must have been held by the business for over one year. ###

5. Caraway Carwash paid $200,000 for business equipment in January 2012. Caraway sells the equipment for $180,000 in October 2012. Caraway had not taken any depreciation on the equipment. How will this transaction be reported?

A. Caraway has a section 1231 loss of $20,000 on the sale of the equipment. This is treated as an ordinary loss.
B. Caraway has a section 1231 loss of $20,000 on the sale of the equipment. This is treated as a capital loss.
C. This is an installment sale, with a loss of $20,000. This is treated as an ordinary loss.
D. Caraway has an ordinary loss.

The answer is D. Because the business asset was held for less than one year, the business has an ordinary loss. The loss will therefore offset ordinary income and is immediately deductible. ###

6. Jennifer operates Right Hair Salon, a sole proprietorship. In 2012, she sells all of her salon chairs for $3,500 in order to buy new ones. She had purchased the chairs seven years ago for $15,000, and they were fully depreciated. Therefore, her basis in the chairs is zero. How should she report this section 1231 transaction?

A. She reports a gain of $3,500 on Form 4797 and Schedule C. The entire $3,500 is treated as depreciation recapture, which is subject to ordinary income tax rates, as well as self-employment tax.
B. She reports a gain of $3,500 on Form 4797 and Schedule C. The entire $3,500 is treated as depreciation recapture, which is subject to ordinary income tax rates but not self-employment tax.
C. She reports a gain of $3,500 on Form 4797 and Schedule C. The entire $3,500 is taxed as a long-term capital gain.
D. She is not required to report this sale.

The answer is B. Since the amount realized from the sale is less than Jennifer's original cost for the chairs, the entire gain is treated as depreciation recapture, which is subject to ordinary income tax rates but not self-employment tax. She reports the sale on Form 4797 and Schedule C. ###

7. Which of the following property types qualifies for section 1031 like-kind exchange?

A. A personal residence.
B. Inventory property.
C. Corporation common stock.
D. An empty lot held for investment.

The answer is D. Real property held for investment qualifies for like-kind exchange treatment. A personal residence, inventory, and common stock do not qualify for section 1031 treatment. ####

8. On January 10, 2012, a rental office building owned by Clovis Investments Corporation burns down. The property had an adjusted basis of $260,000, and Clovis receives an insurance reimbursement of $310,000. Clovis buys another rental office property for $290,000 in March 2012. What is Clovis's recognized gain as a result of this transaction?

A. $0.
B. $20,000.
C. $30,000.
D. $50,000.

The answer is B. This transaction is treated as an involuntary conversion. Clovis recognizes a taxable gain of $20,000 ($310,000 - $290,000), equal to the portion of the insurance reimbursement that was not reinvested in replacement property. Clovis's unrecognized gain is $30,000, the difference between the $50,000 realized gain and the $20,000 recognized gain. The basis of the new property is as follows:

Cost of replacement property	$290,000
Minus gain not recognized	($30,000)
Basis of replacement property	**$260,000**

If Clovis had reinvested all the insurance proceeds into a new property, the entire gain would have been deferred, and the involuntary conversion would have been completely nontaxable. ###

9. Barbara exchanges an apartment building with an adjusted basis of $125,000 for a business office building. The fair market value of Barbara's property is $500,000. The fair market value of the business office building, the property Barbara receives, has an FMV of $475,000. What is Barbara's basis in the new building?

A. $125,000.
B. $475,000.
C. $500,000.
D. $525,000.

The answer is A. Generally, an exchange of real property qualifies as a nontaxable exchange under section 1031. In a nontaxable exchange situation, the FMV of the buildings has no bearing on the basis. In this case, the basis of the new property is the same as the basis of the old property ($125,000). ####

10. Scott has a plane that he used in his business for two years. Its adjusted basis is $35,000, and its trade-in value is $45,000. He trades his old plane for a new plane that costs $200,000 and pays the dealer an additional $155,000 in cash. What is Scott's basis of the new plane?

A. $35,000.
B. $155,000.
C. $190,000.
D. $200,000.

The answer is C. Scott's basis is $190,000 ($155,000 of cash paid plus the $35,000 adjusted basis of the old plane). ###

11. The Karabell Company trades a delivery truck with an adjusted basis of $11,000 and cash of $6,000 for a new truck with a fair market value of $25,000. How much gain must Karabell recognize in this exchange, and what is its basis in the new truck?

Gain	Basis of New Truck
A. $0	$17,000
B. $0	$25,000
C. $8,000	$17,000
D. $8,000	$25,000

The answer is A. This exchange qualifies as a nontaxable exchange. Any gain on the exchange is deferred until the new asset is later sold or exchanged again. The $6,000 of cash is added to the basis of the old truck to determine the basis of the new truck. ###

12. Which of the following property exchanges does not qualify as a like-kind exchange?

A: Exchange of an apartment building for an office building.
B. Exchange of livestock of different sexes.
C: Exchange of improved property for unimproved property.
D: Exchange of farm machinery for factory machinery.

The answer is B. The exchange of livestock of different sexes does not qualify. The exchange of real estate for real estate and the exchange of business property for similar business property are exchanges of like-kind property. ###

13. Fran and Zachary are mother and son who complete a section 1031 exchange in March 2012. On January 29, 2013, Fran dies, and her property is inherited by her husband, who promptly sells it. Which of the following statements is true?

A. Since one of the properties in the exchange has been sold before the two-year time limit for related parties, the section 1031 exchange is disallowed, and both parties must pay tax on the transaction.
B. The exchange is still valid.
C. Since this was a related party exchange, the section 1031 exchange is still valid for Zachary, but Fran's estate must pay tax on the exchange, since her husband disposed of the property before the two-year waiting period.
D. The nonrecognition treatment is lost for both parties, but Fran's husband is liable for the tax on the exchange, since he was the owner of the property when it was sold.

The answer is B. In a related-party exchange, the nonrecognition treatment will be lost if either property in the exchange is disposed of within two years. However, there are exceptions to this rule. The section 1031 exchange will still be valid if either party in the transaction dies, or if the property is subject to an involuntary conversion. ###

14. Which of the following trades qualifies as a nontaxable like-kind exchange?

A. The exchange of a vacant lot in the city with farmland in the country.
B. The exchange of a Toyota Prius owned by one car dealer for a Ford C-Max Hybrid owned by another car dealer.
C. The exchange of shares of stocks for units of bonds.
D. The exchange of an apartment building in New York City for an apartment building in Mexico City.

The answer is A. The exchange of a vacant lot for a tract of farmland qualifies for like-kind exchange treatment. Section 1031 specifically excludes exchanges of inventory; stocks, bonds, notes, other securities, or evidence of indebtedness; partnership interests; livestock of different sexes; and property used predominantly in the United States and property used predominantly outside the United States. Properties are like-kind if they are of the same nature or character, even if they differ in grade or quality. ###

15. Special rules apply to like-kind exchanges between related persons. For purposes of a section 1031 exchange, what qualifies as a related person?

A: The taxpayer and the taxpayer's spouse.
B: The taxpayer and a corporation in which the taxpayer has a 51% ownership.
C: A partnership in which the taxpayer owns a 53% interest, and a partnership in which the taxpayer's spouse owns a 52% interest.
D: All of the above.

The answer is D. The taxpayer and a member of his immediate family are related persons for purposes of like-kind exchanges. Any business where the taxpayer has beneficial ownership (over 50%) is also considered a related party. ###

16. Caliper Corporation purchases a machine to use in its business operations in July 2012. The cost of the machine is $250,000, not including $18,500 in sales tax. The entire purchase of the machine is financed with a small business loan. During 2012, Caliper Corporation pays interest of $10,500 on the loan. What is the proper treatment of this transaction?

A. Caliper Corporation must capitalize $279,000 as the total cost of the machine, and record depreciation expense each year.
B. Caliper Corporation may take a deduction for the interest paid on the loan ($10,500). The other costs, including sales tax, should be capitalized and depreciated.
C. Caliper Corporation may deduct all the costs, including the machine purchase, as a current business expense in 2012.
D. Caliper Corporation may deduct the sales tax and the loan interest as business expenses.

The answer is B. Caliper Corporation can take a deduction for the interest paid on the loan. However, the sales tax is not deductible. It must be added to the cost of the depreciable asset and depreciated over the useful life. The interest on a business loan, however, is a current expense and should be treated separately from the basis of the asset. ###

17. Sergio is a self-employed carpenter who owns a compressor for use in his business. He trades the compressor (adjusted basis $3,000) for a large table saw (FMV $7,500) and pays an additional $4,000 cash to the seller in a qualified exchange. What is Sergio's basis in the saw?

A. $7,000.
B. $7,500.
C. $4,000.
D. $3,000.

The answer is A. The basis of the saw is $7,000 (the $3,000 basis of the old asset plus the $4,000 paid). ###

18. Angelina trades a laser printer used in her tax practice for a new color model. The cost of the original printer was $5,000 and she had taken $1,000 of depreciation. She exchanged her old printer as a trade-in and paid an additional $2,000 in cash to complete the exchange. What is Angelina's basis in the new printer?

A. $1,000.
B. $2,000.
C. $6,000.
D. $7,000.

The answer is C. The adjusted basis of the old printer was $4,000 ($5,000 - $1,000 depreciation). Then she paid an additional $2,000 to acquire the new printer. Therefore, the basis of the new model is:

Original model adj. basis	$4,000
Cash paid	$2,000
Basis of new model	**$6,000**

###

19. Sadie owns a gym. She sells some used fitness equipment in 2012 for $65,000. She had purchased the equipment in 2008 for $90,000. She has taken $60,000 of depreciation, which includes a section 179 deduction of $10,000. Which of the following will Sadie report on the sale of the equipment?

A. Ordinary loss of $25,000.
B. Long-term capital gain of $35,000.
C. Ordinary income of $35,000.
D. Ordinary income of $10,000 and long-term capital gain of $25,000.

The answer is C. Sadie has a gain of $35,000, equal to the difference between her sales proceeds of $65,000 and her adjusted basis of $30,000 (cost of $90,000 less accumulated depreciation of $60,000). Although she has had the property for more than one year, it is personal property classified as section 1245 property and therefore is subject to depreciation recapture to the extent of the entire amount of depreciation (and section 179 deductions) taken. Since this amount exceeds her gain, the entire amount of the gain is treated as ordinary income. ###

20. Cecil operates an electronics repair business as a sole proprietorship. During 2012, Cecil sold property that was acquired for use in the business for $10,000. The purchase price of the property was $20,000 and Cecil had claimed the following deductions: section 179 deduction of $5,000 and depreciation of $8,000.

Based upon the information provided, what amount of taxable income will result from the sale of this property?

A. Capital gain of $3,000.
B. Ordinary income of $3,000.
C. $0.
D. Ordinary income of $10,000.

The answer is B. The disposition of the property results in a gain of $3,000 (equal to the proceeds of $10,000 less adjusted basis of $7,000 representing the purchase price of $20,000 less depreciation and section 179 deductions of $13,000). The gain is characterized as ordinary income to the lesser of the actual gain or the amount of depreciation and section 179 expenses recaptured ($13,000). ###
Supporting calculations:

Purchase price	$20,000
Less depreciation and section 179 deductions	($13,000)
Adjusted basis at date of sale	**$7,000**

Proceeds	$10,000
Gain on sale	$3,000
Depreciation recapture (as ordinary income)	**$13,000**

####

Unit 11: Partnerships in General

| More Reading: |
| Publication 541, *Partnerships* |

Partnership Basics

An unincorporated business with two or more members is generally classified as a partnership for federal tax purposes. A partnership is a pass-through entity. Its major advantage is that it is not directly taxed on its income. Instead, income and loss are determined at the partnership level and are only taxable to the individual partners. In this respect, a partnership is similar to a sole proprietorship.

Unlike a corporation, a partnership does not require any formal legal documents. A partnership must have at least two partners and at least one of them must be a general partner. A joint undertaking merely to share expenses is not a partnership. For example, co-ownership of rental property is not a partnership unless the co-owners provide services to the tenants.

> **Example:** Will and Todd are brothers, and they co-own a single residential rental that they inherited from their mother. They use a management company to run the property. Will and Todd are not partners, and their co-ownership of the property does not automatically create a partnership.

As described in Unit 1, certain entities with different legal structures may be classified as partnerships for tax purposes, either based upon their election by filing Form 8832, *Entity Classification Election,* or by default (as in the case of a domestic LLC with at least two members that is classified as a partnership unless it files Form 8832 and elects to be treated as a corporation). However, the following organizations are prohibited from being classified as partnerships:

- A corporation (although a corporation can be a partner in a partnership)
- Any joint-stock company or joint-stock association
- An insurance company
- Certain banks
- A government entity
- An organization required to be taxed as a corporation by the IRS
- Certain foreign organizations
- Any tax-exempt (nonprofit) organization
- Any real estate investment trust (REIT)
- Any organization classified as a trust or estate
- Any other organization that elects to be classified as a corporation by filing Form 8832

The Partnership Agreement

The term "partnership agreement" refers to any written document or oral agreement that bears on the underlying economic arrangement of the partners, including allocations of income, gain, loss, deductions, and credits. Examples of such documents include:

- Loan and credit agreements
- Assumption agreements
- Indemnification agreements
- Subordination agreements
- Correspondence with a lender concerning terms of a loan
- Loan guarantees

A partnership agreement may be modified during the tax year and even after the tax year has closed. However, the partnership agreement cannot be modified after the due date for filing the partnership return for the year, not including extensions.

> **Example:** Terry and Dawn run a cash-basis, calendar-year partnership. They split the proceeds 50-50. In 2012, they decide to alter the partnership agreement. They have until the due date of the partnership return to change the partnership agreement. Filing for an extension does not give them additional time.

A Partnership's Tax Year

A partnership generally must conform to the tax year of the partners. This means that partnerships typically report income on a calendar year basis. However, a partnership may request a fiscal year based on a legitimate business purpose. In order to qualify as a legitimate business purpose, the partnership must be able to prove that the decision to adopt a different tax year is not simply to defer income recognition by the partners.

A partnership may request a fiscal tax year based on a natural business year so that it closes its books after its busiest or most profitable period. A natural business year is a 12-month period where at least 25% of total gross receipts are received in the last two months of the year.

> **Example:** John and Kate run a seasonal business making pool equipment. Their busiest time of the year is during the summer months, and more than 60% of their income is received during June and July. John and Kate may request a fiscal year based on a legitimate business purpose—that is, the natural tax year of their seasonal business.

In the absence of a legitimate business purpose, a partnership may still request a fiscal year that does not conform to the tax year of its partners by making a section 444 election (explained previously in Unit 3).

Partnership Filing Requirements

Every partnership must file a tax return unless it has no activity whatsoever, (with no income or losses during the year). A partnership reports its income and loss on Form 1065, which is due on the 15th day of the fourth month following the close of the tax year. Since most partnerships are calendar-year partnerships, their tax returns are due on the same day as individual returns. A partnership may request a five-month extension to file (unlike individuals and corporations that may request a six-month extension). Therefore, a calendar-year partnership can request an extension until September 15 to file its tax return. The extension is requested on Form 7004, *Automatic Extension of Time to File Certain Business Income Tax, Information, and Other Returns.*

The partnership return must show the name and address of each partner and the partner's distributive share of taxable income (or loss) on Schedule K-1. The partnership is also required to furnish a copy of each partner's Schedule K-1 to every partner by the due date (including extensions) of the partnership tax return. The individual partner then reports his share of partnership income on Schedule E of Form 1040.

> **Example:** Lovett Partnership is a calendar-year, cash-basis partnership that is required to file a Form 1065 every year. The partnership has five partners and each partner receives a Schedule K-1 for his share of partnership income and losses, which are then reportable on the partners' individual tax returns. Each partner must receive his Schedule K-1 by the due date of the partnership return (or the extended due date, if the partnership requests an extension).

The IRS requires partnerships with more than 100 partners (Schedules K-1) to file their returns electronically. If a partnership fails to do so, it may be subject to penalty unless it was unable to file electronically (because the e-filing was rejected, the return required paper attachments, etc.)

The partnership return must be signed by a general partner.

The penalty for late filing is $195 per month, per partner, for up to 12 months. For example, if a partnership has four partners and files its tax return two months late, it would be liable for a late filing penalty of $1,560 ($195 × 2 months × 4 partners). Additional penalties may apply if the partnership fails to furnish Schedules K-1 to its partners, fails to supply a tax identification number, or fails to furnish information on tax shelters. These penalties may not be imposed if the partnership can show reasonable cause for its failure.

Partners who work in the business are not employees and do not receive a Form W-2. No withholding is taken out of their distributions to pay the income and self-employment taxes that they report on their Forms 1040. General partners are considered to be self-employed and therefore must pay estimated payments just like other self-employed individuals. Limited partners are subject to self-employment tax only on guaranteed payments, such as salary and professional fees for services rendered.

General Partnership vs. Limited Partnership

A partnership can either be a general partnership or a limited partnership. In a general partnership, all the partners have unlimited liability for partnership debts. In a limited partnership, at least one partner is a limited partner who is only liable for partnership liabilities up to his investment in the partnership. Limited partners generally cannot participate in the management or the day-to-day administration of the partnership.

A limited partner has no obligation to contribute additional capital to the partnership and therefore does not have an economic risk of loss in partnership liabilities. In this respect, a limited partner is like an investor in a corporation. A limited partner is not subject to self-employment tax on his distributive share of income.

A limited partnership (LP or LLP) is formed under state limited liability law. A limited partnership can have an unlimited number of investors, but there must always be at least one general partner. Usually, the owners of limited liability partnerships offer professional services (attorneys, doctors, etc.) This entity type protects individual partners from liability for the malpractice of other partners. However, all the partners remain liable for the general debts of the partnership.

Capital Interests

A capital interest in a partnership is an interest in its assets that is distributable to the owner of the interest in either of the following situations:

- The owner withdraws from the partnership
- The partnership liquidates

The right to share in earnings and profits is not itself a capital interest in the partnership.

Example: Rasheda and Aaron form a partnership in order to open a restaurant. Aaron is an experienced restaurant manager, but he has no money to invest. Rasheda owns the building and the restaurant equipment. Her basis in the assets is $100,000. Therefore, Rasheda has a capital interest in the partnership. Aaron does not.

Family Partnerships

Members of a family can be legitimate partners and form a partnership together. However, family members will be recognized as partners only if one of the following requirements is met:

- If capital is a material income-producing factor, the family members must have acquired their capital interest in a bona fide transaction (even if by gift or purchase from another family member); actually own the partnership interest; and actually control the interest. This means that a family member who acquires a partnership interest from another family member needs to treat the activity as a bona fide business activity.

- If capital is not a material income-producing factor, the family members must have joined together in good faith to conduct a business. They must have agreed that contributions of each entitle them to a share in the profits and that some capital or service is provided by each partner.

Capital (investment) is a material income-producing factor if a substantial part of the gross income of the business comes from the use of capital. For example, this would apply if the operation of the business requires substantial inventories or investment in a plant, machinery, or equipment. In general, capital is not a material income-producing factor if the income of the business consists principally of fees, commissions, or other compensation for personal services performed by members or employees of the partnership.

Related Persons and Partnership Losses

For purposes of determining a partner's distributive share, an interest purchased by one family member from another family member is considered a gift from the seller. The fair market value of the purchased interest is considered donated capital. For this purpose, members of a family include only spouses, ancestors, and lineal descendants (grandson, daughter, son, stepson, etc.)

A loss on the sale or exchange of property between related persons is not deductible. Under the related party transaction rules, an individual is considered as also owning the partnership interest directly or indirectly owned by his family. Members of a family, for this purpose, include only brothers, sisters, half-brothers, half-sisters, spouses, ancestors, parents, and lineal descendants (children, grandchildren).

Husband and Wife Businesses

An unincorporated business jointly owned by a husband and wife is generally classified as a partnership for federal tax purposes. However, a married couple can elect instead to be treated as a "qualified joint venture." In order to make this election, both spouses must materially participate in the business, they must be the only members in the venture, and they must file a joint tax return. If this election is made, they do not file Form 1065. Instead, all items of income and loss are divided between the spouses based on their respective interests in the venture.

Each spouse reports his or her respective share of these items as a sole proprietor on Schedule C or Schedule F (Form 1040) and reports self-employment income on Schedule SE.

Costs of Organizing and Starting a Partnership

The costs to organize a partnership and to start up a business are treated much like similar costs incurred by other types of businesses. Limited amounts of organizational and start-up costs can be deducted in the year the partnership's active trade or business begins. Amounts not deducted can be amortized ratably over a period of 180 months. The election to either amortize or capitalize these costs is irrevocable and applies to all organizational and start-up costs related to the trade or business. The partnership must complete and attach Form 4562, *Depreciation and Amortization*, to its tax return.

A partnership can amortize an organizational cost only if it meets all the following tests:

- It is for the creation of the partnership itself and not for starting or operating the partnership trade or business.
- It is chargeable to a capital account.
- It is incurred by the due date of the partnership return (excluding extensions) for the first tax year in which the partnership is in business.
- It is for a type of item normally expected to benefit the partnership throughout its entire life.

Qualifying partnership organizational costs include the following fees:

- Legal fees for services related to the organization of the partnership, such as negotiation and preparation of the partnership agreement.
- Accounting fees for services related to the organization of the partnership.
- Filing fees.

The following costs cannot be deducted or amortized:

- The cost of acquiring assets for the partnership or transferring assets to the partnership

- The cost of admitting or removing partners, other than at the time the partnership is first organized
- The cost of making a contract concerning the operation of the partnership trade or business including a contract between a partner and the partnership
- Syndication costs for issuing and marketing interests in the partnership, such as brokerage, registration, and printing costs

If a partnership is liquidated (ceases operations) before the end of the amortization period, the unamortized amount of qualifying organizational costs can be deducted in the partnership's final tax year, but only to the extent they qualify as a loss from a business.

Start-up costs include amounts paid or incurred in connection with an existing activity engaged in for profit and for the production of income in anticipation of the activity becoming an active trade or business. Start-up costs include amounts paid for the following:

- An analysis or survey of potential markets, products, labor supply, transportation facilities, etc.
- Advertisements for the opening of the business.
- Salaries and wages for employees who are being trained and their instructors.
- Travel and other necessary costs for securing prospective distributors, suppliers, or customers.
- Salaries and fees for executives and consultants, or for similar professional services.

Special Partnership Allocations

Unlike S corporations, which must report all income and expenses in proportion to stock ownership, partnerships allow more flexibility. Special allocations of income, gain, loss, or deductions can be made between the partners based on their partnership agreement.

Partnership agreements can be written to reflect whatever economic sharing and risk sharing arrangements the parties wish. Special allocations permit partners to assume different levels of risk and to set the timing of income in accordance with their preferences.

For example, the partnership agreement may allocate all of the depreciation deductions to one partner or specify that the partners share capital, profits, and losses in different ratios. Further, the sharing of profits does not have to coincide with the sharing of losses.

Example: Pandora, who has design and sewing skills, forms a partnership with Jayne, who has the money to invest in developing a clothing line. Jayne contributes $100,000 in cash to the partnership. Pandora and Jayne agree to split the business profits 20/80 until Jayne recovers her entire investment; thereafter, profits will be split 50/50. These special allocations are written into their partnership agreement.

Example: Nico and Rhoda form a partnership. Nico contributes $1,000 and Rhoda contributes $99,000. Due to Nico's expertise in management and his daily participation in the partnership's business, the partnership agreement provides that he will be allocated 20% of the partnership taxable income and 2% of the partnership loss. Thus, although Nico owns only 1% in partnership capital, his profit sharing ratio is 20%. This tax allocation between Nico and Rhoda is allowable so long as the distribution of economic benefits between the two is also in the same ratio (i.e., 20% to Nico and 80% to Rhoda).

Example: Alicia and Danni form a partnership to run a cupcake bakery. The bakery is opened during the year, and the partnership has ordinary income of $10,000. The partnership agreement states that they will share income and loss equally (50/50). Alicia and Danni agree that the $10,000 income will be distributed equally between them. However, for tax purposes, they want the income to be specially allocated as $7,500 to Alexia and $2,500 to Danni. The tax allocation (75/25) is not consistent with the underlying economic agreement on their partnership agreement (50/50). Unless the partnership agreement contains other provisions that justify this allocation, it has no economic effect and must be reallocated to the partners based on their true economic sharing ratio (50/50).

Guaranteed Payments

A partnership may be required by the terms of the partnership agreement to make guaranteed payments to one or more partners without regard to whether the partnership has income or loss for the year.

Guaranteed payments are not the same as partnership distributions. They may compensate the partner for services or for the use of capital, as if they were made to a person who is not a partner. Guaranteed payments are generally deducted by the partnership on Form 1065 as a business expense and reported on Schedule K-1.

The partner who receives a guaranteed payment reports the full amount of the payment as ordinary income on Schedule E (Form 1040) of his individual tax return for the tax year in which the partnership's tax year ends, and also reports his distributive share of the partnership's ordinary income or loss. Guaranteed payments are not subject to income tax withholding.

> **Example:** Erica is a partner in the Bookertown Partnership. Under the terms of her partnership agreement, she is entitled to a guaranteed payment of $10,000 per year, regardless of how profitable the partnership is. In 2012, Erica's distributive share of partnership income is 10%. Bookertown Partnership has $50,000 of ordinary income after deducting Erica's guaranteed payment. She must include ordinary income of $15,000 ($10,000 guaranteed payment + $5,000 [$50,000 × 10%] for her distributive share) on her individual income tax return (Form 1040).

Separately Stated Items

Many of the individual components of a partnership's income are calculated similarly to those of an individual. However, some deductions are not allowed at the partnership level, and certain items of income and loss must be separately stated on the tax return. These separately stated items flow through to the partners with a specific character. For example, if a partnership makes charitable contributions, it must list the charitable contributions as a separately stated item. The individual partners then report their share of the charitable contributions on their individual Schedule A.

In order to determine taxable income, all partnership income must first be divided into:

- **Separately stated items, and**
- **Ordinary income or loss.**

The following items must be separately stated:

- Net short-term capital gains and losses
- Net long-term capital gains and losses
- Charitable contributions
- Dividends eligible for a dividends-received deduction
- Taxes paid to a foreign country
- Taxes paid to a U.S. possession (Guam, Puerto Rico, etc.)
- Section 1231 gains and losses
- Section 179 deductions and bonus depreciation
- Any tax-exempt income and expenses related to the tax-exempt income
- Investment income and related investment expenses
- Rental income, portfolio income, and related expenses
- Any recovery items, such as bad debts

Any item of income that is not a separately stated item is a component of ordinary income.

Taxable income includes ordinary income, all the separately stated items, and any other adjustments, such as business expenses and cost of goods sold.

Example: The Stevenson Partnership operates as an accrual-based business. Its gross receipts for 2012 were $250,000. In addition to those gross receipts, the company also had the following items of income and expenses:

- Liability insurance   ($5,000)
- Charitable contributions   ($2,000)
- Continuing education   ($9,000)
- Rental income $25,000
- Guaranteed payments to partners   ($15,000)

The ordinary income for the Stevenson partnership is figured as follows:

Gross income	$250,000
Liability insurance	($5,000)
Continuing education	($9,000)
Guaranteed payments to partners	($15,000)
The ordinary income of the partnership is therefore:	**$221,000**

The rental income and charitable contributions are not considered in determining ordinary income of the partnership. Instead, these are separately stated items that pass through to the partners and retain their character, just as they would for a sole proprietorship. The separately stated items are reported on each individual partner's return (Form 1040).

Guaranteed payments are deductible to the partnership because they are treated like wages and are taxable to the partners.

Cash and Property Contributions to a Partnership

When a partnership is formed, the partners contribute property or cash in exchange for their partnership interests. Generally, neither the partner nor the partnership recognizes gain or loss in connection with contributions, whether made in connection with the partnership's formation or after it is operating. However, a partner's contribution can result in gain or loss recognition in the following situations:

- When property is contributed to a partnership that would be treated as an investment company if it were incorporated. A partnership is treated as an investment company if over 80% of the value of its assets is held for investment in cash or readily marketable items.

- When contributed property is distributed to a different partner within seven years of the original contribution date. The contributing partner would recognize gain on the difference between the fair market value and the adjusted basis of the property as of the contribution date. The character of the gain or loss will be the same as would have resulted if the partnership had sold the property to the distributee partner. This rule is designed to prevent partners from shifting assets around in order to mask revenue.

- When a partner contributes cash or property to a partnership and then receives a distribution of different property. In this case, the transaction may be considered a disguised sale. A disguised sale is not treated as a contribution and a subsequent distribution, but as a sale of property, if:
  o The distribution would not have been made if the initial contribution had not occurred; and
  o The partner's right to the distribution does not depend on the success of partnership operations.

When a partner contributes property to a partnership, the partnership's basis is generally the same as the adjusted basis of the partner, including any gain recognized by the partner in connection with the contribution. The partner's holding period for the property is also carried over. For example, if a partner contributes a building with an FMV of $100,000 and a basis of $50,000, the basis of the building in the hands of the partnership would generally be $50,000.

Contribution of Services to a Partnership

A partner can acquire an interest in a partnership as compensation for services performed or to be performed. The tax treatment depends upon whether the partner receives a capital interest or a profits interest. If a partner receives a capital interest as compensation for services, the partner must recognize ordinary income equal to the fair market value of a partnership interest that is transferred in exchange for services. The amount is treated as a guaranteed payment and is included in the partner's gross income in the first tax year during which the partner can transfer the interest. If a partner receives a profits interest as compensation for services, the receipt may not be taxable to the partner or the partnership, except in certain circumstances.

Example: Greer is an attorney who contributes her services to a partnership in exchange for a 10% partnership interest. It is deemed a capital interest, as the partnership agreement provides for distribution of assets to Greer in the event she withdraws from the partnership or the partnership liquidates. The fair market value of the partnership interest is $3,000. Greer is required to recognize $3,000 in ordinary income, and her basis in the partnership is $3,000. The payment is deducted by the partnership as a guaranteed payment and is taxable to Greer as ordinary income.

Basis of a Partner's Interest

A partner's basis in his partnership interest may be referred to as **outside basis**. This is in contrast to the partnership's basis in its assets, which is known as **inside basis**.[50]

The initial basis of a partnership interest is generally equal to the cash plus the adjusted basis of any property the partner contributed. The adjusted basis of a partner's partnership interest is ordinarily determined at the end of the partnership's tax year. However, if there is a sale or exchange of all or part of a partner's interest or a liquidation of his entire interest in a partnership, the adjusted basis must also be determined on the date of liquidation.

The following items increase a partner's basis in the partnership:

- The partner's additional cash contributions to the partnership
- The partner's increased liabilities
- The partner's increased share (or assumption of) partnership liabilities
- The partner's distributive share of partnership income
- The partner's distributive share of the excess of the deductions for depletion over the basis of the depletable property

Sometimes a partner will be required to recognize a gain when he contributes an asset to the partnership that is subject to liability (such as the contribution of a building that is subject to a mortgage). If the partner must recognize a gain as a result of his partnership contribution, this gain is added to the basis of his partnership interest.

Any increase in a partner's individual liabilities because of his assumption of partnership liabilities is treated as if it were a contribution to the partnership by the partner. If a partner's share of partnership liabilities increases, this increase is treated as if the partner contributed cash or property to the partnership.

> **Example:** Sam and Abdul have a partnership. Sam contributes a machine to his partnership that has an adjusted basis of $400 and an FMV of $1,000. Abdul contributes $1,000 cash. Each partner has increased his capital account by $1,000, which will be reflected in the partnership books. However, the adjusted basis of Sam's interest is only $400 and Abdul's partnership interest is $1,000.

A partner's basis in the partnership is *decreased* by the following items:

- The money and adjusted basis of property distributed to the partner by the partnership.
- The partner's distributive share of the partnership losses.

---

[50] On the EA exam, these two terms may be used in questions in which you must determine partnership or partner basis.

- The partner's distributive share of nondeductible partnership expenses that are not capital expenditures. This includes the partner's share of any section 179 expenses, even if the partner cannot deduct the entire amount on his individual income tax return.
- The partner's deduction for depletion for any partnership oil and gas wells, up to the proportionate share of the adjusted basis of the wells allocated to the partner.

If a partner's share of partnership liabilities decreases or the partnership assumes any of the individual partner's liabilities, the amounts are treated as distributions to the partner by the partnership.

If contributed property is subject to a debt and the debt is assumed by the partnership, the basis of the contributing partner's interest is reduced (but not below zero) by the portion of the liability assumed by the other partners. The partner must reduce his basis because the assumption of the liability is treated as a distribution to him. The other partners' assumption of the liability is treated as a contribution by them to the partnership.

Example: Al acquired a 20% interest in a partnership by contributing a moving van that had an adjusted basis to him of $8,000 and a related $4,000 loan balance. The partnership assumed the loan. The basis of Al's interest is:

Adjusted basis of contributed property	$8,000
Minus: Auto loan assumed by other partners (80% × $4,000)	($3,200)
Basis of Al's partnership interest	**$4,800**

A partner's basis can never go below zero. So, in order to prevent a negative basis, a partner must recognize gain equal to the amount that the decrease in a partner's share of liability exceeds his basis.

Example: Raymond acquired a 20% interest in a partnership by contributing an asset that had an adjusted basis to him of $8,000 and a related $12,000 loan. Since the value of the asset is less than the amount of the loan, Raymond's partnership basis is zero. The $1,600 difference between the loan assumed by the other partners, $9,600 (80% × $12,000), and his basis of $8,000 is treated as capital gain from the sale or exchange of a partnership interest. However, this gain would not increase the basis of his partnership interest. His partnership basis would remain zero.

Partnership Loss Limitations

The amount of a partnership's loss that a partner is allowed to deduct on his individual tax return is dependent on the partner's basis in the partnership. In general, a partner cannot deduct losses that exceed his partnership basis. Losses disallowed due to insufficient basis are carried forward until the partner can deduct them in a later year.

However, debts on behalf of the partnership can *increase* a partner's individual basis. So, for example, if a partner takes out a $50,000 loan in order to finance partnership operations and he personally guarantees the debt, the partner is allowed to take losses due to his debt basis.

Example: Rebecca invests $1,000 in the Andrews Partnership in return for a 10% partnership interest. The Andrews Partnership takes out a $500,000 loan and incurs $100,000 in losses during the first year. Rebecca's share of partnership liabilities would increase her basis to $51,000 [$1,000 cash investment + ($500,000 × 10%). Rebecca's share of the loss is $10,000 ($100,000 × 10%). Rebecca is allowed to deduct the entire loss, because her partnership basis was increased by debt basis.

This only applies if the partner is at risk for the loss. If the partner does not have any personal liability to satisfy the debt, deductible losses are limited by the at-risk rules**.** The at-risk rules limit the deductibility of losses to the partner's basis *reduced* by his share of any nonrecourse debt.

This means that a partner is prohibited from taking losses based on partnership liabilities unless the partner would be forced to satisfy the debt with his personal assets. This is intended to prevent abusive deductions from real estate and other tax shelter activities.

Partnership Liabilities

If a partner's share of partnership liabilities increases, or a partner's individual liabilities increase because he assumes partnership liabilities, this increase is treated as a contribution of money by the partner to the partnership. A partner (or related person) is considered to assume a partnership liability when:

- He is personally liable for it,
- The creditor knows that the liability was assumed by the partner or related person,
- The creditor can demand payment from the partner or related person, and
- No other partner or person related to another partner will bear the economic risk of loss on that liability immediately after the assumption.

> **Example:** Gary and Stanton form a general partnership, with cash contributions of $2,000 from each. Under the partnership agreement, they share all partnership profits and losses equally. The partnership also borrows an additional $10,000 and purchases equipment. Both partners are liable for the debt. This debt is included in the partners' basis in the partnership. Each partner's basis would include his allocated share of the liability of $5,000. Therefore, each partner's basis is now $7,000 (the initial $2,000 contribution + $5,000 share of the liability).

The effect of liabilities on the individual partner's basis depends mainly on two factors:

- Whether or not the liability is recourse or nonrecourse
- Whether or not the partner is a general or limited partner

A nonrecourse liability is usually secured by an asset or property, and its terms provide that the creditor has no claim against the owner of the property. At most, the creditor may have a claim against the property. An example of this would be a home loan where the bank's only recourse in case of default is to repossess the house. A partnership liability is considered a nonrecourse liability if no partner has an economic risk of loss for that liability.

> **Example:** Reuben purchases a used van for his business but he is unable to make the payments. The loan is a nonrecourse loan because the only action the lender can take is to repossess the vehicle. The lender cannot seek payment from Reuben for the balance of the loan.

A partner's share of nonrecourse liabilities is proportionate to his share of partnership profits. A partner's basis in a partnership interest includes the partner's share of a partnership liability only if, and to the extent, the liability:

- Creates or increases the partnership's basis in any of its assets,
- Gives rise to a current deduction to the partnership, or
- Is a nondeductible, noncapital expense of the partnership.

In a cash-basis partnership, any liabilities that are accrued but unpaid are not included in the basis calculation for each individual partner.

A partnership liability is a recourse liability when the individual partners have an economic risk of loss. A partner has an economic risk of loss to the extent that partner or a related person would be obligated to make payments to a creditor in the event of a constructive liquidation. Generally, in a constructive liquidation, the following events are treated as occurring at the same time:

1. All partnership liabilities become payable in full
2. All of the partnership's assets have a value of zero, except for property contributed to secure a liability

3. All property is disposed of by the partnership in a fully taxable transaction for no consideration
4. All items of income, gain, loss, or deduction are allocated to the partners
5. The partnership liquidates

Partners generally share recourse liabilities based on their ratios for sharing losses. A limited partner has no obligation to contribute additional capital to the partnership, and therefore does not have an economic risk of loss in partnership recourse liabilities. Therefore, unless a limited partner guarantees a partnership liability or makes a loan to the partnership, his basis will generally not be affected by the partnership's recourse liabilities.

Unit 11: Questions

1. In 2012 Raj and Ellie formed Spring Lawn, a calendar-year partnership, to provide yard maintenance to residential customers. Before they began operations in November 2012, they incurred legal fees of $2,000 and consulting expenses of $1,000 to draft the partnership agreement and file the required forms. They also paid a commission of $600 to a broker to market partnership interests. How much of these expenses may be deducted or amortized?

A. $0.
B. $600.
C. $3,000.
D. $3,600.

The answer is C. The partnership may choose to deduct the amounts for legal fees and consulting expenses ($2,000 + $1,000 = $3,000). However, the amount paid in commissions to a broker to market partnership interests must be capitalized and cannot be amortized or deducted. The costs for marketing and issuing interests in the partnership such as brokerage, registration, legal fees, and printing costs are syndication costs that are not deductible or amortizable. ###

2. Which of the following statements is true?

A. The IRS requires partnerships with more than 100 partners to file their returns electronically.
B. The IRS requires all partnerships to file electronically.
C. The IRS requires limited partnerships with more than 10 partners to file their returns electronically.
D. The IRS requires partnerships with 100 or more partners to file electronically.

The answer is A. The IRS requires partnerships with more than 100 partners (Schedules K-1) to file their returns electronically. Partnerships with 100 or fewer partners are not required to electronically file their returns. ###

3. Which of the following statements regarding limited partnerships is correct?

A. A limited partner has an economic liability for damages and an economic risk of loss.
B. A limited partner does not have an economic risk of loss in partnership recourse liabilities.
C. A limited partner does not have an economic risk of loss in partnership recourse liabilities; however, a limited partner is required to contribute additional capital.
D. A limited partner is treated just like a general partner when it comes to recourse liability.

The answer is B. A limited partner generally has no obligation to contribute additional capital to the partnership and therefore does not have an economic risk of loss in partnership recourse liabilities. Thus, absent some other factor such as the guarantee of a partnership liability by the limited partner or the limited partner making a loan to the partnership, a limited partner generally does not have an economic risk of loss from the partnership recourse liabilities. ###

4. Otto and Janelle form a cash-basis general partnership with cash contributions of $20,000 each. Under the partnership agreement, they share all partnership profits and losses equally. They borrow $60,000 and purchase depreciable business equipment. However, Otto has poor credit, so Janelle is the only signer on the loan. Janelle is required to pay the creditor if the partnership defaults, so she has an economic risk of loss related to the loan. The payments on the loan are made out of the partnership bank account. What is Janelle's basis in the partnership, and what is Otto's basis?

A. Janelle: $80,000, Otto: $20,000.
B. Janelle: $60,000, Otto: $20,000.
C. Janelle: $20,000, Otto: $20,000.
D. Janelle: $60,000, Otto: $60,000.

The answer is A. This loan amount is included in Janelle's basis in the partnership because she has an economic risk of loss related to this liability. An additional $60,000 of basis in the partnership's depreciable property was created as a result of incurring this debt. Her basis in the partnership would be $80,000 ($20,000 + $60,000), while Otto's basis would be only $20,000. ###

5. Polly and Diane form P&D Partnership in 2012. Polly contributes $16,000 cash and Diane contributes equipment with a fair market value of $15,000 and an adjusted basis of $5,000. What amount should Diane report as a gain as a result of this transaction?

A. $0.
B. $3,000.
C. $5,000.
D. $8,000.

The answer is A. Usually, neither the partner nor the partnership recognizes a gain or loss when property is contributed to the partnership in exchange for a partnership interest. This applies whether a partnership is being formed or is already operating. However, if an asset is encumbered by a liability, such as a mortgage, there is a possibility that the partner will recognize a gain in connection with the contribution. ###

6. Daniel is a general partner in the Vrettos Partnership. During the year, Daniel personally assumes $100,000 of the partnership's liabilities. Which of the following statements regarding partnership liabilities is true?

A. The assumption of partnership debt by Daniel is treated as a distribution of cash to Daniel, and it decreases Daniel's partnership basis.
B. The assumption of partnership debt by Daniel increases his basis.
C. Daniel cannot assume partnership liabilities.
D. Only limited partners are allowed to assume partnership liabilities.

The answer is B. The assumption of partnership debt by Daniel increases his basis. If a partner's share of partnership liabilities increases, or a partner's individual liabilities increase because he assumes partnership liabilities, this increase is treated as if the partner made a contribution to the partnership.###

7. If a partnership requests additional time to file its return, for how long will the filing deadline be extended?

A. Three months.
B. Five months.
C. Six months.
D. Nine months.

The answer is B. Form 7004, Automatic Extension of Time to File Certain Business Income Tax, Information, and Other Returns, is used by partnerships to extend their filing deadline for five months. ###

8. Roadhouse Partnership forms in 2012. Roadhouse decides to amortize its organizational costs. Which of the following costs would not be considered an organizational or start-up cost qualified for amortization?

A. The costs of transferring a building to the partnership.
B. Legal fees to draft the partnership agreement.
C. Accounting fees for services related to the organization of the partnership.
D. The cost of training employees before the business opens.

The answer is A. The expenses for acquiring or transferring assets to a partnership cannot be amortized. They must instead be included in the basis of a partnership interest. The other choices are all costs that may be amortized or deducted as qualifying start-up or organizational costs. ###

9. When payments are made by a partnership to partners that are without regard to partnership income, these payments are called:

A. Capital gains.
B. Ordinary distributions.
C. Passive income.
D. Guaranteed payments.

The answer is D. Guaranteed payments are those made by a partnership to a partner that are determined without regard to the partnership's income. A partnership treats guaranteed payments for services, or for the use of capital, as a business expense, just as if they were made to a person who is not a partner. ###

10. Which of the following increases the basis of a partner's interest in a partnership?

A. A partner's share of tax-exempt interest from municipal bonds owned by the partnership.
B. A decrease in the partner's share of liabilities.
C. A distribution of $2,000 in cash to the partner.
D. A property distribution with an FMV of $5,000.

The answer is A. Partnership income, including tax-exempt interest, increases a partner's basis in his partnership interest. ####

11. The G&H Partnership has two partners, Gil and Hassid. They share profits and losses equally (50/50). The partnership has the following activity during the year.

Gross income from operations:	$200,000
Business expenses:	$30,000
Tax-exempt interest income:	$10,000
Rental income:	$120,000
Charitable contributions:	$4,000

What is Hassid's share of the partnership ordinary income?

A. $85,000.
B. $91,000.
C. $100,000.
D. $105,000.

The answer is A. The rental income, tax exempt income, and charitable contributions are all separately stated items. They do not affect the calculation of ordinary income. Instead, each partner's share of the separately stated items is passed through to the individual partners. Hassid's share of the partnership's ordinary income is split evenly with Gil, so his portion is figured as follows:

($200,000 - $30,000) = $170,000
$170,000 X 50% =$85,000 ###

12. José and Carlos form a partnership. Each contributes $20,000 during the initial formation of the partnership. Their partnership agreement states that José will receive 35% of the distributive income, and Carlos will receive 65%. In 2012, the partnership has a net profit of $200,000. What is each partner's distributive share of the partnership profits?

A. José: $70,000, Carlos: $130,000.
B. José: $100,000, Carlos: $100,000.
C. José: $35,000, Carlos $65,000.
D. Some other amount.

The answer is A. The profits are allocated according to the partnership agreement. Jose's distributive share is calculated as follows: 35% X $200,000 = $70,000. Carlos's share is figured as follows: 65% X $200,000 = $130,000. ###

13. John, Robin, Shanette, and Theresa form a partnership. Each partner contributes $10,000 and receives an equal interest in the partnership (25%). Under the partnership agreement, they share partnership profits and losses equally. The partnership borrows $135,000 and purchases business equipment. All the partners except for Theresa personally guarantee the liability. What is each partner's basis after this transaction?

A. Theresa's basis is zero, and the other partners each have a basis of $58,333.
B. Theresa's basis is $10,000, and the other partners each have a basis of $43,750.
C. Theresa's basis is $10,000, and the other partners each have a basis of $55,000.
D. Each partner has a basis of $43,750.

The answer is C. If a partner's share of partnership liabilities increases, this increase is treated as a contribution of money by the partner to the partnership. This debt is included in the partners' basis in the partnership because incurring it creates an additional $135,000 of basis in the partnership's depreciable property. However, since Theresa does not have an economic risk of loss for this liability, the liability does not increase her basis. The basis for each of the remaining partners would include his or her share of the liability ([$135,000 ÷ 3 partners] = $45,000 + $10,000 their original investment). ###

14. Racing Horses Partnership has seven partners. The partnership files its tax return three months late. What is the IRS penalty for late filing of the partnership return?
A. $0.
B. $585.
C. $780.
D. $4,095.

The answer is D. The penalty for late filing is $195 per month, for each partner, for up to 12 months. The penalty is calculated as follows: $195 X 3 months X 7 partners = $4,095. ###

15. Carolyn and Jerome form a partnership in 2012. Each contributes $5,000 for an equal partnership interest. Their partnership agreement states that they will share income and loss equally. However, because of her accounting expertise, Carolyn will receive a guaranteed payment each year of $21,000, regardless of the partnership's income or loss. In 2012, the partnership earns $50,000 before deducting the guaranteed payment. What is Jerome's distributive share of partnership profits for 2012?

A. $0.
B. $14,500.
C. $22,500.
D. $25,000.

The answer is B. The guaranteed payment must be deducted before figuring each partner's distributive share. The answer is figured as follows:
$50,000 - $21,000 = $29,000
$29,000 X 50% = $14,500
Guaranteed payments are deducted from partnership income before determining the distributive share of income or loss for each partner. ###

16. The D&D Healthy Pet Stores operates as an accrual-based partnership and files a Form 1065 for 2012. In addition to receipts from pet food sales of $250,000, the partnership has the following items of income and expenses for 2012:

- Salaries $50,000
- Insurance $5,000
- Charitable contributions $5,000
- Licenses $5,000
- Rental income $25,000
- Guaranteed payments $75,000

What is the correct ordinary income or loss that D&D Healthy Pet Stores should report on line 22 of their 2012 Form 1065?

A. $85,000.
B. $115,000.
C. $100,000.
D. $150,000.

The answer is B. All of the items listed are included in the calculation of ordinary income except the charitable contributions and the rental income, both of which must be separately stated on Form 1065. Thus, ordinary income will be $115,000 ($250,000 - $50,000 - $5,000 - $5,000 - $75,000). Like the other deductions listed, guaranteed payments to partners are treated as a deduction in determining ordinary income or loss. ###

17. Monica contributes property with a fair market value of $7,000, an adjusted basis of $4,000, and a related mortgage of $1,000 which the partnership assumes, to a partnership for a 40% interest in the partnership. What is Monica's basis in her partnership interest?

A. $4,000.
B. $3,000,
C. $6,000.
D. $3,400.

The answer is D. The basis of Monica's interest is the adjusted basis of the property she contributes ($4,000) less the portion of the related mortgage liability assumed by the other partners (60% x $1,000 = $600), or $3,400. ###

18. A partner is not considered at risk for which of the following amounts?

A. The money and adjusted basis of any property the partner contributed to activity.
B. The partner's share of net income retained by the partnership.
C. A partnership's nonrecourse liability.
D. Certain amounts borrowed by the partnership for use in the activity if the partner is personally liable for repayment.

The answer is C. The at-risk rules limit the deductibility of losses to the partner's basis reduced by his share of any of the partnership's nonrecourse debt. ###

19. Bea acquired a 30% interest in a partnership by contributing property that had an adjusted basis to her of $25,000, fair market value of $50,000, and a $40,000 mortgage. The partnership assumed the liability. What is Bea's gain or loss on the contribution of her property to the partnership?

A. $0.
B. $3,000 gain.
C. $12,000 gain.
D. $10,000 loss.

The answer is B. The basis of Bea's partnership interest should be the adjusted basis of the property contributed ($25,000) less the portion of the mortgage liability assumed by the other partners (30% x $40,000 = $28,000). However, this would result in a basis of negative $3,000, and a partner's basis can never go below zero. In order to prevent a negative basis, Bea must recognize a gain of $3,000. ###

20. Hatam Persian Restaurant operates as a calendar-year partnership. Hatam's two partners, Afsar and Ted, share profits and losses 60% and 40% respectively. For tax year 2012, Hatam Restaurant had the following income and expense:

•Gross sales	$270,000
•Cost of goods sold	$80,000
•Bank interest income	$2,500
•Wages paid	$50,000
•Short-term capital loss	$5,000

Compute the partnership's ordinary income and flow-through amounts to the partners:

A. Afsar: ordinary income $85,500 and short-term capital loss $3,000; Ted: ordinary income $57,000 and short-term capital loss $2,000.

B. Afsar: ordinary income $82,500; Ted: ordinary income $55,000.

C. Afsar: ordinary income $81,000, interest income $1,500, and short-term capital loss $3,000; Ted: ordinary income $54,000, interest income $1,000, and short-term capital loss $2,000.

D. Afsar: ordinary income $84,000, interest income $1,500, and short-term capital loss $3,000. Ted: ordinary income $56,000, interest income $1,000, and short-term capital loss $2,000.'

The answer is D. Interest income and short-term capital losses are separately stated items that flow through to each partner, and retain their character. The other items listed are components of ordinary income, determined as follows: gross sales of $270,000, less cost of goods sold of $80,000 and wages of $50,000 = ordinary income of $140,000. Absent any provisions in the partnership agreement to the contrary, both ordinary income and the separately stated items would be allocated according to the 60%/40% profit-sharing arrangement. ###

21. The Bissinger Cosmetics Partnership generated income and expenses as stated below. What is the amount of ordinary income (loss) from trade or business activities that Bissinger should report for 2012?

- Employee wages: $15,000
- Rental real estate income: $20,000
- Charitable contributions: $500
- Cost of goods sold: $10,000
- Income from cosmetics sales: $75,000

A. $65,000.
B. $69,500.
C. $50,000.
D. 30,000.

The answer is C. Bissinger's ordinary income for 2012 is equal to its sales income less cost of goods sold and wages ($75,000 - $10,000 - $15,000 = $50,000). The income from rental real estate and the charitable contributions must be separately stated on the partnership's tax return. ###

22. Davisville Partnership sold a capital asset to Winters Partnership at a loss of $50,000. Davisville had held the property for five months. Davisville is owned 30% by Marvin, 30% by LaTroy, and 40% by Geoff, Marvin's brother. Winters Partnership is owned 80% by Dixon Corporation. Marvin owns 25% of the stock of Dixon Corporation and Geoff's daughter owns 60% of Dixon Corporation. How much of the loss should Davisville Partnership recognize for tax purposes on their tax return for the year of the sale?

A. $0.
B. $3,000.
C. $35,000.
D. $50,000.

The answer is A. A loss is not allowed from a sale or exchange of property directly or indirectly between a partnership and a person whose direct or indirect interest in the capital or profits of the partnership is more than 50%. In this case, Marvin and Geoff own a combined interest of 70% in the Davisville Partnership, and they indirectly own over 50% in Winters Partnership. (Since Marvin and Geoff's daughter own a combined interest of 85% in Dixon Corporation, their indirect interest in Winters Partnership is 85% times 80%, or 68%.) ###

Unit 12: Partnership Distributions & Liquidations

> **More Reading:**
> Publication 541, *Partnerships*

Partnership Distributions

Partnership distributions include the following:

- Distributions of the partnership's earnings for the current or prior years
- A withdrawal by a partner in anticipation of the current year's earnings
- A complete or partial liquidation of a partner's interest
- A distribution to all partners in a complete liquidation of the partnership

A partnership is not a taxable entity, and its income and loss flow through and are reported on the partners' individual tax returns. Each partner is taxed on his distributive share of income, whether or not it is actually distributed. Therefore, when distributions are made to the partners in connection with these earnings, they are generally not taxable.

A partnership distribution is not taken into account in determining the partner's distributive share of the partnership income or loss. If any gain or loss from the distribution is recognized by the partner, it must be reported on his return for the tax year in which the distribution is received. Cash or property withdrawn by a partner in anticipation of the current year's earnings is treated as a distribution received on the last day of the partnership's tax year. A partner's adjusted basis in his partnership interest is decreased (but not below zero) by the cash and adjusted basis of property distributed to the partner.

A partnership generally does not recognize any gain or loss because of distributions it makes to partners. The partnership may be able to elect to adjust the basis of its undistributed property.

Example: The adjusted basis of Angela's partnership interest is $14,000. She receives a distribution of $8,000 cash and land that has an adjusted basis of $2,000 and a fair market value of $3,000. The distribution decreases the basis of her partnership interest to $4,000 [$14,000 − ($8,000 + $2,000)]. Because the cash received does not exceed the basis of her partnership interest, Angela does not recognize any gain on the distribution. Any gain on the land will be recognized when she later sells it.

Unless there is a complete liquidation of a partner's interest, the basis of property (other than cash) distributed to the partner is its adjusted basis to the partnership immediately before the distribution. However, the basis of the property distributed to the partner cannot be more than the adjusted basis of his interest in the partnership, reduced by any cash received in the same transaction.

> **Example:** The basis of Mike's partnership interest is $10,000. He receives a distribution of $4,000 cash and a parcel of land that has an adjusted basis to the partnership of $8,000. His basis for the land is limited to $6,000 ($10,000 - $4,000, the cash he receives), since the total amount cannot exceed his partnership interest. After the distribution, his partnership basis would be zero.

When a partnership distributes the following items, the distribution may be treated as a sale or exchange of property rather than a distribution:

- Unrealized receivables or substantially appreciated inventory items distributed in exchange for any part of the partner's interest in other partnership property, including cash
- Other property, including cash, distributed in exchange for any part of a partner's interest in unrealized receivables or substantially appreciated inventory items

This treatment does not apply to the following distributions:

- A distribution of property to the partner who contributed the same property to the partnership
- Payments made to a retiring partner or successor in interest of a deceased partner that are the partner's distributive share of partnership income or guaranteed payments

Any gain or loss on a sale or exchange of unrealized receivables or inventory items a partner received in a distribution is treated as ordinary income or loss.

> **Example:** Marcia was a partner in Illuminated, a business that sold handmade candles. In 2010, the store closed and Marcia received, through dissolution of the partnership, inventory that has a basis of $19,000. She sells the entire inventory for $24,000. The $5,000 gain is taxed as ordinary income. If she had held the inventory for more than five years, her gain would have been capital gain, provided the inventory was a capital asset in her hands at the time of sale.

Distributions in Excess of Basis

A partner cannot have a negative partnership basis. If a partner has distributions that exceed his adjusted basis during any tax year, the excess is generally treated as a capital gain to the partner. This can occur, for example, when a partner's share of the decrease in partnership liabilities during the taxable year and the cash distributions received by the partner during the taxable year exceed the basis of the partner's partnership interest.

However, if a partner's losses for the year exceed his basis, the losses are limited to the basis of his partnership interest (with some exceptions to this rule in a partnership liquidation). Any partnership losses and deductions that exceed the partner's basis may be carried forward indefinitely until the partner's basis in the partnership increases.

If a partnership acquires a partner's debt and extinguishes the debt by distributing it to the partner, the partner will recognize capital gain or loss to the extent the fair market value of the debt differs from the basis of the debt. The partner is treated as having satisfied the debt for its fair market value. If the issue price of the debt exceeds its FMV when distributed, the partner may have to include the excess amount in income as canceled debt.

Sale of a Partnership Interest

A partnership interest is a capital asset. Typically that means any gain or loss on the sale or exchange of a partnership interest is treated as a capital gain or loss. Gain or loss is calculated as the difference between the amount realized and the adjusted basis of the partner's interest in the partnership. If the selling partner is relieved of any partnership liabilities, he must include the liability relief as part of the amount realized for his interest.

An exchange of partnership interests generally does not qualify as a nontaxable exchange of like-kind property. This applies regardless of whether they are general or limited partnership interests or interests in the same or different partnerships.

> **Example:** Selene became a partner in the Rincon Partnership by contributing cash to the formation of the partnership. The adjusted basis of her partnership interest at the end of 2012 is $20,000, which includes her $15,000 share of partnership liabilities. Selene sells her interest in the partnership for $10,000 in cash on December 31, 2012. At the time of the sale, she had been paid her share of the partnership income for the tax year. Selene realizes $25,000 from the sale of her partnership interest ($10,000 cash payment + $15,000 liability relief). She must report $5,000 ($25,000 realized − $20,000 basis) as a capital gain.

Liquidation of a Partnership

When a partnership dissolves or stops doing business, it is called a partnership liquidation. A partnership can dissolve when a partner dies, or when one partner drops out of the business.

The basis of property received in complete liquidation of a partner's interest is the adjusted basis of the partner's interest in the partnership reduced by any cash distributed to the partner in the same transaction. A partner's holding period for property distributed to him includes the period held by the partnership, and if contributed to the partnership by a partner, the period held by that partner also.

> **Example:** Tim's basis in his partnership interest is $20,000. In a distribution in liquidation of his entire interest, he receives a delivery truck and a utility trailer (neither of which is inventory or unrealized receivables). The truck has an adjusted basis to the partnership of $15,000 and an FMV of $15,000. The trailer has an adjusted basis to the partnership of $15,000 and an FMV of $5,000. To figure his basis in each property, Tim first assigns a basis of $15,000 to the truck and $15,000 to the trailer. This leaves a $10,000 basis decrease (the $30,000 total of the assigned basis minus the $20,000 allocable basis). He allocates the entire $10,000 to the trailer (its unrealized depreciation). Tim's basis in the truck is $15,000, and his basis in the trailer is $5,000 ($15,000 - $10,000).

Sometimes, a partnership will dissolve with unamortized organizational or start-up expenses. If a partnership is liquidated before the end of the amortization period, the unamortized amount of qualifying organizational costs and start-up expenses can be deducted in the partnership's final tax year.

Liquidation at Partner's Retirement or Death

Payments made by the partnership to a retiring partner or a deceased partner's estate or in liquidation of the interest of a retiring or deceased partner in exchange for his interest in partnership property are considered a distribution, not a distributive share or guaranteed payment that could give rise to a deduction for the partnership. A retiring partner or deceased partner is treated as a partner until his interest in the partnership has been completely liquidated.

Recognizing Loss on Liquidating Distribution

In a partnership liquidation, the liquidating distributions are similar to regular distributions except that the partner may recognize a loss if the total basis of the cash and property received is less than the partner's basis in the partnership. A partner cannot recognize a loss on a partnership distribution unless all of the following requirements are met:

- The adjusted basis of the partner's interest in the partnership exceeds the distribution.
- The partner's entire interest in the partnership is liquidated.
- The distribution is in cash, unrealized receivables, or inventory items.

Partnership Termination

A partnership generally terminates when one of the following events takes place:

- All its operations are discontinued and no part of any business, financial operation, or venture is continued by any of its partners in a partnership.
- At least 50% of the total interest in partnership capital and profits is sold or exchanged within a 12-month period, including a sale or exchange to another partner.

The partnership's tax year ends on the date of termination. If a partnership is terminated before the end of its regular tax year, Form 1065 must be filed for the short tax year from the beginning of the tax year through the date of termination. The return is due the fifteenth day of the fourth month following the date of termination.

If a partnership is converted into an LLC classified as a partnership, the conversion does not terminate the partnership, and there is no sale, exchange, or termination of partnership interests. The partnership's tax year does not close, and the LLC can continue to use the partnership's taxpayer identification number.

If a business partnership breaks up and one of the former partners is insolvent and cannot pay any of the partnership's debts, existing partners will sometimes be forced to pay more than their share of the liabilities. If a partner pays any part of the insolvent partner's share of the debts, he can take a bad debt deduction.

Related Party Transactions

A partnership cannot deduct a loss on the sale or trade of property if the transaction is directly or indirectly between related parties. Losses will not be allowed from a sale or exchange of property (other than an interest in the partnership) directly or indirectly between a partnership and a person whose direct or indirect interest in the capital or profits of the partnership is more than 50%.

If the sale or exchange is between two partnerships in which the same persons directly or indirectly own more than 50% of the capital or profits interests in each partnership, no deduction of a loss is allowed.

Example: George and Lynn are siblings. Lynn is a 60% partner in the Buildrite Machinery Partnership, and George is a 55% partner in the Schlutter Partnership. If the partnerships sell property to each other, no loss will be allowed in the transaction, because the partnerships are considered related parties. Losses will instead be suspended until the property is eventually disposed of in a nonrelated party transaction.

The basis of each partner's interest in the partnership is decreased (but not below zero) by the partner's share of the disallowed loss.

If the purchaser later sells the property, only the gain realized that is greater than the loss not allowed will be taxable. If any gain from the sale of the property is not recognized because of this rule, the basis of each partner's interest in the partnership is increased by the partner's share of that gain.

Unit 12: Questions

1. The adjusted basis of Tammy's partnership interest is $24,000. She receives a distribution of $9,000 cash and machinery that has an adjusted basis of $1,000 and a fair market value of $7,000. How much gain should Tammy recognize on this distribution?

A. $0.
B. $1,000.
C. $2,000.
D. $7,000.

The answer is A. No gain or loss is recognized in this transaction. Because the sum of cash received and adjusted basis does not exceed the basis of her partnership interest, Tammy does not recognize any gain on the distribution. Any gain on the machinery will be recognized when she sells it. ###

2. The adjusted basis of Steve's partnership interest is $10,000. He receives a distribution of $4,000 cash and a utility van that has an adjusted basis to the partnership of $9,000 and a fair market value of $12,000. This was not a liquidating distribution. What is Steve's basis in the van?

A. $5,000.
B. $6,000.
C. $12,000.
D. $16,000.

The answer is B. Steve's basis for the van is limited to $6,000 ($10,000 basis – $4,000, the cash he receives). His basis in the van is limited by Steve's basis in his partnership interest. ###

3. Marty is permanently retiring from Sunnyside Partnership this year. His adjusted basis in the partnership is $50,000. He receives a distribution of $65,000 in cash. How would Marty report this transaction?

A. $15,000 gain upon distribution.
B. $50,000 gain upon distribution.
C. $65,000 capital gain.
D. $65,000 ordinary income.

The answer is A. Marty must recognize $15,000 of gain. This is the difference between his adjusted basis in the partnership and the amount of his distribution ($65,000 - $50,000). Upon receipt of the distribution, a retiring partner or the successor in interest of a deceased partner recognizes gain to the extent that any cash (and marketable securities treated as cash) distributed is more than the partner's adjusted basis in the partnership. ###

4. Bart and Ellen are equal partners in B&E Partnership. In 2012, the partnership breaks up. Bart is insolvent, and Ellen becomes responsible for paying a portion of his partnership debt. Which of the following statements is true?

A. Ellen cannot take a bad debt deduction for any debt that the partnership incurred.
B. Bart is not responsible for paying any of his liabilities after dissolution.
C. Ellen can take a bad debt deduction for any amount that she must pay that is not her share of the partnership liability.
D. None of the above.

The answer is C. Ellen is allowed to take a bad debt deduction for the liabilities she must pay that are not her share of partnership liabilities. If a business partnership dissolves and one of the former partners is insolvent and cannot pay his share of the partnership's debts, other partners may have to pay more than their respective shares. If a partner pays any part of the insolvent partner's share of the debts, he can take a bad debt deduction for the amount paid. ###

5. The adjusted basis of Hugo's partnership interest is $150,000. He receives a nonliquidating distribution of $80,000 cash and land that has an adjusted basis to the partnership of $100,000. What is the basis of the land in Hugo's hands?

A. $70,000.
B. $100,000.
C. $120,000.
D. $150,000.

The answer is A. Hugo's basis for the distributed property is limited to $70,000 ($150,000 - $80,000, the cash received). In a nonliquidating distribution, the basis of property (other than cash) distributed to the partner by a partnership is the adjusted basis to the partnership immediately before the distribution. However, the basis of the property distributed to the partner cannot be more than the adjusted basis of his interest in the partnership. ###

6. Bill owns a 75% capital interest in the Shanahan Partnership. Bill's wife, Veronica, is a 65% owner in the Underdahl Partnership. Bill and Veronica file separate tax returns and keep all their books and records separate. Shanahan Partnership sells Underdahl Partnership a factory machine for $7,600. Shanahan's partnership basis in the machinery is $10,000. What is Shanahan Partnership's deductible loss?

A. $0.
B. $2,400.
C. $7,600.
D. $10,000.

The answer is A. Shanahan Partnership's loss of $2,400 is not deductible. A loss on the sale or exchange of property between related persons is not deductible. This applies to both direct and indirect transactions. The fact that Bill and Veronica file separate tax returns does not prevent them from being related parties for purposes of this transaction. ###

7. In 2012, Laney sold her partnership interest for $45,000. Her adjusted basis at the time of the sale was $29,500, which includes her $12,500 share of partnership liabilities. When she initially invested in the partnership, she contributed $10,000 worth of equipment. There was no profit or loss at the partnership level at the time she sold her interest. What is the amount and nature of her income or loss from the sale of her partnership interest in 2012?

A. $7,500 ordinary loss.
B. $10,000 capital gain.
C. $12,500 ordinary income.
D. $28,000 capital gain.

The answer is D. When Laney sold her partnership interest, she was relieved of her $12,500 share of the partnership's liabilities, so her adjusted basis for purposes of calculating her gain on sale of the interest is $17,000 ($29,500 - $12,500). Thus, her gain is $28,000 (proceeds of $45,000 less adjusted basis of $17,000). Approached differently, the amount of liability relieved from Laney upon sale of her interest might be viewed as additional proceeds, but her gain would still be $28,000 ($45,000 + $12,500 - $29,500). As a partnership interest is a capital asset, any gain or loss recognized on the sale of the interest is typically treated as a capital gain or loss. ###

8. The adjusted basis of Adrian's partnership interest is $17,500. He received a distribution of $9,000 cash and a piece of land with an adjusted basis of $2,500 to the partnership and a fair market value of $4,000. What is the gain to be recognized at the time of these distributions?

A. $0.
B. $1,500.
C. $4,500.
D. $6,000.

The answer is A. Because the total of cash and the basis of property distributed ($9,000 + $2,500 = $11,500) does not exceed Adrian's adjusted basis of $17,500 in his partnership interest, he will recognize no gain as a result of the distribution. He assumes the partnership's adjusted basis of $2,500 in the property received, and will recognize gain or loss if he later sells this property. ###

9. Alice's outside basis in Dogan Tiles Partnership on January 1, 2012 was $11,000. She is a 50% partner and shares profits and losses in the same ratio. For 2012, the partnership's ordinary business income was $40,000 and tax-exempt interest income was $700. If the partnership were to liquidate on December 31, 2012, what would be Alice's basis for determining gain or loss?

A. $24,900.
B. $30,750.
C. $31,350.
D. $30,300.

The answer is C. Alice's basis on December 31, 2012 would be determined as follows:

Basis at January 1, 2012	$11,000
50% share of ordinary business income	$20,000
50% share of tax-exempt interest income	$350
Basis at December 31, 2012	$31,350

Calculation:
($11,000 + $20,000 + $350 = $31,350) ###

10. Nora, a partner in the Maass Partnership, receives $1,000 cash and property worth $2,000, in which Maass has a basis of $1,500. Nora's outside basis at the time of the distribution is $20,000. The partnership has assets of $40,000 and no outstanding liabilities. This distribution is made at the end of the year after partnership income (loss) has been recorded. How much gain should Nora recognize on the distribution and what is her basis in the property received?

A. Nora recognizes a gain of $500 on the property received and her basis in the property is $2,000.
B. Nora recognizes gain of $1,500 on the property and cash received. Her basis in the property received is $3,500.
C. Nora recognizes no gain on the property received. Her basis in the property received is $1,500.
D. Nora recognizes a gain of $1,000. Her basis in the property received is $1,500.

The answer is C. Nora recognizes no gain because the total of cash and the basis of property received does not exceed her basis in the partnership. She assumes the partnership's basis of $1,500 in the property received, and may recognize gain or loss if she later sells the property.
###

Unit 13: C Corporations in General

More Reading:
Publication 542, *Corporations*
Publication 544, *Sales and Other Dispositions of Assets*
Instructions for Form 1120, *U.S. Corporation Income Tax Return*

Most major companies are C corporations, which are taxed under sub-chapter C of the Internal Revenue Code. A C corporation can own property in its own name and it can be sued directly. The shareholders who own stock in a corporation do not own its individual assets. Individual shareholders are pro-tected from legal liability, except in very unusual circumstances.

The IRS requires certain businesses to be taxed as corporations. The fol-lowing businesses formed after 1996 are automatically treated as corporations:

- A business formed under a federal or state law that refers to it as a corporation
- A business formed under a state law that refers to it as a joint-stock company or joint-stock association
- Insurance companies
- Certain banks
- A business owned by a state or local government
- A business specifically required to be taxed as a corporation by the IRC (for example, certain publicly-traded partnerships)
- Certain foreign businesses
- Any other business that elects to be taxed as a corporation and files Form 8832, *Entity Classification Election*

Basic Concepts

1. A C corporation enjoys perpetual life and limited liability.
2. Earnings of a C corporation may be taxed twice: first at the corporate level and again at the shareholder level if they are distributed as dividends. Shareholders of a C corporation cannot deduct corporate losses. A corpora-tion must maintain a list of all its shareholders, and generally must conduct at least one shareholder meeting per year.
3. A C corporation must file a charter, issue stock, and be overseen by a board of directors. A C corporation may have a single owner-shareholder or mil-lions of shareholders.
4. Corporate existence starts when the articles of incorporation are filed with the state office that handles incorporations (e.g., usually the Secretary of State), along with any required filing fees.

5. If a C corporation liquidates, it will recognize gain or loss on the sale or distribution of its assets. Corporate shareholders then recognize gain or loss on the surrender of their stock to the corporation.

6. A C corporation may sell common or preferred stock with different voting rights.

7. One of the major advantages of a C corporation is the ability for shareholder-employees to receive tax-free employee fringe benefits that are 100% deductible to the corporation as a business expense.

C Corporation Filing Requirements

All domestic corporations in existence for any part of a tax year (including corporations in bankruptcy) must file an income tax return, regardless of their taxable income. A C corporation typically files Form 1120, *U.S. Corporation Income Tax Return*, but it may file Form 1120-A if its gross receipts, total income, and total assets are each under $500,000.

A corporation must continue to file tax returns even if there is no business activity or profits. However, it does not have to file after it has formally dissolved. The only exception to this filing requirement is for tax-exempt organizations (which may be organized as corporations). Exempt organizations file Form 990 rather than Form 1120.

A corporation filing a short-period return (for example, a corporation that dissolves in the middle of the year) must generally file by the fifteenth day of the third month after the short period ends. This means that a calendar-year corporation must file its tax return by March 15 of the following year.

Example: Greenbook Inc. is a domestic corporation with a fiscal year tax year-end of March 31. Greenbook must file Form 1120 by June 15.
Example: Finman Design Corporation's tax year ends December 31. It must file its Form 1120 by March 15.

Electronic filing using the Electronic Federal Tax Payment System (EFTPS) is *mandatory* for C corporations that have $10 million or more in assets and at least 250 or more returns of any type, including information returns such as Forms W-2 or Forms 1099.

A corporation must file Form 7004, *Automatic Extension of Time to File Certain Business Income Tax, Information, and Other Returns,* to request a six-month extension of time to file its income tax return. Form 7004 does not extend the time for paying the tax due on the return. Interest, and possibly penalties, will be charged on any part of the tax due and not paid. The interest is figured from the original due date of the return to the date of payment.

A penalty for late filing is assessed at 5% of any unpaid tax for each month the return is late, up to a maximum of 25% of the unpaid tax on the return. The late filing penalty is reduced by any late payment penalty for the same period. The minimum penalty for any return that is over 60 days late is the *smaller* of the tax due on the return, or $135. The penalty for late payment of corporate income tax is one half of 1% of the unpaid tax for each month that the tax is not paid, up to a maximum of 25% of the unpaid tax.

These penalties will not be imposed if the corporation shows reasonable cause for not paying or filing on time.

Estimated Tax Payments

Corporations are required to make estimated tax payments if they expect their tax due to be $500 or more during the taxable year. Penalties apply if estimated tax payments are not made on time. Most business entities, including corporations, are now required to use EFTPS to make their estimated tax payments. Installments are due on a quarterly basis, on the fifteenth day of the fourth, sixth, ninth, and twelfth months of the corporation's taxable year. So, for example, a calendar year corporation is required to make estimated payments on April 15, June 15, September 15, and December 15.

Example: Longinotti Textiles Corporation's tax year ends January 31. Estimated tax payments are due on May 15, July 15, October 15, and January 15 (of the following year).

There is no penalty for underpayment of estimated tax if the tax is less than $500, or if each quarterly estimated tax payment is *at least* 25% of the corporation's current-year tax.

There is also no underpayment penalty if each estimated tax installment is at least 25% of the income tax on the prior year return. However, this provision will not apply in the following instances:

- If the prior tax year was a short year (less than 12 months)
- If the corporation did not file a return for the prior year
- If the prior year tax return showed zero tax liability
- If the corporation had at least $1 million of taxable income in any of the last three years

Corporate Refunds and Amended Returns

Corporations may use Form 1139, *Corporate Application for Tentative Refund,* or Form 1120X, *Amended U.S. Corporation Income Tax Return,* to apply for a refund. A corporation can get a refund faster by using Form 1139.

The corporation cannot file Form 1139 before filing the return for a corporation's capital loss year, but it must file Form 1139 no later than one year after the year it sustains the capital loss.

If the corporation does not file Form 1139, it must file Form 1120X (an amended return) to apply for a refund. The corporation must file Form 1120X within three years of the due date, including extensions, for filing the return for a year in which it sustains a loss.

If a corporation accidentally overpays its estimated tax, it may use Form 4466, *Corporation Application for Quick Refund of Overpayment of Estimated Tax,* to obtain a quick refund of its estimated tax payments. Form 4466 may be used if a corporation's overpayment is at least 10% of its anticipated tax liability and at least $500.

Corporate Taxation

Unlike a partnership or an S corporation, a C corporation is not a pass-through entity. This means that the earnings of a C corporation are taxed twice. Corporate income is taxed when it is earned and then taxed again when it is distributed to shareholders as dividends. A corporation does not receive a tax deduction for the distribution of dividends to its shareholders.

Income does not retain its character when it is distributed to the shareholders. A corporation can have revenue from many different sources, including sales of products, services, and investment income. If, for example, a C corporation has rental income, it pays tax on this and any other sources of income at the corporate level.

When its after-tax income is distributed to shareholders, the rental income does not retain its character as rental income. It is distributed merely as a dividend. This is true even if the income is tax-exempt income to the corporation. For example, a C corporation may earn tax-exempt income from investing in municipal bonds. However, if this income is used to make distributions to shareholders, the distributions will be taxed as dividends to the shareholders.

> **Example:** In 2012, Riden Paper Products receives tax-exempt income from bonds. The C corporation subsequently distributes income to its shareholders as taxable dividends. Even though a portion of the income was originally tax-exempt, it does not retain its tax-exempt character when distributions are made to the shareholders. In contrast, in the case of an S corporation or a partnership, the income would have retained its character when it was passed through to the partners or S corporation shareholders.

> **Example:** Super Sailing Inc. is a calendar-year C corporation with 20 shareholders. After deducting business expenses, Super Sailing has $150,000 in taxable net income in 2012. The corporation also earns $4,000 in interest from municipal bonds. The $4,000 of tax-exempt bond interest is excluded from the corporation's taxable income. In December 2012, Super Sailing also distributes $120,000 to its shareholders. The company cannot take a tax deduction for the distribution. Each shareholder has an equal stake in the company, so each one receives $6,000 in dividend income ($120,000 ÷ 20 = $6,000). Each shareholder is required to recognize $6,000 in dividend income for 2012.

Accumulated Earnings Tax

A corporation is allowed to accumulate its earnings for a possible expansion or other bona fide business reasons. However, a corporation may be subject to the accumulated earnings tax if it does not distribute enough of its profits to shareholders. This tax was instituted to prevent corporations from hoarding income in order to avoid income tax for its shareholders by permitting earnings to accumulate instead of being distributed.

The tax is levied at a rate of **15% of accumulated taxable income**. If the accumulated earnings tax applies, interest is also assessed from the date the corporate return was originally due, without extensions.

An accumulation of $250,000 or less is generally considered reasonable for most businesses. However, for PSCs, the limit is $150,000. Reasonable needs of the business include the following:

- Specific, definite, and feasible plans for use of the earnings accumulation in the business.
- The amount necessary to redeem the corporation's stock included in a deceased shareholder's gross estate, if the amount does not exceed the reasonably anticipated total estate and inheritance taxes and funeral and administration expenses incurred by the shareholder's estate.

The absence of a bona fide business reason for a corporation's accumulated earnings may be indicated by many different circumstances, such as a lack of regular distributions to its shareholders or withdrawals by the shareholders classified as personal loans. However, actual moves to expand the business generally qualify as a *bona fide* use of the accumulated income. Examples of qualified accumulations include:

- The expansion of the company to a new area or a new facility
- Acquiring another business through the purchase of stock or assets
- Providing for reasonable estimates of product liability losses

The fact that a corporation has an unreasonable accumulation of earnings is sufficient to establish liability for the accumulated earnings tax unless the corporation can show the earnings were not accumulated to allow its individual shareholders to avoid income tax.

Corporate Alternative Minimum Tax

The tax laws give special treatment to some types of income and allow special deductions and credits for some types of expenses. As these laws allow some corporations with substantial economic income to significantly reduce their regular tax liabilities, the corporate alternative minimum tax (AMT) is intended to ensure that corporations pay at least a minimum amount of tax on their income. A corporation owes AMT if its tentative minimum tax is more than its regular tax.

Small corporations are exempt from corporate AMT. Most corporations will automatically qualify for the exemption in their first year of existence. After its first year, a corporation is considered a small corporation if its average annual gross receipts for the prior three years (or portion thereof) do not exceed $7.5 million ($5 million for its first three-year period).

If the corporation fails the $7.5 million test for any year, the corporation will become ineligible for the AMT exemption for that year and all subsequent years. If a corporation fails to qualify under the first year's $5 million limit, it will never qualify for the AMT exemption even if its gross receipts remain under the $7.5 million exemption limit.

The starting point for the determination of income for AMT purposes is the corporation's regular taxable income. Regular taxable income is modified by a series of additional computations called adjustments and preferences. Adjustments can either increase or decrease taxable income, whereas preferences are calculated on a property-by-property basis and only apply to the extent that they are positive.

Adjustments include a portion of accelerated depreciation on buildings and equipment, amortization of pollution control facilities, mining exploration and development expenses, income reported under the completed contract method of accounting, and installment sales income.

Corporations use Form 4626, *Alternative Minimum Tax-Corporations*, to figure their minimum tax for AMT purposes. Corporations use Form 8827, *Credit for Prior Year Minimum Tax*, to figure the minimum tax credit, if any, for alternative minimum tax incurred in prior tax years and any minimum tax credit carry forward. A minimum AMT tax credit may be carried forward indefinitely.

Accounting Methods for C Corporations

Like other entity types, C corporations may use any permissible accounting method for keeping track of income and expenses. Permissible methods include:

- Cash
- Accrual
- Special methods of accounting for certain items of income and expenses
- Hybrid method using elements of the methods above

A corporation with more than $5 million in average annual gross receipts is required to use the accrual method. If a corporation produces inventory, then the accrual method is generally required for sales and purchases of merchandise, unless average gross receipts are $1 million or less.

Nonaccrual Experience Method for Bad Debts

The nonaccrual experience method is a method of accounting for bad debts. If a corporation uses the accrual method of accounting and qualifies to use the nonaccrual experience method for bad debts, it is not required to accrue service-related income that it expects to be uncollectible.

Accrual-method corporations are not required to maintain accruals for certain amounts from the performance of services that, on the basis of their experience, will not be collected, if:

- The services are in the fields of health, law, engineering, architecture, accounting, actuarial science, performing arts, or consulting (personal service corporations); or
- The corporation's average annual gross receipts for the three prior tax years do not exceed $5 million.

This provision does not apply if the corporation charges interest on late payments, or if the business charges customers any penalty for failure to pay an amount timely. A business is permitted to use the nonaccrual experience method only for amounts earned for performing services. It cannot use this method for amounts owed from activities such as lending money, selling goods, or acquiring receivables.

Reconciliation of Book Income vs. Tax Income

Differences in accounting rules for financial reporting (book income) and tax reporting can lead to differences in the amounts of income reported to shareholders and tax authorities. Preparation of a C corporation's income tax return includes a reconciliation of book income to taxable income. The differences in book and taxable income are reconciled in Schedule M-1 of Form 1120 by small corporations with less than $10 million in assets. Larger corporations with over $10 million in assets use Schedule M-3.[51] Schedule M-3 provides additional information and contains three main sections:

- Financial statement reconciliation
- Detail of income/loss items
- Detail of expenses/deductions

Some examples of items that would be included in the reconciliation on Schedule M-1 or Schedule M-3, if applicable, are:

- Charitable contribution carryover (the amount of charitable contributions that are disallowed for tax purposes and must be carried over to the next taxable year.)
- Travel and entertainment in excess of the allowable 50% limit.
- Income subject to tax that is not included in the books.
- Federal income taxes paid or accrued, which are deductible for accounting purposes but not for tax purposes.
- Advance rental income.

Corporate Formation

A corporation is formed initially by a transfer of money, property, or services by prospective shareholders in exchange for stock in the corporation. For example, when a business is created using a corporate structure or a business previously operated as a partnership or sole proprietorship opts to become a corporation, a transfer of assets to the corporation usually takes place. The transfers of property to corporations have tax consequences to both the corporation and the shareholders.

Contributions to the capital of a corporation are not taxable transactions to the corporation, whether or not they are made by the shareholders. A shareholder will not recognize gain when a cash contribution is made for stock. This is just like when a person purchases stock on the open market for cash. The shareholder's basis in the stock is the amount of cash contributed. However, if a shareholder contributes property to a corporation, he generally recognizes gain and the basis of the contributed property to the corporation is the same as the basis that the shareholder had in the property, after increases for any gain that the shareholder recognized in the exchange.

The basis of property contributed to capital by anyone other than a shareholder is zero.

---

[51] A domestic corporation with total assets of $10 million or more is required to file Schedule M-3, *Net Income (Loss) Reconciliation for Corporations with Total Assets of $10 million or More,* along with its main return.

> **Example:** The city of Omaha, Nebraska gives Madera Corporation a plot of land as an enticement to locate its business operations there. Madera accounts for the property as a contribution to capital. The land has zero basis since the property was contributed by a non-shareholder.

If stock is exchanged for services, the recipient of the stock recognizes taxable income based upon fair market value of the services provided, and that amount is his basis in the stock.

> **Example:** Justin is a web designer who provides web design services to a corporation. He agrees to accept stock as payment, rather than cash. The stock is valued at $5,000. Justin must recognize ordinary income of $5,000 as payment for services he rendered to the corporation. His basis in the stock is $5,000.

There is an exception, however, for situations when property is contributed and the shareholder controls the corporation immediately after the transfer. This is called a *Section 351 transfer,* and is explained next.

Nontaxable Corporate Transfers: Section 351

If a taxpayer transfers property to a corporation in exchange for stock and immediately afterward the taxpayer controls the corporation, the exchange may not be taxable. This rule applies both to individuals and to entities that transfer property to a corporation. The rule also applies whether the corporation is being formed or is already in operation. The effect is to allow the investing shareholder to contribute assets to a corporation without immediate tax consequences, and defer recognition of taxable gain until the stock received is later disposed. This nonrecognition rule does not apply in the following situations:

- The corporation is an investment company.
- The taxpayer transfers the property in a bankruptcy proceeding in exchange for stock that is used to pay creditors.
- The stock is received in exchange for the corporation's debt (other than a security, such as a bond) or for interest on the corporation's debt (including a security) that accrued while the taxpayer held the debt.

In order to be considered in control of a corporation immediately after the exchange, the transferors must own at least 80% of the total combined voting power of all classes of stock entitled to vote and at least 80% of the outstanding shares of each class of nonvoting stock.

> **Example:** Mandy owns an office building. Her basis in the building is $100,000. She organizes a corporation when the building has a fair market value of $300,000. Mandy transfers the building to the corporation for all its authorized capital stock. No gain is recognized by Mandy or the corporation on the transfer.

> **Example:** Aaron and Pedro transfer property with a basis of $100,000 to a corporation in exchange for stock with a fair market value of $300,000. This represents only 75% of each class of stock of the corporation. The other 25% was already issued to someone else. Aaron and Pedro must recognize a taxable gain of $200,000 on the transaction.

This nonrecognition rule does not apply when services are rendered in exchange for stock. The value of stock received for services is income to the recipient.

> **Example:** Wayne is an architect. In 2012, he transfers property worth $35,000 and renders services valued at $3,000 to a corporation in exchange for stock valued at $38,000. Right after the exchange, Wayne owns 85% of the outstanding stock. No gain is recognized on the exchange of property. However, Wayne must recognize ordinary income of $3,000 as payment for services he rendered to the corporation.

If, in addition to stock, the shareholder receives money or property in exchange for the contribution of property, he would recognize gain to the extent of any money received plus the fair market value of property received.

Both the corporation and certain stockholders involved in a nontaxable exchange of property for stock must attach to their income tax returns a complete statement of all facts pertinent to the exchange. Based upon revised regulations issued in 2012, the reporting requirement now applies to stockholders that own 5% or more of a public company or 1% or more of a privately held company.

Assumption of Shareholder Liabilities in a Section 351 Exchange

Generally, when an entity assumes a liability for a taxpayer, this is treated as if the taxpayer had received cash in the amount of the liability relief. However, in the case of a section 351 exchange, a corporation may assume a shareholder's liability without triggering any gain, so long as the liability is less than the shareholder's adjusted basis.

The shareholder's basis in his stock must be reduced by the amount of the liability assumed by the corporation. If the liability assumed exceeds the contributing shareholder's basis, the excess is treated as a gain to the shareholder.

> **Example:** Casey transfers machinery to a corporation in exchange for all of the corporation's outstanding stock. The machinery's FMV at the time of the transfer is $200,000. Casey's basis in the machinery is $80,000. The machinery is encumbered by an outstanding loan of $30,000, which the corporation assumes. In this example, the section 351 exchange is valid, and no gain or loss is recognized in the transaction. Casey's basis in the stock is $50,000 ($80,000 basis of property contributed minus the $30,000 loan that was assumed by the corporation.)

Exclusions from Nonrecognition Treatment

This nonrecognition rule does not apply when the property transferred is of a relatively small value when compared to the value of stock already owned, and the main purpose of the transfer is to qualify for the nonrecognition of gain or loss. Property transferred will not be considered to be of small value if its FMV is at least 10% of the FMV of the stock already owned or to be received by the transferor.

If a group of transferors exchanges property for corporate stock, each transferor does not have to receive stock in proportion to his interest in the property transferred. If a disproportionate transfer takes place, it will be treated for tax purposes in accordance with its true nature. It may be treated as if the stock were first received in proportion and then some of it used to make gifts, pay compensation for services, or to satisfy the transferor's obligations.

If there is no good business reason for the corporation to assume a shareholder's liabilities, or if the main purpose of the exchange is to avoid federal income tax, the assumption is taxable to the shareholder.

If a corporation transfers its stock in satisfaction of indebtedness and the fair market value of its stock is less than the indebtedness, the corporation has income to the extent of the difference from the cancellation of indebtedness. For example, if stock is given to an individual in order to pay for a debt, the transfer does not qualify for nonrecognition treatment.

Corporate Start-up and Organizational Costs

Capital expenditures are costs that cannot be deducted in the year in which they are paid or incurred, and must be capitalized. The general rule is that if the property acquired has a useful life longer than the taxable year, the cost must be capitalized. The cost is then amortized or depreciated over the life of the asset.

The following items related to corporate equity transactions cannot be amortized or deducted:

- Costs associated with issuing and selling stock or securities, such as commissions, professional fees, and printing costs
- Costs associated with the transfer of assets to the corporation

For qualified start-up and organizational costs, a corporation may elect to take an immediate deduction for up to $5,000 of business start-up costs and up to $5,000 of organizational costs, rather than amortize the costs. Any remaining costs must be amortized ratably over a 180-month period. The amortization period starts with the month the corporation begins operating. The $5,000 deduction is reduced (but not below zero) by the amount the total start-up or organizational costs exceed $50,000. If the costs exceed $55,000 or more, the deduction is reduced to zero.

The election is generally made on the corporation's first income tax return, filed by the due date (including extensions) for the tax year in which business begins. However, if the corporation files its return on time without making an election, it can still make an election by filing an amended return within six months of the due date of the return (excluding extensions).

The election to either amortize or capitalize these costs is *irrevocable* and applies for the current tax year and all subsequent years. The corporation must complete and attach Form 4562, *Depreciation and Amortization,* to its corporate tax return. Start-up costs include expenses such as:
- Advertising the business before it actually opens
- Wages for training new employees
- Wages paid to employees during training, and the costs of the training itself

Start-up costs do not include research and development expenses.

To qualify as an organizational cost it must be:
- For the creation of the corporation
- Chargeable to a capital account
- Amortizable over the life of the corporation
- Incurred before the end of the first tax year in which the corporation is in business

Examples of qualifying organizational costs are:
- The cost of temporary directors
- The cost of organizational meetings
- State incorporation fees
- The cost of legal services for writing the corporate bylaws or the corporate charter

If a corporation dissolves or is disposed of before the amortization period is complete, the remaining unamortized costs can be deducted on the corporation's final return.

Unit 13: Questions

1. Carrera Italian Foods Corporation incurred $40,000 in start-up costs when it opened for business in 2012. Instead of deducting the costs, the corporation elected to amortize all of them. What is the minimum period over which these expenses can be recovered?

A. 12 months.
B. 36 months.
C. 60 months.
D. 180 months.

The answer is D. A corporation can choose to amortize start-up expenses over 180 months. ###

2. The accumulated earnings tax is imposed on C corporations that accumulate earnings beyond the reasonable needs of their businesses. Which of the following reasons would not be an example of a qualified accumulation?

A. The expansion of the company to a new area or a new facility.
B. Acquiring another business through the purchase of stock or other assets.
C. Allowing the shareholders to take bona fide loans from the corporation.
D. Providing for reasonable estimates of product liability losses.

The answer is C. Allowing shareholders to draw personal loans from a corporation is not a valid reason for a corporation to accumulate earnings. In fact, this is one of the items the IRS looks for that may lead to imposing the accumulated earnings tax upon a corporation. Making loans to shareholders would allow them to access the corporation's earnings without taking taxable distributions. The accumulated earnings tax is imposed when a corporation tries to avoid income tax by permitting earnings and profits to accumulate instead of being divided or distributed. ###

3. If a corporation's tentative minimum tax (AMT) exceeds the regular tax, the excess amount is:

A. Payable instead of the regular tax.
B. Carried back to abate losses from prior years.
C. Payable in addition to the regular tax, unless a corporation is insolvent.
D. Payable in addition to the regular tax.

The answer is D. If a corporation's tentative minimum tax exceeds the regular tax, the excess amount is payable in addition to the regular tax. ###

4. Which of the following types of domestic business entities will be automatically taxed as a corporation?

1. A joint stock company.
2. An insurance company.
3. Any business formed under a state law that refers to it as a corporation.
4. A single member limited liability company (LLC).

A. All of the above.
B. 1, 2, and 3 only.
C. 3 only.
D. 2 and 3 only.

The answer is B. A single member LLC will be taxed as a sole proprietorship unless an election is made by filing Form 8832, Entity Classification Election. The rest of the choices are automatically required to be taxed as corporations. ###

5. BRB Corporation's fiscal tax year ends June 30. Not counting extensions, what is the due date for its tax return?

A. September 15.
B. April 15.
C. October 15.
D. January 15.

The answer is A. The due date for BRB Corporation's income tax return is September 15. Generally, a corporation must file its income tax return by the fifteenth day of the third month after the end of its tax year. ###

6. The accumulated earnings tax is levied at a rate of _____ on accumulated taxable income.

A. 5%.
B. 10%.
C. 15%.
D. 50%.

The answer is C. The accumulated earnings tax is levied at a rate of 15% of accumulated taxable income. ###

271

7. Nell transfers property with a basis of $200,000 and an FMV of $350,000 to a corporation in exchange for stock with a fair market value of $300,000. This represents 65% of the stock of the corporation. How much gain is recognized by Nell on this transaction?

A. $0.
B. $50,000.
C. $100,000
D. $150,000.

The answer is C. Nell must recognize a taxable gain of $100,000 ($300,000 FMV of stock minus $200,000 basis) on the transaction. IRC section 351 provides that no gain or loss will be recognized if property is transferred to a corporation solely in exchange for stock and immediately after the exchange the shareholder is in control of the corporation. However, Nell did not control the corporation after the transfer. In order to be in control of a corporation, the transferor must own, immediately after the exchange, at least 80% of the total combined voting power of all classes of stock entitled to vote and at least 80% of the outstanding shares of each class of nonvoting stock. Since Nell only has control over 65% of the shares, the exchange is taxable. ###

8. Lisa transfers property worth $35,000 and renders services valued at $3,000 to a corporation in exchange for stock valued at $38,000. Right after the exchange, Lisa owns 85% of the outstanding stock. How much income, if any, must Lisa recognize in this transaction?

A. $0.
B. $3,000.
C. $35,000.
D. $38,000.

The answer is B. Lisa recognizes ordinary income of $3,000 as payment for services she rendered to the corporation. Normally, the exchange of money or property for a controlling interest in a corporation is treated as a nontaxable exchange. However, the exchange of services for stock does not qualify for this treatment. The value of stock received in exchange for services is taxed as income to the recipient. ###

9. What is the penalty for a corporation that fails to make estimated tax payments?

A. One-half of 1% per month, up to a maximum of 25%.
B. 5% per month, up to a maximum of 25%.
C. 5% per month, up to a maximum of 35%.
D. 5% per month, up to a maximum of 100%.

The answer is A. If a corporation fails to make estimated tax payments, there is a late payment penalty of one-half of one percent per month, up to a maximum of 25%. ###

10. Topcare Pet Products, a cash-basis corporation that operates on the calendar year, is required to make estimated tax payments. What are the due dates for the estimated payments?

A. April 15, June 15, September 15, and December 15.
B. January 15, March 15, June 15, September 15, and December 15.
C. March 1, June 1, September 1, and December 1.
D. None of the above.

The answer is A. Installments for corporations are due by the fifteenth day of the fourth, sixth, ninth, and twelfth months of the year. So, for example, a calendar-year corporation would have estimated tax due dates of April 15, June 15, September 15, and December 15. ###

11. Metro Street Cars Corporation had a profitable 2012 and was required to make estimated payments during the year totaling $19,000. However, because of serious economic difficulties, Metro expects to post a loss in 2013. Which statement is true about Metro's required estimated payments?

A. Metro must make a minimum estimated tax payment of $500.
B. Metro must make estimated payments of at least 90% of the prior year's tax liability.
C. Metro is required to pay 100% of the prior year tax liability.
D. Metro is not required to make estimated payments in 2013.

The answer is D. Metro Street Cars Corporation does not have to make estimated payments if it expects to post a loss during the year. A corporation must make installment payments of estimated tax only if it expects its estimated tax for the year to be $500 or more. However, it should be noted that payment of 100% of the prior year's liability, as is answer C, would provide a safe harbor in the event that the corporation's tax liability exceeds the amount estimated. ###

12. Multitasker Corporation realized net income of $300,000 for book purposes in 2012. Included in book net income are the following:

Federal income taxes	$4,000
Excess of capital losses over capital gains	$10,000
Tax exempt interest income	$5,000

What is Multitasker's taxable income?

A. $290,000.
B. $304,000.
C. $280,000.
D. $309,000.

The answer is D. Multitasker's taxable income is determined as follows:

Net income per books	$300,000
Plus federal income tax expense per books	$4,000
Plus excess of capital losses over capital gains	$10,000
Less tax exempt interest income	($5,000)
Taxable income	**$309,000**

###

13. Lori and Marcus each transfer property with a basis of $10,000 to a corporation in exchange for stock with a fair market value of $30,000. The total stock received by them represents 75% of the corporation's stock. The other 25% of the corporation's stock was issued earlier to Anne, an unrelated person. The taxable consequences are:

A. None, because it is a transfer of property for stock.
B. Lori and Marcus each recognize a gain of $20,000.
C. Lori and Marcus each recognize a gain of $30,000.
D. 80% of the transaction is recognized as a taxable gain.

The answer is B. If a shareholder contributes property to a corporation, he generally recognizes gain. The basis of the contributed property to the corporation is the same as the basis that the shareholder had in the property, after increase for any gain that the shareholder recognized in the exchange. There is an exception for situations in which property is contributed and the shareholder controls the corporation immediately after the transfer. In order to be considered in control of a corporation immediately after the exchange, the transferors must own at least 80% of the total combined voting power of all classes of stock entitled to vote and at least 80% of the outstanding shares of each class of nonvoting stock. In this case, Lori and Marcus do not own at least 80% of the corporation immediately afterward, so the exception does not apply. ###

14. Kathleen transferred a factory building with an adjusted basis of $70,000 and a fair market value of $110,000 to the Carpentaria Corporation in exchange for 100% of Carpenteria Corporation stock and $20,000 cash. The building was subject to a mortgage of $25,000, which Carpenteria Corporation assumed. The fair market value of the stock was $75,000. Which is the amount of Kathleen's realized gain and recognized gain?

A. $25,000 realized gain; $25,000 recognized gain.
B. $50,000 realized gain; $40,000 recognized gain.
C. $50,000 realized gain; $20,000 recognized gain.
D. $35,000 realized gain; $20,000 recognized gain.

The answer is C. In situations where a shareholder contributes property for stock in a corporation and then controls the corporation immediately after the transfer, she typically would not recognize gain. However, if the shareholder receives money or property in addition to the corporation's stock in exchange for her contribution of property, she would recognize gain to the extent of any money received plus the fair market value of property received. In this case, Kathleen's realized gain is calculated as follows:

Fair value of stock received	$75,000
Cash received	$20,000
Mortgage assumed by corporation	$25,000
Total fair value received	$120,000
Adjusted basis of property	($70,000)
Realized gain	**$50,000**

Kathleen recognizes gain only to the extent of the cash received ($20,000). ###

Unit 14: Corporate Transactions

More Reading:
Publication 542, *Corporations*

Unlike S corporations and partnerships, a C corporation is not a pass-through entity. For federal income tax purposes, a C corporation is recognized as a separate taxpaying entity. A corporation conducts business, realizes net income or loss, pays taxes, and distributes profits to its shareholders. Certain items are unique to C corporations, which we will review in this unit.

Capital Gains and Losses

C corporations are subject to their own tax rate schedules, which may vary from year to year as Congress adjusts the lowest and highest rates.

Unlike the capital gains of individuals, the capital gains of corporations are taxed at the same rate as ordinary income. A corporation figures its capital gains and losses much like an individual. However, in the case of a C corporation, capital losses are only deductible up to the amount of its capital gains. A C corporation is not allowed to offset capital losses against its other income the way individuals can (up to a limit).

If a corporation has an excess capital loss, it may carry the loss back or forward to other tax years and deduct it from any net capital gains that occurred in those years. The default election is for a corporation to carry back its capital losses to the earliest of three preceding years in which it had net capital gains; any remaining losses may be carried forward a maximum of five years.

A capital loss from another year cannot produce or increase a net operating loss in the year to which it is carried back. In other words, corporations can carry capital losses only to years that would otherwise have had a net capital gain.

There are some instances in which longer carryback and carryforward periods are allowed. Capital losses that are a result of foreign expropriation[52] may not be carried back, but may be carried forward for ten years. In the case of a regulated investment company (RIC), net capital losses may be carried forward eight years.

When a corporation carries back or carries forward a capital loss, the loss does not retain its character as a long-term loss. All capital loss carryforwards and carrybacks are treated as short-term losses. A C corporation cannot carry back capital losses to any year when it was previously an S corporation.

---

[52] This is when a foreign nation expropriates a corporation's assets for its own use.

Example: In 2012, a calendar-year corporation has a capital gain of $3,000 and a capital loss of $9,000. The capital gain offsets some of the capital loss, leaving a net capital loss of $6,000. The corporation treats this $6,000 as a short-term loss when carried back or forward. The corporation carries the $6,000 short-term loss back one year. In the prior year the corporation had a short-term capital gain of $8,000 and a long-term capital gain of $5,000 (a total of $13,000 in capital gains). It carries back the loss and subtracts the $6,000 short-term loss (carryback) first from the net short-term gain. This results in a net capital gain of $7,000. This consists of a net short-term capital gain of $2,000 ($8,000 - $6,000) and a net long-term capital gain of $5,000 for the prior year, which allows the corporation to receive a refund of income tax paid in the prior year.

Net Operating Losses (NOLs)

A corporation figures and deducts a net operating loss (NOL) the same way an individual, estate, or trust does. The same carryback (two years) and carryforward (up to 20 years) periods apply, and the same sequence applies when the corporation carries two or more NOLs to the same year. A corporation must carry back an NOL to the earliest of the two years prior to the year the NOL is generated that had taxable income. If the NOL is not fully used against taxable income from the prior two years, the remaining NOL can be carried forward for up to 20 years.

A corporation figures a net operating loss the same way it figures taxable income. It starts with gross income and subtracts its deductions. If its deductions are more than its gross income, the corporation has an NOL. However, the following rules apply for figuring NOL:

- A corporation cannot increase its current year NOL by carrybacks or carryovers from other years in which it has a loss.
- A corporation cannot use the domestic production activities deduction to create or increase a current year NOL.
- A corporation can take the deduction for dividends received, without regard to the aggregate limits that normally apply.
- A corporation can figure the deduction for dividends paid on certain preferred stock of public utilities without limiting it to its taxable income for the year.

An NOL will only reduce income tax. If the corporation owes other taxes or penalties from a prior year, a carryback will not reduce the penalties.

> **Example:** The Artisan Cheese Company has been in business for five years. In the prior year, the corporation had net income of $30,000. However, business slowed, and Artisan Cheese has a net operating loss of $20,000 in 2012. The company decides to carry back its net operating loss in order to recover all of the income taxes it paid in the prior year. In the prior year, the Artisan Cheese also incurred a $1,200 penalty for failing to remit estimated taxes on time. The corporation cannot recover the amount paid for the estimated tax penalty. An NOL carryback will not abate interest and penalties from a prior year. An NOL will only offset income tax.

A C corporation with a net operating loss can file for a refund by using Form 1139 or by amending its corporate tax return using Form 1120X. If a corporation elects to waive carryback and instead carry forward its NOL, it enters the carryover on Form 1120, Schedule K. If the corporation is filing a consolidated return, it must also attach a required statement or the election will not be valid.

If a corporation reasonably expects to have a net operating loss in its current year, it may automatically extend the time for paying income tax liability for the preceding year by filing IRS Form 1138, *Extension of Time For Payment of Taxes by a Corporation Expecting a Net Operating loss Carry Back.*

Charitable Contributions of a C Corporation

C corporations may deduct charitable contributions that are made to qualified organizations, up to 10% of taxable income. A corporation figures its taxable income for the purposes of this limit *without regard to* the following:

- The deduction for charitable contributions
- The dividends-received deduction
- The domestic production activities deduction
- Any net operating loss carryback to the tax year
- Any capital loss carryback to the tax year

The rules regarding what qualifies as a charitable organization are the same for corporations as they are for individuals. Generally, no deduction is allowed for any charitable contribution of $250 or more unless the corporation gets a receipt from the donee organization. The written receipt or acknowledgment should show the amount of cash contributed or a description of the property contributed. The receipt or acknowledgment should also give a description and a good faith estimate of the value of any goods or services provided in return for the contribution, or state that no goods or services were provided in return for the contribution.

If a corporation (other than a closely held or personal service corporation) claims a deduction of more than $500 for contributions of property other than cash, a schedule describing the property and the method used to determine its fair market value must be attached to the corporation's return. In addition the corporation should keep a record of:

- The approximate date and manner of acquisition of the donated property.
- The cost or other basis of the donated property held by the donor for less than 12 months prior to contribution.
- Any donation of a used vehicle, boat, or similar property if it takes a deduction larger than $500 for the donated vehicle.

If the deduction claimed for donated property exceeds $5,000, the corporation must complete Form 8283, *Noncash Charitable Contributions,* and attach it to its tax return. A corporation must obtain a qualified appraisal for all deductions of property claimed in excess of $5,000. A qualified appraisal is not required for the donation of cash, publicly traded securities, or inventory.

A corporation using the accrual method of accounting can deduct unpaid contributions if the board of directors authorized the contributions, and the corporation pays the contributions within 2.5 months after the close of the year. A declaration stating that the board of directors adopted the resolution during the tax year must accompany the return. The declaration must include the date the resolution was adopted.

Example: Ladera Corporation is a calendar-year, accrual-basis corporation. Ladera's board of directors approves a charitable contribution of $5,000 to the United Way on December 15, 2012. Ladera Corporation deducts the contribution on its 2012 corporate tax return. Ladera does not have to actually pay the contribution until March 15, 2013, 2.5 months after the close of its tax year.

A corporation using the cash method of accounting deducts contributions in the tax year they are paid.

Carryover of Excess Charitable Contributions

A corporation can carry over charitable contributions made during the current year that exceed the 10% limit to each of the subsequent five years, subject to the same 10% limitation in each year. A corporation loses any excess contributions not used within that five-year period. No carryback is allowed for charitable contributions. A corporation cannot deduct a carryover of excess contributions to the extent it increases a net operating loss carryover.

> **Example:** Hernandez Sporting Goods has net income of $600,000 in 2012 before taking into account its charitable contribution. The corporation donated $80,000 to a qualified charity in 2012. It also has a net operating loss carryover of $100,000 from a prior year. Therefore, the corporation's charitable deduction is limited to $50,000. The allowable contribution deduction is figured as follows:
> ($600,000 - $100,000 = $500,000) × 10% = $50,000
> The charitable contribution that is not allowed in the current tax year can be carried forward up to five years. If Hernandez Sporting Goods does not use the remainder at the end of five years, the deduction is lost.

> **Example:** Gromwell Corporation, a calendar-year C corporation, makes a large charitable contribution in 2012. As a result, the corporation has a carryover of excess contributions paid in 2012 and it does not use all the excess on its return for 2013. Gromwell Corporation can carry the rest over to 2014, 2015, 2016, and 2017. After that time, it can no longer carry over the excess 2012 charitable contributions.

Dividends-Received Deduction

A corporation can deduct a percentage of certain dividends received from other corporations in which it has an ownership stake. The dividends-received deduction (DRD) is designed to reduce the consequences of double taxation. Without this deduction, corporate profits would be taxed to the corporation that earned them, then to its corporate shareholder, and then *again* to the individual shareholders of the corporation.

The DRD complements the consolidated return regulations, which allow affiliated corporations to file a single consolidated return for U.S. federal income tax purposes. It is only available to C corporations and not to LLCs, S corporations, partnerships, or individuals.

Generally, if a corporation receives dividends from another corporation, it is entitled to a deduction of 70% of the dividends it receives. If the corporation receiving the dividend owns 20% of the other corporation, the deduction increases to 80% of the dividends received.

If the corporation receiving the dividends owns more than 80% of the distributing corporation, it is allowed to deduct 100% of the dividends it receives, making the dividends essentially nontaxable to the receiving corporation.

To summarize, the deduction for dividends received is based on the percentage of stock ownership in the distributing corporation:

Percentage of ownership	Dividends-Received Deduction
Less than 20%	70%
20 - 80%	80%
Greater than 80%	100%

The percentage of stock ownership is determined without regard to preferred stock.

> **Example:** The Quincy Corporation owns 25% of LightStar Corporation. The Quincy Corporation has taxable income of $70,000 *before* taking into account its dividend income. In 2012, Quincy received $100,000 in dividends from LightStar. Quincy receives an 80% dividends-received deduction, figured as follows: $80,000 = ($100,000 × 80%). Therefore, the Quincy Corporation only has to recognize $20,000 of the dividends received from LightStar Corporation. In 2012, the Quincy Corporation's taxable net income is $90,000 ($70,000 + $20,000).

If a corporation is entitled to a 100% DRD, there is no taxable income limitation, and the corporation may deduct the full amount of the dividends received. However, if a corporation is entitled to a 70% DRD, it can deduct amounts only up to 70% of its taxable income. If a corporation is entitled to an 80% DRD, it can deduct amounts only up to 80% of its taxable income. In each case, the corporation would determine taxable income *without* the following items:

- The DRD
- The net operating loss deduction
- The domestic production activities deduction
- Any adjustment due to the nontaxable part of an extraordinary dividend
- Any capital loss carryback to the tax year

> **Example:** Jamestown Corporation owns 85% of the outstanding stock in Humboldt Corporation. In 2012, Jamestown Corporation receives $250,000 in dividends from Humboldt Corporation. Because Jamestown Corporation has over 80% ownership of Humboldt Corporation, the dividends are not taxable. Jamestown Corporation may claim the dividends-received deduction for the dividends received from Humboldt Corporation.

Corporations cannot take a deduction for dividends received from the following entities:

- A real estate investment trust (REIT)
- A tax-exempt corporation
- A corporation whose stock was held less than 46 days

- A corporation whose preferred stock was held less than 91 days
- Any corporation, if another corporation is under an obligation to make related payments for positions in substantially similar property

Dividends on deposits in domestic building and loan associations, mutual savings banks, cooperative banks, and similar organizations are taxed as interest income—not dividends. They do not qualify for the DRD.

Small business investment companies can deduct 100% of the dividends received from taxable domestic corporations.

Effect of NOL on the Dividends-Received Deduction

If a corporation has an NOL for a tax year, the DRD must be figured differently. The limit of 80% (or 70%) of taxable income does not apply if use of the unlimited DRD by the receiving corporation would result in a net operating loss.

> **Example:** Verde Eco-Products Corporation loses $25,000 from its own business operations in 2012. Verde Eco-Products also receives $100,000 in dividend income from a 20%-owned corporation. Therefore, Verde Eco-Product's taxable income in 2012 is $75,000 ($100,000 - $25,000 loss) *before* the DRD. If Verde Eco-Products claims the full DRD of $80,000 ($100,000 × 80%) and combines it with a loss from operations of $25,000, it will create an NOL of ($5,000). Therefore, the 80% of taxable income limit does not apply. The corporation can deduct the full $80,000 DRD.

> **Example:** Redwood Patio Corporation has a loss of $15,000 from business operations in 2012. However, it also has dividends of $100,000 from a corporation in which it holds an interest of 50%. Therefore, Redwood's taxable income is $85,000 *before* applying the DRD. After claiming the DRD of $80,000 ($100,000 × 80%), its taxable income is $5,000. Because Redwood will not have an NOL after applying a full DRD, its allowable DRD is limited to 80% of its taxable income, or $68,000 ($85,000 × 80%).

Related Party Transactions

Strict rules apply to related party transactions. A corporation that uses an accrual method of accounting cannot deduct business expenses and interest owed to a related person who uses the cash method until the corporation makes the related payment and the amount is included in the related person's income. These rules also deny the deduction of a loss on the sale or trade of property (other than in the complete liquidation of a corporation) between related persons.

For purposes of these rules, the following persons are considered related to a corporation:

- A corporation that is a member of the same controlled group.

- An individual who owns, directly or indirectly, more than 50% of the value of the outstanding stock of the corporation.
- A partnership, if the same persons own more than 50% of the value of the outstanding stock of the corporation and more than 50% of the partnership.
- An S corporation, if the same persons own more than 50% of the value of the outstanding stock of each corporation.
- A trust fiduciary, when the trust or its grantor owns, directly or indirectly, more than 50% of the value of the outstanding stock of the corporation.
- An employee-owner of a personal service corporation, regardless of the amount of stock owned.

In determining whether a person directly or indirectly owns any of the outstanding stock of a corporation, the following rules apply:

- Stock directly or indirectly owned by or for a corporation, partnership, estate, or trust is considered owned proportionately by or for its shareholders, partners, or beneficiaries.
- An individual is considered to own the stock that is directly or indirectly owned by or for his family. Family includes only brothers and sisters (including half-brothers and half-sisters), a spouse, ancestors, and lineal descendants.
- An individual owning any stock in a corporation is considered to own the stock that is directly or indirectly owned by his partner.

> **Example:** Robert is a 90% owner in Nampa Boots Corporation. His wife, Eileen, is a 55% owner of Terabyte Corporation. For tax purposes, Robert is considered a related person for the purposes of ownership in Terabyte Corporation. Therefore, for the related-party transaction rules, Robert is also considered a 55% owner in Terabyte Corporation and Eileen is considered a 90% owner in Nampa Boots Corporation.

Closely Held Corporations and the At-Risk Rules

A closely held corporation generally has a small number of shareholders (usually family) and no public market for its corporate stock. The corporate ownership and management often overlap. A corporation is considered to be closely held if all of the following apply:

- It is not a personal service corporation.
- At any time during the last half of the tax year, more than 50% of the value of its outstanding stock is, directly or indirectly, owned by or for

five or fewer individuals. An individual in this case includes certain trusts and private foundations.

The reason why this issue is important to the IRS is because of the application of the at-risk rules. These rules dictate that losses are only allowed up to the amount at risk of financial loss. If the corporation does not have a risk of financial loss in an activity, the losses are not deductible. The amount at-risk generally equals:

- The money and the adjusted basis of property contributed by the taxpayer to the activity, and
- The money borrowed for the activity.

The at-risk amount also includes the FMV of any property (adjusted for any liens or encumbered mortgages) that is pledged as security or collateral for the debts of the activity.

> **Example:** Allworth Corporation is a closely held C corporation with only two shareholders: a father and son. Allworth Corp. invests $50,000 in a business venture, and also pledges the value of a factory building as collateral for a $100,000 loan that is used in the business venture. Allworth's factory building has a fair market value of $150,000 but is also secured by a lien of $125,000. Allworth Corp.'s amount at-risk in the business venture is only $75,000 ($50,000 plus the $25,000 ($150,000 - $125,000) equity in the building).

The following items increase an entity's amount at-risk:

1. A contribution of additional cash (or property) to the venture.
2. Any recourse loan for which the corporation is liable for repayment.

The amount at-risk is decreased by the following items:

1. An investor's withdrawal of cash or property from the activity.
2. A nonrecourse loan where the corporation is not liable for repayment.

The amount at risk cannot be decreased below zero. If this occurs, suspended losses from prior years must be reduced.

Controlled Groups

A controlled group is a group of corporations that are related through common ownership, typically as either parent-subsidiary or brother-sister. A parent-subsidiary controlled group involves a parent corporation that owns at least 80% or more of the voting power of at least one other corporation (with possible additional corporations that are at least 80% owned by either the common parent or one of the subsidiary entities). A brother-sister controlled group involves situations in which five or fewer individuals, estates, or trusts own 80% or more of the combined voting power for multiple corporations, and have identical common ownership within the individual corporations of at least 50%.

A controlled group is allowed a single set of graduated income tax brackets, a single exemption amount for AMT purposes, and a single accumulated earnings credit of $250,000. In each case, these amounts must be allocated among the members of the group. Members of controlled groups are also subject to rules regarding related party transactions that may require deferral of recognition for losses or expenses incurred by one party.

Unit 14: Questions

1. The Farber Corporation owns 10% of the Lewisville Corporation. In 2012, Farber receives $10,000 in dividends on Lewisville stock. What is the amount of the dividends-received deduction that Farber Corporation can take?

A. 10%.
B. 50%.
C. 70%.
D. 80%.

The answer is C. The dividends deduction for less-than-20% owned stock is generally 70%. ###

2. The Surf's Up Corporation had an NOL of $110,000. Which of the following statements is true?

A. The corporation can forgo the carryback period and choose to carry the entire loss forward to the next 20 years.
B. The corporation is required to carry back losses for two years and then forward for 15 years.
C. The corporation can carry back losses five years and carry them forward for 25 years.
D. A corporation cannot carry back losses. It can only carry them forward.

The answer is A. A corporation is not required to carry back losses. It may elect to forgo the carryback period. Net operating losses can be carried back to the two years before the loss year and forward to the 20 years following the loss year. ###

3. BMD Corporation is a calendar-year corporation that uses the accrual method of accounting. What is the last day that the corporation can make a charitable contribution and still deduct it on its 2012 tax return?

A. December 31, 2012.
B. April 15, 2012.
C. January 15, 2013.
D. March 15, 2013.

The answer is D. The corporation has until March 15 of the following year to pay the contribution. A corporation using the accrual method can choose to deduct unpaid contributions for the tax year if the board of directors authorizes the contribution during the tax year, and the corporation pays the contribution within 2.5 months after the close of the year. ###

4. In 2012, Mansour Corporation has a $15,000 loss from its business operations. In addition, Mansour has received $100,000 in taxable dividends from a 30%-owned corporation. Therefore, its taxable income is $85,000 before applying the dividends-received deduction. What is the corporation's dividends-received deduction?

A. $15,000.
B. $68,000.
C. $80,000.
D. $100,000.

The answer is B. The corporation would not have an NOL after applying the full dividends-received deduction, so its allowable dividends-received deduction is limited to 80% of its taxable income (before applying the DRD), or $68,000 ($85,000 × 80%). ###

5. Davidson Corporation owns 50% of Nguyen Corporation's outstanding common stock. Davidson has taxable income of $8,000, which includes dividends received of $10,000 from its investment in Nguyen Corporation. What is Davidson Corporation's taxable income after applying the dividends-received deduction?

A. $0.
B. $1,600.
C. $6,400.
D. $8,000.

The answer is B. Davidson Corporation cannot deduct the full $8,000 (80% × $10,000) dividends-received deduction that would normally apply based upon its 50% ownership because doing so would not result in a net operating loss. The deduction is instead limited to 80% of taxable income (before applying the DRD), which is $6,400 (80% × $8,000).

Taxable Income:	$8,000
Minus DRD:	($6,400)
Income after DRD:	**$1,600**

###

6. In 2012 Real Time Corporation made contributions totaling $20,000 to qualified charitable organizations. Due to income limitations, Real Time Corporation could only deduct $15,000 of the contributions on its return. Which of the following statements regarding the excess contributions of $5,000 is correct?

A. Excess charitable contributions can be carried back two years and carried forward 20 years.
B. Excess charitable contributions can be carried forward 20 years
C. Excess charitable contributions can be carried back three years and carried forward ten years.
D. Excess charitable contributions can be carried forward five years. They cannot be carried back.

The answer is D. The corporation can carry over excess charitable contributions made during the year that result from the 10% limit on deductibility to each of the subsequent five years. Any excess charitable contributions that are not used in this five-year period are lost. A corporation cannot carry back excess charitable contributions. ###

7. Xena Corporation is a cash-basis, C corporation. In 2012, the corporation has a net short-term capital gain of $23,000 and a net long-term capital loss of $29,000. How should these capital gains and losses be treated?

A. The corporation may deduct a $6,000 long-term capital loss on its 2012 tax return.
B. The corporation may carry back the $29,000 long-term capital loss to a prior year, where it may only be deducted against long-term capital gains.
C. The corporation may carry back the $6,000 net capital loss to a prior year, where it may be deducted against short-term capital gains.
D. The corporation must carry forward the entire capital loss to the following tax year. Carryback of capital losses is not allowed.

The answer is C. The corporation may carry back the $6,000 capital loss to the earliest of the three preceding years, where it may be deducted against short-term capital gains. Any remaining losses can be carried forward for up to five years. The corporation treats this $6,000 as a short-term loss when carried back or forward, because capital loss carrybacks and carryforwards do not retain their original character. ###

8. The Capital Cross Corporation is a calendar-year C corporation. In 2012, Capital Cross has $4,000 in charitable contributions that it cannot use on the current year return because of income limitations. How should this unused contribution be treated?

A. The corporation can carry over unused charitable contributions for five years.
B. The corporation can carry over unused charitable contributions for 20 years.
C. The corporation can carry over unused charitable contributions for 10 years.
D. The corporation can carry back unused charitable contributions for three years, and carry them forward for five years.

The answer is A. A corporation can carry over charitable contributions for five years. It loses any unused amounts after that period. Corporate charitable contributions cannot be carried back. ###

9. Redd Beauty Products and Helena Mountain Coffee are domestic corporations. Redd Beauty owns 25% of Helena Mountain Coffee. Redd Beauty's income from its business operations in 2012 is $500,000. In addition to its business income, Redd Beauty received dividends from Helena Mountain Coffee of $100,000. What is Redd Beauty's dividends-received deduction?

A. $70,000.
B. $80,000.
C. $100,000.
D. $20,000.

The answer is B. Generally, if a corporation receives dividends from another corporation in which it owns an interest of 20% to 80%, it is entitled to a deduction of 80% of the dividends received, subject to limitation based upon its taxable income without regard to the DRD and certain other items. Since Redd owns 25% of Helena, its DRD is 80% of $100,000, or $80,000. ###

10. The Arbabi Plastics Corporation is a calendar-year C corporation. In 2012, it has $400,000 of taxable income before consideration of the following additional items:
•$50,000 of charitable contributions
•A dividends-received deduction of $70,000
•A domestic production activities deduction of $40,000

What portion of the charitable contributions is deductible in 2012?

A. $50,000.
B. $29,000.
C. $40,000.
D. $36,000.

The answer is C. Arbabi Plastics' deductible charitable contributions are limited to 10% of its taxable income, before consideration of the following items:

•The deduction for charitable contributions
•The dividends-received deduction
•The domestic production activities deduction
•Any net operating loss carryback to the tax year
•Any capital loss carryback to the tax year

Calculation: $400,000 X 10% = $40,000 ($10,000 would be carried over to the next year). Qualifying contributions in excess of this limitation can be carried over for five years. ###

11. Which of the following statements about a controlled group of corporations is true?

A. Members of a controlled group are entitled to only one accumulated earnings tax credit.
B. A parent corporation and its 80% owned subsidiary would be considered members of a controlled group.
C. Members of controlled groups are subject to rules regarding related party transactions that may require deferral of recognition for losses or expenses incurred by one party.
D. All of the above.

The answer is D. A parent-subsidiary controlled group involves a parent corporation that owns at least 80% or more of the voting power of at least one other corporation. A controlled group is allowed a single set of graduated income tax brackets, a single exemption amount for AMT purposes, and a single accumulated earnings credit of $250,000. ###

13. McClimate Corporation owns 25% of Wilson Foods Corporation. In 2012, McClimate received $10,000 dividends from Wilson Foods stock. Assuming no other limitations apply, McClimate's dividends-received deduction is _____:

A. $7,000.
B. $8,000.
C. $2,000.
D. $0.

The answer is B. If a corporation receiving dividends owns 20% of the corporation issuing the dividends, it generally qualifies for a dividends-received deduction equal to 80% of the dividends received. It can deduct amounts up to 80% of its taxable income, calculated without regard to the DRD itself and certain other items. ###

12. During 2012, Bernardino Jewelry, a domestic C corporation, had the following income, expenses, and deductions:

Gross receipts:	$95,000
Net capital gains:	$10,000
Business expenses, (not including charitable contributions):	$65,000
Charitable contribution:	$20,000
NOL carryover from 2011:	$30,000

What is the amount of Bernardino Jewelry's allowable charitable contribution deduction for 2012?

A. $1,000.
B. $20,000.
C. $4,000.
D. $3,000.

The answer is A. A C corporation may deduct charitable contributions made to qualified organizations, up to 10% of taxable income. Taxable income for this purpose is determined without regard to certain items, including the charitable contribution deduction itself and any net operating loss carryback (but not carryforward) to the tax year. Therefore, Bernardino Jewelry's charitable contribution deduction would be determined as follows:

Gross receipts	$95,000
Expenses	($65,000)
Net capital gains	$10,000
NOL from 2011	($30,000)
Taxable income before contribution deduction	$10,000
Deduction limit at 10%	$1,000

###

Unit 15: Corporate Distributions & Liquidations

More Reading:
Publication 542, *Corporations*

Corporate Distributions

Corporate distributions or dividends occur when cash, stock, or other property is distributed to shareholders based on the shareholders' ownership of stock. When a corporation earns profits, it can retain the profits in the business (as retained earnings), or it can pay all or a portion of the profits as dividends to shareholders. The amounts a corporation pays as dividends are not deductible expenses. Dividends are most commonly paid in cash. However, a dividend can take the form of stock or other property.

The most common kinds of corporate distributions are:

- Ordinary dividends (either in cash or in property)
- Capital gain distributions
- Nondividend distributions
- Distributions of stock or stock rights

A distribution is calculated by adding the amount of any cash paid to the shareholder plus the fair market value of any property transferred to the shareholder. The distribution amount is reduced by the following liabilities:

- Any liability of the corporation the shareholder assumes
- Any liability that the property is subject to upon distribution, such as mortgage debt the shareholder assumes in connection with distribution of ownership in a building

The amount of a distribution can never go below zero, no matter how much liability a shareholder assumes. The FMV of the distributed property becomes the shareholder's basis in the property.

Ordinary dividends are generally paid out of the earnings and profits of a corporation and are taxable as ordinary income to the shareholders rather than capital gains.

Distribution Reporting Requirements

A corporation must file Form 1099-DIV, *Dividends and Distributions*, with the IRS for each shareholder who receives a dividend of $10 or more during a calendar year. A corporation must send Forms 1099-DIV to the IRS along with Form 1096, *Annual Summary and Transmittal of U.S. Information Returns*, by February 28 (March 31 if filing electronically) of the year following the year of the distribution.

The corporation is also required to furnish Forms 1099-DIV to shareholders by January 31 of the year following the close of the calendar year during which the corporation made the distributions.

The corporation is allowed to furnish Forms 1099-DIV early to shareholders. A business may furnish Forms 1099-DIV to shareholders any time after April 30 of the year of the distributions if the corporation has made its final distributions for the calendar year.

Distributions from Earnings and Profits

The amount of corporate earnings and profits (E&P) determines the tax treatment of corporate distributions to shareholders. Distributions of a C corporation are deducted first from current E&P, and then from any accumulated E&P from prior years. Any part of a distribution from current-year earnings and profits or accumulated earnings and profits is reported as dividend income to the shareholder.

Corporate distributions in excess of E&P are nontaxable to the shareholder to the extent of the shareholder's stock basis. The starting point for determining corporate E&P is initially increased by the corporation's taxable income. The following transactions *increase* the amount of E&P:

- Long-term contracts reported on the completed contract method

- Intangible drilling costs deducted currently

- Mine exploration and development costs deducted currently

- Dividends-received deduction

The following transactions *reduce* the amount of E&P:

- Corporate federal income taxes

- Life insurance policy premiums on a corporate officer

- Excess charitable contribution (over 10% limit)

- Expenses relating to tax-exempt income

- Excess of capital losses over capital gains

- Corporate dividends and other distributions

Accumulated Earnings and Profits

Accumulated earnings and profits are earnings that the corporation accumulated before the current year and has not distributed to its shareholders. Sometimes a corporation will make a distribution that exceeds its current E&P. If a corporation's current E&P are less than the total distributions made during the year, part or all of each distribution is treated as a distribution of accumulated earnings and profits.

If accumulated earnings and profits are reduced to zero, the remaining part of each distribution reduces the adjusted basis of the shareholder's stock. This is referred to as a nondividend distribution and it is not taxable to the shareholder until his basis in the stock is fully recovered. This nontaxable portion is considered to be a return of capital that he had previously invested in the corporation. If the corporation makes nondividend distributions to a shareholder that exceed the adjusted basis of his stock, the excess distribution is treated as a gain from the sale or exchange of property and is taxable to the shareholder as capital gain.

If nondividend distributions are made to shareholders, the corporation must report these distributions to the IRS on Form 5452, *Corporate Report of Nondividend Distributions*.

Example: Tobias is the only shareholder of Seaside Corporation, a calendar-year corporation. During the year, Seaside makes four $1,000 distributions to Tobias. At the end of the year (before subtracting distributions made during the year), the corporation has $10,000 of current year profits. Since the corporation's current year earnings and profits ($10,000) were more than the amount of the distributions it made during the year ($4,000), all of the distributions are treated as distributions of current year earnings and profits. The corporation must issue Form 1099-DIV to Tobias by January 31 to report the $4,000 distributed to him as dividends. Seaside Corporation must use Form 1096, *Annual Summary and Transmittal of U.S. Information Returns*, to report this transaction to the IRS by February 28 (March 31 if filing electronically). The corporation does not deduct these dividends on its income tax return.

Stock Distributions

Stock distributions or stock dividends occur when a corporation issues additional shares of its own stock to shareholders, rather than paying a cash dividend or distributing property.

Stock rights, also known as stock options, may be distributed by a corporation to some or all of its shareholders to allow them to purchase additional shares at a set price.

Distributions by a corporation of its own stock or stock rights are generally tax-free to shareholders and not deductible by the corporation. However, they may be treated as property distributions in certain situations, including when:

- The shareholder has the choice to receive cash or other property instead of stock or stock rights.

- The distribution gives cash or other property to some shareholders and an increase in the percentage interest in the corporation's assets or earnings and profits to other shareholders.
- The distribution is in convertible preferred stock.
- The distribution gives preferred stock to some shareholders and common stock to other shareholders.
- The distribution is on preferred stock.

A corporation must capitalize, rather than deduct, the expenses of issuing a stock dividend, such as printing, postage, and any fees for listing on stock exchanges.

Constructive Distributions

A constructive distribution may occur when a corporation confers a benefit upon a shareholder. A transaction may initially be recorded by the corporation as an expense and the IRS may re-categorize it instead as a constructive distribution. This would make the transaction nondeductible to the corporation and in many instances taxable to the shareholder. Examples of constructive distributions include:

- **Unreasonable compensation:** If a corporation pays an employee-shareholder an unreasonably high salary considering the services actually performed, the excessive part of the salary may be treated as a distribution.

- **Unreasonable rents:** If a corporation rents property from a shareholder and the rent is unreasonably higher than the shareholder would charge a stranger for use of the same property, the excessive part of the rent may be treated as a distribution.

- **Cancellation of a shareholder's debt:** If a corporation cancels a shareholder's debt without repayment by the shareholder, the amount canceled may be treated as a distribution.

- **Property transfers for less than FMV:** If a corporation transfers or sells property to a shareholder for less than its FMV, the excess may be treated as a distribution.

- **Below market or interest-free loans**: If a corporation gives a shareholder an interest-free loan or at a rate below the applicable federal rate, the uncharged interest may be treated as a distribution.

Transfers of Property to Shareholders

A property distribution is treated as if the corporation had sold the property to the shareholder. A corporation (either a C corporation or an S corporation) recognizes gain on a distribution of property to a shareholder if the FMV of the property is more than its adjusted basis. For this purpose, the FMV is considered to be the greater of the property's actual FMV or the amount of liabilities the shareholder assumes in connection with the distribution. If the distributed property was depreciable or amortizable, the corporation may have to treat all or a portion of the gain as ordinary income from depreciation recapture.

The transaction is taxable to the shareholder at FMV and is reported on Form 1099-DIV and Form 5452, *Corporate Report of Nondividend Distributions*. A corporation generally cannot recognize a loss on a distribution of property (i.e., where the property's FMV is less than the adjusted cost basis). However, a corporation is allowed to recognize losses when depreciated property is distributed to shareholders in complete liquidation (when the corporation ceases operations).

Stock Redemptions

A stock redemption occurs when a corporation buys back its own stock from a shareholder in exchange for cash or property. The stock acquired may be canceled, retired, or held as treasury stock.

A shareholder is required to treat the amount realized on a stock redemption as either a dividend or a sale of stock. Stock redemptions are generally treated as dividends unless certain conditions are met, as follows:

- The redemption is not equivalent to a dividend, meaning that the shareholder's proportionate interest and voting power in the corporation has been substantially reduced.
- There was a substantially disproportionate redemption of stock, meaning that the amount received by the shareholder is not in proportion to his stock ownership.
- The redemption was due to a complete termination of a shareholder's interest in the corporation.
- The redemption is of stock held by a non-corporate shareholder and was part of a partial liquidation.
- The distribution is received by estate and does not exceed the sum of death taxes plus funeral and administration expenses to be paid by the estate.

The corporation must realize a gain from the redemption, as if the property were sold at its fair market value to the shareholder. The corporation must recognize income on the distribution of depreciated property to the extent of depreciation or the amount realized, whichever is less. The corporation may not recognize a loss on a stock redemption unless:

- The redemption occurs in a complete liquidation of the corporation, or
- The redemption occurs on stock held by an estate.

Corporate Liquidations and Dissolution

Liquidating distributions are distributions received by a shareholder during a complete or partial dissolution of a corporation. When a corporation dissolves, it redeems all of its stock in a series of distributions.

Complete liquidation occurs when the corporation ceases to be a going concern and its activities are merely for the purpose of winding up its affairs, paying its debts, and distributing any remaining balance to its shareholders. In certain cases in which the buyer is a corporation in control of the distributing corporation, the distribution may not be taxable. A corporate dissolution or liquidation must be reported on Form 966, *Corporate Dissolution or Liquidation*, within 30 days after the resolution or plan is adopted to dissolve the corporation or liquidate any of its stock. Exempt entities are not required to file Form 966, even if they are organized as corporations.

When property is distributed in a complete liquidation, the transaction is treated as if the corporation sold the assets to a buyer at fair market value. The corporation recognizes gain or loss on the liquidation in an amount equal to the difference between the FMV and the adjusted basis of the assets distributed. A corporation is allowed to recognize losses during the liquidation, except for losses resulting from transactions with related parties.

Amounts received by the shareholder in complete liquidation of a corporation are treated as full payment in exchange for the shareholder's stock. A liquidating distribution is considered a return of capital and is not taxable to the shareholder until the shareholder recovers all of his basis in the stock. After the basis of the stock has been reduced to zero, shareholders must report the liquidating distribution as a capital gain.

If a dissolving corporation distributes property that is subject to a liability, the gain or loss is adjusted to reflect assumption of the liability. If the liability is greater than the FMV of the property, the amount of the liability is treated as the FMV of the property. A corporation is required to provide each shareholder a Form 1099-DIV from the corporation showing the amount of the liquidating distribution.

A corporation must file an annual return for the year it goes out of business, even if it has no income or business activity in that year. The IRS ordinarily has three years from the date an income tax return is filed (or its due date, whichever is later) to charge any additional tax that is due.

If a dissolving corporation is filing a final return, the corporation can request a prompt assessment from the IRS after filing the return. In the case of a deceased taxpayer whose estate is a shareholder in a dissolving corporation, the fiduciary representing a dissolving corporation or a decedent's estate may request a prompt assessment of tax. In either instance, this reduces the time for making the assessment to 18 months from the date the written request for prompt assessment was received.

Example: The Maurer Farm Equipment Corporation is going through a complete liquidation. Saul, a shareholder, receives a liquidating distribution of property (a tractor). Maurer Corporation's basis in the tractor is $3,000. The fair market value of the tractor is $13,000. However, the tractor is encumbered by a liability of $15,000 (an unpaid loan), which Saul assumes. Because the remaining loan amount is more than the FMV of the tractor, the amount of the liability is treated as the FMV. The corporation must recognize a $12,000 gain on the distribution ($15,000 loan - $3,000 basis), and Saul is treated as having received a liquidating distribution of $15,000.

Unit 15: Questions

1. Which of the following statements about stock distributions is correct?

A. Stock distributions must be treated as a cash distribution that is taxable to the shareholder.
B. Stock distributions are usually taxable to the corporation when distributed to shareholders.
C. Stock distributions are deductible by a corporation as an expense.
D. Stock distributions are generally not taxable to shareholders and not deductible by the corporation.

The answer is D. Generally, distributions of stock and stock rights are not taxable to shareholders and not deductible by the corporation. ###

2. April bought corporate stock five years ago for $1,000. In 2011, she received a return of capital of $800. April did not include this amount in her income, but correctly reduced the basis of her stock to $200. She received another return of capital of $300 in 2012. The first $200 of this amount reduced April's stock basis to zero. How should she report the remaining $100 in distributions?

A. April must report $100 in long-term capital gain in 2012.
B. April does not have to report the additional return of capital.
C. April must report the $100 as ordinary income.
D. April must report any additional return of capital as a capital loss.

The answer is A. When the basis of a shareholder's stock has been reduced to zero, the shareholder must report any additional return of capital received as a capital gain. Since April has held the stock for more than one year, the gain is reported as a long-term capital gain. ###

3. Three years ago, Mark purchased 100 shares of Rock Star, Inc. for $10 per share. In 2012 Rock Star, Inc. completely liquidated and distributed $20,000 to Mark in exchange for all of his stock. Mark must report this distribution as:

A. A $20,000 long-term capital loss.
B. A $19,000 short-term capital gain.
C. A $19,000 long-term capital gain.
D. A $19,000 ordinary gain.

The answer is C. Mark has a $19,000 long-term capital gain. His basis in the stock was $1,000 [100 shares stock x $10]. So his gain is figured as follows: ($20,000 - $1,000). Gain or loss that is recognized to shareholders on distributions in a corporate liquidation is generally determined by the difference between the total of the cash and property received by the shareholders and the basis of the stock they surrendered. The gain or loss will be long-term or short-term depending on the length of time the stock was held. Since Mark purchased the shares several years ago, his holding period exceeds one year and is therefore recognized as long-term capital gain on his return. ###

4. Geraldine owns 1,000 shares of Kimball Software Corporation. Her shares were all acquired three years ago, and her basis in the stock is $20,000. Kimball Software completely liquidated in 2012 and distributed $56,000 in two payments to Geraldine. Geraldine received $16,000 in December 2012 and $40,000 in January 2013. How much gain or loss is recognized by Geraldine in 2012 and 2013?

A. $4,000 loss in 2012 and $40,000 gain in 2013.
B. $4,000 loss in 2012 and $44,000 gain in 2013.
C. No gain or loss in 2012 and $40,000 gain in 2013.
D. No gain or loss in 2012 and $36,000 gain in 2013.

The answer is D. The liquidating distribution is not taxable until the shareholder's stock basis ($20,000) has been recovered. Geraldine recovered $16,000 of her basis in 2012 and the remaining balance of $4,000 in 2013. Her recognized gain is $36,000 ($56,000 total distribution - $20,000 basis), and she will recognize no gain or loss in 2012. Geraldine will recognize $36,000 of capital gain in 2013. ###

5. Ryan is a shareholder in PRK Corporation with a basis of $20,000 in his stock. He also has an outstanding $10,000 loan that he owes to the corporation. In 2010, Ryan files for bankruptcy and defaults on the loan. PRK Corporation cancels Ryan's debt in 2012. How should this cancellation of debt be reported?

A. The debt cancellation is a $10,000 distribution to Ryan.
B. The debt cancellation is considered a return of capital to Ryan.
C. The debt cancellation is a charitable contribution to Ryan.
D. The debt cancellation is a $10,000 capital gain to Ryan.

The answer is A. If a corporation cancels a shareholder's debt without repayment by the shareholder, the amount canceled is treated as a distribution to the shareholder. In this instance, the distribution would likely be treated as ordinary income. ###

6. Party Time Corporation distributes to a shareholder $75,000 in cash and a delivery truck with a $40,000 adjusted basis and a $60,000 FMV. What gain or loss, if any, must Party Time Corporation recognize?

A. No gain or loss is recognized in this transaction.
B. $20,000 gain.
C. $40,000 gain.
D. $20,000 loss.

The answer is B. A corporation will recognize a gain on the distribution of property to a shareholder if the FMV of the property is more than its adjusted basis ($60,000 FMV - $40,000 adjusted basis = $20,000). This is the same treatment the corporation would receive if the property were sold for its FMV. ###

7. All of the examples below are considered corporate distributions except?

A. Ordinary dividends to a shareholder.
B. Capital gain distributions to a shareholder.
C. Constructive distributions to an employee-shareholder.
D. Wage compensation to an employee-shareholder.

The answer is D. Salaries or wages to an employee-shareholder is not considered a distribution. Instead, the wages would be treated as a business expense just like wages for the corporation's other employees. The wages are deductible by the corporation and then taxable to the employee-shareholder. ###

8. The Red Dog Corporation paid dividends to the following shareholders in 2012:

•Marie: $1,000 in dividends.
•Rose: $90 in dividends.
•Laura: $9.75 in dividends.
•Timothy: $100 in dividends.

The Red Dog Corporation is required to issue a Form 1099-DIV to which shareholders?

A. All shareholders must receive a Form 1099-DIV.
B. Marie and Timothy only.
C. Timothy, Marie, and Rose only.
D. Only Marie.

The answer is C. A C corporation is required to issue a Form 1099-DIV with the IRS for each shareholder who is paid dividends of $10 or more during a calendar year. Since Laura did not receive at least $10 in dividends, a Form 1099-DIV is not required. ###

9. Six years ago, Sabine purchased 100 shares of Vitality Nature Corporation stock for $50 per share. In 2012, the corporation liquidated. After paying all of its outstanding liabilities, Vitality Nature distributed $10,000 in cash and appreciated property worth $90,000 to all of its shareholders. Sabine's portion of the distributed assets and cash was $12,000. What must she report from this liquidating distribution in 2012?

A. $0 gain.
B. $3,000 capital gain.
C. $7,000 capital gain.
D. $10,000 capital gain.

The answer is C. The capital gain is figured as follows: Her basis is $5,000 ($50 x 100 shares). The excess of her portion of the distribution over her basis: ($12,000 distribution - $5,000 basis) results in a $7,000 capital gain. ###

10. Distributions of stock rights are generally tax-free to shareholders. Which of the following statements is not correct?

A. Even if a shareholder has a choice to receive cash instead of stock rights, so long as the shareholder chooses to receive stock rights, the distribution will be tax-free.
B. Stock rights are distributions by a corporation of rights to acquire its own stock.
C. Stock rights are sometimes called stock options.
D. Stock rights can be taxable in some circumstances.

The answer is A. If the shareholder has a choice to receive cash instead of stock rights, the distributions of stock and stock rights are taxable. ###

11. Buffalo Corporation displays a collection of fine artwork in its main office. When the 75% shareholder retires, he is presented with his choice from the art collection. He selects a painting with a fair market value of $250,000. Buffalo Corporation's basis in the painting is $100,000. How should the transaction be reported on the Buffalo Corporation's tax return?

A. $150,000 loss.
B. $150,000 distribution.
C. $150,000 taxable gain.
D. $250,000 taxable gain.

The answer is C. The corporation must recognize a gain for any property distributed that has an FMV higher than its adjusted basis. This is the same treatment the corporation would receive if the property were sold for its FMV. The answer is figured as follows:

FMV of distribution $250,000
Subtract adjusted basis ($100,000)
Recognized gain $150,000

It should be noted that the FMV of $250,000 is also reported as a distribution to the shareholder, and will be his basis in the painting. ###

12. Millerton Software is a C corporation that was formed in 2003. At the beginning of 2012, Millerton Software had accumulated earnings and profits of $100,000. The company makes a $5,000 distribution to its 100% shareholder in the first month of each quarter. In 2012, Millerton Software had $150,000 in gross income and $140,000 in expenses from ordinary business operations. Millerton also received $5,000 in fully tax-exempt interest from state bonds. What part of the second quarter distribution is treated as a distribution of accumulated earnings and profits?

A. $1,250.
B. $2,500.
C. $3,750.
D. $5,000.

The answer is A. Distributions from a C corporation are deducted first from current E&P, and then from any accumulated E&P from prior years. Any part of a distribution from current-year E&P or accumulated E&P is reported as dividend income to the shareholder. If a corporation's current earnings are less than the total distributions made during the year, part or all of each distribution is treated as a distribution of accumulated E&P. Since Millerton's distributions during the year ($20,000) were more than its current year E&P of $15,000 ($150,000 - $140,000 + $5,000), the amount of each distribution is treated as having been paid partially from current year E&P (in the ratio of current E&P for the year to total distributions for the year ($15,000/$20,000 x $5,000 = $3,750). The remainder of each distribution ($5,000 - $3,750 = $1,250) is treated as having been paid from accumulated E&P. ###

13. The Midwestern Grain Corporation distributes property with an adjusted basis of $1,000 and a fair market value of $4,000 subject to a liability of $6,000 to Joseph, a shareholder. What is the gain or loss, if any, Midwestern Grain must recognize as a result of the distribution?

A. $3,000 gain.
B. $1,000 loss.
C. $5,000 gain.
D. $0.

The answer is C. A distribution of property to a shareholder is treated as if the corporation had sold the property to the shareholder. The corporation recognizes gain on the distribution if the FMV of the property is more than its adjusted basis. The FMV is considered to be the greater of the property's actual FMV or the amount of liability the shareholder assumes in connection with the distribution. In this case, the FMV is considered to be the liability of $6,000 assumed by Joseph, so Midwestern Grain must recognize a gain of $5,000 ($6,000 − adjusted basis of $1,000). ###

Unit 16: S Corporations

More Reading:
Form 1120S and Instructions

The rules governing S corporations are found in subchapter S of the Internal Revenue Code. An S corporation has similarities to both a C corporation and a partnership. Like a partnership, an S corporation is a pass-through entity and is generally not taxed on its earnings. Instead, earnings and losses pass through to shareholders. Like a C corporation, an S corporation enjoys liability protection that a partnership does not.

S corporations do have some drawbacks. They are less flexible than partnerships. There are some instances in which an S corporation is forced to pay tax on its earnings. There are restrictions on the number and type of shareholders an S corporation can have. For example, the number of S corporation shareholders is limited to 100, while a C corporation may have an unlimited number of shareholders and a partnership may have an unlimited number of partners.

Electing S Corporation Status

In order to become an S corporation, a business must file an S election on Form 2553, *Election by a Small Business Corporation.* The filing must be made within 2.5 months of the start of its tax year in order for the election to be effective at the beginning of the year. An election made after the first 2.5 months of the tax year becomes effective on the first day of the following tax year, unless the corporation receives IRS approval to make the election retroactive to the beginning of the tax year. The IRS will generally accept a late S election, so long as the following requirements are met:

- The entity must qualify for S corporation status, except for not having filed Form 2553 in a timely manner.
- The entity had intended to be classified as an S corporation as of the effective date of the S corporation election.
- The entity applies for relief no later than six months following the due date of the tax return.
- The corporation either had reasonable cause or inadvertently failed to file Form 2553 in a timely manner.
- The corporation has not yet filed tax returns for the first tax year for which it intends to file as an S corporation, or the corporation has filed its first tax return using Form 1120S and the shareholders properly reported their share of income in a manner consistent with the corporation's intention to be an S corporation.
- No shareholder has reported inconsistencies with the S election.

If the S election is made during the corporation's tax year for which it first takes effect, any individual stockholder who holds stock at any time during the part of that year before the election is made must also consent to the election, even though the person may have sold or transferred his stock before the election is made.

> **Example:** Ron, Tara, and William are all equal shareholders in a C corporation. In March 2012, William decides to retire and sells all his shares in the C corporation to Sandra, an unrelated person. In April, Ron, Tara, and Sandra vote to elect S corporation status. All the current shareholders must agree to the election. William must also agree, even though he sold his stock before the election was made.

An S corporation may choose to use the cash or accrual method of accounting if it meets the requirements. However, an S corporation may not use the cash method if it is a tax shelter.

S Corporation Requirements

The main requirements for S corporation status are:

- It cannot have more than 100 shareholders.
- Shareholders must be U.S. citizens or residents, if individuals, or certain kinds of trusts, banks, estates, or certain tax-exempt corporations. Corporate shareholders and partnerships are excluded. (In contrast, an S corporation is allowed to own a partnership interest or own stock in a C corporation).
- A business must meet the definition of a small business corporation, per IRC section 1361.
- An S corporation can only have one class of stock, but that stock can be voting or nonvoting. The difference in voting rights allows one group of shareholders to retain voting control, while still allowing other shareholders to benefit from corporate earnings. However, all the stock of an S corporation must possess identical rights to distribution and liquidation proceeds.
- Profits and losses must be allocated to shareholders in proportion to each one's interest in the business.
- Nonresident aliens cannot be shareholders in an S corporation.
- All shareholders of an S corporation must give written consent for the S election.

> **Example:** A husband and wife own 90% of an S corporation and their son owns the remaining 10% of the stock. The son announces his marriage to a nonresident alien, to whom he gifts one-half of his stock. The S corporation's status is revoked, because a nonresident alien cannot hold stock ownership in an S corporation.

For the purpose of the 100-shareholder limit, related persons are considered one shareholder. Spouses are automatically treated as a single shareholder. Families, defined as individuals descended from a common ancestor, plus spouses and former spouses of either the common ancestor or anyone lineally descended from that person, are considered a single shareholder so long as any family member elects such treatment.

When a shareholder dies, the deceased shareholder's spouse and the estate are still considered one shareholder for the purpose of the shareholder limit. A husband and wife cannot be considered a single shareholder if they divorce, or if the marriage is dissolved for any other reason than death. Therefore, a shareholder's divorce can potentially increase the number of shareholders to a number in excess of the 100-shareholder limit. When an S corporation fails to meet these restrictions, the S election is considered terminated, and the S corporation ceases to be an S corporation and is instead taxed as a C corporation. The following entities cannot elect S corporation status:

- A bank or thrift institution that uses the reserve method of accounting for bad debts
- An insurance company
- A domestic international sales corporation (DISC)
- Any foreign entity

Termination of an S election

Once the S election is made, it stays in effect until terminated. The election will terminate automatically in any of the following cases:

- The corporation no longer qualifies as a small business corporation.[53]
- For each of three consecutive tax years, the corporation
    - Has accumulated earnings and profits,[54] and
    - Derives more than 25% of its gross receipts from passive investment income. The election terminates on the first day of the first tax year beginning after the third consecutive tax year.

---

[53] This termination of an election is effective as of the day the corporation no longer meets the definition of a small business corporation. A statement notifying the IRS of the termination and the date it occurred is attached to Form 1120S for the final year of the S corporation.

[54] This only applies to S corporations that were once C corporations. That is because an S corporation cannot accumulate earnings and profits as a C corporation can. However, it is possible for a C corporation to elect S corporation status and still have accumulated earnings and profits at the time of the election.

In addition, the corporation must pay a tax for each year it has excess net passive income.
- The shareholders willingly revoke the S election.
- The corporation creates a second class of stock.

An S election can be revoked only with the consent of the *majority* shareholders. This means that, at the time the revocation is made, the revoking shareholders hold more than 50% of the corporation's stock (including nonvoting stock).

A shareholder revocation may specify an effective revocation date that is on or after the day the revocation is filed. If no date is specified, the revocation is effective at the start of a tax year if the revocation is made on or before the fifteenth day of the third month of that tax year.

If no date is specified and the revocation is made after the fifteenth day of the third month of the tax year, the revocation is effective at the start of the next tax year. To voluntarily revoke an S election, the corporation must file a statement of revocation with the IRS. The statement must be signed by each shareholder who consents. A revocation may also be rescinded before it takes effect.

When an S corporation terminates its election, it creates two short tax years. The corporation must allocate income and loss on a pro rata basis between the period it operated as an S corporation and the period as a C corporation that was created when the S election was terminated. The entity must file Form 1120S for the S corporation's short year by the due date (including extensions) of the C corporation's short year return.

> **Example:** On May 1, 2012, Zander Corporation, a calendar-year S corporation, exceeded 100 shareholders. This will create two short tax years—one for the S corporation and one for the C corporation. Zander must file a Form 1120S and a Form 1120.

Inadvertent Termination of an S Election

An S corporation may unintentionally lose its S status and revert to a C corporation. If the IRS deems that the revocation was inadvertent (that the shareholders did not mean to revoke their S election or that the revocation was accidental), the corporation may be allowed to correct the error and retain its S election status.

> **Example:** In 2012, Morrison Window Blinds, a calendar-year S corporation, inadvertently terminates its S status. The S corporation shareholders immediately correct the problem. Therefore, the S corporation status is considered to have been continuously in effect, and no termination is deemed to have occurred. Only a single S corporation tax return will need to be filed for tax year 2012.

A terminating event will be considered inadvertent if the event was not within the control of the corporation, and the shareholders did not plan to terminate the election. In order to qualify after a terminating event, all of the following must occur:

- The S election must have involuntarily terminated either because:
  - The corporation no longer qualified as a small business corporation, or
  - It had accumulated earnings and profits from past C corporation activities.
- The IRS must agree that the termination was inadvertent.
- The corporation must take reasonable and immediate steps to correct the issue.
- The shareholders and the corporation must agree to any adjustments proposed by the IRS.
- The corporation must request a private letter ruling from the IRS for any inadvertent termination relief.

If the status of an S corporation is terminated, either because the shareholders elect to become a C corporation or because a terminating event has occurred, the S corporation cannot elect to become an S corporation again for at least five years. However, the IRS may waive the five-year restriction.

Filing Requirements

An S corporation files its tax return on IRS Form 1120S, *U.S. Income Tax Return for an S Corporation*. Individual items of income, deductions, and credits pass through to individual shareholders and are reported on Schedule K-1. The return must be signed and dated by an authorized corporate officer or, in certain instances, by a fiduciary such as a receiver, trustee, or assignee, on behalf of the corporation.

An S corporation is always required to file a tax return, regardless of income or loss. The filing requirement ends only when the corporation is totally dissolved. The IRS mandates electronic filing for S corporations with $10 million or more in assets that file 250 or more returns of any type (W-2, 1099, K-1) per year. The tax return is due on the fifteenth day of the third month following the tax year end. For a calendar-year corporation, the tax return is due March 15. A corporation that has dissolved must generally file by the fifteenth day of the third month after the date it dissolved.

A six-month extension of time to file can be requested using Form 7004, *Automatic Extension of Time to File Certain Business Income Tax, Information, and Other Returns*.

Shareholders are required to pay estimated tax for their individual returns. S corporations are only required to pay estimated tax if $500 or more of certain corporate-level taxes apply.

S Corporations: Required Tax Year

An S corporation must use one of the following as its tax year:

- A calendar year
- A natural business year
- A fiscal year duly elected and approved by the IRS under section 444
- An ownership tax year (the tax year that coincides with <50% ownership of the corporation)
- A 52-53 week year that ends with reference to a year listed above

An S corporation may always use a calendar year, or any other tax year for which it establishes a bona fide business purpose.

A new S corporation must use Form 2553, *Election by a Small Business Corporation*, to elect a tax year. An existing S corporation that wishes to change its existing tax year may use Form 1128, *Application to Adopt, Change, or Retain a Tax Year*.

However, Form 8716, *Election to Have a Tax Year Other Than a Required Tax Year*, is used to apply for a tax year change under section 444.

S Corporation Income and Expenses

As with a partnership, all the income of an S corporation must be allocated to the shareholders, even if it is not distributed. Income, gains, losses, deductions, and credits are allocated to a shareholder on a pro-rata basis, according to the number of shares of stock held by the shareholder on each day of the corporation's tax year, and retain their character when they are passed through. The shareholder then reports the items on his individual tax return (Form 1040).

Some of the items that pass through to shareholders on a pro rata basis and retain their character must be separately stated on an S corporation's tax return. These include:

- Net income or loss from rental real estate activity (rental income)
- Portfolio income or loss that includes:
    - Interest income

- o Dividend income
- o Royalty income
- Capital gains or losses
- Section 1231 gain or loss
- Charitable contributions
- Section 179 expense deduction
- Foreign taxes paid or accrued
- Expenses related to portfolio income or loss
- Credits, including:
  - o Low-income housing credit
  - o Qualified rehabilitation expenses
- Investment interest expense
- Tax preference and adjustment items needed to figure a shareholder's AMT
- Nonbusiness bad debts

Unlike a C corporation, an S corporation is not eligible for a dividends-received deduction.

Limited Taxation of S Corporations

S corporations generally are not subject to taxation since they are primarily pass-through entities. However, in certain cases, S corporations are subject to taxes. A subchapter S corporation may have to pay income tax due to:

- Excess net passive investment income
- Built-in gains
- Investment credit recapture
- LIFO recapture

None of these taxes are deductible as business expenses by the S Corporation.

An S corporation may also be responsible for other taxes, such as payroll taxes if it has employees, and penalties, such as late filing penalties.

Excess Net Passive Investment Income: An S corporation that had been a C corporation previously and had accumulated earnings and profits (E&P) during that period may have to pay tax at the corporate level on excess net passive income (ENPI). Further, if the corporation has passive investment income for three consecutive tax years, it may lose its S status.

If an S corporation that was formerly a C corporation has accumulated E&P at the end of the tax year and has passive investment income in excess of 25% of its gross receipts for three consecutive taxable years, the S election is terminated as of the beginning of the fourth year.

Example: For 2010, 2011, and 2012, Herzing Corporation, a calendar-year S corporation, earned passive investment income in excess of 25% of its gross receipts. If Herzing Corporation has accumulated E&P from earlier years in which it was a C corporation, its S election would be terminated as of January 1, 2013, and the corporation would be taxed as a C corporation as of January 1, 2013.

The purpose of this requirement is to discourage a corporation with accumulated earnings and profits (E&P) from becoming or functioning as a holding company in order to obtain favorable tax treatment as an S corporation. For this purpose, passive investment income includes interest, dividends, and royalties. If income is generated in the ordinary course of business, it is non-passive, or active, income.

Example: Trailblazer Inc. is an S corporation with accumulated E&P from earlier years when it was a C corporation. In 2012, Trailblazer's first taxable year as an S corporation, it has gross receipts of $75,000:
- $5,000 is royalty payments from Trademark A
- $8,000 is royalty payments from Trademark B
- $62,000 is gross receipts from regular operations

Trailblazer created Trademark A, but Trailblazer did not create Trademark B or perform significant services with respect to the development or marketing of Trademark B. Because Trailblazer created Trademark A, the royalty payments from Trademark A are derived in the ordinary course of business and are not considered passive income for purposes of determining Trailblazer's passive investment income. However, the royalty payments for Trademark B are included within the definition of royalties for purposes of determining Trailblazer's passive investment income. Trailblazer's passive investment income for the year is $8,000.

If the corporation has always been an S corporation, the ENPI tax would not apply. The tax rate on excess net passive income is 35%. This tax is applied on passive income from activities such as royalties, rents, dividends, and interest. The tax is applied against the lesser of:
- Excess net passive income, or
- Taxable income figured as though the corporation were a C corporation.

Built-in Gains (BIG) Tax: The built-in gains (BIG) tax may apply to the following S corporations:
- An S corporation that was a C corporation before it elected to be an S corporation.

- An S corporation that acquired an asset with a basis determined by reference to its basis (or the basis of any other property) in the hands of a C corporation (a transferred-basis acquisition).

The built-in gains tax requires an S corporation to measure the amount of unrecognized appreciation that existed at the time an S election is made or an asset was acquired. The amount of unrecognized gain is determined for each asset. The net of unrecognized built-in gains and built-in losses is the company's unrecognized built-in gain.

The S corporation then pays taxes at the highest corporate rate based on the recognized built-in gain. The tax is reported on Form 1120S. The amount of the tax is a deduction for the shareholders.

The built-in gains tax is imposed on assets sold by an S corporation that it held when it was converted from a C corporation, unless the assets are held by the S corporation for a certain period of time. The current statutory period is five years after conversion from a C corporation to an S corporation.

The built-in gains tax only applies to corporations that elected S status after 1986, and it only affects property dispositions during the recognition period.[55] The applicable recognition period is the five-year period beginning:

- On the first day of the first tax year for which the corporation is an S corporation, for an asset held when the S corporation was a C corporation, or
- On the date the asset was acquired by the S corporation, for an asset with a basis determined by reference to its basis in the hands of a C corporation.

Investment Credit Recapture: Business credit recapture is generally the responsibility of the entity that claims the credit. If the company is an S corporation when the credit originates, the credit passes through to the shareholders and they must report the recapture on IRS Form 4255, *Recapture of Investment Credit*. However, if a C corporation claims the General Business Credit and then converts to S status, the S corporation itself may be responsible for the recapture.

LIFO Recapture Tax: Corporations that account for inventory using the last in, first out (LIFO) method are subject to a LIFO recapture tax in the final year before making an S corporation election. This tax is intended to address built-in gains on inventory that might not otherwise be recognized during the normal recognition period. The taxable LIFO recapture amount is the amount by which

---

[55] The American Taxpayer Relief Act of 2012 extended this temporary five-year recognition period to sales occurring in 2012 and 2013.

the amount of inventory assets calculated under the first in, first out (FIFO) method exceeds the amount under the LIFO method.

"Inventory assets" refers to stock in trade of the corporation, or other property of a kind that would properly be included in the inventory of the corporation if on hand at the close of the taxable year.

The LIFO recapture tax is paid in four equal installments, beginning on the due date of the final C corporation return. The three subsequent installments are payable on the due date of the first three S corporation returns. If the LIFO value is higher than the FIFO value, no negative adjustment is allowed.

S Corporation Basis

In computing stock basis, the shareholder starts with his initial capital contribution to the S corporation or the initial cost of the stock purchased (the same as for a C corporation). A shareholder's basis in his S corporation stock may vary based on how the stock was acquired (by purchase, gift, or inheritance). In general, a shareholder's basis in S corporation stock is determined as follows:

Stock Acquired	How Stock Basis is Determined
Stock Purchase	If the S corporation shares were purchased outright, initial basis is the cost of the shares.
S corporation capitalized	If the shares were received when the S corporation was formed under IRC §351, the basis in the stock is equal to the basis of the property transferred to the corporation, reduced by the amount of property received from the corporation, increased by gain recognized on the transfer, and decreased by any boot received (IRC §358).
Prior C corporation	Initial basis in S corporation stock is the basis in the C corporation stock at the time of conversion.
Gift	The recipient's basis in shares received by gift is generally the donor's basis (IRC §1015). Suspended passive activity losses can increase the basis of a gift (IRC §469).
Inheritance	The basis of inherited stock is its fair market value at the date of death or, if elected, the alternate valuation date (IRC §1014).
Services rendered to the S corporation	Basis in stock received in exchange for services is measured by the stock's fair market value, rather than by the value of the services (Treas. Reg. §1.61-2).

The order in which stock basis is increased or decreased is important. Both the taxability of a distribution and the deductibility of a loss are dependent on stock basis, and there is an ordering rule for computing stock basis. Stock basis is adjusted annually, on the last day of the S corporation year, in the following order:

- Increased for income items and excess depletion
- Decreased for distributions
- Decreased for nondeductible, noncapital expenses and depletion
- Decreased for items of loss and deductions

S corporation shareholders must pay taxes on their share of the corporation's current year income, whether or not the amounts are distributed. The shareholder's Schedule K-1 reflects the income, loss, and deductions that are allocated to him but does not state the taxable amount of a distribution. The taxable amount of distributions is contingent upon the shareholder's stock basis and it is the shareholder's responsibility to track his individual basis.

S corporation distributions are generally not treated as dividends, except in rare cases where a corporation has accumulated earnings and profits from years before it elected to become an S corporation. S corporation distributions (except dividend distributions) are considered a return of capital and reduce the shareholder's basis in the stock of the corporation.

If a shareholder receives a nondividend distribution from an S corporation, the distribution is tax-free to the extent it does not exceed his stock basis; his debt basis is not considered. If the amount distributed exceeds the shareholder's basis in the stock, the excess is treated as a capital gain from the sale or exchange of property.

A shareholder's deduction for his share of losses is limited to the adjusted basis of his stock and any debt the corporation owes the shareholder. Any loss or deduction not allowed because of basis limitations is carried over and treated as a loss or deduction in the next tax year. A shareholder's basis can never be reduced below zero.

The basis adjustment rules under IRC §1367 are similar to the partnership rules. However, while a partner has a unitary basis in his partnership interest, the adjustments to the basis of stock of an S corporation are applied on a separate share basis. A loss, deduction, or distribution will decrease stock basis. Here are the rules for figuring shareholder basis in an S corporation:

- Nondeductible expenses reduce a shareholder's stock and debt basis before loss and deduction items. If nondeductible expenses exceed basis, they do not get carried forward.
- If the current year has different types of losses and deductions that exceed the shareholder's basis, the allowable losses and deductions must be allocated pro rata based on the size of the particular loss and deduction items.

- A shareholder is not allowed to claim losses and deductions in excess of stock and debt basis. Losses and deductions not allowable in the current year are suspended due to basis limitations.
- Suspended losses and deductions due to basis limitations retain their character in subsequent years. Any suspended losses or deductions in excess of stock and debt basis are carried forward indefinitely until basis is increased in subsequent years or until the shareholder permanently disposes of the stock.
- In determining current year allowable losses, current year loss and deduction items are combined with the suspended losses and deductions carried over from the prior year, though the current year and suspended items should be separately stated.
- A shareholder is only allowed debt basis to the extent he has personally lent money to the S corporation. A "loan guarantee" is not sufficient to allow the shareholder debt basis.
- Part or all of the repayment of a reduced basis debt is taxable to the shareholder.
- If stock is sold, suspended losses due to basis limitations are lost forever. The sales price does not have an impact on the stock basis. A stock basis computation should be reviewed in the year stock is sold or disposed of.

S corporation shareholders are required to compute both stock basis and debt basis. For losses and deductions that exceed a shareholder's stock basis, the shareholder is allowed to deduct the excess up to his basis in loans he personally made to the S corporation. Debt basis is computed similarly to stock basis, but there are some differences.

If a shareholder has S corporation losses and deductions in excess of stock basis and those losses and deductions are claimed based on debt basis, the debt basis of the shareholder will be reduced by the claimed losses and deductions. If an S corporation repays reduced basis debt to the shareholder, part or all of the repayment is taxable to the shareholder.

The amount of loss that is deductible on a shareholder's tax return is limited to the shareholder's at-risk basis. These limits (and the order in which they apply) are the adjusted basis of:

- Cash and the adjusted basis of property that the shareholder contributed to the S corporation, and
- Any loans the shareholder makes to the corporation or any amounts that are borrowed for use by the S corporation for which the shareholder is directly liable.

An S corporation that engages in rental activity or an S corporation with a shareholder who does not materially participate in S corporation activities is subject to passive activity loss rules.

These rules provide that losses and credits from passive activities can generally be applied only against income and tax from passive activities. Passive activity loss limitations do not apply to S corporations but to its individual shareholders. If the passive activity loss rules apply, the shareholders' at-risk amount must be reduced by the full amount allowable as a current deduction.

Reasonable Wages

An S corporation may wish to pay little or no wages to employees or officers who are also shareholders, as wages are subject to employment taxes while distributions to shareholders are not. However, if an S corporation is not paying a reasonable salary to a shareholder-employee, distributions to him may be reclassified as wages subject to employment taxes. Therefore, an S corporation will be at risk if it attempts to avoid paying employment taxes by having its officers treat their compensation as cash distributions, payments of personal expenses, or loans rather than as wages.

There are no specific guidelines for reasonable compensation in the IRC or in IRS regulations. Factors considered by the courts in determining reasonable compensation for employees or officers of an S corporation include:

- Training and experience
- Duties and responsibilities
- Time and effort devoted to the business
- Dividend history
- Payments to non-shareholder employees
- Timing and manner of paying bonuses to key people
- Amounts that comparable businesses pay for similar services
- Compensation agreements
- The use of a formula to determine compensation

The regulations provide an exception for an officer of a corporation who does not perform any services or performs only minor services and receives no compensation. Such an officer would not be considered an employee for tax purposes.

Health Insurance Premiums for Shareholders

Fringe benefits paid to employees that are not shareholders or who have ownership of less than 2% are generally deductible by the S corporation and tax-free to the employee. However, for shareholder-employees that have at least 2% ownership, health and accident insurance premiums paid on their behalf are deductible by the S corporation as fringe benefits and are reportable as wages for income tax withholding purposes on the shareholder-employee's Form W-2. The S corporation can exclude the value of these health benefits from the employee's wages subject to Social Security, Medicare, and FUTA taxes.

A 2% shareholder-employee is eligible for an AGI deduction for amounts paid during the year for medical care premiums if the medical care coverage is established by the S corporation. If the medical coverage plan is in the name of the shareholder and not in the name of the S corporation, a medical care plan can still be considered to be established by the S corporation if:

- The S corporation either paid or reimbursed the shareholder for the premiums, and
- Reported the premium payment as wages on the shareholder's Form W-2.

Neither Schedule K-1 (Form 1120S) nor Form 1099 can be used as an alternative to Form W-2 to report this additional compensation.

> **Example:** Victory Sports Drinks, an S corporation, provides fringe benefits such as health insurance to its two owner-shareholders. Victory paid $5,000 in insurance premiums. The corporation treats the shareholders as having received the health insurance as additional compensation and includes the insurance expenditure as W-2 wage income. The shareholders report the health insurance as income.

The S corporation cannot take a deduction for amounts incurred during periods in which the owner-shareholder is eligible to participate in any subsidized health plan maintained by another employer (or the spouse's employer).

> **Example:** CJ is the single owner-shareholder in an S corporation. He pays the health insurance for himself and his wife. CJ's wife works full-time for an employer who has offered to provide family health coverage. Franklin and his wife declined the coverage because they do not want to switch doctors. Because Franklin has the option to participate in an employer plan (through his wife), he cannot deduct the health insurance premiums provided by his S corporation.

Corporate Distributions

The amount of an S corporation distribution is equal to the sum of all cash and the fair market value of the property received by a shareholder. If an S corporation distributes appreciated property (such as stocks), the S corporation and the shareholder must treat the distribution as a sale to the shareholder. To the extent the FMV of the property exceeds the shareholder's basis, he would recognize capital gain. Gain is determined when the final year-end reconciliations are made and the shareholder has adjusted his stock basis for any increases but before any decreases attributable to the current year are deducted.

Distributions from an S corporation with no accumulated earnings and profits are generally treated as a nontaxable return of capital.

Distributions up to the shareholder's adjusted stock basis are treated as a nontaxable return of capital. Distributions that exceed the shareholder's adjusted stock basis are reported as a capital gain and must be reported on the individual shareholder's Schedule D.

Distributions from an S corporation are not subject to payroll tax. Withdrawals from an S corporation in the form of dividends are subject to federal taxes at ordinary income tax rates. Wages are subject to employment taxes and income tax at the shareholder level.

Distributions from an S corporation must be paid to all shareholders on the same date, as a pro rata distribution based on each shareholder's individual ownership percentage.

The Accumulated Adjustments Account (AAA)

If a C corporation elects to become an S corporation, it may have an accumulated adjustments account (AAA). The AAA is a corporate account and does not belong to any particular shareholder. The S corporation maintains the account to track undistributed income that has been taxed during the period its S election is in effect.

S corporations with accumulated E&P must maintain the AAA to determine the tax effect of distributions during S years and the post-termination transition period. It is not mandatory to track AAA if the S corporation does not have prior year C corporation earnings and profits (E&P) (IRC section 1368). Nevertheless, if an S corporation without accumulated E&P engages in certain transactions where an AAA account is required, such as a merger into an S corporation with accumulated E&P, the S corporation must be able to calculate its AAA at the time of the merger. Therefore, it is recommended that the AAA be maintained by all S corporations. The AAA may have a negative balance at year end.

Termination of a Shareholder's Interest

A shareholder may sell or liquidate his stock interest in an S corporation. The sale is treated the same way as the sale of stock in a C corporation. The shareholder reports the sale of the stock on Schedule D. The gain or loss that is recognized by the shareholder is the difference between the shareholder's basis and the sale price of the stock.

If a shareholder in an S corporation terminates his interest in a corporation during the tax year, the corporation, with the consent of all affected shareholders (including those whose interest is terminated), may elect to allocate income and expenses as if the corporation's tax year consisted of two separate short tax years, the first of which ends on the date of the shareholder's termination.

To make this election, the corporation must attach a statement to a timely filed original or amended Form 1120S for the tax year for which the election is made and state that it is electing to treat the tax year as if it consisted of two separate tax years.

The statement must also explain how the shareholder's entire interest was terminated (e.g., sale or gift), and state that the corporation and each affected shareholder consent to the election. A single statement may be filed for all terminating elections made for the tax year. If this election is made, the taxpayer should write "Section 1377(a)(2) Election Made" at the top of each affected shareholder's Schedule K-1.

Unit 16: Questions

1. Danielle is a 50% owner in Goodpaster Software Corporation, an S corporation. Danielle's basis is $5,000 in the corporation. At the end of 2012, Goodpaster Corporation reports $10,000 in ordinary income. In December 2012, Goodpaster makes a distribution to Danielle of appreciated property. It is a rare motorcycle originally purchased for $1,000 but now worth $8,000. How much income does Danielle have to report on her individual return?

A. $0.
B. $1,000.
C. $2,000.
D. $8,000.

The answer is A. If an S corporation distributes appreciated property, the S corporation and the shareholder will treat the distribution as a sale to the shareholder. The distribution lowers Danielle's stock basis to $2,000.

Danielle's adjusted basis:	$5,000
S corp. income × 50%:	$5,000
Adjusted basis 12/31/12:	$10,000

Distribution

FMV of property:	$8,000
Less: Shareholder's basis:	$10,000
Capital gain	**$0**

####

2. Close family members can be treated as a single shareholder for S corporation purposes. A family member in this instance includes:

A. A nonresident alien spouse.
B. A first cousin.
C. The estate of a deceased shareholder's spouse.
D. A divorced spouse.

The answer is C. Spouses are automatically treated as a single shareholder, and when a shareholder dies, the deceased shareholder's spouse and the estate are still considered one shareholder for the purpose of the shareholder limit. A husband and wife cannot be considered a single shareholder if they divorce, or if the marriage is dissolved for any other reason than death. An S corporation cannot have a nonresident alien member, so a nonresident alien spouse would not qualify. ###

3. All of the following statements about S corporations are true except:

A. S corporations cannot have more than 100 shareholders.
B. S corporations can own stock in a C corporation.
C. S corporations have only one class of stock.
D. A C corporation can own stock in an S corporation.

The answer is D. An S corporation can own shares in a C corporation, but a C corporation cannot own shares in an S corporation. ###

4. A calendar-year S corporation operating on the accrual basis has the following income items and expenses. What is the income of this S corporation, not counting the separately stated items?

Gross receipts: $300,000
Interest income: $25,000
Royalty income: $10,000
Salary paid to shareholder: $20,000

A. $55,000.
B. $280,000.
C. $320,000.
D. $345,000.

The answer is B. Ordinary income would reflect the gross receipts of $300,000 less salary expense to the shareholder of $20,000, or $280,000. Interest income and royalty income would be separately stated items on Form 1120S, but would not be considered in determining ordinary income or loss. The amount is figured as follows: ($300,000 - $20,000 = $280,000). ###

5. In which circumstance is a C corporation unable to elect to become an S corporation?

A. The C corporation has 50 shareholders.
B. The C corporation is incorporated in Canada.
C. The C corporation has common stock with voting and nonvoting rights.
D. The C corporation is on a fiscal year with a legitimate business purpose.

The answer is B. A C corporation can elect to become an S corporation if it otherwise qualifies. Only domestic U.S. corporations are allowed to elect S status. An S corporation can only have one class of stock, but differences in voting rights are allowed. An S corporation can have a fiscal year if it has a legitimate business purpose for doing so. ###

6. All S corporations, regardless of when they became an S corporation, must use a permitted tax year. A permitted tax year is any of the following except:

A. The calendar year.
B. A tax year elected under section 444.
C. A fiscal tax year with a legitimate business purpose.
D. A short tax year.

The answer is D. A short tax year is only applicable when an S corporation is in its first year or its S status is terminated. ###

7. Which of the following items is not a separately stated item on an S corporation return?

A. Charitable contributions.
B. Net short-term capital gains or losses.
C. Interest income.
D. Interest expense on a business loan.

The answer is D. Charitable contributions, interest income, and short-term capital gains and losses are all separately stated items. The interest on a business loan is not a pass-through item; it is a business expense, as it would be for any other entity. ###

8. On January 15, 2012, Elliott decides to voluntarily terminate his corporation's S status, switching to a C corporation. The termination was approved by the IRS. A year later, he changes his mind and wishes to elect S corporation status again. How long does Elliott have to wait to elect S corporation status again?

A. 18 months.
B. Two years.
C. Four years.
D. Five years.

The answer is D. A corporation must generally wait five years to make another election. ###

9. On December 31, 2011, Adrienne had a $2,000 basis in Liaison Corporation, an S corporation. She owns 50% of Liaison's outstanding stock. At the beginning of 2012, Adrienne contributed a patent that she had acquired for $1,000 to Liaison Corp. During 2012 Liaison Corp received $5,000 in royalty income from that patent. Liaison also had $2,500 of ordinary income and $500 of section 179 deductions. At the end of 2012, Liaison returned ownership of the patent, which now had a fair market value of $5,000, to Adrienne. What is Adrienne's basis in Liaison Services at the end of 2012?

A. $1,000.
B. $1,500.
C. $2,500.
D. $5,000.

The answer is B. Adrienne's basis is calculated as follows:

Basis at December 31, 2011	$2,000
Contribution of patent	$1,000
50% share of 2012 income:	
•Royalty income	$2,500
•Ordinary income	$1,250
Basis prior to consideration of distribution	6,750
Distribution of patent, at FMV	($5,000)
Subtotal	**$1,750**
50% share of section 179 deduction	($250)
Basis at December 31, 2012	**$1,500**

###

10. S corporations are generally not subject to taxation and are primarily pass-through entities. But in certain cases, S corporations are subject to taxes. Which of the following taxes do not apply to S corporations?

A. Excess net passive investment income.
B. Built-in gains tax.
C. Self-employment tax.
D. LIFO recapture.

The answer is C. S corporations are not subject to self-employment tax. Self-employment tax only applies to individuals. The S corporation may have to pay tax due to:

•Excess net passive investment income
•Built-in gains
•Investment credit recapture
•LIFO recapture ###

11. Bettendorf River Company is a calendar-year C corporation that wishes to elect S corporation status in 2012. What is the latest date that Bettendorf River Company can elect S status for tax year 2012?

A. March 15, 2012.
B. March 15, 2013.
C. February 15, 2012.
D. December 31, 2012.

The answer is A. An eligible corporation must make an S election within two months and 15 days of its tax year (or within 2.5 months of its inception) to become an S corporation. Since Bettendorf is a calendar-year corporation, its tax year begins January 1. It must make the election on or before March 15. ###

12. A C corporation may not elect to become an S corporation if:

A. It is a domestic corporation.
B. It has voting and nonvoting stock.
C. It has two classes of stock.
D. It has common stock.

The answer is C. A corporation may not elect S corporation status if it has two classes of stock. A corporation may have both voting and nonvoting stock because they are not considered different classes of stock. A corporation must be a domestic corporation in order to qualify for S corporation status. ###

13. On January 1, 2012, Seth purchased 50% of the stock of Rancho Sendero, an S corporation, for $100,000, and also loaned the corporation $20,000. At the end of 2012, Rancho Sendero incurred an ordinary loss of $180,000. How much of the loss can Seth deduct on his personal income tax return for 2012?

A. $ 90,000.
B. $180,000.
C. $ 0.
D. $120,000.

The answer is A. An S corporation shareholder may deduct his share of the corporation's losses only to the extent of his stock and debt basis. Before consideration of Rancho Sendero's 2012 loss, Seth's stock basis and debt basis were $100,000 and $20,000, respectively. Therefore, he can deduct his entire 50% share of the company's ordinary loss. ###

14. In January 2012, Christopher and Eva are shareholders in Garabedian Company, a C corporation. Christopher owns 65% of the corporate stock and Eva owns the remainder. Christopher decides that he wants to convert to an S corporation. Which of the following statements is true regarding the conversion?

A. Christopher and Eva must both consent to the conversion to the S corporation.
B. The election to become an S corporation is taken on Form 1120S.
C. Christopher may choose, on his own, to convert the C corporation to an S corporation because he owns the majority interest (more than 50% of the stock).
D. Christopher and Eva cannot elect S corporation status, because a C corporation cannot elect to become an S corporation.

The answer is A. All the shareholders must consent to an S election. ###

15. Which of the following events would cause the termination of an S corporation's status?

A. An S corporation that has an estate as a shareholder.
B. An S corporation that has a nonprofit corporation 501(c)(3) shareholder.
C. An S corporation that issues one share of stock to a C corporation.
D. An S corporation that owns one share of stock in a C corporation.

The answer is C. An S corporation cannot issue stock to a C corporation. S corporation shareholders must be U.S. citizens or U.S. residents, and must be physical entities (persons), so corporate shareholders and partnerships are generally excluded. Certain estates and trusts can also be shareholders. Certain tax-exempt corporations, notably 501(c)(3) corporations, are permitted to be shareholders. An S corporation may own stock in a C corporation. ###

16. Which of the following will not terminate an S corporation's status?

A. The S corporation no longer qualifies as a small business corporation.
B. The S corporation, for each of three consecutive tax years, has accumulated earnings and profits, and derives more than 25% of its gross receipts from passive investment income.
C. The S corporation creates a second class of stock.
D. The S corporation earns the majority of its revenue from passive activities.

The answer is D. All of the following actions will terminate an S election:

•When the corporation no longer qualifies as a small business corporation.
•For each of three consecutive tax years, the corporation
•Has accumulated earnings and profits, and
•Derives more than 25% of its gross receipts from passive investment income.
•The S election may be willingly revoked by the shareholders.
•An S election will be terminated if the corporation creates a second class of stock (such as common and preferred stock). ###

17. Given the following information, what is the total amount of separately stated income items of this S corporation?

Rental real estate income	$ 300,000
Interest income	$25,000
Royalty income	$10,000
Section 1231 gain	$20,000
Gross receipts	$700,000

A. $355,000.
B. $345,000
C. $700,000.
D. $720,000.

The answer is A. All of the income, except for the gross receipts, must be separately stated on the S corporation's tax return. The total of the separately stated items is figured as follows:

Rental activities:	$300,000
Interest income	$25,000
Royalty income	$10,000
Section 1231 gain	$20,000
Total	**$355,000**

###

18. On January 1, 2012, Gloria, Kristin, and Nancy are all equal shareholders in Fairview Heights Corporation, a calendar-year C corporation that has been in existence for four years. On March 1, 2012, Gloria sells her entire stock interest in the corporation to an unrelated party, Irving. Irving immediately wants to convert the corporation to an S corporation. What is required in order for the corporation to convert to S status?

A. Irving may convert the corporation into an S corporation so long as Kristin and Nancy consent.
B. Gloria must also consent to the election, along with Kristin and Nancy.
C. Irving may convert the corporation to an S corporation on his own.
D. The corporation cannot convert to S status until it has been in existence for five years.

The answer is B. In order for the election to be made, Gloria must also consent to the election, even though she has sold all of her shares to Irving. All the shareholders must consent to the election. If the S election is made during the corporation's tax year for which it first takes effect, any individual stockholder who holds stock at any time during the part of that year before the election is made must also consent to the election, even though the person may have sold or transferred his stock before the election is made. ###

19. How much is the tax on excess net passive income?

A. 10%.
B. 15%.
C. 25%
D. 35%.

The answer is D. Excess net passive income is taxed at a rate of 35% to S corporations. ###

20. Francisco is the single employee-shareholder in his S corporation. At the beginning of the year, his stock basis was $50,000. The corporation had zero income in 2012. The corporation distributed property to Francisco with an FMV of $75,000 and an adjusted basis of $62,000. What is the treatment of the distribution?

A. $50,000 as a return of capital and $25,000 taxable capital gain.
B. $50,000 as a return of capital and $12,000 taxable capital gain.
C. $60,000 as a return of capital and $15,000 taxable capital gain.
D. $62,000 as a return of capital and $0 taxable gain.

The answer is A. The distribution is figured as follows:

Francisco's adjusted basis:	$50,000
S corporation income	$0
Adjusted basis 12/31/12:	$50,000

Distribution

FMV of property:	$75,000
Less: shareholder's basis:	$50,000
Capital gain:	**$25,000**

Francisco must report $25,000 in capital gain income on his personal tax return. The distribution reduces the shareholder's basis in his stock, and the remaining amount exceeding the basis is treated as capital gain. ###

21. Fisherton Textiles, a qualified S corporation, has no accumulated earnings and profits. In 2012, Fisherton Textiles distributed property to Lydia, its sole shareholder, with a fair market value of $75,000 and an adjusted basis of $62,000. After recognizing her share of Fisherton's current year income, Lydia's adjusted basis in the company's stock at the end of the year was $60,000. How should Lydia handle the distribution?

A. $60,000 as return of capital and $15,000 as nontaxable distributions.
B. $60,000 as return to capital and $2,000 as taxable capital gain.
C. $60,000 as return to capital and $15,000 as taxable capital gain.
D. $60,000 as a nontaxable distribution.

The answer is C. Distributions from an S corporation with no accumulated earnings and profits are generally treated as a nontaxable return of capital, up to the amount of the shareholder's adjusted stock basis. However, if an S corporation distributes appreciated property, the distribution is treated as a sale to the shareholder. To the extent the FMV of the property exceeds the shareholder's basis, he would recognize capital gain. Gain is determined when the final year-end reconciliations are made and the shareholder has adjusted his stock basis for any increases but before any decreases attributable to the current year are deducted. The gain is reported as a capital gain on the shareholder's Schedule D. ###

22. Sydney owns 50% of the Verrengia Company, a calendar-year S corporation. At the beginning of the year, Sydney's stock basis is $3,000. At the end of 2012, Verrengia has $2,000 in income and distributes a large machine with an FMV of $7,000 to Sydney. How much income must Sydney report on her individual tax return for this distribution?

A. $0.
B. $3,000.
C. $5,000.
D. $6,000.

The answer is B. After recognizing her 50% share of Verrengia's income for the year, the basis of Sydney's stock is $4,000. Since the FMV of the property distribution exceeds her basis, she recognizes capital gain to the extent of the excess amount ($3,000). The distribution is figured as follows:

Sydney's adjusted basis	$3,000
S Corp income X 50%	$1,000
Adjusted basis 12/31/2012	$4,000

Distribution

FMV of machine	$7,000
Less: shareholder's basis	($4,000)
Her capital gain	**$3,000**

###

23. Greenhouse Gardens is an S corporation. It has four shareholders: Jordan, Mai, Simon, and Nora. The corporation has 10,000 shares outstanding. The shareholders have the following ownership:

Shareholder	Ownership
Jordan	4,500 shares
Mai	2,000 shares
Simon	2,000 shares
Nora	1,500 shares
Total	**10,000 shares**

Nora and Jordan wish to terminate the S election, but Mai and Simon do not. What statement is true?

A. Jordan can elect to terminate the corporation's S status on his own.
B. All of the shareholders must agree to terminate the election.
C. Nora and Jordan have enough stock ownership to terminate the election.
D. At least 75% of the shareholders with active ownership must agree to the termination.

The answer is C. An S election may be revoked if shareholders holding more than 50% of the stock agree to the termination. Since Nora and Jordan own more than 50% of the outstanding stock, they can elect to revoke the S election. ###

Unit 17: Farmers and Farming Corporations

More Reading:
Publication 225, *Farmer's Tax Guide*

Congress has enacted many tax laws specific to farming that reflect the highly unpredictable nature of the business and that treat farming differently from other businesses. For example, farmers have a different schedule for paying estimated taxes; they may postpone gain or income in certain cases that other businesses cannot; they may deduct a higher percentage of mileage expenses than other businesses; and they are given special tax considerations when disaster strikes.

Farming businesses as sole proprietorships report income and loss on Schedule F, *Profit or Loss from Farming*. Farmers are generally considered self-employed and must pay self-employment tax on their earnings. Schedule F is also used by self-employed fishermen.

Self-employed farmers must complete Schedule SE (self-employment tax) to figure out how much they should pay in taxes for Social Security and Medicare. A farmer is usually self-employed if he operates his own farm or rents farmland from others to engage in the business of farming.

A farming business may also be organized as a partnership or a corporation. Farming businesses are primarily engaged in crop production, animal production, or forestry and logging. A farm includes stock, dairy, poultry, fish, fruit, and tree farms. It also includes plantations, ranches, timber farms, and orchards.

Certain associated businesses are not considered "farming businesses" and instead must file on Schedule C. Examples of businesses that are not considered farming businesses include:

- Veterinary businesses
- Businesses that only supply farm labor
- Businesses that raise or breed dogs, cats, or other household pets
- Businesses that are only in the business of breeding
- Businesses that provide agricultural services such as soil preparation and fertilization

Examples of true farming businesses include:

- Fruit and tree nut farming
- Crop farming
- Forest nurseries and timber tracts
- Aquaculture farms
- Beef cattle ranching

- Crop shares for use of the farmer's land

Farm income does not include any of the following:

- Wages received as a farm employee
- Income received under a contract for grain harvesting with workers and machines furnished by the taxpayer
- Gains received from the sale of farm land and depreciable farm equipment
- Gains from the sale of securities, regardless of who owns the securities

Rents from Farming, Including Crop Shares

If a farmer rents his farmland for someone else to use, it is generally rent income, not farm income. This is true of crop shares too, when a tenant farmer pays a proportion of crop harvest proceeds to the land owner for use of his farmland. This passive income is reported on Form 4835, *Farm Rental Income and Expenses.*

However, if a farmer *materially participates* in farming operations on the land he owns, the rent is considered farm income and is reported on Schedule F.

Special Rules for Estimated Taxes

Special rules apply to the payment of estimated tax by qualified farmers and fishermen.

If at least two-thirds of the business's gross income comes from farming or fishing activity, the business qualifies under the special rules for estimated tax, and the following rules apply:

- The taxpayer does not have to pay estimated tax if he files his return and pays all the tax owed by the first day of the third month after the end of his tax year (usually March 1).
- If the taxpayer must pay estimated tax, he is required to make only one estimated tax payment (called the "required annual payment") by the fifteenth day after the end of his tax year (usually January 15).

For the 2012 tax year only, the IRS announced an extension in the filing deadline for qualified farmers or fishermen. Many typically file by March 1 under the special rules that allow them to avoid making quarterly tax payments during the year. However, the late tax changes of the fiscal cliff legislation[56] affected the IRS's ability to process some of the forms farmers and fisherman use, particularly those for depreciation.

---

[56] Formally called the American Taxpayer Relief Act of 2012, passed on January 2, 2013.

Because of this, the IRS will waive penalties for the 2012 tax year for those farmers and fishermen who miss the March 1, 2013 deadline, so long as they file their returns and pay the tax due by April 15, 2013.

Accounting Methods for Farming

Most small farming businesses operate using the cash method of accounting. However, since farming usually requires an inventory (of crops or livestock, for example), larger farming businesses are required to use the accrual method.

Farmers generally choose an accounting method when they file their first income tax return. They are allowed to use any of the following accounting methods:

- **Cash method**
- **Accrual method**
- **Special methods (the Crop method)**
  - o **The Crop method** is a special inventory valuation method that is only allowed for farming businesses. If crops are not harvested and disposed of in the same tax year they are planted, with IRS approval a farmer may use the crop method of accounting. Under the crop method, the farmer may deduct the entire cost of producing the crop, including the expense of seed or young plants, in the year income is realized from the crop. This method is not allowed for timber.
- **Combination (hybrid) method:** The IRS allows businesses to use a hybrid combination of the cash method and the accrual method. For instance, companies may use the accrual accounting method to satisfy tax requirements and the cash basis method for all other transactions.

Example: Ernie is a self-employed farmer who uses the accrual method of accounting. He keeps his books on the calendar-year basis. Ernie sells grain in December 2012, but he is not paid until January 2013. Ernie must include the sale and also deduct the costs incurred in producing the grain on his 2012 tax return.

Example: Miguel is also a self-employed farmer, but he uses the cash method of accounting. Miguel sells livestock in December 2012, but he is not paid until January 2013. Since Miguel uses the cash method and there was no constructive receipt of the sale proceeds until 2013, he does not report the income from the livestock sale on his 2012 return. Under this method, Miguel includes the sale proceeds in income in 2013, the year he receives payment.

The accrual method is required for certain large farm corporations and partnerships. The following farming businesses must use the accrual method:

- A corporation (*other than* a family farming corporation) that had gross receipts of more than $1 million for any tax year
- A family farming corporation that had gross receipts of more than $25 million for any tax year
- A partnership with a corporate partner
- A tax shelter (of any size or income)

Special Rules for Family Farming Corporations

Farming businesses are required to use the accrual method if they reach a gross receipts' threshold of $1 million (since farming businesses typically carry inventory). However, a special exception is made for family farming corporations. Qualified family farming corporations are still allowed to use the cash method so long as their average annual gross receipts are $25 million or less.

To qualify as a family farming corporation, the business must meet at least one of the following requirements:
- Members of the same family must own at least 50% of the corporation's stock
- Members of two families must have owned, either directly or indirectly, at least 65% of the corporation's stock
- Members of three families must have owned, either directly or indirectly, at least 50% of the corporation's stock

Example: Dave and Raymond are brothers. They are also the two sole shareholders of Da-Ray Farms Corporation, which is a qualified family farming corporation. Da-Ray Farms raises cattle, and in 2012 it has $20 million in gross receipts. Since Da-Ray is a qualified family farm, the entity is allowed to use the cash method of accounting.

Farm Inventory Methods in General

Farmers may use the same inventory methods that are available to other businesses, such as cost and lower of cost or market, which were covered in Unit Three under inventory methods. However, there are two other inventory methods that are unique to farming businesses:
- **Farm-price method**
- **Unit-livestock-price method**

Farm-Price Method: Under the farm-price method, each item, whether raised or purchased, is valued at its market price less the cost of disposition. The costs of disposition include broker's commissions, freight, hauling to market, and other marketing costs. If a farming business chooses to use the farm-price method, it must use it for the entire inventory, except that livestock can be inventoried under the unit-livestock-price method.

Unit-Livestock-Price Method: The unit-livestock-price method is an easier inventory method that allows farmers to group livestock together, rather than tracking costs of each individual animal. A farmer may classify livestock according to type and age, and then use a standardized unit price for each animal within a class. The unit price must reasonably approximate the costs incurred in producing the animal. If a farming business uses the unit-livestock-price method, it must include all raised livestock in inventory, regardless of whether it is held for sale or for draft, breeding, sport, or dairy purposes. This method accounts only for the costs incurred while raising an animal to maturity. It does not provide for any decrease in the animal's market value after it reaches maturity.

Livestock in Inventory

All livestock purchased primarily for sale must be included in inventory. If the livestock was purchased primarily for draft, breeding, sport, or dairy purposes, the farmer can choose to depreciate it, or include the livestock in inventory. Regardless of the method chosen, it must be consistent from year to year.

If a farmer values his livestock inventory at cost or the lower-of-cost or market, he does not need IRS approval to change to the unit-livestock-price method. However, if he values his livestock inventory using the farm-price method, then he must obtain permission from the IRS to change to the unit-livestock-price method.

All harvested and purchased farm products held for sale, such as grain, hay, or tobacco, must be included in inventory. Supplies acquired for sale or that become part of the items held for sale must be included in inventory. A business may expense the cost of supplies consumed in operations during the year.

Uniform Capitalization Rules (UNICAP)

Farming businesses are subject to the uniform capitalization rules (UNICAP).[57] A farmer can determine costs required to be allocated under UNICAP by using the farm-price or unit-livestock-price inventory method.

If a farming business uses the accrual method of accounting, it is subject to the following uniform capitalization rules:

- The rules apply to all costs of raising a plant, even if the pre-productive period of raising a plant is two years or less.
- The rules apply to all costs related to animals.

---

[57] UNICAP was covered in Unit 3, *Accounting Methods*.

Included in Farm Inventory

Farm inventory includes all items that are held for sale, purchased for resale, and for use as feed or seed, such as the following:

- Eggs in the process of hatching
- Harvested farm products that are held for sale, such as grain, cotton, hay, or tobacco
- Supplies that become a physical part of an item held for sale, such as containers, wrappers, or other packaging
- Any livestock that is held primarily for sale or purchased for resale
- Fur-bearing animals, such as mink, fox, or chinchilla, that are being held for breeding
- Purchased farm products that are being held for seed or feed

Not Included in Farm Inventory

Farm inventory does not include real property, such as land or buildings, or depreciable equipment, such as tractors.

Currently growing crops are generally *not required* to be included in inventory. However, if the crop has a pre-productive period of more than two years, the farmer may have to capitalize (or include in inventory) the costs associated with the crop.

Also not included in inventory is most livestock held for draft, breeding, dairy, or sport. These are business assets, and as such are subject to depreciation and generally not included in inventory.

Sales of Farm Products and Farm Assets

When a farmer sells products raised on a farm, the entire amount is reported on Schedule F. This is similar to any other self-employed taxpayer who sells regular inventory and reports the sales proceeds on Schedule C. When a farmer sells farm products bought for resale, his profit or loss is the difference between his basis in the item (usually cost) and any payment received for it.

> **Example:** In 2011, Oscar bought 20 feeder calves for $6,000 for resale. He sold them in 2012 for $11,000. Oscar reports the $11,000 sales price, subtracts his $6,000 basis, and reports the resulting $5,000 profit on his 2012 Schedule F.

Income reported on Schedule F does not include gains or losses from sales or other dispositions of the following farm assets:

- Land
- Depreciable farm equipment
- Buildings and structures

- Livestock held for draft, breeding, sport, or dairy purposes (this is live-stock that is not held primarily for sale)

The sale of these assets is reported on Form 4797, *Sales of Business Property*, and may result in ordinary or capital gains or losses.

Dispositions of Farm Property and Real Estate

When a farming business disposes of depreciable property (section 1245 property or section 1250 property) at a gain, the taxpayer may have to recognize ordinary income under the depreciation recapture rules. Any gain remaining after applying the depreciation recapture rules is a section 1231 gain, which may then be taxed as a capital gain. This is the same treatment as other businesses when they sell depreciable business property.

Section 1245: Part or all of the gain of the sale of section 1245 property is treated as ordinary income under the rules of depreciation recapture. Buildings and structural components are excluded under section 1245. However, "single purpose agricultural (livestock) or horticultural structures" are section 1245 property. So, for example, a barn that houses different animals and is used to store supplies would not be section 1245 property because it is not a single purpose facility. However, a greenhouse that is used only to grow plants would be single purpose, and thus section 1245 property. If a cash register is installed in the greenhouse so that a farmer can sell plants in addition to growing them there, the greenhouse would no longer be section 1245 property because it is no longer single purpose.

Other examples of farming-related section 1245 property include a grain silo, fencing for the confinement of livestock, and wells for providing water to livestock.

Section 1231 Transactions Specific to Farming Businesses

Gain or loss on the following farm-related transactions is subject to section 1231 treatment:

1. Sale or exchange of cattle or horses held for draft, breeding, dairy, or sporting purposes and held for 24 months or longer.

2. Sale or exchange of other livestock held for draft, breeding, dairy, or sporting purposes and held for 12 months or longer. Other livestock includes hogs, mules, sheep, and goats, but does not include poultry.

3. Sale or exchange of depreciable property used in the farming business and held for longer than one year. Examples include farm machinery and trucks.

338

4. Sale or exchange of real estate used in the farming business and held for longer than one year. Examples are a farm or ranch, including barns and sheds.

5. Sale or exchange of unharvested crops.

6. Sale from cut timber.

7. The condemnation of business property held longer than one year. Condemnations of business property usually qualify for nonrecognition treatment if replacement property is purchased within a certain time period, under the involuntary conversion rules.

Postponing Gain Due to Disaster Provisions

There are special rules for farmers regarding the postponement of gain due to weather conditions. If a farmer sells or exchanges *more* livestock (including poultry), than he *normally would* in a year because of a drought, flood, or other weather-related condition, he may postpone reporting the gain from the *additional* animals until the following year. The taxpayer must meet all the following conditions to qualify:

- The principal trade or business must be farming.
- The farmer must use the cash method of accounting.
- The farmer must be able to show that he would not have sold or exchanged the additional animals this year except for the weather-related condition.
- The area must be designated as eligible for federal disaster assistance.

The livestock does not have to be raised or sold in the affected area for the postponement to apply. However, the sale must occur solely because the weather-related condition affected the water, grazing, or other requirements of the livestock. The farmer must figure the amount to be postponed separately for each generic class of animals—for example, hogs, sheep, and cattle.

Example: Yolanda is a calendar-year farmer, and she normally sells 100 head of beef cattle a year. As a result of drought, she sells 135 head during 2011 and realizes $70,200 from the sale. On November 9, 2011, because of drought, the affected area is declared a disaster area eligible for federal assistance. The income Yolanda can postpone until 2012 is $18,200 [($70,200 ÷ 135) × 35], which is the portion of the gain attributed to the additional animals that she sold over her normal amount.

A weather-related sale or exchange of livestock held for draft, breeding, or dairy purposes *may* also qualify as an involuntary conversion (in this case, this does not include poultry). Livestock that is sold or exchanged because of disease may not trigger taxable gain if the proceeds of the transaction are reinvested in replacement animals within two years of the close of the tax year in which the diseased animals were sold or exchanged. This would qualify as an involuntary conversion.

> **Example:** Paulo is a farmer who owns 3,000 head of cattle. In 2012, his herd is struck by viral disease and he is forced to send 1,500 to slaughter. His insurance reimburses his losses, and he promptly reinvests all the insurance proceeds into new livestock. This is treated as an involuntary conversion.

Postponing Gain from a Weather-Related Condition

To postpone gain, the farmer must attach a statement to his tax return for the year of the sale. The statement must have the following information for each class of livestock for which the taxpayer is postponing gain:

- A declaration that the postponement of gain is based on section 451(e) of the IRC
- Evidence of the weather-related conditions that forced the early sale or exchange of the livestock
- An explanation of the relationship of the area affected by the weather-related condition to the farmer's early sale or exchange of the livestock
- The number of animals sold in each of the three preceding years
- The number of animals the farmer would have sold in the tax year had he followed normal business practices in the absence of weather-related conditions
- The total number of animals sold and the number sold because of weather-related conditions during the tax year
- A computation, as described earlier, of the income to be postponed for each class of livestock

In order to postpone gain, the farmer must file this statement along with the tax return by the due date of the return, including extensions.

However, for sales that qualify as an involuntary conversion, the farmer can file this statement at any time during the replacement period. The replacement period for the sale of livestock due to weather-related conditions is four years, and up to five years if the property is subject to an involuntary conversion in a federally declared disaster area.

Crop Insurance and Disaster Payments

Insurance proceeds, including government disaster payments, are generally taxable in the year they are received. These payments are made as a result of the destruction or damage to crops or the inability to plant crops because of drought, flood, or other natural disaster.

340

The farmer can elect to postpone reporting the income until the following year if he meets all of these conditions:

- The farming business must use the cash method of accounting.
- Crop insurance proceeds were received in the same tax year the crops were damaged.
- Under normal business practices, the farming business would have reported income from the damaged crops in any tax year following the year the damage occurred.

A statement must be attached to the tax return indicating the specific crops that were damaged and the total insurance payment received.

In order to make this election to postpone income, the farmer must be able to prove that the crops would have been harvested or otherwise sold in the following year.

Sometimes, farmers choose to forgo the planting of crops altogether. These farmers may then receive agricultural program payments from the government. An agricultural program payment is reported on Schedule F, and the full amount of the payment is subject to self-employment tax.

Other Unique Tax Rules for Farmers

There are many other rules that are unique to farming businesses. Other examples of special tax breaks afforded to farmers are:

1. **Car and truck expenses:** Farmers can claim 75% of the use of a car or light truck as business use *without any records* (such as a mileage log) so long as the vehicle is used in a farming business.
2. **Soil conservation:** Farmers can choose to deduct as a business expense land-related expenses for soil or water conservation or for the prevention of erosion. Examples include leveling, eradication of brush, removal of trees, or planting of windbreaks. Normally, these expenses are capital expenses that are added to the basis of the land, but farming businesses may choose to deduct them instead.
3. **Net operating losses:** Farming losses qualify for longer carryback periods. The carryback period for farming losses is five years. Other businesses are allowed to carryback their losses only two years.
4. **Farm income averaging:** Certain farmers may average all or some of their current year's farm income by allocating it to the three prior years. This may lower a farmer's current year tax if the current year is high and his taxable income from one or more of the three prior years was low. Income averaging is only available to farming businesses that are sole proprietorships or

partnerships. Farmers use Schedule J, *Income Averaging for Farmers and Fishermen,* to figure their 2012 income tax by income averaging.

5. **Excise tax credits:** Farmers may be eligible to claim a credit or refund of federal excise taxes on fuel used on a farm.

Unit 17: Questions

1. Isaac is a calendar-year, self-employed farmer on the cash basis. For purposes of the estimated tax for qualified farmers, all of the following statements are true except:

A. Isaac does not have to make any estimated payments if he files by April 15 and pays all his taxes with his return.
B. Isaac is a qualified farmer if at least two-thirds of his previous year's gross income is from farming.
C. The required annual estimated tax payment for farmers is due on the fifteenth day after the close of their tax year.
D. The required annual payment is two-thirds of the current year's tax or 100% of the previous year's tax.

The answer is A. If a farmer waits until April 15 to file his return, he must pay estimated taxes just like any other business. If the taxpayer is a qualified farmer, he can either:

•Pay all his estimated tax by the fifteenth day after the end of his tax year (this date is usually January 15)
•File his return and pay all the tax owed by the first day of the third month after the end of his tax year (usually March 1).

*Note: For tax year 2012, however, the IRS announced that it is waiving penalties for farmers and fishermen who miss the March 1, 2013 filing tax deadline, as long as they file their returns and pay the tax due by April 15, 2013. This is because of delays in IRS processing due to the last-minute tax changes of the fiscal cliff legislation. ###

2. Joel is a qualified farmer who usually sells 500 beef cattle every year. However, because of a severe drought, he was forced to sell 800 beef cattle. Which of the following statements is true?

A. Joel may choose to postpone all of the gain in this transaction.
B. Joel may choose to postpone a portion of his gain in this transaction.
C. Joel must use the accrual method of accounting in order to postpone gain.
D. Postponement of gain is not allowed.

The answer is B. Joel may postpone a portion of his gain to the following year. If a farmer sells or exchanges more livestock, including poultry, than he normally would in a year because of a drought, flood, or other weather-related condition, he may postpone reporting the gain from the additional animals until the next year. The farmer must use the cash method of accounting in order to postpone gain in this manner. ###

3. All of the following should be included in farming inventory except:

A. Farming equipment and machinery.
B. Livestock held primarily for sale.
C. Farm products held for feed or seed.
D. Supplies that become a physical part of items held for sale.

The answer is A. Farming equipment is an asset. Equipment is depreciated and therefore not included in inventory. ###

4. Which of the following statements about farmers is true?

A. Gross income from farming includes capital gains from the sale of equipment.
B. A farmer who is a sole proprietor may use income averaging to reduce his tax liability.
C. A farmer does not have to report income from crop insurance payments.
D. An individual who owns livestock as a hobby and grows a large garden can be considered a farmer for tax purposes.

The answer is B. Certain farmers may average all or some of their current year's farm income by allocating it to the three prior years. This may lower a farmer's current year tax if the current year is high and his taxable income from one or more of the three prior years was low. Income averaging is only available to farmers and fishermen who operate as sole proprietors or partnerships. It is reported on Schedule J, Income Averaging for Farmers and Fishermen. ###

5. All of the following are acceptable methods for valuation of farm inventory except:

A. Cost.
B. Harvest discount.
C. Farm-price method.
D. Unit-livestock-price method.

The answer is B. The harvest discount method does not exist. All of the other inventory valuation methods listed are allowed for farming businesses. ###

6. Jon owns a dairy business and has income from the following sources:

- Income from milk production: $50,000
- Sale of old dairy cows: $20,000
- Sale of feed: $15,000
- Sale of used machinery: $4,000

What amount of income should be reported on Jon's Schedule F, Profit or Loss from Farming?

A. $50,000.
B. $65,000.
C. $74,000.
D. $85,000.

The answer is B. The farming income reported is from milk production and sale of feed ($50,000 + $15,000 = $65,000) Gross income from farming activity is reported on Schedule F, and includes farm income, farm rental income, and gains from livestock that were raised specifically for sale on the farm, or purchased specifically for resale. The sale of old dairy cows and the sale of used machinery do not qualify. The sale of depreciable machinery is not reported on Schedule F, and likewise, the sale of livestock used for dairy purposes results in a capital gain (or loss) and is not reported on Schedule F. Instead, these amounts should be reported on Form 4797, Sales of Business Property. ###

7. Hope is a qualified farmer who grows soybeans. In 2012, her soybean crop was destroyed by flood. If the crop had not been destroyed, she would have harvested it in 2013. Hope receives federal disaster payments in 2012. Which of the following is true?

A. Hope can choose to postpone the income from this disaster payment until 2013.
B. Disaster payments are not taxable income.
C. Hope must report the income on her 2012 return.
D. Hope may delay recognition of the gain for two years.

The answer is A. She can delay recognizing income on the payment until the following year. Payments for disaster relief may be included in income in the tax year following the year in which they were awarded. In order to make this election, the farmer must be able to prove that the crops would have been harvested or otherwise sold in the following year. ###

8. Oliver is a farmer and has decided to refrain from growing any crops in 2012. He receives agricultural program payments for this activity. How should these payments be reported?

A. As "other income" on the taxpayer's individual Form 1040.
B. On Schedule E, Supplemental Income and Loss.
C. As farm income, but not subject to self-employment tax.
D. As farm income on Schedule F, subject to self-employment tax.

The answer is D. An agricultural program payment is reported on Schedule F, and the full amount of the payment is subject to self-employment tax. ###

9. Luke is a qualified farmer. A bull calf was born on his farm on 2011. Luke raised the calf for breeding purposes. Luke spent $750 in feed for the calf and it was sold for $5,000 for breeding use in 2012. How much is Luke's gain from the sale of the bull calf?

A. $0.
B. $4,250.
C. $4,750.
D. $5,000.

The answer is D. The basis of livestock is generally cost. However, since the bull calf was born on the farm, the basis of the calf is $0. The cost of the feed is deductible and is listed on the return as a regular business expense and as a deduction from gross income. The cost of the feed is not added to the basis of the calf. The sale of livestock held for breeding is not included in regular farming income. Special rules apply to the sale of livestock held for draft, breeding, sport, or dairy purposes. In this case, the sale resulted in a capital gain of $5,000. Farmers report these sales on Form 4797, Sales of Business Property. ###

10. Andy owns 150 acres of farmland that he rents to other farmers. He does not actively participate in any of the farming activity. How should the income from this activity be reported?

A. As rental income on Form 4835.
B. As farming income on Schedule F.
C. As ordinary income on Schedule C.
D. As passive income on Schedule 4797.

The answer is A. The rent received for the use or rental of farmland is generally rental income, not farm income. If the farmer does not materially participate in operating the farm, the income is reported on Form 4835, Farm Rental Income and Expenses, and the income is not subject to self-employment tax. ###

11. To be eligible as a qualified farmer and not have to pay quarterly estimated taxes during the year, at least _____ of a farmer's gross income must be from farming.

A. Half.
B. Two-thirds.
C. Three-quarters.
D. 80%

The answer is B. An individual is a qualified farmer for 2012 if at least two-thirds of his or her gross income from all sources for 2011 or 2012 was from farming. ###

12. All of the following would be considered section 1245 property except:

A. A greenhouse.
B. A grain silo.
C. A wire chicken coop.
D. A barn that houses cows and horses.

The answer is D. Section 1245 typically excludes buildings and other structural components. However, there is an exception for single purpose agricultural or horticultural structures. A barn for cows and horses is not a single purpose structure so it would not qualify for section 1245 treatment. ###

347

13. Merle is a sheep farmer, and also has income from other sources. In 2012, he had the following total gross income amounts:

•Taxable interest: $3,000
•Dividends: $500
•Rental Income (Schedule E): $41,500
•Farming income (Schedule F): $75,000
•Gain (Form 4797): $5,000

Total income: $125,000
Total farming income: $75,000

Merle's Schedule D showed gain from the sale of sheep carried over from Form 4797 ($5,000) in addition to a loss from the sale of corporate stock ($2,000). Is Merle a "qualified farmer" according to IRS rules?

A. Yes.
B. No.
C. Only if his 2011 income was greater than his 2012 income.
D. Cannot be determined given the information provided.

The answer is B. Merle is not a qualified farmer for IRS purposes. The loss from the sale of corporate stock is not netted against the gain to figure Merle's total gross income or his gross farm income. His gross farm income is 64% of his total gross income ($80,000 ÷ $125,000 = .64). This means that Merle does not qualify for the special treatment for estimated taxes that is available to farmers and fishermen. An individual is a "qualified farmer" only if at least two-thirds (66%) of his or her gross income from all sources was from farming###

14. The carryback period for farming losses is _____:

A. Two years.
B. Four years.
C. Five years.
D. Farmers are not allowed to carryback their losses.

The answer is C. The carryback period for farming losses is five years. Other businesses are allowed to carry back their losses only two years. ###

15. Farm income averaging is computed on Schedule J, which may be filed:

A. For the current year when a taxpayer files Schedule F showing a farm loss.
B. For the current year, which includes a Schedule F showing net income from farming.
C. For the current year, along with Schedule C.
D. As an amended return showing the past three years of farming income.

The answer is B. If a farmer or fisherman elects income averaging, he must file Schedule J along with a Schedule F showing his net farming income for 2012. ###

Unit 18: Exempt Organizations

More Reading:
Publication 4220, *Applying for 501(c)(3) Tax-Exempt Status*
Publication 557, *Tax-Exempt Status for Your Organization*
Publication 4221-PC, *Compliance Guide for 501(c)(3) Public Charities*
Publication 598, *Tax on Unrelated Business Income of Exempt Organizations*

Nonprofit organizations may qualify for exemption from the requirement to pay income taxes, but they are still subject to certain filing and record-keeping requirements under federal tax law. There are several different types of exempt organizations; all are tax exempt, but not all qualify to receive contributions that are deductible by the donor.

IRC Section 501(c)(3)

The majority of nonprofit organizations qualify for tax-exempt status under section 501(c)(3) of the IRC. These nonprofits are exempt from paying income tax in connection with their charitable activities, and they are eligible to receive tax-deductible charitable contributions. To qualify for these benefits, most organizations must file an application with the IRS to seek recognition as a 501(c)(3). There are three key components for an organization to be exempt from federal income tax under 501(c)(3):

- **Organization:** It must be organized as a corporation, trust, or unincorporated association, and its purpose must be limited to those described in section 501(c)(3). A nonprofit entity may not be organized as a partnership or sole proprietorship.
- **Operation:** A substantial portion of its activities must operate to further its exempt purpose. A 501(c)(3) organization:
  - must refrain from participating in political campaigns of candidates
  - must restrict its lobbying activities to an "insubstantial" part of its total activities
  - must ensure that its earnings do not benefit any private shareholder or individual
  - must not operate for the benefit of private interests such as those of its founder, the founder's family, or its shareholders
  - must not operate for the primary purpose of conducting a trade or business that is not related to its exempt purpose
- **Exempt purpose:** It must have one or more exempt purposes as listed under section 501(c)(3): charitable, educational, religious, sci-

entific, literary, fostering national or international sports competition, preventing cruelty to children or animals, and testing for public safety.

Applying for 501(c)(3) Status

Before applying for tax exemption, the organization must be created using an *organizing document*. This document must limit the organization's purposes to those set forth in section 501(c)(3) and must specify that the entity's assets will be permanently dedicated to an exempt purpose. The organizing document should also contain a provision for distributing funds if it dissolves.

To request exempt status under section 501(c)(3), entities use Form 1023, *Application for Recognition of Exemption*. Organizations that do not qualify for exemption under section 501(c)(3) may still qualify for tax-exempt status by filing Form 1024, *Application for Recognition of Exemption Under 501(a)*.

In order to qualify for tax exemption, an organization must generally request exemption from the IRS by the end of the fifteenth month after it was created, with a 12-month extension available. A small organization is not required to file Form 1023 unless its annual gross receipts are more than $5,000.

An organization must file Form 1023 to request formal exemption within 90 days of the end of the year in which it exceeds this threshold. However, a private foundation is always required to request exemption, regardless of the amount of its gross receipts.

Example: An animal rescue organization that was created five years ago did not exceed the $5,000 gross receipts threshold until September 30, 2012. The organization must file Form 1023 to request formal tax exemption by March 30, 2013.

An organization that files its application before the deadline may be recognized as tax-exempt from the date of its creation. An organization that files an application after the deadline also may be recognized as tax-exempt from the date of the application by requesting exemption retroactive as of the date of creation.

The IRS will review an organization's application and determine if it meets the requirements for exemption. If the decision is affirmative, the IRS will then issue a letter recognizing the organization's exempt status and providing its public charity classification.

While an organization's Form 1021 is pending approval, the organization may operate as if it were tax-exempt. Donor contributions made while an application is pending would qualify if the IRS determines the entity should have 501(c)(3) status. However, if the application is not approved, these contributions would not qualify. The organization would also be liable for filing federal income tax returns unless its income is otherwise excluded from federal taxation.

Other Section 501(c) Organizations

Not all tax-exempt organizations are 501(c)(3) organizations. There are other organizations that qualify for tax-exempt status, but may or may not qualify to accept donor-deductible contributions.

Other examples of nonprofit entities that are not 501(c)(3) organizations include:

- 501(c)(4) Civic leagues and social welfare organizations
- 501(c)(5) Labor unions, agricultural, and horticultural organizations
- 501(c)(6) Business leagues
- 501(c)(7) Social and recreation clubs
- 501(c)(8) and 501(c)(10) Fraternal beneficiary societies
- 501(c)(4), 501(c)(9), and 501(c)(17) Employees' associations
- 501(c)(12) Local benevolent life insurance associations
- 501(c)(13) Nonprofit cemetery companies
- 501(c)(14) Credit unions and other mutual financial organizations
- 501(c)(19) Veterans' organizations
- 501(c)(20) Group legal services plan organizations
- 501(c)(21) Black lung benefit trusts
- 501(c)(2) Title-holding corporations for single parents
- 501(c)(25) Title-holding corporations or trusts for multiple parents
- 501(c)(26) State-sponsored high-risk health coverage organizations
- 501(c)(27) State-sponsored workers' compensation reinsurance organizations

To be exempt under IRC section 501(c)(7), a social club must be organized for pleasure, recreation, and other similar nonprofit purposes, and substantially all of its activities must be for these purposes.

Filing Requirements

Every exempt organization must file an annual information return on Form 990, *Return of Organization Exempt from Income Tax*, with the IRS, unless it is specifically exempt from the filing requirement. The organizations that are not required to file Form 990 are:

- Churches and their affiliated organizations
- Government agencies

Small tax-exempt organizations with gross receipts of $50,000 or less are required to file Form 990-N, *Electronic Notice for Tax Exempt Organizations Not Required to File Form 990.* This form is also called an "e-postcard" because it is filed electronically and is short. A small tax-exempt organization may also voluntarily choose to file a long form (Form 990) instead.

Exempt Entities: Financial Activity	Annual Information Return Required
Gross receipts normally < $50,000	Form 990-N (e-postcard)
Gross receipts < $500,000 and Total assets < $1.25 million	Form 990-EZ or 990
Gross receipts $500,000 (or greater), or Total assets ≥ $1.25 million	Form 990
Private foundation (must file every year, regardless of financial activity)	Form 990-PF
Churches and similar religious organizations	No yearly filing requirement, but may still be required to file payroll returns if the entity has employees

An exempt entity may choose to file on a fiscal year or a calendar year basis. The applicable annual information return is due by the fifteenth day of the fifth month after the year ends. For a calendar-year entity, the due date is May 15. If the organization has been dissolved, the return is due by the fifteenth day of the fifth month after the dissolution.

Extensions of Time to File

An exempt entity may request a three-month extension of time to file by filing Form 8868, *Application for Extension of Time to File an Exempt Organization Return.* The organization may also apply for an additional three-month extension, if needed, using the same form. When filing a request for the first three-month extension, neither a signature nor an explanation is required. However, when filing an additional three-month extension, both a signature and an explanation are required.

An organization must file Form 990 electronically if it files at least 250 returns during the calendar year and has total assets of $10 million or more at the end of the tax year. A private foundation is required to file Form 990-PF electronically if it files at least 250 returns during the calendar year.

Section 501(c)(3) organizations must make their application (Form 1023) and the three most recent annual returns (Form 990) available to the public. The IRS also makes these documents available for public inspection and copying.

Every tax-exempt entity must have an EIN whether it has employees or not.

Penalties for Late Filing and Failure to File

An exempt organization that fails to file a required return must pay a penalty of $20 a day for each day the return is late. The same penalty will apply if the organization provides incorrect information on the return. The maximum penalty for any year is the smaller of:

- $10,000, or

- 5% of the organization's gross receipts for the year.

However, for an organization that has gross receipts of more than $1 million for the year, the late filing penalty is $100 a day, up to a maximum of $50,000.

An organization's exempt status may be revoked for failure to file. Failure to file an annual information return for three years in a row will result in the automatic revocation of exempt status. In this case, the organization would be required to reapply for exemption.

No penalty will be imposed if reasonable cause for failure to timely file can be shown.

Retroactive Reinstatement

If an organization's tax-exempt status was automatically revoked for failing to file a return or notice for three consecutive years, it must apply to have its tax-exempt status reinstated by filing either Form 1023 or Form 1024 and paying the appropriate fee.

In 2012, smaller organizations—defined as having annual gross receipts of $50,000 or less in their most recent tax year—that lost their tax-exempt status by failing to file the e-postcard were eligible for transitional relief. This relief included possible retroactive reinstatement and a reduced user fee.[58]

Employment Tax Returns for Exempt Organizations

The basic requirements for tax and wage reporting compliance, calculating withholding, making deposits, and keeping tax and reporting records apply to exempt organizations just like other businesses.

Even though some organizations (such as a church or other religious organization) are not required to file Form 990, any entity with employees must withhold and remit Social Security and Medicare taxes on its employees' wages, and some exempt organizations are also responsible for Federal Unemployment Tax (FUTA).

---

[58] IRS Notice 2011-43.

> **Example:** Trinity Methodist Church is not required to file an application for exemption in order to be recognized as tax-exempt by the IRS. Trinity applies for an EIN as an exempt entity and begins regular worship. In 2012, Trinity Church hires three employees: a part-time pastor, a Sunday child care worker, and a music leader. Although Trinity does not have to file Form 990, the church is still required to file employment tax returns and remit and collect employment taxes from its employees. In this way, the exempt organization is treated like every other employer.

Public Charity or Private Foundation?

Every organization that qualifies for tax-exempt status under section 501(c)(3) of the IRC is further classified as either a public charity or a private foundation. Tax-exempt entities are automatically presumed to be private foundations, unless they are specifically excluded.

For some organizations, the primary distinction between classification as a public charity or a private foundation is the organization's source of financial support. Generally, a public charity has a broad base of support while a private foundation has very limited sources of support.

This classification is important because different tax rules apply: the deductibility of contributions to a private foundation is more limited than deductibility of contributions to a public charity.

A private foundation is a charitable organization that is set up as a holding entity for donated assets. Private foundations receive less preferential tax treatment than public charities and religious organizations because they are not always seen as operating for the good of the public.

Some organizations are automatically excluded from being classified as private foundations. As listed in IRC section 509(a)(1), these organizations are not considered private foundations:

- Any church
- An educational organization, such as a school or college
- A hospital or a medical research organization operated in conjunction with a hospital
- Endowment funds operated for the benefit of colleges and universities
- Any domestic governmental organization
- A publicly-supported organization
- Organizations organized and operated exclusively for testing for public safety

Any exempt organization will not be considered a private foundation if it receives more than one-third of its annual support from its own members and/or the general public.

All private foundations must file Form 990-PF, *Return of Private Foundation*, every year regardless of their income.

There is an excise tax on the net investment income of domestic private foundations. Certain foreign private foundations are also subject to a tax on investment income derived from domestic sources. This excise tax is reported on Form 990-PF, and must be paid annually or in quarterly estimated tax payments if the total tax for the year is $500 or more.

Unrelated Business Income Tax (UBIT)

Although an exempt organization must be operated primarily for a tax-exempt purpose, it may engage in unrelated income-producing activities so long as these activities are not a substantial part of the organization's regular activities. Income from unrelated business activity is subject to a federal tax called the unrelated business income tax (UBIT). For most organizations, an activity is considered an unrelated business and subject to UBIT if:

- It is a trade or business,
- It is regularly carried on, and
- It is not substantially related to furthering the exempt purpose of the organization.

An exempt organization that has $1,000 or more of gross income from an unrelated business must file Form 990–T by the fifteenth day of the fifth month after the tax year ends. An exempt organization must make quarterly payments of estimated tax on unrelated business income if it expects its tax for the year to be $500 or more.

Example: A university enters into a multi-year contract with a company to be its exclusive provider of sports drinks for the athletic department and concessions. As part of the contract, the university agrees to perform various services for the company, such as guaranteeing that coaches make promotional appearances on behalf of the company. The university itself is a qualified nonprofit organization, but the income received from the exclusive contract is subject to UBIT. The university is therefore required to file Form 990-T.

Example: A college negotiates discounted rates for the soft drinks it purchases for its cafeterias in return for an exclusive provider arrangement. Generally, discounts are considered an adjustment to the purchase price and do not constitute gross income to the purchaser. Thus, the amount of the negotiated discount is not includable in UBIT. The college is not required to file Form 990-T.

Unit 18: Questions

1. Which of the following organizations do not qualify for tax-exempt status?

A. A charitable organization.
B. A religious organization.
C. A private foundation.
D. An educational partnership.

The answer is D. A partnership does not qualify for exemption from income tax. A tax-exempt organization cannot be organized as a partnership or sole proprietorship. ###

2. Cat Rescue Inc. is a calendar year nonprofit organization that helps prevent cruelty to animals. It is required to file Form 990 in 2012. What is the due date of its tax return, not including extensions?

A. April 15.
B. March 15.
C. May 15.
D. October 15.

The answer is C. Since Cat Rescue is on a calendar year, its tax return is due May 15. Each tax-exempt organization is required to file by the fifteenth day of the fifth month after its fiscal year ends. ###

3. Which of the following statements is true?

A. Any exempt organization that qualifies for tax-exempt status with the IRS receives contributions that are fully deductible by the donor.
B. A church is not required to file an annual information return (Form 990).
C. A religious entity does not have to file payroll tax returns if it has employees.
D. A church may be organized as a sole proprietorship.

The answer is B. A religious organization is not required to file an annual information return. However, a religious organization with employees is still responsible for filing employment tax returns. ###

4. Most organizations seeking recognition of exemption from federal income tax must use specific application forms prescribed by the IRS. Which form must be filed in order to request recognition as a 501(c)(3) nonprofit organization by the IRS?

A. Form 1023.
B. Form 1024.
C. Form 1040.
C. Form 990.

The answer is A. The form required by the IRS to apply for 501(c)(3) status is Form 1023, Application for Recognition of Exemption Under Section 501(c)(3) of the Internal Revenue Code. ###

5. Which of the following exempt organizations is not required to file an annual information return?

A. A church with gross receipts exceeding $250,000.
B. An exempt literary organization with $6,000 in gross receipts.
C. A Chamber of Commerce with $26,000 in gross receipts.
D. A private foundation with income of less than $5,000.

The answer is A. Only the church would not be required to file a tax return. Tax-exempt organizations must file a Form 990 or Form 990-N (e-postcard) unless specifically exempt. Private foundations must file a Form 990-PF, regardless of income. ###

6. All of the organizations listed below would qualify for tax-exempt status under the Internal Revenue Code except:

A. A Christian church with only eight members.
B. A political action committee.
C. A trust for a college alumni association.
D. A local boys club.

The answer is B. A political action committee would not qualify. In general, if a substantial part of an organization's activities includes attempting to influence legislation, the organization's exemption from federal income tax will be denied. ###

7. The Blue Lake Sailing Club is a social club promoting the social activity of sailing. Which of the following is true?

A. The Blue Lake Sailing Club may apply and be recognized as exempt from federal income tax.
B. A social club cannot qualify for IRS exemption.
C. This type of organization only qualifies for exemption if it is organized as a religious organization.
D. None of the above.

The answer is A. The sailing club can apply for exemption from income tax. To be exempt under IRC section 501(c)(7), a social club must be organized for pleasure, recreation, and other similar non-profit purposes and substantially all of its activities must be for these purposes. It should file Form 1024 to apply for recognition of exemption from federal income tax. Donations under 501(c)(7) are not deductible as charitable contributions. ###

8. The local Catholic church has two employees: Martha, who works as a secretary in the church rectory, and Jack, who is the church custodian. Which return(s) must the church file in order to fulfill its IRS reporting obligations?

A. Form 990.
B. Form 8300.
C. Employment tax returns.
D. Form 990-PF.

The answer is C. Exempt churches, their integrated auxiliaries, and conventions or associations of churches are not required to file information returns. However, every employer is responsible for filing employment tax returns. ###

9. Which of the following organizations may request exempt status under the Internal Revenue Code as a section 501(c)(3) organization?

A: A Catholic organization.
B: A Hindu organization.
C: A children's rescue organization.
D: All of the above.

The answer is D. Nonprofit organizations that are exempt from federal income tax under section 501(c)(3) of the Internal Revenue Code include entities organized exclusively for religious, charitable, scientific, testing for public safety, literary or educational purposes, fostering national or international amateur sports competition, or for the prevention of cruelty to children or animals. ###

10. A charitable organization has $2,000 in unrelated business income in the current year. How is this income reported?

A. The organization must file a business tax return for the unrelated business income.
B. The organization is required to file Form 990-T.
C. The organization will have its exempt status revoked.
D. The organization must file Schedule C to correctly report the business income.

The answer is B. An exempt organization that has $1,000 or more of gross income from unrelated business activity must file Form 990–T. ###

11. What does an organization that wishes to be recognized as a 501(c)(3) charity need to file with the IRS?

A. Form 990.
B. Form 990 and its organizing document.
C. Form 1023 and its organizing document.
D. Form 1023, its organizing document, a listing of its board of directors, and its bylaws.

The answer is C. Form 1023, Application for Recognition of Exemption Under Section 501(c)(3 of the Internal Revenue Code, must be filed with the IRS, along with the entity's organizing document. This document should contain the required information as to purposes and powers of the organization and disposition of its assets upon dissolution. ###

12. Which kind of organization is allowed to file an e-postcard?

A. A private foundation.
B. A nonprofit with gross receipts of $25,000 or less.
C. A nonprofit with gross receipts of $50,000 or less.
D. A nonprofit with gross receipts of $100,000 or less.

The answer is C. A tax-exempt organization with gross receipts of $50,000 or less may file the short "e-postcard" Form 990-N, Electronic Notice for Tax Exempt Organizations Not Required to File Form 990, instead of the longer information return, Form 990, if it so chooses. ###

13. What action does the IRS take if a nonprofit with $500,000 in gross receipts fails to file its required information returns or notices?

A. Nothing. Information returns are voluntary.
B. A maximum penalty of up to $10,000 or 5% of the organization's gross receipts for the year.
C. Automatic revocation of tax-exempt status if the organization fails to file returns or notices for three consecutive years.
D. Both B and C.

The answer is D. Exempt organizations are subject to both substantial failure-to-file penalties and automatic revocation when returns are not filed for three consecutive years. For exempt organizations with gross receipts of less than $1 million for the year, the maximum penalty is up to $10,000 or 5% of the organization's gross receipts for the year. For exempt organizations with gross receipts of more than $1 million a year, the maximum penalty is increased to a $50,000. ###

Unit 19: Retirement Plans for Businesses

More Reading:
Publication 560, *Retirement Plans for Small Business*

Employers set up retirement plans as a fringe benefit for their employees. Self-employed taxpayers are also allowed to set up retirement plans for themselves. There are numerous forms of retirement plans that employers can choose; these include Simplified Employee Pension (SEP) plans, Savings Incentive Match Plan for Employees (SIMPLE) plans, and qualified plans.

The term "qualified" refers to certain IRS requirements to which the plan and the employer must adhere in order to qualify for tax-favored status. SEP and SIMPLE plans must also meet certain requirements, but they are much less complex than those that apply to qualified plans.

Deductibility Rules for Business

If retirement plans are structured and operated properly, businesses can deduct retirement contributions they make on behalf of their employees. Both the contributions and the earnings are generally tax-free to the employees until distribution.

The rules vary depending on the type of business. Any business, including a sole proprietorship or a partnership, can deduct retirement plan contributions made on behalf of employees, even if the business has a net operating loss for the year.

However, in the case of a sole proprietorship or partnership, if the owners of the business contribute to *their own* retirement accounts, they must take the deduction on Form 1040, and only if they have self-employment income. Self-employment income for the purpose of this deduction means net profits from Schedule C or Schedule F, or self-employment income from a partnership.

Since an S corporation is a pass-through entity, shareholder-employees in an S corporation are also required to report these deductions on their individual returns.[59] However, as a C corporation is not a pass-through entity, the corporation deducts the expense on Form 1120, *US Corporation Income Tax Return,* whether it is made for an employee-shareholder, an officer, or a regular employee.

---

[59] In the case of an S corporation, this rule applies to employee-shareholders who own more than 2% of the S corporation stock.

> **Example:** Gemma is self-employed and reports her income and losses from her dress shop on Schedule C. She has a retirement account set up for herself and her five employees. In 2012, Gemma's dress shop showed a loss from operations on her Schedule C, and Gemma has no other source of taxable income. She made regular contributions to her employees' retirement accounts in 2012, and she may deduct these contributions as a regular business expense. However, Gemma cannot make a retirement contribution for *herself* in 2012 because she has no self-employment income. Since her business showed a loss, she has no qualifying income for purposes of her own retirement plan contribution.

Simplified Employee Pension (SEP)

A SEP plan provides the simplest and least expensive method for employers to make contributions to a retirement plan for themselves and their employees.

A SEP may be established as late as the due date (*including extensions*) of the company's income tax return for the year the employer wants to establish the plan. Employers must also make their contributions to the plan by the due date, including extensions. There is no requirement for a "plan document" such as those needed for qualified retirement plans. However, the employer must execute a formal written agreement to provide benefits to all eligible employees under the SEP. Except in certain circumstances, including when the employer also maintains a qualified plan, this can be done using IRS Form 5305-SEP. Using this form will typically eliminate the need to file annual information forms with the IRS and the Department of Labor. Contributions to a SEP can vary from year to year, so it is a very flexible option for small employers.

A SEP can be set up for an individual person's business even if he participates in another employer's retirement plan.

> **Example:** Mitch works full time for the post office as a mail carrier, and also runs a profitable catering business with his wife on the weekends. They have self-employment income from the business. Mitch may set up a SEP for himself and his spouse, even though he is already covered by the post office plan.

Under a SEP, employers make contributions to an Individual Retirement Arrangement (called a SEP-IRA), which must be set up for each eligible employee. The SEP-IRA is owned and controlled by the employee, and the employer makes contributions to the financial institution where the SEP-IRA is maintained. The SEP-IRAs are funded exclusively by contributions from the employer.

A SEP does not require employer contributions every year, but it cannot discriminate in favor of highly compensated employees (HCEs). This means that a business cannot choose to fund the SEP-IRAs of its highly-paid executives, while ignoring its other workers.

An eligible employee is one who meets all the following requirements:

- Has reached age 21
- Has worked for the employer in at least three of the last five years
- Has received at least $550 in compensation in 2012

If an employer sets up a SEP, then all the employees who are eligible employees must also be allowed to participate. An employer can use *less restrictive* participation requirements than those listed, but not *more restrictive* ones.
The following employees can be excluded from coverage under a SEP:

- Employees covered by a union agreement
- Nonresident alien employees who have received no U.S. source income from the employer

As with traditional IRAs, money withdrawn from a SEP-IRA (and not rolled over to another qualified retirement plan or account) is subject to income tax for the year in which an employee receives a distribution. If an employee withdraws money from a SEP-IRA before age 59½, a 10% additional tax generally applies. Further, a participant in a SEP-IRA must begin receiving required minimum distributions by April 1 of the year following the year the participant reaches age 70½. However, unlike a traditional IRA, contributions can be made to participants over age 70½.

Example: Quincy Company decides to establish a SEP for its employees. Quincy has chosen a SEP because its industry is cyclical in nature. In good years, Quincy can make larger contributions for its employees, and in down years it can reduce or eliminate contributions. Quincy knows that under a SEP, the contribution rate (whether large or small) must be uniform for all employees. The financial institution that Quincy has identified to be the trustee for its SEP has several investment funds for employees to choose from. Individual employees have the opportunity to divide their employer's contributions to their SEP-IRAs among these fund options.

Contributions to a SEP

Contributions to a SEP must be made in cash; an employer cannot contribute *property* to a SEP. However, plan participants may be able to transfer or roll over certain property from another retirement plan account to a SEP-IRA. When employers contribute to a SEP, they must contribute to the SEP-IRAs of all participants who had qualified compensation, including employees who die or terminate employment before the contributions are made. A SEP-IRA cannot be a Roth IRA. Employer contributions to a SEP-IRA will not affect the amount an individual can contribute to a Roth or traditional IRA. The following SEP limits apply in 2012:

- For an employee: Contributions cannot exceed the lesser of 25% of the employee's compensation or $50,000.
- For a self-employed individual: Contributions cannot exceed the lesser of 20% of net self-employment income, after considering both the deduction for self-employment tax and the deduction for the SEP-IRA contribution, or $50,000.

Employees have control over their own SEP-IRAs, so employers cannot prohibit distributions from a SEP-IRA. Further, employers cannot make contributions conditional, or require that any part of the contribution be kept in the employee's account after the business has made its contributions.

SEP Snapshot

	Rules for Employers	Rules for Employees
Eligibility	Any business or self-employed individual may set up a SEP.	All employees aged 21 or older who have worked for the business for three out of the last five years and earned at least $550 in the current year.
Contributions	Vesting is immediate.	Only employers and self-employed individuals can contribute to a SEP. Employees cannot contribute to a SEP. Vesting is immediate.
Pros	Contributions can vary from year to year. Inexpensive to set up and administer.	Employers cannot prohibit distributions from a SEP, because vesting is immediate.
Drawbacks	A SEP must cover all qualifying employees. Employers cannot discriminate in favor of HCEs. Only employers can contribute.	Employees cannot contribute.

SIMPLE Plan

A SIMPLE (Savings Incentive Match Plan for Employees) plan provides an employer and his employees with a simplified way to contribute toward retirement. SIMPLE plans have lower start-up and annual costs than most other types of retirement plans.

If a business has 100 or fewer employees who received $5,000 *or more* in compensation during the preceding year, it can establish a SIMPLE plan.[60] The business cannot maintain another retirement plan, unless the other plan is for a union workforce.

The business must continue to meet the 100-employee limit each year. However, if a business maintains a SIMPLE plan for at least one year and subsequently fails to meet the 100-employee limit, the business is allowed a two-year grace period to establish another retirement plan. Another exception may apply if the business fails to meet the 100-employee limit as a result of an acquisition, disposition, or similar transaction.

Employees can choose to make retirement plan contributions by allocating a portion of their salaries, and businesses can contribute matching or nonelective contributions. SIMPLE plans can only be maintained on a calendar-year basis. A SIMPLE plan can be structured in one of two ways: using SIMPLE IRAs or as part of a 401(k) plan (SIMPLE 401(k) plan).

SIMPLE IRA

Unlike a SEP, SIMPLE IRAs allow employee contributions and they mandate employer contributions.

A SIMPLE IRA must be set up for *each eligible employee*. An eligible employee is generally one who received at least $5,000 in compensation during any two years preceding the current calendar year and reasonably expected to receive at least $5,000 in the current calendar year, except for:

- Employees covered by a union agreement
- Nonresident alien employees who have received no U.S. source income from the employer

Prior to an election period (generally 60 days) preceding the start of the calendar year, employees must receive formal notice of their right to participate and make salary reduction contributions, and information regarding the employer's planned contributions.

During the election period, an employee may execute or modify a salary reduction agreement to defer a portion of his contribution (up to $11,500 for 2012.) Employees age 50 or over can also make a catch-up contribution of up to $2,500 (for a total of up to $14,000 for 2012). The salary reduction contributions under a SIMPLE IRA plan are elective deferrals that count toward an overall annual limit on elective deferrals an employee may make to this and other plans permitting elective deferrals.

---

[60] For purposes of the 100-employee limitation, all employees employed at any time during the year are taken into account, regardless of whether all of them are eligible to participate in the SIMPLE plan.

Contributions to a SIMPLE IRA

Each year, the employer must choose to make either matching contributions or nonelective contributions. Employer matching of the employee's salary reduction contributions is generally required on a dollar-for-dollar basis up to 3% of the participant's compensation. The employer may elect to make matching contributions at less than 3%, but not lower than 1%, for no more than two years within a five-year period.

Instead of matching contributions, the employer may choose to make nonelective contributions of 2% of each eligible employee's compensation. An individual employee's compensation used for this contribution is limited to $250,000 in 2012. If the employer chooses to make nonelective contributions, it must make them for all eligible employees *whether or not* they make salary reduction contributions. The employer must notify employees of its choice to make nonelective contributions within a specified period prior to the employees' annual period for making their own salary reduction contribution elections.

An eligible employee may choose not to make salary reduction contributions for a given year, in which case the employee would accrue no employer matching contributions, but would receive an employer nonelective contribution if the employer elects to make this type of contribution for the year. No other contributions may be made under a SIMPLE IRA plan.

Employee and employer contributions are 100% vested—that is, the money an employee has put aside plus employer contributions and net earnings from investments cannot be forfeited, and the employee has the right to withdraw at any time, even though those withdrawals may be subject to tax.

Salary reduction contributions must be deposited with the applicable financial institution within 30 days after the end of the month in which they would otherwise have been paid to the employee. Matching or nonelective contributions must be made by the due date (including extensions) for filing the company's income tax return for the year.

An employer can set up a SIMPLE IRA plan effective on any date from January 1 through October 1 of a year, provided the employer did not previously maintain another SIMPLE IRA plan. A new employer may set up a SIMPLE IRA plan as soon as administratively feasible after the business comes into existence.

> **Example:** Riley works for the Skidmore Tire Company, a small business with 75 employees. Skidmore Tire has decided to establish a SIMPLE IRA plan and will make a 2% nonelective contribution for each of its employees. Under this option, even if Riley does not contribute to her own SIMPLE IRA, she would still receive an employer nonelective contribution to her SIMPLE IRA equal to 2% of salary. Riley has a yearly salary of $40,000 and has decided that this year she cannot afford to make a contribution to her SIMPLE IRA. Even though she does not make a contribution this year, Skidmore must make a nonelective contribution of $800 (2% of $40,000). The financial institution partnering with Skidmore on the SIMPLE IRA has several investment choices, and Riley has the same investment options as the other plan participants.

> **Example:** Rockland Quarry Company is a small business with 50 employees. Rockland has decided to establish a SIMPLE IRA plan for all of its employees and will match its employees' contributions dollar-for-dollar up to 3% of each employee's salary. Under this option, if a Rockland employee does not contribute to his SIMPLE IRA, the employee does not receive any matching employer contributions. Elizabeth is an employee of Rockland Company. She has a yearly salary of $50,000 and decides to contribute 5% of her salary to her SIMPLE IRA. Elizabeth's yearly contribution is $2,500 (5% of $50,000). The Rockland matching contribution is $1,500 (3% of $50,000). Therefore, the total contribution to Elizabeth's SIMPLE IRA that year is $4,000 (her $2,500 contribution plus the $1,500 contribution from Rockland).

Withdrawals from a SIMPLE IRA

Distributions from a SIMPLE IRA are subject to income tax for the year in which they are received. If a participant takes a withdrawal from a SIMPLE IRA before age 59½, an additional tax of 10% generally applies. If the withdrawal occurs within two years of beginning participation in the SIMPLE IRA plan, the additional tax is increased to 25%.

SIMPLE IRA contributions and earnings may be rolled over tax-free from one SIMPLE IRA to another. A rollover may also be made from a SIMPLE IRA to another type of IRA, or to another employer's qualified plan, but it will be tax-free only if it is made after two years of participation in the SIMPLE IRA plan.

A participant in a SIMPLE IRA plan must begin receiving required minimum distributions by April 1 of the year following the year the participant reaches age 70½.

SIMPLE IRA Snapshot

	Rules for Employers	Rules for Employees
Eligibility	Any employer with 100 employees or more who received $5,000 or less in the preceding year. The employer cannot maintain another retirement plan in addition to the SIMPLE IRA.	All employees who have earned over $5,000 in any two prior years and who is expected to earn at least $5,000 in the current year.
Contribution Thresholds	Employers may choose to make either matching contributions, at 1% to 3% of compensation for employees that make salary deferral contributions, or nonelective contributions at 2% of compensation for all eligible employees.	An employee can contribute up to $11,500 of his salary (or self-employment earnings, for a self-employed owner), plus an additional $2,500 if 50 or older for a total of $14,000.
Pros	Employees can make contributions. Vesting is immediate.	Employees can make contributions. Vesting is immediate.
Drawbacks	Employer matching is mandatory.	Employees with higher salaries may prefer a retirement plan option that allows them to contribute more.

A business cannot suspend its employer matching contributions mid-year or terminate its SIMPLE IRA plan mid-year. The business must maintain the plan for a full calendar year (except in the year the business first establishes the plan). The employer is required to make the contributions that were promised to the employees.

A SIMPLE IRA plan may not require a participant to be employed on a specific date to receive an employer contribution. If a participant terminates employment during the year after making a salary reduction contribution, he would still be entitled to an employer contribution.

SIMPLE IRA contributions are not included in the "Wages, tips, other compensation" box of Form W-2, *Wage and Tax Statement*. However, salary reduction contributions must be included in the boxes for Social Security and Medicare wages.

SIMPLE 401(k) Plan

A SIMPLE plan can be adopted as part of a traditional 401(k) plan (see below) if the business meets the 100-employee limit discussed above for SIMPLE IRA plans and does not maintain another qualified retirement plan.

An employee can elect to make salary reduction contributions as a percentage of his compensation, but not more than $11,500 for 2012. An employee age 50 or over can also make a catch-up contribution of up to $2,500 (for a total of up to $14,000 for 2012).

Unlike a regular 401(k) plan, the employer must make either:

- A matching contribution up to 3% of compensation for each employee who makes a salary reduction contribution, or
- A nonelective contribution of 2% of compensation for each eligible employee who receives at least $5,000 of compensation from the employer that year.

Participants are fully vested in all contributions. SIMPLE 401(k) plans must file Form 5500 annually.

Pros and Cons of a SIMPLE 401(k):
•The plan is not subject to the discrimination rules that apply to traditional 401(k) plans.
•The plan may offer optional participant loans and hardship withdrawals to add flexibility for employees.
•No other retirement plans can be maintained.
•Withdrawal and loan flexibility adds an administrative burden for the employer.

Qualified Plans

There are two basic kinds of qualified retirement plans, defined contribution plans and defined benefit plans, and different rules apply to each. An employer is allowed to have more than one type of qualified plan, but maximum contributions cannot exceed annual limits.

All qualified plans are subject to federal regulation under the Employee Retirement Income Security Act (ERISA). The federal government does not require an employer to establish any type of retirement plan, but it provides minimum federal standards for qualified plans.

ERISA mandates minimum funding requirements to ensure that benefits will be available to employees when they retire. For defined benefit plans, it also requires that plan funding be certified by an actuary. ERISA covers qualified retirement plans, as well as health and welfare benefit plans. Among other things, ERISA requires that individuals who manage plans (and other fiduciaries) meet certain standards of conduct. The law also contains detailed provisions for reporting to the government and for disclosure to participants. Further, there are provisions aimed at assuring plan funds are protected and participants receive their benefits.

ERISA also mandates that qualified plans meet specific requirements regarding eligibility, vesting, and communications with participants. The administrator of an employee benefit plan subject to ERISA must file an information return for the plan each year. Form 5500, *Annual Return/Report of Employee Benefit Plan*, must be filed by the last day of the seventh month after the plan year ends.

Defined Benefit Plans (Pension Plans)

A defined benefit plan (often called a traditional pension plan) promises a specified benefit amount or annuity after retirement. Most federal and state governments offer defined benefit plans to their employees. However, fewer companies now offer defined benefit plans because they are costly to administer and inflexible. The benefits in many defined benefit plans are protected by federal insurance. Contributions to a defined benefit plan are not optional. Contributions are typically based on actuarial calculations. Contributions for self-employed taxpayers are limited to 100% of compensation. If the business does not have any income for the year, no contribution can be made.

Defined Benefit Plan Snapshot

Rule	Rules for Employers	Rules for Employees
Eligibility	Any business or employer.	All employees who have worked at least 1,000 hours in the past year.
Contribution Thresholds	There is no set limit for contributions to defined benefit plans. However, the annual benefit for a participant may be limited.	Employees cannot contribute to this type of plan.
Pros	Vesting is determined by the employer. Shareholder-employees of closely held corporations can contribute and deduct more per year than in a defined contribution plan.	Employees can be guaranteed a fixed payout after retirement.
Drawbacks	This plan can be expensive to administer. Annual reporting is required. Future benefits are dependent on contributions and investment performance.	Employer contributions can take years to vest.

Defined Contribution Plans

A defined contribution plan provides an individual account for each participant in the plan. It provides benefits to the participant based on the amounts contributed to the participant's account, and subsequent income, expenses, gains, losses, and, in some instances, allocations of forfeitures among participant accounts. The participant, the employer, or sometimes both may contribute to the individual account on the employee's behalf. The value of the account will fluctuate due to the changes in the value of investments that have been made with the amounts contributed.

A participant's retirement benefits depend primarily on the amount of contributions made on his behalf, rather than upon his years of service with the employer or his earnings history. Examples of defined contribution plans include 401(k) plans, 403(b) plans, and 457 plans.

Comparison of Defined Benefit and Defined Contribution Plans		
Rule	**Defined Benefit Plan**	**Defined Contribution Plan**
Employer Contributions	Employer contributions are required based upon actuarial calculation of amounts needed to fund benefits.	The employer may choose to match a portion of employee contributions or to contribute without employee contributions.
Employee Contributions	Employees generally do not contribute.	Many plans require the employee to contribute.
Managing the Investments	The employer must ensure that contributions to the plan plus investment earnings will be enough to pay the promised benefits.	The employee often is responsible for managing the investment of his account, choosing from investment options offered by the plan. For some plans, the plan administrator is responsible for investing the plan's assets.
Benefits Paid Upon Retirement	A promised benefit is based on a formula, often using a combination of the employee's age, years worked, and salary history.	The benefit depends on contributions made by the employee and/or the employer and investment earnings on the contributions.
Type of Retirement Benefit Payments	Traditionally, these plans pay the retiree monthly annuity payments that continue for life.	The retiree may transfer the account balance into an Individual Retirement Account (IRA) from which the retiree withdraws money. Some plans also offer monthly payments through an annuity.
Guarantee of Benefits	The government, through the Pension Benefit Guaranty Corporation (PBGC), may partially guarantee benefits.	No federal guarantee of benefits.

Traditional 401(k) Plans

A 401(k) plan is a defined contribution plan that allows employees to defer receiving a portion of their salary, which is instead contributed on their behalf to the 401(k) plan. Deferrals generally are made on a pretax basis, although some plans allow employees the option to make them on an after-tax basis.

Pretax deferrals are not subject to income tax withholding, and they are not included in taxable wages on the employee's Form W-2. However, they are subject to Social Security, Medicare, and federal unemployment taxes.

Sometimes the employer will make matching contributions. Employee deferrals and any employer matching contributions are accounted separately for each employee. Earnings on the retirement account grow tax-free until distribution. 401(k) plans can vary significantly in their complexity. However, many financial institutions administer 401(k) plans, which can lessen the administrative burden on individual employers of establishing and maintaining these plans.

Prohibited Transactions

A prohibited transaction is a transaction between a plan and a disqualified person that is prohibited by law. A disqualified person may include the following:

- A fiduciary of the plan
- A person providing services to the plan
- An employer, any of whose employees are covered by the plan
- An employee organization, any of whose members are covered by the plan
- An indirect or direct owner of 50% or more of the applicable employer or employee organization
- A member of the family of anyone described in the bullet points above
- A corporation, partnership, trust, or estate of which any direct or indirect owner described in the bullet points above holds a 50% or more interest
- An officer, director, 10% or more shareholder, or highly compensated employee of the entity administering the plan

An initial 15% tax is applied on the amount involved in a prohibited transaction for each year in a taxable period. If the transaction is not corrected within the taxable period, an additional tax of 100% of the amount involved is imposed. These taxes are payable by any disqualified person who takes part in a prohibited transaction. If more than one person takes part, each can be jointly and severally liable for the entire amount of tax. Prohibited transactions include the following:

- A transfer of plan income or assets to, or use for the benefit of, a disqualified person
- Any act of a fiduciary by which plan income or assets are used for his own benefit
- The receipt of money or property by a fiduciary for his own account from any party dealing with the plan in a transaction that involves plan income or assets
- The sale, exchange, or lease of property between a plan and a disqualified person
- Lending money between a plan and a disqualified person
- Furnishing goods or services between a plan and a disqualified person

> **Example:** A plan fiduciary had a prohibited transaction by investing in a life insurance company's group annuity contract, resulting in a 10% commission paid to his company on the investment. This is a prohibited transaction between a plan fiduciary and a retirement plan.

If a prohibited transaction is *not corrected* during the taxable period, the taxpayer usually has an additional 90 days after the day the IRS mails a notice of deficiency for the 100% tax to correct the transaction. This correction period (the taxable period plus the 90 days) can be extended if one of the following occurs:

- The IRS grants a reasonable time needed to correct the transaction.
- The taxpayer petitions the U.S. Tax Court.

If the transaction is corrected within this period, the 100% tax may be abated.

Required Minimum Distributions

A participant in a qualified retirement plan must begin receiving distributions by April 1 of the first year following the later of:

- The calendar year in which he reaches age 70½
- The calendar year in which he retires from employment with the employer maintaining the plan

However, the plan may require distributions by April 1 of the year after the participant reaches age 70½ even if he has not retired. Further, if the participant is a 5% owner of the employer, he must begin receiving distributions by April 1 of the year after the year he reaches age 70½.

Penalties for not taking required minimum distributions (RMDs) can be severe. Penalties are assessed if an account owner fails to withdraw an RMD, fails to withdraw the full amount of the RMD, or fails to withdraw the RMD by the applicable deadline. The penalty is 50% of the amount that is not withdrawn from the account when required.

Distributions from Qualified Plans

Generally, distributions cannot be made from a 401(k) plan until one of the following occurs:

- The employee retires, dies, becomes disabled, or otherwise terminates employment
- The plan terminates
- The employee reaches age 59½ or suffers financial hardship

Unless a distribution is properly rolled over into another retirement plan or individual retirement account, it will be subject to income tax upon receipt.

If a distribution is made to an employee before he reaches age 59½, the employee may have to pay a 10% additional tax on the distribution. However, the additional 10% tax would not apply in the following situations:

- Distributions are for the taxpayer's medical care, up to the amount allowed as a medical deduction.
- Disability or death.
- Distributions in the form of an annuity.
- Distributions are made because of an IRS levy on the plan.
- Distributions are made to a qualified reservist (an individual called up to active duty).

Even though these distributions will not be subject to the additional 10% tax, they will still be subject to tax at the taxpayer's applicable rate.

Example: Lauren, age 43, takes a $5,000 distribution from her traditional IRA account. She does not meet any of the exceptions to the 10% additional tax, so the $5,000 is an early distribution. Lauren must include the $5,000 in her gross income for the year the distribution is received and pay income tax on it. She must also pay an *additional* tax of $500 (10% × $5,000).

Overall Limits on Benefits and Contributions

For 2012, the following limits apply:

The annual benefit for a participant in a defined benefit plan cannot exceed the lesser of $200,000 or 100% of the participant's average compensation for his highest three consecutive calendar years.

A combined limit of $17,000 applies to each employee's elective deferrals and salary reduction contributions, other than catch-up contributions, to all defined contribution retirement plans and any SIMPLE IRA plan under which he is covered. If the limit is exceeded, the amount that would otherwise have been nontaxable must be included in the employee's gross income. Catch-up contributions are limited to $2,500 for each participant in a SIMPLE plan and $5,500 for each participant in other defined contribution plans.

Annual contributions to the account of a participant in a defined contribution plan cannot exceed the lesser of $50,000 or 100% of the participant's compensation.

An employer's deduction for contributions to a defined contribution plan cannot be more than 25% of the compensation paid or accrued during the year for the eligible employees. The maximum compensation that can be considered for each employee is $250,000.

Employer Credit for Pension Start-up Costs

Employers may be able to claim a tax credit equal to 50% of the cost to set up and administer the plan, up to a maximum of $500 per year, for each of the first three years of the plan.

Employers can choose to start claiming the credit in the tax year before the tax year in which the plan becomes effective. In order to qualify for this credit, the employer must have had 100 or fewer employees who received at least $5,000 in compensation for the preceding year.

Further, the employees cannot be substantially the same group covered by another retirement plan sponsored by essentially the same employer during the preceding three-year period. This credit is part of the general business credit, which can be carried back or forward to other tax years if it cannot be used in the current year.

Retirement Savings Contributions Credit

Retirement plan participants (including self-employed individuals) who make contributions to their own retirement plan may *also* qualify for the Retirement Savings Contributions Credit. The credit is 10% to 50% of eligible contributions up to $1,000 ($2,000 for MFJ). It is subject to specified limits on AGI.

Unit 19: Questions

1. Hurley Biomedical Corporation maintains a SIMPLE IRA for its employees. A former employee, Grace, quit her job on January 27, 2012, after the business had already deducted $75 from her wages based upon her election to contribute to its SIMPLE IRA plan. Hurley Biomedical makes a 3% matching contribution, and Grace had earned $2,000 in wages before she quit. How must Hurley Biomedical treat this $75 deduction from Grace's wages?

A. Hurley must return Grace's $75 salary reduction contribution.
B. Hurley must deposit Grace's salary reduction contribution in her SIMPLE IRA account. The company must also match Grace's salary reduction contributions up to 3% of her $2,000 compensation ($60).
C. Hurley must deposit Grace's salary reduction contribution in her SIMPLE IRA account. However, the company is not required to make a matching contribution for an employee who has terminated employment.
D. Hurley is required to remit the $75 to the U.S. Treasury.

The answer is B. Hurley Biomedical Corporation must deposit Grace's salary reduction contribution in her SIMPLE IRA account. The company must also match Grace's salary reduction contributions up to 3% of her $2,000 compensation ($60). An employer cannot return a salary reduction contribution after it has already deducted it from wages as a SIMPLE IRA plan contribution. A SIMPLE IRA plan may not require a participant to be employed on a specific date to receive an employer contribution. If a participant terminates service during the year after making a salary reduction contribution, he or she would still be entitled to an employer contribution, regardless of whether it is matching or nonelective. ###

2. What types of employers cannot establish a SEP?

A. A self-employed taxpayer without any employees.
B. A corporation with 90 employees.
C. A nonprofit entity with five employees.
D. All of the above can establish a SEP.

The answer is D. Any employer or self-employed individual can establish a SEP. ###

3. "Prohibited transactions" are transactions between a retirement plan and a disqualified person. Which of the following is exempt from the prohibited transaction rules?

A. A fiduciary of the plan.
B. A person providing services to the plan.
C. An employer whose employees are covered by the plan.
D. A disqualified person who receives a benefit to which he is entitled as a plan participant.

The answer is D. It is not a prohibited transaction if a disqualified person receives a benefit to which he is entitled as a plan participant or beneficiary. ###

4. Sarah runs her own business, and sets up a new qualified defined benefit plan for her ten employees. In 2012, what is the maximum tax credit Sarah can receive for qualified retirement plan start-up costs?

A. $100.
B. $500.
C. $1,000.
D. $2,000.

The answer is B. The maximum annual credit amount is $500. Employers may claim a tax credit of up to 50% of the first $1,000 of qualified start-up costs if starting a new SEP, SIMPLE, or qualified plan. ###

5. Ram is a sole proprietor whose tax year is the calendar year. He made a contribution to his SIMPLE IRA on May 15, 2013. What is the earliest year for which he can deduct this contribution?

A. His 2013 tax return.
B. His 2012 tax return.
C. The contribution is not deductible on his tax return because it was made late.
D. None of the above.

The answer is B. Taxpayers can deduct contributions for a particular tax year if they are made by the due date (including extensions) of the federal income tax return for that year. Assuming the contributions made in May 2013 were within the applicable limits based upon his compensation for 2012, he could make deductible contributions until his extended due date of October 15, 2013 for his 2012 tax return. ###

6. Maura, age 26, began participating in a SIMPLE IRA retirement account on March 10, 2011. She took an early distribution from the account on December 26, 2012. She does not qualify for any of the exceptions to the early withdrawal penalty. The distribution amount was $10,000. What is the amount of additional tax that Maura must pay on the early distribution?

A. $1,000.
B. $1,500.
C. $2,500.
D. $3,000.

The answer is C. Early withdrawals generally are subject to an additional tax of 10%. However, the additional tax is increased to 25% if funds are withdrawn within two years of beginning participation in a SIMPLE IRA. The answer is ($10,000 × 25% = $2,500). ###

7. Brenda owns the Berry Company, a sole proprietorship with 150 employees. All of the following plans are available for Brenda's company except:

A. A qualified plan.
B. A defined benefit plan.
C. A SIMPLE IRA.
D. None of the above.

The answer is C. Brenda cannot set up a SIMPLE IRA for her employees, because her company exceeds the 100-employee threshold, unless at least 50 of the employees earned less than $5,000 in the prior year. ###

8. Which of the following statements regarding a SEP-IRA is true?

A. Money can be withdrawn from a SEP-IRA by the employee at any time without tax or penalty.
B. Money can be withdrawn from a SEP-IRA by the employee at any time, but taxes may apply.
C. An employee must wait at least two years to withdraw money from a SEP-IRA.
D. An employee must wait at least three years to withdraw money from a SEP-IRA.

The answer is B. Although income tax may apply, including an additional 10% tax for withdrawals prior to age 59½, participants are allowed to withdraw money from a SEP-IRA at any time. Withdrawals can be rolled over tax-free to another SEP-IRA, another traditional IRA, or another employer's qualified retirement plan. ###

9. Marcelo owns Perez Body Shop and sets up a SEP-IRA for all of his employees. In his benefits handbook, he makes the following statements regarding the shop's SEP-IRA plan. All are correct except:

A. Only employees age 21 and older are eligible.
B. An employee cannot withdraw from his SEP-IRA while he is employed by Perez Body Shop.
C. A SEP-IRA will be set up for all eligible employees.
D. An employee must have worked for Perez for at least three of the last five years to be eligible.

The answer is B. Employers cannot prohibit distributions from a SEP-IRA. Employers also cannot make their contributions contingent on the condition that any part of them must be kept in the account. All of the other statements are correct regarding SEP-IRA plans. ###

10. The Azalea City Partnership has 15 employees and contributes to their retirement accounts. How is this transaction reported?

A. The business can take the deduction for its contributions to its employees' retirement accounts on Form 1065, Partnership Income Tax Return.
B. The business cannot take a deduction for its contributions to its employees' retirement accounts. Instead, the amounts contributed are added to the partnership basis.
C. The individual partners are allowed to deduct contributions to the employee retirement plans on their individual returns.
D. None of the above.

The answer is A. A partnership may deduct contributions to an employee's retirement plan, just as it would deduct any other ordinary business expense. However, the rules are different for contributions to the retirement accounts of the partners. Contributions made on behalf of the partners are passed through to each of them on Schedule K-1. ###

11. Huang Software, Inc. decides to establish a SEP for its employees. All of the following statements about Huang's retirement plan are correct except:

A. In good years, Huang can make larger contributions for its employees, and in down times it can reduce the amount.
B. Individual employees have the opportunity to divide the employer's contributions to their SEP-IRAs among the funds made available to Huang employees.
C. Under a SEP, the contribution rate can be different for each employee, based on length of service and sales performance.
D. Only employers and self-employed individuals can make contributions to SEPs.

The answer is C. Under a SEP, the contribution rate (whether large or small) must be uniform for all employees. Employers may contribute less when they have less income, but the plan cannot discriminate among employees. ###

12. The Esslinger Carpet Company has started a SEP plan for its employees. The company currently has four employees. Which of the following employees is the company not required to cover under the SEP plan?

A. Faye, 45 years old, a full-time employee for the last five years.
B. Larry, 25 years old, a part-time employee for the last three years.
C. Randolph, 20 years old, a full-time employee for the last three years.
D. Mack, 42 years old, a seasonal employee for the last six years.

The answer is C. Randolph is not an automatically eligible employee because he is not at least 21 years old. For purposes of a SEP, an eligible employee is an individual who meets all the following requirements:

• Has reached age 21
• Has worked for the employer in at least three of the last five years
• Has received at least $550 in compensation

An employer can use less restrictive participation requirements than those listed, but not more restrictive ones. ###

13. Leah is a sole proprietor with two employees. She establishes a 401(k) SIMPLE plan. Leah has a net loss in 2012 on her Schedule C. Which of the following is true?

A. Because the business shows a loss, she is prohibited from contributing to her retirement account, as well as the retirement accounts of her employees.
B. Because the business shows a loss, she is prohibited from contributing to her retirement account, but she may contribute to the retirement accounts of her employees.
C. Leah may make a retirement contribution to her own retirement account as well as the accounts of her employees.
D. None of the above.

The answer is B. Leah is self-employed, so she must have compensation in order to contribute to her own retirement plan. However, she is not prohibited from contributing to her employees' retirement plan, even if the business has a loss. ###

14. Theresa is a small business owner who maintains a SEP plan for her employees. Which of the following employees can be excluded from the plan, if Theresa chooses?

A. Stan, a 32-year-old part-time employee who has worked for Theresa for five years.
B. Aldo, a 42-year-old seasonal employee and U.S. resident alien who has worked for Theresa for three years.
C. Noel, a 21-year-old part-time employee who is also a union member.
D. Millie, a 55-year-old full-time employee who has worked for Theresa for four years.

The answer is C. Employers may choose to exclude employees covered by a union agreement. Since Aldo is a resident alien, he still qualifies to participate. Only nonresident aliens who do not have any U.S.-source income may be excluded. ###

15. All of the following are requirements of ERISA (the Employee Retirement Income Security Act) except:

A. ERISA requires that employers file an annual report on Form 5500 for their sponsored retirement plans.
B. ERISA requires employers to set up retirement plans for their employees.
C. ERISA requires minimum funding standards for retirement plans.
D. ERISA requires certain communications with plan participants.

The answer is B. ERISA does not require that employers set up retirement plans for their employees. No employer is forced to offer a retirement plan. All of the other answers are correct. ###

16. Can a SIMPLE IRA plan be maintained on a fiscal-year basis?

A. Yes, if the business is on a fiscal year.
B. Yes, even if the business uses a calendar year.
C. Yes, but only if the business requests a 444 election
D. No, a calendar year must be used.

The answer is D. A SIMPLE IRA plan may only be maintained on a calendar-year basis. ###

17. Josie works full-time and participates in her employer's retirement plan. She also has her own graphic design business. She does not have any employees. Can Josie set up a SEP for self-employment income, even though she is already participating in her employer's plan?

A. Yes, Josie can still set up a SEP for her catering business.
B. No, Josie cannot set up a SEP because she is covered by an employer plan.
C. No, Josie cannot set up a SEP because she is a prohibited individual.
D. Josie can set up a SEP only if she hires employees.

The answer is A. Josie can set up a SEP. A SEP can be established for a person's independent business activity even if she participates in an employer's retirement plan. ###

18. What happens if an eligible employee entitled to a contribution is unwilling to set up a SIMPLE IRA?

A. Eligible employees may decline to participate in an employer's SIMPLE IRA.
B. Eligible employees may not opt out of a SIMPLE IRA.
C. Eligible employees may choose to set up a ROTH IRA in lieu of a SIMPLE IRA.
D. None of the above.

The answer is B. An eligible employee may not opt out of participation. However, any eligible employee may choose not to make salary reduction contributions for a year. In that case the employee would accrue no employer matching contributions for the year, but would still receive an employer nonelective contribution (if the plan provides for such contributions for the year.) ###

19. What are the penalties imposed on a disqualified person who takes part in a prohibited transaction?

A. 25% tax of the amount involved.
B. 50% tax of the amount involved.
C. An initial tax of 15% and an additional tax of 100% of the amount involved, if the transaction is not corrected within the taxable period.
D. An initial tax of 25% and an additional tax of 100% of the amount involved, if the transaction is not corrected within the taxable period.

The answer is C. An initial 15% tax is applied on the amount involved in a prohibited transaction for each year in a taxable period. If the transaction is not corrected within the taxable period, an additional tax of 100% of the amount involved is imposed. These taxes are payable by any disqualified person who takes part in a prohibited transaction. ###

20. All of the following statements are true regarding defined benefit plans except:

A. Employees receive a fixed payout upon retirement.
B. Generally, employers, not employees, contribute to defined benefit plans.
C. Defined benefit plans can be expensive to administer and have strict reporting requirements.
D. An employee must have worked 500 hours in the prior year to be eligible for the plan.

The answer is D. Under a defined benefit plan, an employee must have worked 1,000 hours in the prior year to be eligible. All of the other statements are correct. ###

21. A 401(k) is a type of _____:

A. SEP-IRA.
B. Government pension plan.
C. Defined contribution plan.
D. Defined benefit plan.

The answer is C. A 401(k) is a very common type of defined contribution plan in which employees contribute to their own accounts, generally on a pretax basis. Earnings grow tax-free until distribution. Employers often supplement or match employee contributions. ###

22. Under the rules for prohibited transactions, all of the following would be considered disqualified persons except:

A. A 5% shareholder of the entity administering the plan.
B. A fiduciary of the plan.
C. An employer whose employees are covered by the plan.
D. A person providing services to the plan.

The answer is A. A 10% or more shareholder of the entity administering the plan would be a disqualified person under the rules for prohibited transactions. ###

23. Channing, age 77, has not taken a required minimum distribution from his qualified retirement plan. What penalty, if any, does he face?

A. Nothing. He is allowed to let the retirement plan funds accumulate so his heirs can inherit the proceeds.
B. A tax of 15% on the amount not withdrawn from the account.
C. A tax of 50% on the amount not withdrawn from the account.
D. A tax of 50% on his balance in the account.

The answer is C. A participant in a qualified retirement plan must begin taking required minimum distributions by April 1 of the first year following the later of:

•The calendar year in which he reaches age 70½, or
•The calendar year in which he retires from employment with the employer maintaining the plan.

The penalty for failing to take an RMD is a tax of 50% on the amount that has not been withdrawn from the account as required. ###

Unit 20: Trusts and Estates

More Reading:
Publication 559, *Survivors, Executors, and Administrators*
Publication 950, *Introduction to Estate and Gift Taxes*
Publication 536, *Net Operating Losses (NOLs) for Individuals, Estates, and Trusts*

Estates and trusts are separate legal entities that are defined by the assets they hold. An estate is created when a taxpayer dies. The estate tax is imposed on certain transfers at death.

A trust is created while the taxpayer is alive or by a taxpayer's last will, and can determine how property will be distributed during his lifetime or at death. A trust can hold title to property for the benefit of one or more persons or entities. Estates and trusts are generally required to obtain an Employer Identification Number (EIN), just like any other legal entity.

Estates in General

For federal tax purposes, an estate is a separate legal entity that is created when a taxpayer dies. The deceased taxpayer's property may consist of items such as cash and securities, real estate, insurance, trusts, annuities, business interests, and other assets. A person who inherits the property from an estate is not taxed on the transfer. Instead, the estate itself is responsible for paying any tax before the property is distributed. However, if the estate's assets are distributed to beneficiaries before applicable taxes are paid, the beneficiaries can be held liable for the tax debt, up to the value of the assets distributed.

Requirements for the Personal Representative

After a person dies, a personal representative, such as an executor named in his will or an administrator appointed by a court, will typically manage the estate and settle the decedent's financial affairs. If there is no executor or administrator, another person with possession of the decedent's property may act as the personal representative.

The personal representative is responsible for filing the final income tax return and the estate tax return, if required.

The personal representative is also responsible for determining any estate tax liability before the estate's assets are distributed to beneficiaries. The tax liability for an estate attaches to the assets of the estate itself, so if the assets are distributed to the beneficiaries before the taxes are paid, the beneficiaries may be held liable for the tax debt, up to the value of the assets distributed.

Either the personal representative or a paid preparer must sign the appropriate line of the return. Current IRS requirements require that the following tax returns be filed:

- The final income tax returns (Form 1040) for the decedent (for income received before death);
- Fiduciary income tax returns (Form 1041) for the estate for the period of its administration; (if necessary) and
- Estate Tax Return (Form 706), if the fair market value of the assets of the estate exceeds the applicable threshold for the year of death.

Example: James was unmarried when he died on April 20, 2012. His only daughter, Lillian, was named as the executor of his estate. James earned wages in 2012 before his death. Therefore, a final tax return is required for 2012. Lillian asks her accountant to help prepare her father's final Form 1040, which will include all the taxable income that James received in 2012 before his death. The accountant also helps Lillian with the valuation of her father's estate. After determining the fair market value of all her father's assets, they conclude that James's gross estate is valued at approximately $7 million. As this exceeds the threshold of $5,120,000 for 2012, an estate tax return (Form 706) is also required to be filed.

The Final Income Tax Return (Form 1040)

The taxpayer's final income tax return is filed on the same form that would have been used if the taxpayer were still alive, but "deceased" is written after the taxpayer's name. The filing deadline is April 15 of the year following the taxpayer's death, just like regular tax returns.

The personal representative must file the final individual income tax return of the decedent for the year of death and any returns not filed for preceding years. If an individual died after the close of the tax year but before the return for that year was filed, the return for that year will not be the final return. The return for that year will be a regular return and the personal representative must file it.

Example: Stephanie dies on March 2, 2013. At the time of her death, she had not yet filed her 2012 tax return. She earned $51,000 in wages in 2012. She also earned $18,000 in wages between January 1, 2013 and her death. Therefore, Stephanie's 2012 and 2013 tax return must be filed by her representative. The 2013 return would be her final individual tax return.

On a decedent's final tax return, the rules for personal exemptions and deductions are the same as for any taxpayer. The full amount of the applicable personal exemption may be claimed on the final tax return, regardless of how long the taxpayer was alive during the year.

Income In Respect of a Decedent

Income in respect of a decedent (IRD) is any taxable income that was earned but *not received* by the decedent by the time of death. IRD is not taxed on the final return of the deceased taxpayer. IRD is reported on the tax return of the person (or entity) that receives the income. This could be the estate, the surviving spouse, or another beneficiary, such as a child. Regardless of the decedent's accounting method, IRD is subject to income tax when the income is received.

IRD retains the same tax nature after death as if the taxpayer were still alive. For example, if the income would have been short-term capital gain to the deceased, it is taxed the same way to the beneficiary. IRD can come from various sources, including:

- Unpaid salary, wages or bonuses
- Distributions from traditional IRAs and employer-provided retirement plans
- Deferred compensation benefits
- Accrued but unpaid interest, dividends, and rent
- Accounts receivable of a sole proprietor

Example: Carlos was owed $15,000 in wages when he died. The check for these wages was not remitted by his employer until three weeks later and was received by his daughter and sole beneficiary, Rosalie. The wages are considered IRD, and Rosalie must recognize the $15,000 as ordinary income, the same tax treatment that would have applied for Carlos.

Example: Beverly died on April 30. At the time of her death, she was owed (but had not yet received) $1,500 in interest on bonds and $2,000 in rental income. Beverly's beneficiary will include $3,500 in IRD in gross income when the interest and rent are received. The income retains its character as passive interest income and passive rental income.

IRD is includible in the decedent's estate and subject to estate tax, and may also be subject to income tax if received by a beneficiary. Therefore, the beneficiary may take a deduction for estate tax paid on the IRD. This deduction is taken as a miscellaneous itemized deduction on Schedule A, and is not subject to the 2% floor, as are most other miscellaneous itemized deductions.

IRS Form 1041, Fiduciary Returns

An estate is a taxable legal entity that exists from the time of an individual's death until all assets have been distributed to the decedent's beneficiaries.

Form 1041 is a fiduciary return used to report the following items for a domestic decedent's estate, trust, or bankruptcy estate:

- Current income and deductions, including gains and losses from disposition of the entity's property;
- A deduction for income that is either accumulated or held for future distribution or distributed currently to the beneficiaries; and
- Any income tax liability.

Current income would include IRD, if it was received by the estate rather than specific beneficiaries. As investment assets will usually continue to earn income after a taxpayer has died, this income, such as rents, dividends and interest, must be reported. Expenses of administering the estate can be deducted either from the estate's income on Form 1041 in determining its income tax, or from the gross estate on Form 706 in determining the estate tax liability, but cannot be claimed for both purposes. Schedule K-1 is used to report any income that is distributed to each beneficiary and is filed with Form 1041, with a copy is also given to the beneficiary.

The due date for Form 1041 is the fifteenth day of the fourth month following the end of the entity's tax year, but is subject to an automatic extension of five months if Form 7004 is filed. The tax year may be either a calendar or fiscal year, subject to the election made at the time the first return is filed. An election will also be made on the first return as to method (cash, accrual, or other) to report the estate's income.

Form 1041 must be filed for any domestic estate that has gross income for the tax year of $600 or more, or a beneficiary who is a nonresident alien (with any amount of income).

The Gross Estate

The estate tax is a tax on the transfer of property from an individual's estate after his death. It applies to the taxable estate, which is the gross estate less certain deductions. The gross estate is based upon the fair market value of the taxpayer's property, which is not necessarily equal to his cost, and includes:

- The FMV of all tangible and intangible property owned by the decedent at the time of death.
- The full value of property held as joint tenants with the right of survivorship (unless the decedent and spouse were the only joint tenants)
- Life insurance proceeds payable to the estate, or for policies owned by the decedent, payable to the heirs.

- The value of certain annuities or survivor benefits payable to the heirs.
- The value of certain property that was transferred within three years before the decedent's death.

The gross estate does not include property owned solely by the decedent's spouse or other individuals. Lifetime gifts that are complete (so that no control over the gifts was retained) are not included in the gross estate.

Deductions from the Gross Estate

Once the gross estate has been calculated, certain deductions (and in special circumstances, reductions to value) are allowed to determine the taxable estate." Deductions from the gross estate may include:

- Funeral expenses paid out of the estate.
- Administration expenses for the estate, including attorney's fees.
- Debts owed at the time of death.
- The marital deduction (generally, the value of the property that passes from the estate to a surviving spouse).
- The charitable deduction (generally, the value of the property that passes from the estate to qualifying charities).
- The state death tax deduction (generally, any inheritance or estate taxes paid to any state).

The following items are not deductible from the gross estate:

- Federal estate taxes paid.
- Alimony paid after the taxpayer's death. These payments would be treated as distributions to a beneficiary.

Property taxes are deductible only if they accrue under state law prior to the decedent's death.

The Marital Deduction

There are special rules and exceptions for transfers between spouses. The marital deduction allows spouses to transfer an unlimited amount of property to one another during their lifetimes or at death without being subject to estate or gift taxes. The marital deduction is a deduction from the "gross estate" in order to arrive at the "taxable estate."

To receive an unlimited deduction, the spouse receiving the assets must be a U.S. citizen, a legal spouse, and have outright ownership of the assets. The unlimited marital deduction is generally not allowed if the transferee spouse is not a U.S. citizen (even if the spouse is a legal resident of the United States). If the receiving spouse is not a citizen, assets transferred are subject to an annual exclusion, which is $139,000 in 2012.

Basis of Estate Property

The basis of property inherited from a decedent is generally one of the following:

- The FMV of the property on the date of death.
- The FMV on an alternate valuation date, if elected by the personal representative.
- The value under a special-use valuation method for real property used in farming or another closely-held business, if elected by the personal representative.
- The decedent's adjusted basis in land to the extent of the value excluded from the taxable estate as a qualified conservation easement.

Property that is jointly owned by a decedent and another person will be included in full in the decedent's gross estate unless it can be shown that the other person originally owned or otherwise contributed to the purchase price. The surviving owner's new basis of property that was jointly owned must be calculated. To do so, the surviving owner's original basis in the property is added to the value of the part of the property included in the decedent's estate. Any deductions for depreciation allowed to the surviving owner on that property are subtracted from the sum.

If property is jointly held between husband and wife as tenants by the entirety or as joint tenants with the right of survivorship (if they were the only joint tenants), one-half of the property's value is included in the gross estate, and there is a step-up in basis for that one-half. If the decedent holds property in a community property state, half of the value of the community property will be included in the gross estate of the decedent, but the entire value of the community property will receive a step-up in basis.

Special Election for Decedent's Medical Expenses

Debts that were not paid before death, including medical expenses subsequently paid on behalf of the decedent, are liabilities of the estate and can be deducted from the gross estate on the estate tax return. However, if medical expenses for the decedent are paid out of the estate during the one-year period beginning with the day after death, the personal representative can alternatively elect to treat all or part of the expenses as paid by the decedent at the time they were incurred, and deduct them on the final tax return (1040) for the decedent.

Estates and Credits

Estates are allowed some of the same tax credits that are allowed to individuals. The credits are generally allocated between the estate and the beneficiaries. However, estates are not allowed the credit for the elderly or the disabled, the child tax credit, or the earned income credit.

Form 706: The Estate Tax Return

An estate tax return is filed using Form 706, *United States Estate (and Generation-Skipping Transfer) Tax Return.* After the taxable estate is computed, the value of lifetime taxable gifts is added to this number and the estate tax is computed. The tax is then reduced by the applicable credit amount. The applicable credit amount, formerly referred to as the unified credit, applies to both the gift tax and the estate tax. It equals the tax on the basic exclusion amount.

- For 2012, the basic exclusion amount is **$5,120,000**.
- The applicable credit amount is **$1,772,800**.

Any portion of the applicable credit amount used against gift tax in a given year reduces the amount of credit that can be used against gift or estate taxes in later years. For estate tax purposes but not for gift taxes, the unified credit amount may also include the tax applicable to the deceased spousal unused exclusion (DSUE). The DSUE is the unused portion of the decedent's predeceased spouse's estate that was not used against gift or estate tax liabilities. The predeceased spouse must have died on or after January 1, 2011 and the DSUE must have been reported on Form 706 filed on behalf of the first spouse's estate.

If required to be filed, the due date for Form 706 is nine months after the decedent's date of death. An automatic six- month extension may be requested by filing Form 4768. However, the tax is due by the due date and interest is accrued on any amounts owed that are not paid at that time.

The assessment period for tax is three years after the due date for a timely filed estate tax return. The assessment period is four years for transfers from an estate.

The GST: Generation-Skipping Transfer Tax (Form 709)

The generation skipping transfer tax (GST) may apply to gifts during a taxpayer's life or transfers occurring after his death, called bequests, made to "skip persons." A skip person is a person who belongs to a generation that is two or more generations *below* the generation of the donor. The most common scenario is when a taxpayer makes a bequest to a grandchild.

The GST tax is assessed when a property transfer is made, including instances in which property is transferred from a trust. The GST tax is based on the amounts transferred to skip persons, after subtracting the allocated portions of the GST tax exemption. In 2012, the GST tax exemption is $5,120,000 and the GST tax rate is set at the maximum estate tax rate of 35%. The GST tax is imposed separately and **in addition** to the estate and gift tax.

Example: Patrick sets up a trust that names his adult daughter, Helene, as the sole beneficiary of the trust. In January 2012, Patrick dies, and the trust passes to Helene. However, later in the year, Helene also dies, and now the trust passes to her children (Patrick's grandchildren). Patrick's grandchildren are "skippersons" for purposes of the GST, and the trust fund property may be subject to the GST.

Any *direct* payments that are made toward tuition or medical expenses are exempt from gift tax or GST tax.

Example: Gordon wants to help support his grandchildren, but he wants to make sure that his gifts are not subject to gift tax, GST tax, or estate tax. So, in 2012, he offers to pay his grandchild's college tuition in full. Gordon writes a check directly to the college in the amount of $25,000. There is no tax consequence for this gift, and no reporting is required.

Trusts in General

A trust is an entity created under the laws of the state in which it is formed. A trust may be created during an individual's life (an inter-vivos trust) or at the time of death under a will (a testamentary trust). The primary benefit of a trust is that it can be created to hold property for the benefit of other persons. A trust may also be created for the benefit of a disabled individual, or can be used to legally avoid certain taxes. The establishment of a trust creates a fiduciary relationship between three parties:

- **The grantor:** The person who contributes property to the trust.
- **The trustee (or fiduciary):** The person or entity charged with the fiduciary duties associated with the trust.
- **The beneficiary:** The person who is designated to receive the trust income or assets.

Example: An elderly individual is having medical problems and decides to put his assets in a trust. He asks his attorney to create the trust and manage the assets. The elderly person then names his grandson as the beneficiary of the trust. In this common scenario, the elderly person is the **grantor**, the lawyer is the **trustee**, and the grandson is the **beneficiary**.

Sometimes, a trust is used to transfer property in a controlled manner. For example, a wealthy parent wishes to transfer ownership of assets to his child, but does not want the child to waste the assets or spend them unwisely. The assets could be transferred to a trust, with the parent as both the grantor and the trustee. The child would be the beneficiary. The parent still has control over the assets, and the child is prevented from using them all up.

The accounting period for a trust is generally the calendar year. The due date for a calendar-year trust is April 15. A trust must file IRS Form 1041, *U.S. Income Tax Return for Estates and Trusts* if it has:

- Any *taxable* income for the year (after subtracting the allowable exemption amount),
- Gross income of $600 or more (regardless of whether the income is taxable), or
- Any beneficiary who is a nonresident alien.

A trust calculates its gross income in a manner similar to an individual taxpayer. Trusts are allowed an exemption, but the amount varies based on the *type* of trust. A trust that must distribute all its income currently (a simple trust) is allowed an exemption of $300. All other trusts are allowed a yearly exemption of $100 per year.

Most deductions and credits allowed to individuals are also allowed to trusts. However, there is one major distinction: a trust is a pass-through entity that is allowed a deduction for its distributions to beneficiaries. The beneficiaries (and not the trust) pay income tax on their distributive share of income. Schedule K-1 (Form 1041) is used to report income that a trust distributes to beneficiaries. The income must then be reported on the beneficiaries' individual income tax returns.

Example: The Smith Family Trust has $400 in tax-exempt interest from municipal bonds during the year. There is no other income. Normally, the trust would not be required to file a tax return because the income earned by the trust is tax-exempt. However, the Smith Family Trust has a beneficiary who is a nonresident alien. Therefore, the trust is required to file a Form 1041.

Distributable Net Income of a Trust (DNI)

Taxable income earned by a trust is taxable to either the trust or the beneficiaries, but not to both. Distributable net income (DNI) is trust income that is currently available for distribution. If the beneficiary receives a distribution in excess of DNI, only the DNI is taxed. The income distribution deduction (IDD) is allowed to trusts (and estates) for amounts that are paid, credited, or required to be distributed to beneficiaries. The income distribution deduction is calculated on Schedule B (Form 1041) and is limited to the lesser of distributions less tax-exempt income or DNI less tax-exempt income.

Simple and Complex Trusts

With regard to income distribution, there are two types of trusts: a simple trust and a complex trust. The Internal Revenue Code defines a simple trust as a trust that:

- Distributes all of its income currently;
- Makes no distributions from principal; and
- Makes no distributions to charity.

Any trust that is not a simple trust is automatically a complex trust. A complex trust:

- Is allowed to accumulate income;
- Can make discretionary distributions of income;
- Can make mandatory (or discretionary) distributions of principal; and
- Can make distributions to charity.

A trust may be a simple trust one year, and a complex trust in another year. For example, if a simple trust fails to distribute all its income in the current year, it becomes a complex trust.

Trust Types (Grantor, Irrevocable, Tax shelters)

Grantor Trusts

A grantor trust is a valid legal entity under state law, but it is not recognized as a separate entity for income tax purposes.

The grantor (also known as trustor, settlor, or creator) creates the trust relationship and retains control over the trust. In the eyes of the IRS, the grantor is considered the owner of the trust for income tax purposes. The grantor establishes the terms and provisions of the trust relationship between the grantor, the trustee, and the beneficiary. These will usually include the following:

- The rights, duties, and powers of the trustee;

- Distribution provisions;

- Ability of the grantor to amend, modify, revoke, or terminate the trust agreement;

- The designation of a trustee or successor trustees; and

- The designation of the state under which the trust agreement is to be governed.

> **Example:** The John Doe Trust is a grantor trust. John Doe is the grantor. During the year, the trust sold 100 shares of ABC stock for $1,010 in which it had a basis of $10 and 200 shares of XYZ stock for $10 in which it had a $1,020 basis. The trust does not report these transactions on Form 1041. Instead, a schedule is attached to Form 1041 showing each stock transaction separately and in the same detail as John Doe (grantor and owner) will need to report these transactions on his Schedule D (Form 1040). The trust may not net the capital gains and losses; nor may it issue John Doe a Schedule K-1 (Form 1041) showing a $10 long-term capital loss.

Revocable Trust

A revocable trust is a trust in which the grantor retains the right to end the trust. The trust assets are subject to estate tax upon the grantor's death. A revocable trust is treated as a grantor trust for income tax purposes. This type of trust is generally created only to manage and distribute property. Many taxpayers use this type of trust instead of a will.

Revocable Living Trust

A revocable living trust is an arrangement created during the life of an individual and can be changed or ended at any time during the individual's life. A revocable living trust is generally created to manage and distribute property. Many people use this type of trust instead of, or in addition to, a will. Because this type of trust is revocable, it is treated as a grantor type trust for tax purposes.

Non-Grantor Trusts

A non-grantor trust is any trust that is not a grantor trust. A non-grantor trust is considered a separate legal entity from the individual or organization that created it. The trust's income and deductions are reported on Form 1041. If a non-grantor trust makes distributions to a beneficiary, in general those distributions carry any taxable income to the beneficiary.

1. **Irrevocable Trusts**: An irrevocable trust is a trust that cannot be revoked after it is created. The transfer of assets into this type of trust is generally considered a "completed gift" subject to gift tax.

2. **Disability Trust:** A qualified disability trust is a non-grantor trust created solely for the benefit of a disabled individual under age 65. In 2012, a qualified disability trust can claim an exemption of up to $3,800. This is a specific exception to the regular exemption of $600 for trusts.

3. **Charitable Trusts:** A charitable trust is a trust devoted to qualified charitable contribution purposes. Charitable trusts are irrevocable.

> **Example:** Hugo creates a charitable trust whose governing instrument provides that the Catholic Church (a qualified religious organization), and the SPCA (a 501(c)(3) charity) are each to receive 50% of the trust income for 10 years. At the end of the 10-year period, the corpus will be distributed to the Red Cross, also a 501(c)(3) organization. Hugo is allowed an income tax deduction for the value of all interests placed in trust.

Abusive Trust Arrangements

Certain trust arrangements purport to reduce or eliminate federal taxes in ways that are not permitted under the law. These are called abuse trusts. Abusive trust arrangements may use trusts to hide the true ownership of assets and income or to disguise the substance of transactions. These arrangements frequently involve more than one trust, each holding different assets of the taxpayer (for example, the taxpayer's business, business equipment, home, automobile, etc.) Some trusts may hold interests in other trusts, purport to involve charities, or be foreign trusts.

When trusts are used for legitimate business, family, or estate planning purposes, either the trust, the beneficiary, or the transferor to the trust will pay the tax on the income generated by the trust. Trusts cannot be used to transform a taxpayer's personal, living, or educational expenses into deductible items. A taxpayer cannot use a trust to avoid tax liability by ignoring either the true ownership of income and assets or the true substance of transactions. Participants and promoters of abusive trust schemes may be subject to civil or criminal penalties.

Termination of Trusts and Estates

Trusts and estates generally terminate when all of the assets and income have been distributed, and all of the liabilities have been paid. If a trust or estate's existence is unnecessarily prolonged, the IRS can step in and terminate it after a reasonable period for completing the final administration.

If an estate or trust has a loss in its final year, the loss can be passed through to the beneficiaries, allowing them a deduction on their returns. Losses cannot be passed through to beneficiaries in a non-termination year.

Unit 20: Questions

1. What is included in the gross estate?

A. The gross estate of the decedent includes everything the taxpayer owns at the date of death.
B. The gross estate of the decedent includes everything the taxpayer owns six months after the date of death.
C. The gross estate of the decedent includes everything the taxpayer owns at the date of death, including income that the taxpayer was owed but had not yet received.
D. The gross estate includes everything the decedent earned in the prior year, as well as income estimates for future years.

The answer is A. The gross estate of the decedent includes everything the taxpayer owns at the date of death. ###

2. The calculation of the gross estate includes all of the following except:

A. Life insurance proceeds payable to the decedent's heirs.
B. The value of certain annuities payable to the estate.
C. Property owned solely by the decedent's spouse.
D. The value of certain property transferred within three years before the taxpayer's death.

The answer is C. The gross estate does not include property owned solely by the decedent's spouse or other individuals. ###

3. What is the due date for Form 706 for a decedent who died in 2012?

A. April 15, 2013.
B. Nine months after the date of death.
C. Twelve months after the date of death.
D. Six months after the date of death

The answer is B. The estate tax return is generally due nine months after the date of death. ###

4. The Franklin Trust is required to distribute all its income currently. What is the yearly exemption amount for the Franklin Trust?

A. $0.
B. $100.
C. $300.
D. $600.

The answer is C. A trust that distributes all its income currently is allowed an exemption of $300. All other trusts are allowed an exemption of $100 per year. ###

5. All of the following are characteristics of a simple trust except:

A. The trust may distribute assets to charity.
B. The trust distributes all its income currently.
C. The trust makes no distributions from principal.
D. The trust makes no distributions to charity.

The answer is A. The Internal Revenue Code defines a simple trust as one that distributes all its income currently, makes no distributions from principal, and makes no distributions to charity. Any trust that is not a simple trust is automatically a complex trust. ###

6. All of the following are required to file Form 1041 except:

A. An estate with gross income of $600.
B. An estate with $700 in exempt income.
C. An estate with $200 in gross income and a beneficiary who is a nonresident alien.
D. An estate with $500 in gross income and a beneficiary who is a resident alien.

The answer is D. An estate with $500 in income and a beneficiary who is a resident alien is not required to file a tax return. Resident aliens (green card holders) are taxed the same way as citizens. An estate with a nonresident alien beneficiary would be required to file Form 1041, regardless of the amount of income earned. ###

7. What is the basic exclusion amount for an estate of an individual who dies in 2012?

A. $1 million.
B. $5 million.
C. $5,120,000.
D. $5,250,000.

The answer is C. For the estate of any decedent during calendar year 2012, the basic exclusion from estate tax amount is $5,120,000. ###

8. What is the amount of the applicable credit in 2012?

A. $100.
B. $600.
C. $1 million.
D. $1,772,800.

The answer is D. The applicable credit amount in 2012 is $1,772,800. A taxpayer must subtract the applicable credit amount from any gift or estate tax he owes. Any applicable credit used against gift tax in one year reduces the amount of credit he can use against gift or estate taxes in a later year. ###

9. What is the maximum estate tax rate for 2012?

A. 10%.
B. 25%.
C. 35%.
D. There is no estate tax in 2012.

The answer is C. The maximum estate and gift tax rate for 2012 is 35%. ###

10. Carlton's will provides that each of his ten grandchildren would receive $1 million. Assuming that none of his GST exemption amount has previously been used in connection with gifts to the grandchildren or other skip persons, what portion of the total amount distributed to the grandchildren after his death in 2012 would be subject to GST?

A. $8,700,000.
B. $5,120,000.
C. $10,000,000.
D. $4,880,000.

The answer is D. The aggregate portion of his estate distributed to his grandchildren ($10 million) would be reduced by his exclusion amount for GST ($5,120,000) and the remainder of $4,880,000 would be subject to GST. ###

11. Parker, a single taxpayer, died on March 3, 2012. Based on the following information, determine the value of his gross estate:

FMV on date of death	
Life insurance on Parker's life (payable to his estate)	$250,000
Parker's revocable grantor trust	$700,000
Liabilities owed by Parker when he died	$ 150,000

A. $250,000.
B. $800,000.
C. $950,000.
D. $1.1 million.

The answer is C. Life insurance payable to a trust and assets held in a grantor trust are included in a decedent's gross estate. Liabilities of the decedent are not included in the gross estate. However, they are an allowable deduction from the gross estate in determining the taxable estate. ###

12. Bianca, who is married, gave a vase worth $40,000 to her brother. Bianca's basis in the vase is $10,000. What amount will she report as the value of the gift on Form 709?

A. $10,000.
B. $20,000.
C. $30,000.
D. $40,000.

The answer is D. Generally, the value of a gift is its fair market value on the date of the gift. In this case, the value of $40,000 exceeds the annual exclusion amount of $13,000 for 2012. Even if Bianca and her husband took advantage of the gift-splitting option for purposes of the gift to her brother, the value would exceed their combined exclusion amount of $26,000, and would need to be reported on Form 709. ###

13. Luis died in March 2012. At the time of his death and when his estate was being settled, none of his basic exclusion amount was used to reduce or eliminate payment of gift or estate taxes. Form 706 was filed in October 2012, and the full amount of deceased spousal unused exclusion (DSUE) was reported thereon. His wife Jenna died in December 2012. As was the case with Luis, none of her basic exclusion amount had been used previously to offset gift taxes that would otherwise have been payable. What amount must Jenna's taxable estate exceed in order to be subject to estate tax?

A. $5,120,000.
B. $1,772,800.
C. $5,000,000.
D. $10,240,000.

The answer is D. When Luis died in 2012, his estate qualified for the full basic exclusion amount of $5,120,000. As a result of having reported the DSUE when Form 706 was filed for his estate, the amount of the DSUE is available in addition to Jenna's basic exclusion amount of $5,120,000. Therefore, the amount of her taxable estate would have to exceed $10,240,000 in order to be subject to estate tax. ###

14. Georgiana died on March 1, 2012. The executor of her estate has elected to file the estate's income tax return on a calendar-year basis. No distributions have been made by the estate. Based on the following, what is the taxable income (Form 1041) of the estate for the December 31, 2012 year-end before consideration of the estate's exemption amount?

•Taxable interest	$2,000
•Tax-exempt interest	$1,000
•Capital gain	$3,000
•Executor's fees	$300

A. $5,700.
B. $4,700.
C. $5,100.
D. $6,000.

The answer is B. Taxable income of $4,700 can be reported for the estate, determined as follows: Taxable interest of $2,000 plus capital gain of $3,000, less executor's fees of $300. The expenses of administering an estate can be deducted either from the estate's income on Form 1041 in determining its income tax or from the gross estate on Form 706 in determining the estate tax liability, but cannot be claimed for both purposes. The tax-exempt interest retains the character that would have applied if it had been reported by the decedent. The estate would be eligible for an exemption amount of $600 in determining its actual taxable income. ###

15. Roberto died on May 3, 2012. The estate's tax year ends on December 31, 2012. The estate had the following items of income during the year:

- Interest $250
- Dividends $150
- Stock-sale proceeds, net of broker's commission $10,000
- Basis of the stock $9,900

The estate made no distributions during 2012. Based upon the information provided, which of the following statements is true?

A. The estate is not required to file an income tax return.
B. The estate is required to file an income tax return.
C. The estate is required to file a return on Form 706.
D. Both B and C.

The answer is A. An income tax return (Form 1041) must be filed for any domestic estate that has gross income for the tax year of $600 or more, or a beneficiary who is a nonresident alien (with any amount of income). Roberto's estate has gross income of $500 ($250 + $150 + $100 gain from stock sale). Since the gross income is below the $600 exemption amount, an income tax return is not required to be filed for 2012. There is insufficient information to determine whether an estate tax return (Form 706) will need to be filed. ###

16. Shane, who had not given taxable gifts in any prior year, gave his five children the following gifts in 2012:

- Car to Pat $14,000
- Cash to Lizzie $12,000
- Stock to Adam $10,500
- Stock to Ben $9,500
- Cash to Kris $5,000

From the information above, determine the amount, if any, of taxable gifts given by Shane.

A. $0.
B. $1,000.
C. $6,500.
D. $41,000.

The answer is B. Only one of the children, Pat, received a gift in excess of the exemption amount of $13,000. The excess portion of $1,000 would be considered a taxable gift for purposes of filing a gift tax return. However, Shane can use a portion of his basic exclusion amount to avoid payment of gift tax in 2012. ###

17. Virgil gave his granddaughter Susannah $30,000. Susannah is 15 years old and lives with her parents. Which of the following statements regarding the generation-skipping transfer tax is true?

A. Because the gift is subject to the generation-skipping transfer tax, it is not subject to the regular gift tax.
B. The gift is subject to both the regular gift tax and the generation-skipping transfer tax.
C. The gift is not subject to the generation-skipping transfer tax because Susannah's parents are still alive.
D. If Virgil had transferred the funds into a trust solely for his granddaughter's benefit, the gift would not be subject to the generation-skipping transfer tax.

The answer is B. The GST tax is imposed separately and in addition to the estate and gift tax. ###

405

Index

S

T

Also Available from PassKey Publications

The Enrolled Agent Tax Consulting Practice Guide:

Learn How to Develop, Market, and Operate a Profitable
Tax and IRS Representation Practice

ISBN-13: 978-0982266045

Available in Kindle and Nook editions and as a paperback

About the Authors

Collette Szymborski is a certified public accountant and the managing partner of Elk Grove CPA Accountancy Corporation. She specializes in the taxation of corporations, individuals, and exempt entities. Elk Grove CPA also does estate planning.

Richard Gramkow is an enrolled agent with more than sixteen years of experience in various areas of taxation. He holds a master's degree in taxation from Rutgers University and is currently a tax manager for a publicly held Fortune 500 company in the New York metropolitan area.

Christy Pinheiro is an enrolled agent, registered tax return preparer, Accredited Business Accountant, and writer. Christy was an accountant for two private CPA firms and for the State of California before going into private practice. She is a member of the California Society of Enrolled Agents and CalCPA.